always up to date

The law changes, but Nolo is always on top of it! We offer several ways to make sure you and your Nolo products are always up to date:

Nolo's Legal Updater

We'll send you an email whenever a new edition of your book is published! Sign up at **www.nolo.com/legalupdater**.

Updates @ Nolo.com

Check **www.nolo.com/update** to find recent changes in the law that affect the current edition of your book.

Nolo Customer Service

To make sure that this edition of the book is the most recent one, call us at **800-728-3555** and ask one of our friendly customer service representatives. Or find out at **www.nolo.com**.

please note

We believe accurate and current legal information should help you solve many of your own legal problems on a cost-efficient basis. But this text is not a substitute for personalized advice from a knowledgeable lawyer. If you want the help of a trained professional, consult an attorney licensed to practice in your state.

1st edition

Home Business Tax Deductions:

Keep What You Earn

By Attorney Stephen Fishman

First Edition	AUGUST 2004
Editor	LISA GUERIN
Cover Design	SUSAN PUTNEY
Book Design	TERRI HEARSH
Proofreading	SUSAN CARLSON GREENE
Index	BAYSIDE INDEXING SERVICE
Printing	DELTA PRINTING SOLUTIONS, INC.

Fishman, Stephen.
    Home Business Tax Deductions: Keep What You Earn / by Stephen Fishman.-- 1st ed.
      p. cm.
    ISBN 1-4133-0079-0
    1. Home-based businesses--Taxation--Law and legislation--United States.--Popular
works. 2. Income tax deductions for home office expenses--United States--Popular works.
I. Title.

    KF6491.F57 2004
    343.7305'23--dc22

                                                             2004050107

Quantity sales: For information on bulk purchases or corporate premium sales, please
contact the Special Sales Department. For academic sales or textbook adoptions, ask for
Academic Sales. Call 800-955-4775 or write to Nolo, 950 Parker Street, Berkeley, CA 94710.

Acknowledgments

Many thanks to:

Lisa Guerin for her superb editing

Terri Hearsh for her outstanding book design and Susan Putney for the eye-catching cover

Bayside Indexing Service for the useful index

Table of Contents

Introduction

Using Tax Deductions to Keep What You Earn

1 Home Business Tax Deduction Basics

2 Are You Really In Business?

12 Medical Expenses

13 Retirement Deductions

14 Additional Home Business Deductions

Index

Using Tax Deductions to Keep What You Earn

John and Jane are next door neighbors. John earns $50,000 per year working as an employee; Jane earns the same amount from her home business. However, John is left with only $40,000 after he pays his federal and state taxes for the year, while Jane keeps $45,000. Why the difference? The tax laws. John and Jane have the same personal deductions, but, because Jane is a business owner, she qualifies for a wide array of business tax deductions that Jack and other wage slaves can only dream about. Jane and the other 11 million home business owners in the United States have discovered how to keep more of what they earn: Pay less in taxes by taking more deductions.

A. Why You Need to Know About Tax Deductions

The United States has two separate and unequal tax systems. One is for wage earners; the other is for business owners. Wage earners—those who work for other people's businesses or for the government—have their income taxes withheld from their paychecks and can take relatively few tax deductions. Business owners, whether they work at home or in outside offices, live in a different tax universe. The vast majority have no taxes withheld from their earnings and can take advantage of a huge array of tax deductions unavailable to employees.

If you have a legitimate home business, you may be able to deduct:

- a portion of your rent or mortgage, utilities, maintenance, and other home office expenses
- car expenses for business trips
- the cost of traveling out of town for business (you may even be able to mix business with pleasure and still take a deduction)
- money you spend for office furniture and equipment
- half the cost of business-related meals and entertainment
- medical expenses for yourself and your family, and
- contributions to special retirement accounts available only to business owners.

All of these deductions—and many others available to home business owners—can add up to substantial tax savings. Depending on your income tax bracket and the state where you live, every $100 you take in tax deductions can save you from about $280 to more than $400 in taxes.

B.   Why You Need This Book

To take advantage of the benefits tax deductions offer, you'll have to figure out which deductions you are entitled to take—and keep proper records documenting your expenses. The IRS will never complain if you don't take all the deductions available to you. In fact, the majority of home business owners miss out on many deductions every year simply because they aren't aware of them—or because they neglect to keep the records necessary to back them up.

That's where this book comes in. It shows you how you can deduct all or most of your business expenses from your federal taxes. This book is not a tax preparation guide—it does not show you how to fill out your tax forms. (By the time you do your taxes, it may be too late to take deductions you could have taken if you had planned the prior year's business spending wisely and kept proper records.) Instead, this book gives you all the information you need to maximize your deductible expenses—and avoid common deduction mistakes. You can (and should) use this book all year long, so that you're ready to take advantage of every available deduction opportunity come April 15th.

Even if you work with an accountant or another tax professional, you need to learn about home business tax deductions. No tax professional will ever know as much about your business as you do; and you can't expect a hired professional to search high and low for every deduction you might be able to take, especially during the busy tax preparation season. The information in this book will help you provide your tax professional with better records, ask better questions, and obtain better advice. It will also help you evaluate the advice you get from tax professionals, websites, and other sources, so you can make smart decisions about your taxes.

If you do your taxes yourself (as more and more home business-people are doing, especially with the help of tax preparation software), your need for knowledge is even greater. Not even the most sophisticated tax preparation program can decide which tax deductions you should take or tell you whether you've overlooked a valuable deduction.

C. The Ever-Changing Tax Laws

Congress is constantly amending the tax laws—and the changes in the last few years have been particularly significant. Some of the most sweeping changes occurred in 2003, particularly for small businesses. This book (which will be updated annually) covers all of the latest tax laws through May 2004.

Some recent significant tax changes that are covered in this book include:

- the vast increase in the amount of equipment and other long-term property businesses can deduct in one year (see Chapter 5)
- the special 50% bonus depreciation for long-term business property purchased during 2004 (see Chapter 5)
- the IRS ruling permitting some businesses to deduct the cost of nonprescription medications as a business expense (see Chapter 12)
- Health Savings Accounts, which provide a whole new tax-advantaged way to pay for health care expenses (see Chapter 12)
- new rules permitting an additional 800,000 small businesses to use the standard mileage rate for their car expense deductions (see Chapter 8)
- new rules exempting most small business owners from having to pay capital gains tax on their profits when they use a portion of their home as a business office (see Chapter 6), and
- increases in retirement deductions (see Chapter 13).

D. Icons Used in This Book

This icon alerts you to a practical tip or good idea.

This is a caution to slow down and consider potential problems.

This refers you to other sources of information about a particular topic covered in the text.   ■

Chapter 1

Home Business Tax Deduction Basics

Once you start your own business, you can begin taking advantage of the many tax deductions available only to business owners. The tax code is full of deductions for businesses—and you are entitled to take them whether you work from home or from a fancy outside office. Before you can start using these deductions to hang on to more of your hard-earned money, however, you need a basic understanding of how businesses pay taxes and how tax deductions work. This chapter gives you all the information you need to get started. It covers:

- how tax deductions work (Section A)
- how businesses are taxed (Section B)
- what expenses businesses can deduct (Section C), and
- how to calculate the value of a tax deduction (Section D).

A. How Tax Deductions Work

A tax deduction (also called a write-off) is an amount of money you are entitled to subtract from your gross income (all the money you make) to determine your taxable income (the amount on which you must pay tax). The more deductions you have, the lower your taxable income will be and the less tax you will have to pay.

1. Types of Tax Deductions

There are three basic types of tax deductions: personal deductions, investment deductions, and business deductions. This book covers only business deductions—the large array of write-offs available to business owners, including those who work out of their homes.

a. Personal Deductions

For the most part, your personal, living, and family expenses are not tax deductible. For example, you can't deduct the food that you buy for yourself and your family. There are, however, special categories of personal expenses that may be deducted, subject to strict limitations. These include items such as home mortgage interest, state and local taxes, charitable contributions, medical expenses above a threshold amount, interest on education loans, and alimony. This book does not cover these personal deductions.

b.   Investment Deductions

Many people try to make money by investing money. For example, they might invest in real estate or play the stock market. These people incur all kinds of expenses, such as fees paid to money managers or financial planners, legal and accounting fees, and interest on money borrowed to buy investment property. These and other investment expenses (also called expenses for the production of income) are tax deductible, subject to some important limitations. (See Chapter 2, Section C, for more on investment deductions.)

c.   Business Deductions

Home business owners usually have to spend money on their businesses—for example, for equipment, supplies, or business travel. Most business expenses are deductible sooner or later. It makes no difference for tax deduction purposes whether you run your business from home or from an outside office or workplace either way, you are entitled to deduct your legitimate business expenses. This book is about the many deductions available to people who are in business and who happen to work from home.

2.   You Pay Taxes Only on Your Business Profits

The federal income tax law recognizes that you must spend money to make money. Virtually every home business, however small, incurs some expenses. Even someone with a low overhead business (such as a freelance writer) must buy paper, computer equipment, and office supplies. Some home businesses incur substantial expenses, even exceeding their income.

You are not legally required to pay tax on every dollar your business takes in (your "gross income"). Instead, you owe tax only on the amount left over after your business's deductible expenses are subtracted from your gross income (this remaining amount is called your "net profit").

Although some tax deduction calculations can get a bit complicated, the basic math is simple: The more deductions you take, the lower your net profit will be, and the less tax you will have to pay.

> **EXAMPLE:** Karen, a sole proprietor, earned $50,000 this year from her consulting business, which she operates from her home office. Fortunately, she doesn't have to pay income tax on the entire $50,000—her gross income. Instead, she can deduct various business expenses, including a $5,000 home office deduction (see Chapter 6) and a $5,000 deduction for equipment expenses (see Chapter 5). She deducts these expenses from her $50,000 gross income to arrive at her net profit: $40,000. She pays income tax only on this net profit amount.

3. You Must Have a Legal Basis for Your Deductions

All tax deductions are a matter of legislative grace, which means that you can take a deduction only if it is specifically allowed by one or more provisions of the tax law. You usually do not have to indicate on your tax return which tax law provision gives you the right to take a particular deduction. If you are audited by the IRS, however, you'll have to provide a legal basis for every deduction you take. If the IRS concludes that your deduction wasn't justified, it will deny the deduction and charge you back taxes, interest, and penalties.

4. You Must Be In Business to Claim Business Deductions

Only businesses can claim business tax deductions. This probably seems like a simple concept, but it can get tricky. Even though you might believe you are running a business, the IRS may beg to differ. If your home business doesn't turn a profit for several years in a row, the IRS might decide that you are engaged in a hobby rather than a business. This may not sound like a big deal, but it could have disastrous tax consequences: People engaged in hobbies are entitled to very limited tax deductions, while businesses can deduct all kinds of expenses. Fortunately, careful taxpayers can usually avoid this unhappy outcome.

(See Chapter 2 for tips that will help you convince the IRS that you really are running a business.)

B. How Businesses Are Taxed

If your home business earns money (as you undoubtedly hope it will), you will have to pay taxes on your profits. How you pay those taxes will depend on how you have structured your business. So before getting further into the details of tax deductions, it's important to understand what type of business you have formed (a sole proprietorship, partnership, limited liability company, or corporation), and how you will pay tax on your business's profit.

Need help figuring out how to structure your business? Although most home businesses are sole proprietorships, that may not be the best business form for you. If you need to decide how to organize a new business or you want to know whether you should change your current business form, refer to *Choosing a Legal Structure for Your Small Business*, by Fred Steingold, or *Choose the Best Legal Structure for Your One-Person Business*, by Stephen Fishman. These are available as electronic downloads from Nolo's website, www.nolo.com.

1. Basic Business Forms

Every business, from a part-time operation you run from home while in your jammies to a Fortune 500 multinational company housed in a gleaming skyscraper, has a legal structure. If you're running a business right now, it has a legal form—even if you never made a conscious decision about how it should be legally organized.

a. Most Home Businesses Are Sole Proprietorships

A sole proprietorship is a one-owner business. According to the Small Business Administration, 90% of all home businesses are sole proprietorships. Unlike the other business forms, a sole proprietorship has no legal existence separate from the business owner. It cannot sue or be sued, own property in its own name, or file its own tax returns. The business owner (proprietor) personally owns all of the assets of the business and controls its operations. If you're running a one-person home business and you haven't incorporated or formed a limited liability company, you are a sole proprietor. However, you can't be a sole proprietor if two or more people own your home business, except in some states where a husband and wife can be co-sole proprietors (see "Home Businesses Owned By Spouses," below).

Home Businesses Owned by Spouses

Many home businesses are co-owned by a husband and wife. These businesses can be organized in a variety of ways—the couple might decide to incorporate as an S or C corporation, form a limited liability company (LLC), or enter into a formal partnership. If you don't take any steps to choose a business form, the IRS will treat your business as a partnership, and you will have to file a partnership tax return.

In most states, spouses who own a business together may not form a sole proprietorship, a form of business ownership usually available only to individuals. However, in a handful of states—those that allow couples to own property as community property—spouses may designate their jointly owned community property business as a sole proprietorship, if they wish. If you don't incorporate or form an LLC, you can choose to treat your business as either a partnership or a sole proprietorship. If you elect proprietorship status, you need not file a partnership tax return. This rule applies only in the seven states that use the community property system of laws to govern ownership of property acquired during marriage: Arizona, California, Idaho, Nevada, New Mexico, Texas, and Washington.

b.   Other Business Forms

Only about 10% of home businesses adopt a business form other than a sole proprietorship. These other forms include:

- **Partnerships:** A partnership is a form of shared ownership and management of a business. The partners contribute money, property, or services to the partnership; in return, they receive a share of the profits it earns, if any. The partners jointly manage the partnership business. A partnership automatically comes into existence whenever two or more people enter into business together to earn a profit and don't incorporate or form a limited liability company. Thus, if you're running a home business with somebody else, you are in a partnership right now (unless you've formed an LLC or corporation). Although many partners enter into written partnership agreements, no agreement is required to form a partnership.

- **Corporations:** Unlike a sole proprietorship or partnership, a corporation cannot simply spring into existence—it can only be created by filing incorporation documents with your state government. A corporation is a legal entity distinct from its owners. It can hold title to property, sue and be sued, have bank accounts, borrow money, hire employees, and perform other business functions. For tax purposes, there are two types of corporations: S corporations (also called small business corporations) and C corporations (also called regular corporations). The most important difference between the two types of corporations is how they are taxed. An S corporation pays no taxes itself—instead, its income or loss is passed on to its owners, who must pay personal income taxes on their share of the corporation's profits. A C corporation is a separate taxpaying entity that pays taxes on its profits (see Section B2, below).

- **Limited Liability Companies:** The limited liability company (LLC) is like a sole proprietorship or partnership in that its owners (called members) jointly own and manage the business and share in the profits. However, an LLC is also like a corporation. Because its owners must file papers with the state to create the LLC, it exists as a separate legal entity, and the LLC structure gives owners some protection from liability for business debts.

2.   Tax Treatment

Your business's legal form will determine how it is treated for tax purposes. There are two different ways that business entities can be taxed: The business itself can be taxed as a separate entity, or the business's profits and losses can be "passed through" to the owners, who include these amounts on their individual tax returns. Sole proprietorships, partnerships, LLCs, and S corporations are all "pass-through entities"; the only type of business that is not a pass-through entity is the C corporation.

a.   Pass-Through Entities: Sole Proprietorships, Partnerships, LLCs, and S Corporations

Sole proprietorships, partnerships, LLCs, and S corporations are all pass-through entities. A pass-through entity does not pay any taxes itself. Instead, the business's profits or losses are passed through to its owners, who include them on their own personal tax returns (IRS Form 1040). If a profit is passed through to the owner, the owner must add that money to any income from other sources, and pay tax on the total amount. If a loss is passed through, the owner can generally use it to offset income from other sources—for example, salary from a job, interest, investment income, or a spouse's income (as long as the couple files a joint tax return). The owner can subtract the business loss from this other income, which leaves a lower total subject to tax.

> **EXAMPLE:** Lisa is a sole proprietor who works part time from home doing engineering consulting. During her first year in business, she incurs $10,000 in expenses and earns $5,000, giving her a $5,000 loss from her business. She reports this loss on IRS Schedule C, which she files with her personal income tax return (Form 1040). Because Lisa is a sole proprietor, she can deduct this $5,000 loss from any income she has, including her $100,000 annual salary from her engineering job. This saves her about $2,000 in total taxes for the year.

Although pass-through entities don't pay taxes, their income and expenses must still be reported to the IRS as follows:

- **Sole proprietors** must file IRS Schedule C, *Profit or Loss From Business*, with their tax returns. This form lists all the proprietor's business income and deductible expenses.

- **Partnerships** are required to file an annual tax form (Form 1065, *U.S. Return of Partnership Income*) with the IRS. Form 1065 is used to report partnership revenues, expenses, gains, and losses. The partnership must also provide each partner with an IRS Schedule K-1, *Partner's Share of Income, Credits, Deductions, etc.*, listing the partner's share of partnership income and expenses (copies of these schedules must also be attached to IRS Form 1065). Partners must then file IRS Schedule E, *Supplemental Income and Loss*, with their individual income tax returns, showing their partnership income and deductions.

- **S corporations** must file information returns with the IRS on Form 1120S, *U.S. Income Tax Return for an S Corporation*, showing how much the business earned or lost and each shareholder's portion of the corporate income or loss.

- **LLCs** with only one member are treated like a sole proprietorship for tax purposes. The member reports profits, losses, and deductions on Schedule C—just like a sole proprietor. An LLC with two or more members is treated like a partnership: The LLC must prepare and file IRS Form 1065, Partnership Return of Income, showing the allocation of profits, losses, credits, and deductions passed through to the members. The LLC must also prepare and distribute to each member a Schedule K-1 form showing the member's allocations of profits, losses, credits, and deductions.

b.   Regular C Corporations

A regular C corporation is the only business form that is not a pass-through entity. Instead, a C corporation is taxed separately from its owners. C corporations must pay income taxes on their net income and file corporate tax returns with the IRS, using Form 1120, *U.S. Corporation Income Tax Return,* or Form 1120-A, *U.S. Corporation Short-Form Income Tax Return.* They also have their own income tax rates (which are lower than individual rates at some income levels).

When you form a C corporation, you have to take charge of two separate taxpayers: your corporation and yourself. Your C corporation must pay tax on all of its income. You pay personal income tax on C corporation income only when it is distributed to you in the form of salary, bonuses, or dividends.

C corporations can take all the same business tax deductions that pass-through entities take. In addition, because a C corporation is a separate tax-paying entity, it may provide its employees with tax-free fringe benefits, then deduct the entire cost of the benefits from the corporation's income as a business expense. No other form of business entity can do this. (Although they are corporations, S corporations cannot deduct the cost of benefits provided to shareholders who hold more than 2% of the corporate stock.)

C.   What Businesses Can Deduct

Business owners, whether they work at home or elsewhere, can deduct four broad categories of business expenses:
- start-up expenses
- operating expenses
- capital expenses, and
- inventory costs.

This section provides an introduction to each of these categories (they are covered in greater detail in later chapters).

You must keep track of your expenses. You may deduct only those expenses that you actually incur. You need to keep records of these expenses to (1) know for sure how much you actually spent, and (2) prove to the IRS that you really spent the money you deducted on your tax return, in case you are audited. Accounting and bookkeeping are discussed in detail in Chapter 15.

1.   Start-Up Expenses

Start-up expenses are expenses you incur to get your home business up and running—such as license fees, advertising costs, attorney and accounting fees, market research, and office supplies expenses. Start-up costs are not currently deductible—that is, you cannot deduct them all in the year in which you incur them. However, you may be entitled to deduct them in equal amounts over the first 60 months you are in business. Most home business owners should be able to avoid incurring substantial start-up expenses. (See Chapter 3 for a detailed discussion of deducting start-up expenses.)

2.   Operating Expenses

Operating expenses are the ongoing day-to-day costs a business incurs to stay in business. They include such things as rent, utilities, salaries, supplies, travel expenses, car expenses, and repairs and maintenance. These expenses (unlike start-up expenses) are currently deductible—that is, you can deduct them all in the year when you pay them. (See Chapter 4 for more on operating expenses.)

3.   Capital Expenses

Capital assets are things you buy for your business that have a useful life of more than one year, such as equipment, vehicles, books, office furniture, machinery, and patents you buy from others. These costs, called capital expenses, are considered to be part of your investment in your business, not day-to-day operating expenses.

Large businesses—those that buy at least several hundred thousand dollars of capital assets in a year—must deduct these costs by using depreciation. To depreciate an item, you deduct a portion of the cost in each year of the item's useful life. Depending on the asset, this could be anywhere from three to 39 years (the IRS decides the asset's useful life).

Small businesses can also use depreciation, but they have another option available for deducting many capital expenses—they can deduct up to $102,000 in capital expenses per year under a provision of the tax code called Section 179. Section 179 and depreciation are discussed in detail in Chapter 5.

Certain capital assets, such as land and corporate stock, never wear out. What you spend to purchase and improve capital assets is not deductible; you have to wait until you sell the asset (or it becomes worthless) to recover these costs. (See Chapter 5 for more on deducting capital assets.)

4. Inventory

If your home business involves making or buying products, you'll have an inventory. Inventory includes almost anything you make or buy to resell to customers. It doesn't matter whether you manufacture the goods yourself or buy finished goods from someone else and resell them to customers. Inventory doesn't include tools, equipment, or other items that you use in your business; it refers only to items that you buy or make to sell.

You must deduct inventory costs separately from all other business expenses—you deduct inventory costs as you sell the inventory. Inventory that remains unsold at the end of the year is a business asset, not a deductible expense. (See Chapter 10 for more on deducting inventory.)

D. Adding It All Up: The Value of Tax Deductions

Most taxpayers, even sophisticated businesspeople, don't fully appreciate just how much money they can save with tax deductions. Of course, only part of any deduction will end up back in your pocket as money saved. Because a deduction represents income on which you don't have to pay tax, the value of any deduction is the amount of tax you would have had to pay on that income had you not deducted it. So a deduction of $1,000 won't save you $1,000 — it will save you whatever you would otherwise have had to pay as tax on that $1,000 of income.

1. Federal and State Income Taxes

To determine how much income tax a deduction will save you, you must first figure out your income tax bracket. The United States has a progressive income tax system for individual taxpayers with six different tax rates (called tax brackets), ranging from 10% of taxable income to 35% (see the chart below). The higher your income, the higher your tax rate.

You move from one bracket to the next only when your taxable income exceeds the bracket amount. For example, if you are a single taxpayer, you pay 10% income tax on all your taxable income up to $7,150. If your taxable income exceeds $7,150, the next tax rate (15%) applies to all your income over $7,150—but the 10% rate still applies to the first $7,150. If your income exceeds the 15% bracket amount, the next tax rate (25%) applies to the excess amount, and so on until the top bracket of 35% is reached.

The tax bracket in which the last dollar you earn for the year falls is called your "marginal tax bracket." For example, if you have $60,000 in taxable income, your marginal tax bracket is 25%. To determine how much federal income tax a deduction will save you, multiply the amount of the deduction by your marginal tax bracket. For example, if your marginal tax bracket is 25%, you will save 25¢ in federal income taxes for every dollar you are able to claim as a deductible business expense (25% x $1 = 25¢). The following table lists the 2004 federal income tax brackets for single and married individual taxpayers and shows the federal income tax savings for each dollar of deductions.

2004 Federal Personal Income Tax Brackets		
Tax Bracket	Income If Single	Income If Married Filing Jointly
10%	Up to $7,150	Up to $14,300
15%	From $7,151 to $29,950	$14,301 to $58,100
25%	$29,951 to $70,350	$58,101 to $117,250
28%	$70,351 to $146,750	$117,251 to $178,650
33%	$146,751 to $319,100	$178,651 to $319,100
35%	All over $319,100	All over $319,100

Income tax brackets are adjusted each year for inflation. For current brackets, see IRS Publication 505, *Tax Withholding and Estimated Tax*. You can obtain this and all other IRS publications by calling the IRS at

800-TAX-FORM, visiting your local IRS office, or downloading the publications from the IRS Internet site at www.irs.gov.

You can also deduct your business expenses from any state income tax you must pay. The average state income tax rate is about 6%, although seven states (Alaska, Florida, Nevada, South Dakota, Texas, Washington, and Wyoming) don't have an income tax. You can find your state's tax rates at www.taxadmin.org/fta/rate/ind_inc.html.

State Income Tax Deductions May Differ

Generally, you may deduct the same business expenses for state tax purposes as you do for your federal taxes. However, there are some exceptions—for example, not all states allow deductions for bonus depreciation (see Chapter 9). You should contact your state tax agency for details. Every state tax agency has a website; you can find links to all of them at www.taxsites.com/state.html.

2.   Self-Employment Taxes

Everyone who works—business owner and employee alike—is required to pay Social Security and Medicare taxes. Employees pay one-half of these taxes through payroll deductions; the employer must pony up the other half and send the entire payment to the IRS. Business owners must pay all of these taxes themselves. Business owners' Social Security and Medicare contributions are called self-employment taxes.

Self-employment taxes consist of a 12.4% Social Security tax on self-employment income up to an annual limit; in 2004, the limit was $87,900. Medicare taxes are levied on all self-employment income at a 2.9% rate. This combines to a total 15.3% tax on self-employment income up to the Social Security tax ceiling. However, the effective self-employment tax rate is lower (about 12%) because you are allowed to deduct half of your self-employment taxes from your net income for income tax purposes.

Like income taxes, self-employment taxes are paid on the net profit you earn from a business. Thus, deductible business expenses reduce the amount of self-employment tax you have to pay by lowering your net profit. This makes business tax deductions doubly valuable.

3.   Total Tax Savings

When you add up your savings in federal, state, and self-employment taxes, you can see the true value of a business tax deduction. For example, if you're in the 25% federal income tax bracket, a business deduction can be worth as much as 25% (in federal taxes) + 12% (in self-employment taxes) + 6% (in state taxes). That adds up to a whopping 43% savings. If you buy a $1,000 computer for your business and you deduct the expense, you save about $430 in taxes. In effect, the government is paying for almost half of your business expenses. This is why it's so important to know all of the business deductions to which you are entitled—and to take advantage of every one.

Don't buy things just to get a tax deduction. Although tax deductions can be worth a lot, it doesn't make sense to buy something you don't need just to get a deduction. After all, you still have to pay for the item, and the tax deduction you get in return will only cover a portion of the cost. If you buy a $1,000 computer, you'll probably be able to deduct less than half the cost. That means you're still out over $500—money you've spent for something you don't need. On the other hand, if you really do need a computer, the deduction you're entitled to is like found money—and it may help you buy a better computer than you could otherwise afford.

The Value of Common Tax Deductions
(Sole Proprietors Earning $25,000-$100,000(2001))

The following table lists the 15 most common tax deductions, and the average amounts for each, taken in 2001 by sole proprietor businesses with annual earnings of $25,000 to $100,000.

Expense	Average Amount	Income Tax Savings (25% bracket)	Self-Employment Tax Savings	Total Federal Tax Savings
1. Car and truck expenses	$6,100	$1,525	$933	$2,458
2. Utilities	$2,100	$525	$321	$856
3. Supplies (other than office supplies)	$3,000	$750	$459	$1,209
4. Office supplies	$1,300	$325	$199	$524
5. Legal and professional services	$700	$175	$107	$282
6. Insurance	$1,600	$400	$245	$645
7. Depreciation	$4,300	$1,075	$658	$1,733
8. Taxes	$1,000	$250	$153	$403
9. Meals and entertainment	$1,000	$250	$153	$403
10. Advertising	$1,600	$400	$245	$645
11. Repairs	$2,200	$530	$337	$867
12. Travel	$2,300	$575	$352	$927
13. Rent on business property	$6,400	$1,600	$979	$2,759
14. Home office	$3,000	$750	$459	$1,209
15. Rent on equipment and machinery	$3,100	$775	$474	$1,249

(Source: *Information on Expenses Claimed by Sole Proprietorships*, Government Accounting Office (GAO-04-304; January 2004.)

Chapter 2

Are You Really In Business?

You must operate a bona fide business (in the eyes of the IRS) to take business deductions. This point may seem obvious, but it has gotten more home businesspeople in trouble with the IRS than almost any other provision of the tax law. By declaring your home activity to be a hobby rather than a business, the IRS can, at one fell swoop, eliminate all of your tax deductions for the activity. Because hobbies are ordinarily conducted at home, home ventures are especially vulnerable to being viewed as hobbies by the IRS. That's why it's so important for you to be able to show the IRS that your home activity is a real business.

A.   Proving That You Are in Business

For tax purposes, a business is an activity you regularly and continuously engage in primarily to earn a profit. You don't have to show a profit every year to qualify as a business. As long as your primary purpose is to make money, you should qualify as a business (even if you show a loss when you're first starting out, and even afterward, depending on the circumstances). Your business can be conducted from home, full time or part time, as long as you work at it regularly and continuously. And you can have more than one business at the same time. However, if your primary purpose is something other than making a profit—for example, to incur deductible expenses or just to have fun—the IRS may find that your activity is a hobby rather than a business. If this happens, you'll face some potentially disastrous tax consequences.

> **EXAMPLE:** Jorge and Vivian Lopez thought that they had found an ideal way to save on their income taxes (and enjoy themselves as well)—they started an Amway distributorship as a sideline business. They ran the distributorship out of their home. While they had a lot of fun socializing with family and friends, they never came close to earning a profit. They claimed a loss from this business of over $18,000 a year for two straight years. They deducted this loss from Jorge's salary as a full-time petroleum engineer, which saved them thousands of dollars in income taxes. Things were going great tax-wise, until the IRS audited the Lopez's tax returns and concluded

that the Amway distributorship was a hobby rather than a business. This meant the Lopezes could no longer deduct their Amway losses from Jorge's salary, and they owed the IRS over $17,000 in back taxes for the deductions they had already taken. (*Lopez v. Comm'r.* T.C. Memo. 2003-142.)

⚠ **Beware of home business tax scams.** Many self-proclaimed tax experts market tax avoidance scams on the Internet and elsewhere. According to the IRS, one of the top 12 tax scams involves setting up a phony business at home and then deducting personal expenses, such as rent or mortgage payments, as business expenses. This scam has been around for years and the IRS is well aware of it—which means you won't get away with it if you're audited. You'll have to pay back the value of any tax deductions you claimed, plus penalties.

Popular home business scams include processing medical insurance claims, online schemes, mail-order scams, envelope stuffing, assembling craft items or sewing, multilevel marketing distributorships, and chain letters. Be extremely skeptical about work-at-home promotions that claim you'll be able to reap substantial tax deductions without making a substantial monetary investment in your home business, working at it regularly, or turning a profit.

Your home-based activity can be a business for tax purposes only if you can show that you are engaged in it to earn a profit, not simply to have fun or pursue a personal interest. If you can't prove a profit motive for the activity, you will be considered a hobbyist and forced to enter tax hell.

The IRS has established two tests to determine whether someone has a profit motive. One is a simple mechanical test that looks at whether you have earned a profit in three of the last five years. The other is a more complex test designed to determine whether you act like you want to earn a profit.

⚠ **Investing is not a business.** Investing, whether in stocks, real estate, collectibles, or anything else that makes money, is not a business, even though most people do it to earn a profit. See Section C, below.

Portrait of a Tax Scam Artist

Linda Borden ran a Florida-based income tax preparation service. According to the United States Justice Department, she promised her clients that they could legally pay zero taxes by using home business deductions. Claiming that she had found a "secret loophole" in the Internal Revenue Code, she told her customers that they could deduct personal expenses as business expenses by creating a fictitious home business. Among other things, she advised her customers (incorrectly) that:

- thinking about a business is the same as starting a business
- helping friends and relatives with their computer problems free of charge was a computer consulting business
- their "businesses" could pay $1,000 per month to them as rent for their homes and deduct the amount as a business expense
- they could characterize Thanksgiving and Christmas parties held at home as business "functions" and deduct the cost as a business expense, and
- they could deduct personal expenses such as haircuts, manicures, and cosmetics because a businessperson must look his or her best.

Borden charged her customers a $2,899 fee to prepare their tax returns. She had them provide a list of their personal assets and values. She then listed the value of these assets, including such items as dining room furniture and home entertainment equipment, as "office expenses" on IRS Schedule C. If necessary, she made up other expenses such as "advertising costs." When she was done, the losses on the customer's Schedule C roughly equaled his or her income from salary, investments, and other sources, so little or no tax was due.

Borden marketed her scheme through radio ads, the Internet, and recruiting seminars held in Florida, New Jersey, and Georgia. She had clients in 22 states. The Justice Department claimed that her tax preparation activities resulted in her customers underpaying their taxes by at least $15 million.

Eventually, the law caught up with Borden. In 2004, the Justice Department obtained an injunction (court order) permanently barring Borden from preparing federal income tax returns for others. She was also required to provide a list of her customers to the Justice Department. (*United States v. Borden*, Civil No. 6:03cv01705, MD FL, April 26, 2004.)

Crime Doesn't Pay, But It May Be Deductible

Back in the 1970s, Jeffrey Edmondson was a successful drug dealer in the Minneapolis area, selling substantial amounts of marijuana, cocaine, and amphetamines. Unfortunately for him, he got caught, convicted, and sentenced to jail. To add insult to injury, the IRS audited him and concluded that he owed over $17,000 in back taxes on his drug earnings, which he had never declared on his income taxes. Although one would have thought that a tax assessment was the least of his problems, Edmondson appealed the audit, claiming that the IRS failed to consider the tax-deductible costs he incurred in conducting his "business." The tax court held that Edmondson was self-employed in the business of selling amphetamines, cocaine, and marijuana. Therefore, he was entitled to a home office deduction because he conducted his "business" from home, and could also deduct the cost of goods sold from his drug dealing income. (*Edmondson v. Commissioner*, T.C. Memo 1981-623.)

In 1982, a special rule was added to the tax law barring tax deductions for expenses incurred in the business of drug trafficking. (IRC Sec. 280F.) However, people operating different types of illegal businesses, such as prostitution or contract killing, are still permitted to deduct their expenses.

1. Profit Test

If your venture earns a profit in three of five consecutive years, the IRS will presume that you have a profit motive. The IRS and courts look at your tax returns for each year you claim to be in business to see whether you turned a profit. Any legitimate profit—no matter how small—qualifies; you don't have to earn a particular amount or percentage. Careful year-end planning can help your business show a profit for the year. If clients owe you money, for example, you can press for payment before the end of the year. You can also put off paying expenses or buying new equipment until the new year.

Even if you meet the three-of-five test, the IRS can still try to claim that your activity is a hobby, but it will have to prove that you don't have a profit motive. In practice, the IRS usually doesn't attack ventures that pass the profit test unless the numbers have clearly been manipulated just to meet the standard.

The presumption that you are in business applies to your third profitable year and extends to all later years within the five-year period beginning with your first profitable year.

> **EXAMPLE:** Tom began to work at home as a self-employed graphic designer in 2000. Due to economic conditions and the difficulty of establishing a new business, his income varied dramatically from year to year. However, as the chart below shows, he managed to earn a profit in three of the first five years that he was in business.

Year	Losses	Profits
2000	$10,000	
2001		$5,500
2002		$9,000
2003	$6,000	
2004		$18,000
2005		$30,000

> If the IRS audits Tom's taxes for 2004, it must presume that he was in business during that year. Tom earned a profit during three of the five consecutive years ending with 2004, so the presumption that Tom is in business extends to 2006, five years after his first profitable year.

Special Rule for Horse Breeders

If you breed, train, show, or race horses at home, you need to show a profit in only two out of seven consecutive years for the IRS to presume that you have a profit motive. Why the special rule for horse breeders? Because it usually takes at least five to ten years to make a profit from horse breeding (and because breeders have an effective lobby in Washington, D.C.)

The IRS doesn't have to wait for five years after you start your activity to decide whether it is a business or hobby—it can audit you and classify your venture as a business or hobby at any time. However, you can give yourself some breathing room by filing IRS Form 5213, *Election to Postpone Determination as to Whether the Presumption Applies That an Activity Is Engaged in for Profit*, which requires the IRS to postpone its determination until you've been in business for at least five years.

Although this may sound like a good idea, it can backfire. Filing the election alerts the IRS to the fact that you might be a good candidate to audit on the hobby loss issue after five years. It also adds two years to the statute of limitations—the period in which the IRS can audit you and assess a tax deficiency. For this reason, almost no one ever files Form 5213. Also, you can't wait five years and then file the election once you know that you will pass the profit test. You must make the election within three years after the due date for the tax return for the first year you were in business—that is, within three years after the first April 15th following your first business year. So if you started doing business in 2005, you would have to make the election by April 15, 2009 (three years after the April 15, 2006 due date for your 2005 tax return).

There is one situation in which it might make sense to file Form 5213. If the IRS has already told you that you will be audited, you may want to file the election to postpone the audit for two years. However, you can do this only if the IRS audit notice is sent to you within three years after the due date for your first business tax return. If you're notified after this time, it's too late to file the election. In addition, you must file your election within 60 days after you receive an IRS audit notice, whenever it is given, or you'll lose the right to make the election.

2.   Behavior Test

If you keep incurring losses and can't satisfy the profit test, don't panic. Millions of business owners are in the same boat, whether they work at home or in outside offices. The sad fact is that many businesses don't earn profits every year or even for many years in a row, especially when they're first starting out. Indeed, over *four million* sole proprietors file a Schedule C tax form each year showing a loss from their business, yet the IRS does not categorize all of these ventures as hobbies.

You can continue to treat your activity as a business and fully deduct your losses, even if you have yet to earn a profit. However, you must take steps to demonstrate that your business isn't a hobby, in case you ever face an audit. You must be able to convince the IRS that earning a profit—not having fun or accumulating tax deductions—is your primary motive for doing what you do. This will require some time and effort on your part. It will be especially difficult if you're engaged in a home-based activity that could objectively be considered fun—such as creating artwork, antique collecting, photography, or writing—but it can be done. People who have incurred losses for seven, eight, or nine years in a row have been able to convince the IRS that they were running businesses.

How does the IRS figure out whether you really want to earn a profit? IRS auditors can't read your mind to establish your motives, and they certainly aren't going to take your word for it. Instead, they look at whether you behave as though you want to make money.

a.   Factors the IRS Considers

The IRS looks at the following "objective" factors to determine whether you are behaving like a person who wants to earn a profit (and therefore, should be classified as a business). You don't have to satisfy all of these factors to pass the test—the first three listed below (acting like a business, expertise, and time and effort expended) are the most important by far. Studies demonstrate that taxpayers who meet these three factors are always found to be in business, regardless of how they do on the rest of the criteria. (See Subsection b, below, for tips on satisfying these factors.)

- **Whether you act like a business.** Among other things, acting like a business means you keep good books and other records and carry on your activities in a professional manner.
- **Your expertise.** People who are trying to make money usually have some knowledge and skill in the field of their endeavor.
- **The time and effort you spend.** People who want to make profits work regularly and continuously. You don't have to work full time, but you must work regularly.

- **Your track record.** Having a track record of success in other businesses—whether or not they are related to your current business—helps show that you are trying to make money in your most recent venture.

- **Your history of profit and losses.** Even if you can't satisfy the profit test described in Section 1, above, earning a profit in at least some years helps show that you have a profit motive. This is especially true if you're engaged in a business that tends to be cyclical—that is, where one or two good years are typically followed by one or more bad years.

- **Your profits.** Earning a substantial profit, even after years of losses, can help show that you are trying to make a go of it. On the other hand, earning only small or occasional yearly profits when you have years of large losses and/or a large investment in the activity tends to show that you aren't in it for the money.

- **Your business assets.** Your profit includes money you make through the appreciation (increase in value) of your business assets. Even if you don't make any profit from your business's day-to-day operations, you can still show a profit motive if you stand to earn substantial profits when you sell your assets. Of course, this rule applies only to ventures that purchase assets that increase in value over time, such as land, collectibles, or buildings.

- **Your personal wealth.** The IRS figures that you probably have a profit motive if you don't have substantial income from other sources. After all, you'll need to earn money from your venture to survive. On the other hand, the IRS may be suspicious if you have substantial income from other sources (particularly if the losses from your venture generate substantial tax deductions).

- **The nature of your activity.** If your venture is inherently fun or recreational, the IRS may doubt that you are in it for the money. This means that you'll have a harder time convincing the IRS that you're in business if your venture involves activities such as art, crafts or sewing, photography, or writing; antique or stamp collecting; or training and showing dogs or horses (for example). However, these activities can still be businesses, if you carry them on in a businesslike manner. Even if they don't qualify as businesses, they can still be classified as income-producing activities, which is better than being a hobby.

b.   How to Pass the Behavior Test

Almost anyone with a home business can pass the behavior test, but it takes time, effort, and careful planning. Focus your efforts on the first three factors listed above. As noted earlier, a venture that can meet these three criteria will always be classified as a business. Here are some tips that will help you satisfy these crucial factors—and ultimately ace the behavior test.

Act Like a Businessperson

First and foremost, you must show that you carry on your activity in a businesslike manner. Doing the things outlined below will not only help you with the IRS, but will also help you actually earn a profit someday (or at least help you figure out that your business will not be profitable).

- **Keep good business records.** Keeping good records of your expenses and income from your activity is the single most important thing you can do to show that you want to earn a profit. Without good records, you'll never have an accurate idea of where you stand financially. Lack of records shows that you don't really care whether you make money or not—and it is almost always fatal in an IRS audit. You don't necessarily need an elaborate set of books; a simple record of your expenses and income will usually suffice. (See Chapter 15 for a detailed discussion of record keeping.)

    > **EXAMPLE:** A computer consultant who sold software on the side (at a loss) was found not to be profit motivated because he didn't keep adequate records. The tax court found that his failure to keep records meant that he was "unaware of the amount of revenue he could expect and had no concept of what his ultimate costs might be or how he might achieve any degree of cost efficiency." (*Flanagin v. Commissioner, T.C. Memo 1999-116.*)

- **Keep a separate checking account.** Open up a separate checking account for your business. This will help you keep your personal and business expenses separate—another factor that shows you want to make money.
- **Create a business plan.** Draw up a business plan with a realistic profit and loss forecast—a projection of how much money your business will bring in, your expenses, and how much profit you expect to make. The forecast should cover the next five or ten years. It should show you earning a profit some time in the future (although it doesn't have to be within five years). Both the IRS and courts are usually impressed by good business plans.

Need help drawing up a business plan? If you are really serious about making money, you will need a business plan. A business plan is useful not only to show the IRS that you are running a business, but also to convince others—such as lenders and investors—that they should support your venture financially. For detailed guidance on putting together a business plan, see *How to Write a Business Plan*, by Mike McKeever (Nolo).

- **Get business cards and letterhead.** It may seem like a minor matter, but obtaining business stationery and business cards shows that you think you are in business. Hobbyists ordinarily don't have such things. You can use software programs to create your own inexpensive stationery and cards.
- **Obtain all necessary business licenses and permits.** Getting the required licenses and permits for your activities will show that you are acting like a business. For example, a home-based inventor who attempted to build a wind-powered ethanol generator in his backyard was found to be a hobbyist partly because he failed to get a permit to produce alcohol from the federal Bureau of Alcohol, Tobacco and Firearms.
- **Obtain a separate phone line for your home office.** Set up a separate phone line for your business. This helps separate the personal from the professional and reinforces the idea that you're serious about making money.
- **Join professional organizations and associations.** Taking part in professional groups and organizations will help you make valuable

contacts and obtain useful advice and expertise. This helps to show that you're motivated to earn a profit.

Expertise

If you're already an expert in your field, you're a step ahead of the game. But if you lack the necessary expertise, you can develop it by attending educational seminars and similar activities and/or consulting with other experts. Keep records of your efforts (for example, a certificate for completing a training course or your notes documenting your attendance at a seminar or convention).

Work Steadily

You don't have to work full time to show that you want to earn a profit. It's fine to hold a full-time job and work at your sideline business only part of the time. However, you must work regularly and continuously rather than sporadically. You may establish any schedule you want, as long as you work regularly. For example, you could work at your business an hour every day, or one day a week, as long as you stick to your schedule.

Although there is no minimum amount of time you must work, you'll have a hard time convincing the IRS that you want to make money if you work fewer than five or ten hours a week. Keep a log showing how much time you spend working. Your log doesn't have to be fancy—you can just mark down your hours and a summary of your activities each day on your calendar or appointment book.

c.   Putting It All Together: A Tale of Two Animal Breeders

Two real cases involving animal breeders demonstrate how the behavior factors covered above can make or break you at audit time. The dog breeder discussed in the first example below never had a chance. But the husband and wife horse breeders discussed in the second example, who incurred losses for 12 straight years, were found to be in business because all of the factors showed that they sincerely wanted to earn a profit.

The Hapless Home Dog Breeder

Dr. Burger, an Indiana surgeon, decided to breed Afghan hounds with his wife. He spent $12,000 on three purebred dogs and established a kennel at his home. Although one of his dogs won best of breed at the prestigious Westminster Dog Show, and he sold a few puppies, Burger was unable to earn a profit from dog breeding. Indeed, he had substantial losses for six straight years, partly because he incurred substantial expenses for such items as a large motor home to drive to dog shows and improvements to his home (such as a $3,550 oriental rug he placed in his home office).

Here's a summary of Burger's expenses and earnings:

	Dog Breeding Income	Dog Breeding Expenses
1975	$0	$13,702
1976	$0	$26,098
1977	$0	$40,299
1978	$0	$46,374
1979	$4,650	$59,249
1980	$3,890	$54,596

The IRS audited Burger and concluded that dog breeding was an expensive hobby for him and his wife, not a business. The tax court agreed. Among the many factors that showed that Burger lacked a profit motive were:

- **Inadequate financial records:** Burger accumulated all of his dog breeding bills and receipts throughout the year and didn't tally them up until the end of the year when he entered them into a ledger under appropriate headings. The court found that Burger created these records simply to back up the expenses he claimed, not to run his business more efficiently. Because the expenses incurred were not posted monthly or allocated among the dogs maintained for sale, it was impossible for Burger to determine whether his business was profitable or what he could do to make more money.
- **Failure to act like a business:** Burger had no telephone directory listing for his dog breeding concern and failed to maintain insurance coverage on any of his dogs.

- **Lack of expertise:** Burger and his wife read many dog breeding books and articles and consulted a few people they considered expert in the field, but the court didn't consider this sufficient expertise to start a new business.
- **Lack of a business plan:** Burger failed to conduct even a basic investigation of what his costs might be or how much money he was likely to earn.
- **History of losses:** The dog breeding activity incurred losses for six straight years and showed no sign of ever becoming profitable, whether from business operations, appreciation of business assets, or some combination of the two.
- **Outside income:** Burger earned a substantial income from his medical practice, and did not need to rely on dog breeding for his livelihood. Indeed, he recouped substantial tax savings by deducting his dog breeding expenses from his other income.
- **Elements of personal gratification:** Burger and his wife exhibited great pride in their dogs' success when they testified in court. The judge concluded that Burger engaged in dog breeding primarily to obtain recognition in the dog breeding community by breeding winners, not to earn a profit. (*Burger v. Comm'r.*, T.C. Memo 1985-523.)

The Serious Home Horse Breeders

Dr. Engdahl, an orthodontist, and his wife decided to breed American saddle horses to supplement their income upon his eventual retirement. At first, they boarded their horses at an outside stable. When this arrangement did not prove profitable, they purchased a two-and-a-half acre ranch where they lived and bred their horses. They made numerous improvements to the ranch to aid their breeding activity, including constructing a stable and installing an irrigation system for pastureland.

Although the Engdahls' brood mares produced 11 live foals, they incurred losses from horse breeding for 12 straight years.

	Horse Breeding Income	Horse Breeding Expenses
1964	$164	$8,820
1965	$770	$13,776
1966	$658	$10,970
1967	$550	$18,343
1968	$115	$23,460
1969	$166	$16,468
1970	$10	$18,620
1971	$454	$17,543
1972	$1,136	$19,925
1973	$490	$19,016
1974	$666	$19,761
1975	$0	$14,916

The IRS audited the Engdahls and claimed they were hobbyists. They appealed to the tax court and won. The court concluded that, despite their long history of losses, the Engdahls were sincerely trying to earn a profit. Among the key factors were:

- **Good records:** The Engdahls kept good financial records, regularly posting their expenses to a separate ledger that was reviewed and summarized each quarter and at the end of each year by their accountant.

- **Changes in operations:** The Engdahls changed their method of operations when their breeding activity initially proved unprofitable: They switched from housing their horses in an outside stable to purchasing a ranch where they lived and stabled their horses. This move reduced their expenses. They also disposed of horses that did not meet their show or breeding expectations and fired a trainer who didn't work out. These changes were strong evidence that they wanted to earn money from horse breeding.

- **Consultation with experts:** They consulted with experts, including a CPA, veterinarians, trainers, and knowledgeable horse breeders, both before and after starting the horse breeding operations. They were advised that the market for breeding American saddle horses was good.

- **Businesslike operations:** The Engdahls regularly exhibited their horses at shows, and advertised their horses for sale and breeding. They also deposited the income they received from breeding in a separate bank account.
- **Expectation of asset appreciation:** The Engdahls' horse breeding assets had appreciated in value; their ranch tripled in value since they bought it and their horses also became more valuable. Thus, they had a reasonable expectation that they could eventually reap profits from the activity. This helped explain their willingness to keep incurring annual losses.
- **Lack of personal gratification:** The facts showed that the couple did not have much fun engaging in horse breeding. They worked 35 to 55 hours a week caring for the horses and mucking out stalls. Moreover, they did not ride their horses or use their ranch for social affairs.
- **Losses due to unforeseen circumstances:** The Engdahl's losses were partly caused by unforeseen circumstances—a change in fashion among horse buyers that depressed the market for their horses, as well as medical problems and the untimely death of some of their stable. (*Engdahl v. Comm'r*, 72 T.C. 659.)

B. Tax Consequences of Engaging In a Hobby

A hobby is something you do primarily for a purpose other than to make a profit—for example, to have fun, learn something, help your community, or impress your neighbors. Almost anything can be a hobby; common examples include creating artwork or crafts, photography, writing, or collecting coins, stamps, or other objects.

You do not want what you consider business activities to be deemed a hobby by the IRS. Because hobbies are not businesses, hobbyists cannot take the tax deductions to which businesspeople are entitled. Instead, hobbyists can deduct their hobby-related expenses only from the income the hobby generates. If you have no income from the hobby, you get no deduction. And you can't carry over the deductions to use in future years when you earn income—you lose them forever.

EXAMPLE: Charles collects antiques from his home. This year, he spent $10,000 buying antiques and earned no income from the activity. The IRS determines that this activity is a hobby. As a result, his $10,000 in expenses can be deducted only from any income he earned from his hobby. Because he earned no money from antique collecting during the year, he can't deduct any of these expenses this year—and he can't carry over the deduction to any future years.

Even if you have income from your hobby, you must deduct your expenses in a way that is less advantageous (and more complicated) than regular business deductions. Hobby expenses are deductible only as a Miscellaneous Itemized Deduction on IRS Schedule A, *Itemized Deductions* (the form that you file with your Form 1040 to itemize your deductions). This means that you can deduct your hobby expenses only if you itemize your deductions instead of taking the standard deduction. You can itemize deductions only if your total deductions are greater than the standard deduction—in 2004, the standard deduction was $4,850 for single people and $9,700 for married people filing jointly. If you do itemize, your hobby expenses can be used to offset your hobby income—but only to the extent that your expenses plus your other miscellaneous itemized deductions exceed 2% of your adjusted gross income (your total income minus business expenses and a few other deductions).

EXAMPLE: Assume that Charles, a single taxpayer, earned $5,000 from his antique collecting hobby this year, and had $10,000 in expenses. He could deduct $5,000 of these expenses—the amount equal to his antique collecting income—as an itemized deduction. However, Charles can only deduct those expenses that, together with his other miscellaneous itemized deductions, exceed 2% of Charles's adjusted gross income (AGI) for the year. If Charles's AGI was $100,000 and he had no other miscellaneous itemized deductions, he could not deduct the first $2,000 in expenses (2% x $100,000 = $2,000). So Charles can deduct only $3,000 of his antique collecting expenses on his Schedule A.

You don't need to understand all of this in great detail. Just be aware that an IRS finding that your activities are a hobby will probably result in tax disaster if you claimed business deductions for your expenses.

C. Investing and Other Income-Producing Activities

You can earn money without being in business. Many people do this all the time (or try to) by engaging in personal investing—for example, by having personal bank accounts that pay interest or investing in stocks that pay dividends and appreciate in value over time (hopefully). Activities like these—that are pursued primarily for profit but aren't businesses— are called income-producing activities. They are neither businesses nor hobbies, and receive their own special income tax treatment.

Many of the money-making activities people engage in at home are income-producing activities, not businesses. The distinction is crucial because income-producing activities generally receive less favorable tax treatment than businesses. Thus, you'll want to avoid this classification if possible.

1. Tax Consequences of Income-Producing Activities

You are entitled to deduct the ordinary and necessary expenses you incur to produce income, or to manage property held for the production of income—for example, real estate rentals. (IRC § 212.) This includes many of the same expenses that business people are allowed (many are covered in later chapters). For example, a person with a real estate rental may deduct maintenance and repair costs; an investor in the stock market may deduct fees for investment advice or accounting services.

However, there are some crucial limitations on deductions for income-producing activities (these restrictions do not apply to businesses):

- **No home office deduction:** You can't take a home office deduction for an income-producing activity. This important deduction is available only for businesses conducted from home. Obviously, this is a significant benefit to having your venture classified as a business.

- **No Section 179 expensing:** In addition, taxpayers involved in income-producing activities may not take advantage of IRC Section 179: the tax code provision that allows business people to deduct up to $102,000 in purchases of long-term personal property in a single year. (See Chapter 5 for more on Section 179.)
- **No seminar or convention deductions:** People with income-producing activities can't deduct their expenses for attending conventions, seminars, or similar events. Thus, for example, the cost of attending a stock market investment seminar is not deductible.
- **Limit on deducting investment interest:** Interest on money you borrow to use for a business is fully deductible (see Chapter 14, Section I). However, interest paid on money borrowed to make an investment is deductible only up to the amount of income you earn from the investment. If you earn no income from the investment, you get no deduction.
- **No deduction for start-up expenses:** Most of the expenses you incur in starting up a business are deductible over the first 60 months you are in business (see Chapter 3). You get no deduction at all for expenses incurred to start up an income-producing activity.
- **Limit on deductions:** If, in the course of an income-producing activity, you incur expenses to produce rents or royalties, you can deduct these expenses directly from your gross income (just like business expenses). What are rents and royalties? Rent is what you earn from renting real estate. Thus, landlords who don't qualify as businesspeople may still fully deduct their expenses. Royalties are income from things like copyrights or patents, or mineral leases.

    However, expenses incurred from any other income-producing activity—for example, investing—are miscellaneous itemized deductions. As such, they are deductible only to the extent they exceed 2% of your adjusted gross income—the same standard used for hobbies. If all your itemized deductions don't exceed the standard deductions, you can't itemize and you get no deduction at all. This is perhaps the unkindest cut of all.

- **Only individuals can deduct expenses from income-producing activities:** Corporations, partnerships, and limited liability companies cannot deduct these expenses.
- **No self-employment tax:** One good tax effect of having an income-producing activity is that you don't have to pay any self-employment tax on your income from the activity. Only people in business have to pay self-employment taxes. This is a substantial savings, because the self-employment tax is 15.3% of your self-employment income, up to an annual ceiling amount.

EXAMPLE: Jane is a wealthy Florida retiree who invests heavily in the stock market. To aid her investing, she subscribes to several very expensive stock market investing newsletters. She creates an office in her home, which she uses exclusively for her investing activities; she stocks it with a computer that she uses exclusively to track her investments. Because investing in stocks is an income-producing activity rather than a business, and her investing activity does not produce rents or royalties, she can deduct these expenses only if she itemizes her deductions, and only to the extent they exceed 2% of her adjusted gross income for the year. She may not take a home office deduction, and she can't use Section 179 to deduct the entire cost of the computer in the current year—instead, she'll have to depreciate it over time. (See Chapter 5 for more on depreciation and Section 179.) Had buying stocks been a business instead of an income-producing activity, Jane could have taken a home office deduction, and deducted the whole cost of the computer in one year. Moreover, her total deduction would not have been limited to the amount that exceeds 2% of her AGI.

When you have an income-producing activity, you don't file an IRS Schedule C, *Profit or Loss from Business*, with your tax return. You don't have a business, so that schedule doesn't apply. Instead, you list your expenses on Schedule A, *Itemized Deductions*. However, if your income comes from real estate or royalties, you list it and your expenses on Schedule E, *Supplemental Income and Loss*. Investors who incur capital gains or losses must file Schedule D, *Capital Gains and Losses*.

Need more information on investment deductions? For detailed guidance on tax deductions for investments, refer to IRS Publication 550, *Investment Income and Expenses*. Like all IRS publications, you can download it from the IRS website at www.irs.gov, or obtain it by calling the IRS at 800-829-3676.

2. Types of Income-Producing Activities

Anything you do primarily to earn a profit is an income-producing activity, unless it constitutes a business. You determine whether an activity is done primarily for profit by applying the three-of-five-year profit test or the behavioral test discussed in Section A above—the same tests used for businesses.

a. Investing

Investing is by far the most common income-producing activity. Investing means making money in ways other than running a business—for example:

- you put your money in a bank and earn interest
- you buy stocks, bonds, or other securities in publicly traded corporations and earn money from dividends or from the securities' appreciation in value over time
- you buy commodities like gold or pork bellies, and earn money from their appreciation in value over time
- you buy real estate and earn money from rents or from appreciation in the property's value over time, or
- you purchase an interest in a privately owned business run by someone else and earn money from the increase in the business's value over time or payments from the business.

What all these activities have in common is that you are not engaged in the active, continuous, and regular management or control of a business. You are passive—you put your money in somebody else's business and hope your investment will increase in value due to their efforts, not yours. Or, you buy an item like gold, and then sit and wait for it to increase in value.

Personal investing is always an income-producing activity for tax purposes, not a business. It makes no difference whether you invest from home or an outside office. Thus, for example, you can't take a home office deduction when you direct your investments from a home office.

b.   Other Activities

Investing is by far the most common and important income-producing activity, but it is by no means the only one. Almost any activity can qualify if your primary motive for engaging in it is making money, but you don't work at it enough for it to rise to the level of a business. You must work continuously and regularly at an activity for it to be a business.

3.   Trading In Stocks as a Business

People who buy stocks, bonds, and other securities as personal investments are not in business for tax purposes. But professional securities dealers and traders in securities are in business because they are not investors.

Such people are not subject to the restrictions on deductions listed in Section C1, above. Thus, for example, a professional stock trader may take a home office deduction (provided, of course, that the other requirements for the deduction are met; see Chapter 6). Professional dealers and traders may not deduct the commissions they pay to buy stocks or other securities; these are added to the basis (value) of the securities for purposes of calculating gain or loss when they are sold. Traders who are sole proprietors list their expenses on Schedule C, *Profit or Loss from Business*. However, they list their income or loss from trading on Schedule D, *Capital Gains and Losses*.

a.   Securities Dealers

A securities dealer is someone who maintains an inventory of stocks, bonds, or other securities and offers them for sale to buyers. Dealers make their money from the fees they charge buyers, not from dividends or appreciation in the value of the securities. Dealers include stock brokers and people who buy and sell securities on the floors of stock exchanges. If you're a dealer in securities, you undoubtedly already know it.

b. Professional Stock Traders

Most people who buy and sell stocks and other securities do it as an investment. Professional stock traders do it as a business. What's the difference between a stock market investor and a professional trader? A trader's profits come from the *very act of trading*; an investor's come from dividends or from the increase in value of his or her holdings over time. The IRS says that to qualify as a professional trader, you must meet these requirements:

- you must seek to profit from daily market movements in the price of securities, not from dividends, interest, or capital appreciation,
- your trading must be substantial, and
- your trading must be continuous and regular.

Key factors the IRS examines are:

- How long you hold your securities before you sell them. Professional traders usually don't hold on to most stocks for long, often selling them the same day they buy them. You don't have to be a day trader to be in business. But if you have a "buy and hold" portfolio, you are not a professional trader. Indeed, you're probably in trouble if you hold on to your stocks for more than two or three months on average.
- How often you trade. Professionals trade frequently. Many accountants use the rule of thumb that a professional investor must execute at least ten trades a day, five days a week; this adds up to at least 3,000 trades a year. However, people who do fewer trades a year may still qualify as professional investors.
- Whether you pursue trading to earn a living. Professionals usually trade to make a living (though they may have other sources of income).
- How much time you devote to trading. Professional traders spend a lot of time trading, though not necessarily all of their time.

Another accountant's rule of thumb is that a professional trader must trade at least five hours a day, five days a week. Moreover, you must trade continuously throughout the year.

EXAMPLE: Martha is a "day trader"—she buys and sells large numbers of stocks every day (hence the appellation). She holds on to her stocks for a very short time—often only a few minutes or hours, and rarely more than a few days. She makes profits (or incurs losses) based on the daily fluctuations of the stock market. She trades from her home office, using online trading services. She executes her trades herself, without the aid of a stock broker. She works full time at trading—usually seven to eight hours a day, all year round—and earns her livelihood from trading. She does substantial amounts of research, studying market trends, and looking for all types of hot investment information. She executes an average of 20 trades per day, and more than 4,000 per year. Martha is a professional stock trader, not an investor. Thus, she may deduct her expenses for her home office as well as other trading-related expenses.

Before the advent of the Internet, few people could afford to engage in the frequent trading required to be a professional trader because the commissions and other transaction costs were too great. Today, however, with inexpensive online trading, millions of people are making frequent stock trades from their homes. However, simply calling yourself a day trader will not make you a businessperson. You must meet the criteria listed above.

Note that being an investor or a professional trader is not an either/or proposition. You can be both. That is, you can hold on to some stocks as personal investments, while you actively trade others as your business. If you do this, be sure to keep the two categories separate.

Any Type of Buying and Selling Can Be a Business

Businesses aren't limited to the buying and selling of stocks. Buying and selling anything can be a business if you earn your money from the buying and selling itself and you engage in the activity regularly and continuously. For example, thousands of people now have businesses buying and selling items on Ebay. However, sporadic buying and selling is not a business, even though it is profitable—for example, occasionally selling items on EBay won't qualify as a business.

4. Real Estate as a Business

Another way people commonly earn money without running a business is by investing in real estate. However, real estate can also qualify as a business if you are actively and regularly involved.

a. Real Estate Dealers

A real estate dealer is anyone who holds property primarily for sale to customers, such as builders or developers. Numerous and frequent sales over an extended time period are the hallmark of a dealer who is engaged in a business, not an income-producing activity.

Being classified as a dealer is often a tax disadvantage because gains from sales of real property by a dealer are usually subject to ordinary income tax rates. In contrast, gains realized by an investor are usually taxed at capital gains rates, which are lower. However, dealers are better off if real estate proves to be a money-losing proposition: a dealer is typically permitted to deduct the full amount of a loss, while an investor's deductions for losses may be strictly limited.

b. Managing Rental Property

You don't have to be a bigshot developer to be in the business of real estate. You can also run a business actively managing rental real estate. But the key word here is active. You can't just sit back and collect rent checks while someone else does all the work of being a landlord. You must be actively involved on a regular, systematic, and continuous basis.

EXAMPLE 1: Carolyn Anderson, a nurse, owned an 80-acre farm that she rented to a tenant farmer. She attempted to deduct her home office expenses by claiming that the rental activity was a business. The IRS and tax court disagreed because Carolyn's landlord activities involved little more than depositing rent checks and occasionally talking to her tenant on the telephone. (*Anderson v. Comm'r*, T.C. Memo 19820576.)

EXAMPLE 2: Edwin Curphey, a dermatologist, owned six rental properties in Hawaii. He converted a bedroom in his home into an office for his real estate activities. Curphey personally managed his rentals, which included seeking new tenants, supplying furnishings, and cleaning and otherwise preparing the units for new tenants. The court held that these activities were sufficiently systematic and continuous to place him in the business of real estate rental. As a result, Curphey was entitled to a home office deduction. (*Curphey v. Comm'r*, 73 T.C. 766 (1980).)

Even if managing real estate is a business, you ordinarily don't file Schedule C, *Profit or Loss From Business*, to report your income and expenses. Instead, you file Schedule E, *Supplemental Income and Loss*. However, you must file Schedule C if you run a hotel, motel, or apartment building where you provide hotel-type services to the occupants (such as maid services).

Need more help with real estate taxation? Taxation of activities relating to real estate is a complex subject that is beyond the scope of this book. A good reference is *The Real Estate Investor's Tax Guide*, by Vernon Hoven (Dearborn). ■

Chapter 3

Avoiding the Start-Up Tax Trap

The tax law contains a trap for the unwary: If you don't plan things right, you may be prevented from immediately deducting the money you spend to start up your business. Instead, you'll have to deduct these costs over five years. Fortunately, however, most home businesspeople should be able to avoid the start-up tax trap, or at least greatly limit its impact.

A. What Are Start-Up Expenses?

To take business deductions, you must actually be running a business (see Chapter 2). This commonsense rule can lead to problems if you want to start (or buy) a new business. The money you spend to get your business up and running is not a currently deductible business operating expense because your business hasn't yet begun.

Instead, business start-up expenses are capital expenses—costs that you incur to acquire an asset (a business) that will benefit you for more than one year. A special tax rule allows you to deduct many of these start-up expenses over the first 60 months that you are in business. Without this special rule for start-up expenses, these costs (capital expenses) would not be deductible until you sold or otherwise disposed of your business. Although being able to deduct your start-up expenses over 60 months is better than getting no deduction at all, it is not nearly as good as being able to deduct your expenses in a single year. That's why most business owners will want to avoid the start-up tax rule, if possible.

Once your business begins, the same expenses that were start-up expenses before your business began become currently deductible business operating expenses. For example, supplies you purchase *after* your home business starts are currently deductible operating expenses, but supplies you buy *before* your business begins are start-up expenses (which you have to deduct over 60 months).

> **EXAMPLE:** Diana Drudge is sick of her office job. She decides to start a business as a home-based independent travel agent. Before her business begins, she spends $5,000 of her life savings on a Yellow Pages ad. Her business finally starts on July 1. Because her ad is a start-up expense, she can't deduct the full cost in her first

year of business—instead, she must deduct it in equal installments over the next 60 months. Diana's business is only in operation for six months in her first year, so she can deduct only one-tenth of her start-up costs that year, or $500.

⚠ **Your business must actually start to have start-up expenses.** If your business never gets started, many of your expenses will not be deductible. So think carefully before spending your hard-earned money to investigate starting a new business venture (see Section E, below).

1.   Common Start-Up Expenses

The vast majority of home business owners (87%, according to a 1999 Small Business Administration study) start new businesses rather than buying an existing venture. Most of the costs of investigating whether, where, and how to start a new business, as well as the cost of actually creating it, qualify as business start-up expenses.

Here are some common types of deductible start-up expenses:

- operating expenses incurred before the business begins, such as home office rent, telephone service, utilities, office supplies, equipment rental, and repairs
- the cost of investigating what it would take to create a successful business, including research on potential markets or products
- advertising costs, including advertising for your business opening
- costs for employee training before the business opens
- expenses related to obtaining financing, suppliers, customers, or distributors
- licenses, permits, and other fees, and
- fees paid to lawyers, accountants, consultants, and others for professional services.

2.   Special Rules for Some Expenses

There are some costs related to opening a business that are not considered start-up expenses. Many of these costs are still deductible, but different rules and restrictions apply to the way they are deducted.

a.   Expenses That Wouldn't Qualify as Business Operating Expenses

You get no deduction at all for pre-opening operating expenses, that are not ordinary, necessary, directly related to the business, and reasonable in amount. (See Chapter 4 for a discussion of business operating expenses.) For example, you can't deduct the cost of pleasure travel or entertainment *unrelated* to your business. These expenses would not be deductible as operating expenses by an ongoing business, so you can't deduct them as start-up expenses either.

b.   Inventory

The largest expense many home businesspeople incur before they start their business is for inventory—that is, buying the goods (or the materials to make them) that they will sell to customers. For example, if you decide to start an EBay business selling items you buy at flea markets, you would treat the items you purchase for resale as inventory. (See Chapter 10 for more on deducting inventory costs.)

c.   Long-Term Assets

Long-term assets are things you purchase for your business that will last for more than one year, such as computers, office equipment, cars, and machinery. Long-term assets you buy before your business begins are not considered part of your start-up costs. Instead, you must treat these purchases like any other long-term asset you buy *after* your business begins—you must either depreciate the item over several years or deduct the cost in one year under IRS Section 179. (Chapter 5 explains how to deduct long-term assets.) However, you can't take depreciation or Section 179 deductions until after your business begins.

Depreciating Long-Term Assets Versus Deducting Start-Up Expenses

Depreciating long-term assets and deducting start-up expenses are two very different things. For example, you must deduct start-up expenses over a 60-month (minimum) period, whereas the period for depreciation varies depending on the nature of the asset—it can be anywhere from three years to 39 years. In addition, the amount you can depreciate each year varies and is usually calculated to give you the biggest deductions in the early years. For start-up expenses, the cost is always spread equally over 60 months. And, many business owners use Section 179 to deduct the cost of their long-term assets in a single year—something you can't do with start-up expenses. (See Chapter 5 for a detailed discussion of depreciation and Section 179.)

d.   Research and Development Costs

The tax law includes a special category for research and development expenses. These are costs a business incurs to discover something new (in the laboratory or experimental sense), such as a new invention, formula, prototype, or process. They include laboratory and computer supplies, salaries, rent, utilities, other overhead expenses, and equipment rental, but not the cost of purchasing long-term assets. Research and development costs are currently deductible under Section 174 of the Internal Revenue Code, even if you incur them before the business begins operations. This tax rule is a particular benefit to home-based inventors.

Want more information on tax deductions for inventors? For a detailed discussion of deductions for research and development, see *The Inventor's Law, Business, and Tax Guide*, by Stephen Fishman (Nolo).

e.   Organizational Costs

Costs you incur to form a partnership, limited liability company, or corporation are technically not part of your start-up costs. However, the rule for deducting these costs is the same: You must spread the deduction for organizational costs out over the first 60 months you are in business, under IRC Section 248.

3.   Buying An Existing Business

Different (and harsher) rules apply if you buy an existing business rather than creating a new one. The money you pay to actually purchase the existing business is not deductible. Instead, it is a capital expense that becomes part of the tax basis of your business. If and when you sell the business, you will be able to deduct this amount from any profit you make on the sale before taxes are assessed. The expenses you incur to decide *whether* to purchase a business and *which* business you should buy are start-up expenses. Few home business owners (only 13%, according to the Small Business Administration) buy existing businesses, so this rule probably won't apply to you.

What's Tax Basis?

Tax basis is accounting lingo for your investment in property for tax purposes. Generally, your tax basis is the amount you paid for the property plus the costs of any improvements you make to it. You need to know your basis to figure your gain or loss on a sale, whether you sell a single item of property or an entire business. Chapter 5 explains how to figure out your tax basis.

---

4.   Expanding an Existing Business

What if you already have a home business and decide to expand your operation? The cost of expanding an existing business is considered a business operating expense, not a start-up expense. As long as these costs are ordinary and necessary, they are currently deductible. However, this rule applies only when the expansion involves a business that is the same as—or similar to—the existing business. The costs of expanding into a new business are start-up costs, not operating expenses.

B. When Does a Business Begin?

The date when your home business begins for tax purposes marks an important turning point. Operating expenses you incur after your business starts are currently deductible, while expenses you incur before this crucial date will have to be deducted over many years, if at all.

A new business begins for tax purposes when it starts to function as a going concern and performs the activities for which it was organized. (*Richmond Television Corp. v. U.S.*, 345 F.2d 901 (4th Cir. 1965).) The IRS says that a venture becomes a going concern when it acquires all of the assets necessary to perform its intended functions and puts those assets to work. In other words, your business begins when you start doing business, whether or not you are actually earning any money.

This is usually not a difficult test to apply. Here are the rules for some common types of home businesses.

1. Home Manufacturers

A manufacturing or other business that produces goods begins when it starts using its assets to make saleable products. The products don't have to be completed, nor do sales have to be solicited or made. For example, a home crafts business begins when materials and equipment are acquired, and work is begun on the crafts. If it takes several days to create a completed craft item (and to find someone willing to buy it), that doesn't matter—the business begins when the process of creating the crafts starts.

2. Knowledge Workers

Writers, artists, photographers, graphic designers, computer programmers, and similar knowledge workers might not think of themselves as manufacturers, but the courts do. For example, courts have held that a home-based writer's business begins when he or she starts working on a writing project. (*Gestrich v. Commr.* 74 T.C. 525, (1982).) Just like a manufacturing business, a writer's business begins when the necessary materials are in place and the work starts—not when the work is finished or sold. Similarly, an inventor's business begins when he or she starts working on an invention in earnest, not when the invention is completed, patented, or sold.

3. Service Providers

If your business involves providing a service to customers or clients— for example, accounting, consulting, financial planning, or law—your business begins when you first offer your services to the public. No one has to hire you; you just have to be available for hire. For example, a consultant's business begins when he or she is available for hire by clients.

4. Existing Businesses

If you buy an existing business, your business is deemed to begin for tax purposes when the purchase is complete—that is, when you take over ownership.

C. Avoiding the Start-Up Tax Rule

By understanding and applying the rules about when a business begins for tax purposes, it should be possible for most home businesses to avoid having most or even all of their initial expenses classified as start-up expenses. The key is simply to avoid spending a lot of money until your business begins. This way, you will be able to deduct your costs in the current year as operating costs, rather than waiting 60 months to deduct them as start-up expenses.

This strategy should be easy for most home businesses to implement. After all, you won't have to lay out money for a place of business— such as a retail store, restaurant, or outside office—before you begin your venture. Here are some tips that will help you avoid the start-up tax trap.

1.   Start Small, Spend Little

Depending on the nature of your business, you may be able to begin your operation without spending much money. If you provide a service, such as accounting, bookkeeping, consulting, law, or marketing, you probably won't need to shell out a lot of money up front. Remember, to start a business for tax purposes, you only have to offer services to customers or clients; it's not necessary for anyone to actually hire you. Don't buy a new computer or anything else you don't absolutely need to get your business going. Once your business begins, you can buy whatever you need and currently deduct it (assuming it qualifies as a business expense).

> **EXAMPLE:** Remember Diana Drudge, who wanted to start a business as a home-based independent travel agent? She wants to buy a Yellow Pages ad for $5,000 to promote her business, but would rather deduct the cost in one year than deduct it over 60 months as a start-up expense. To do this, she begins her business by offering her services to the public, and then buys the Yellow Pages ad. The $5,000 is now a currently deductible operating expense, not a start-up expense, so she gets to deduct the full amount in one year.

2.   Don't Pay Your Bills Until You're in Business

If you have to buy something before you start your business, try to avoid paying for it until after your business begins. This way, you can currently deduct the expense. (This assumes you're a cash basis taxpayer—someone who reports income and expenses on the date they are actually paid, not on the date when an agreement to pay is made—which most home businesses are; see Chapter 15.) If you can get your business started quickly, your creditors should not have to wait long to be paid.

> **EXAMPLE:** Instead of beginning her travel agent business before buying her Yellow Pages ad, Diana buys the ad before she starts operations; but she doesn't pay for it until after her business begins, one month later. Because Diana is a cash basis taxpayer, the ad is a currently deductible operating expense.

Proving When Your Business Begins

Your business begins when you make your services available to the public (or are ready to sell and/or produce a product). There are many ways you can do this. Being able to show the IRS a copy of an advertisement for your business is a great way to prove you were open for business. But you don't need to buy an expensive Yellow Pages ad like Diana in the example above; a free ad in the local Penny Saver will do. You can also mail out brochures or other promotional materials. If you don't want to pay for postage, you can leave them on your neighbors' doors or car windshields.

You don't have to advertise to show you are open for business—simply handing out business cards is sufficient. Have cards made up and start giving them out. Give your first cards to friends and associates who could testify for you if you're audited by the IRS.

Establish your home office to show you are ready to take on clients or customers. Take a photo of it with a digital camera (which will be date-stamped).

If you're selling a product, you can start with a small inventory. Keep invoices and other documents showing the date you purchased the inventory. Photograph your equipment and inventory with your digital camera.

If you are making a product at home, your business begins when you have all the equipment and materials ready to start production. Keep invoices and other documents showing when you obtained these items.

D. How to Deduct Start-Up Expenses

If you do incur start-up expenses, you can start deducting them once your business begins. You can deduct them in equal amounts over the first 60 months you're in business. This process is called amortization. Sixty months is the minimum amortization period, but you can choose a longer period if you wish.

1.   Making a Section 195 Election

You must indicate that you want to deduct start-up costs on your tax return by making a Section 195 election. (Section 195 is the tax law governing start-up expenses). To deduct your start-up expenses, you must do two things: (1) File IRS Form 4562, *Depreciation and Amortization*, and (2) attach a statement (called a Section 195 statement) to your tax return listing your start-up expenses, the dates you incurred them, the date your business began, the number of months in the amortization period, and a description of your business. If you forget to list all of your start-up costs in your Section 195 statement, you can file an amended statement later listing any items you omitted. However, you may not list any expenses that you have already claimed were deductible under other tax laws—for example, as ordinary and necessary operating expenses.

> **EXAMPLE:** Tom failed to list a $1,000 accounting fee as a start-up expense in his Section 195 statement. Instead, he mistakenly deducted the fee as a currently deductible business operating expense. Three years later, he is audited. The auditor says Tom should have listed the fee as a start-up cost, not a currently deductible operating expense, and disallows the deduction. Tom cannot amend his Section 195 statement to add the fee as a start-up expense because he has already claimed, albeit mistakenly, that the fee was deductible under another tax rule. Even though Tom made an innocent mistake, he won't get any deduction for his accounting fee.

The moral is this: Be very careful when you prepare your first tax return after your business opens. Figure out how to categorize each of your expenses, and make sure to list every start-up expense in your Section 195 election.

You must make a timely election to deduct start-up expenses. If you want to deduct your start-up expenses, you must file your election (IRS Form 4562 and Section 195 statement) on or before the due date for your first tax return after you start your business. For example, if your business begins in 2004, you must file the election with your 2004 tax return, due April 15, 2005 (or later if you receive an extension). If you miss this deadline, you have one last chance to make your election: You may file an amended return making the election within six months after the date your original return was due.

If you don't make a Section 195 election, your start-up costs become part of the tax basis of your business. This might be advantageous if you don't expect your business to earn a profit for many years or you want to reduce your deductions in order to show a profit. Deducting your start-up expenses will decrease your business profits for the first 60 months, because they will be deducted from your business income. Forgoing the deduction will therefore increase the profit your business earns over that time. This might be advisable, for example, if you fear that the IRS will claim your venture is a hobby instead of a business. Earning profits is the best way to show that an activity is a real business. (See Chapter 2 for more on how to prove that you are running a business.)

2.   If Your Business Doesn't Last 60 Months

Not all home businesses last for 60 months. In fact, most small businesses don't last this long. But you don't lose the value of your deductions if you sell or close your business before you have had a chance to deduct all of your start-up expenses.

If you sell your business or its assets, your leftover start-up costs will be added to your tax basis in the business. This is just as good as getting a tax deduction. If you sell your business at a profit, you can subtract the remaining start-up costs from your profits before taxes are assessed, which reduces your taxable gain. If you sell at a loss, you can add the start-up costs to the money you lost—because this shortfall is deductible, a larger loss means a larger deduction, and therefore lower taxes.

If you simply go out of business with no assets to sell, you can deduct your leftover start-up expenses as ordinary business losses. This means that you can deduct them from any income you have that year, deduct them in future years, or deduct them from previous years' taxes.

Keep Good Expense Records

Whether you intend to start a new business or buy an existing one, you should keep careful track of every expense you incur before the business begins. Obviously, you should keep receipts and canceled checks. You should also keep evidence that will help show that the money went to investigate a new business—for example, correspondence and e-mails with accountants, attorneys, and consultants; marketing or financial reports; and copies of advertisements. You will need these records to calculate your deductions and to prove your expenses to the IRS if you face an audit.

E.   Expenses For Businesses That Never Begin

Many people investigate starting a home business, but the venture never gets off the ground. While this is no doubt disappointing, you might be able to recoup some of your expenses in the form of tax deductions.

1.   General Start-Up Costs

General start-up costs are expenses you incur *before* you decide to start a new business or acquire a specific existing business. They include all of the costs of doing a general search for, or preliminary investigation of, a business—for example, costs you incur analyzing potential markets. If you never start the business, these costs are personal and not deductible. In other words, they are a dead loss.

> **EXAMPLE:** Bruno would like to start his own home business as a fashion designer. He buys several books on fashion, attends a fashion design course, and travels to New York City, where he stays several nights in a hotel, to speak to people in the fashion industry. However, he ultimately decides to keep his day job. None of the expenses he incurred in investigating the fashion design business idea are deductible.

One intended effect of this rule is that you can't deduct travel, entertainment, or other "fun" expenses by claiming that you incurred them to investigate a business *unless you actually start the business.* Otherwise, it would be pretty tough for the IRS to figure out whether you were really considering a new venture or just having a good time.

> **EXAMPLE:** Kim spends $5,000 on a two-week Hawaii vacation. While there, she attends a one-hour seminar on how to make money by stuffing envelopes at home. However, she never starts the business. The cost of her trip is not a start-up expense.

Corporations can deduct general start-up costs. A corporation can deduct general start-up expenses as a business loss, even if the business never gets going.

2. Costs to Start or Acquire a Specific Business

The expenses you incur to actually start or acquire a particular business (that ultimately never begins operations) are not deductible as start-up expenses. Expenses such as accounting and legal fees may be deducted as investment expenses, which are generally deductible only as itemized miscellaneous deductions (IRC § 165; see Chapter 2 for more information on deducting investment expenses). Costs incurred to acquire a specific asset for your future business—for example, equipment—are capital expenses. You get no direct tax deduction for these costs, but you may recover them when you sell or otherwise dispose of the asset. ■

Chapter 4

Home Business Operating Expenses

This chapter covers the basic rules for deducting business operating expenses—the bread and butter expenses virtually every home business incurs for things like home office expenses, supplies, and business-related travel. If you don't maintain an inventory or buy expensive equipment, these day-to-day costs will probably be your largest category of business expenses (and your largest source of deductions).

A. Requirements for Deducting Operating Expenses

There are so many different kinds of business operating expenses that the tax code couldn't possibly list them all. Instead, if you want to deduct an item as a business operating expense, you must make sure the expenditure meets certain requirements. If it does, it will qualify as a deductible business operating expense. To qualify, the expense must be:

- ordinary and necessary
- current
- directly related to your business, and
- reasonable in amount. (IRC § 162.)

1.   Ordinary and Necessary

The first requirement is that the expense must be ordinary and necessary. This means that the cost is common, "helpful and appropriate" for your business (*Welch v. Helvering*, 290 U.S.111 (1933)). The expense doesn't have to be indispensable to be necessary; it need only help your business in some way—even if it's minor. A one-time expenditure can be ordinary and necessary.

> **EXAMPLE:** Bill, a home-based marketing consultant, hires a freelance researcher for two weeks to help him write a marketing report for a client. Hiring such assistance is a common and accepted practice among consultants. The researcher's fee is deductible as an ordinary and necessary expense for Bill's business.

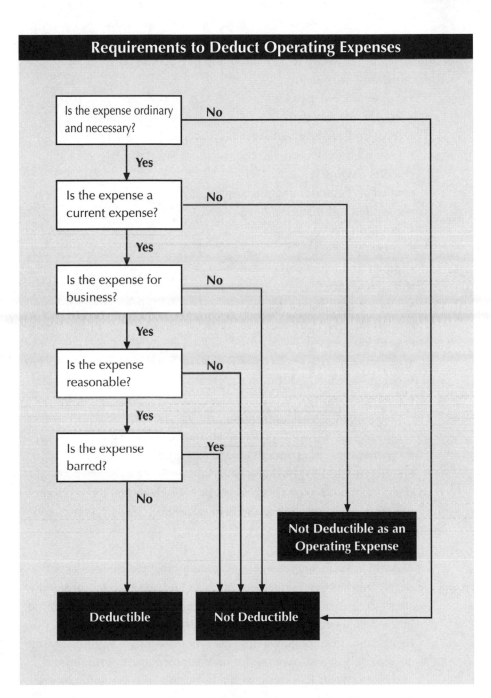

It's usually fairly easy to figure out whether an expense passes the ordinary and necessary test. Some of the most common types of operating expenses include:

- home office expenses
- equipment rental
- legal and accounting fees
- car and truck expenses
- travel expenses
- meal and entertainment expenses
- supplies and materials
- publications
- subscriptions
- repair and maintenance expenses
- business taxes
- interest on business loans
- licenses
- banking fees
- advertising costs
- business-related education expenses
- postage
- professional association dues
- business liability and property insurance
- payments to independent contractors, and
- software used for business.

Generally, the IRS won't second-guess your claim that an expense is ordinary and necessary, unless the item or service clearly has no legitimate business purpose.

> **EXAMPLE:** An insurance agent claimed a business deduction for part of his handgun collection because he had to go to "unsafe job sites" to settle insurance claims, and there was an unsolved murder in his neighborhood. The Tax Court disallowed the deduction explaining, "A handgun simply does not qualify as an ordinary and necessary business expense for an insurance agent, even a bold and brave Wyatt Earp type with a fast draw who is willing to risk injury or death in the service of his clients." (*Samp v. Comm'r*, TC Memo 1981-1986.)

The following chart lists the 15 most common operating expenses claimed in 2001 by sole proprietor business owners who earned $25,000 to $100,000 that year.

15 Most Common Operating Expenses for Small Businesses	
Expense	Percentage of Business Owners Who Claimed the Expense
1. Car and truck expenses	81%
2. Utilities	68%
3. Supplies (other than office supplies)	60%
4. Office supplies	60%
5. Legal and professional services	60%
6. Insurance	54%
7. Taxes	51%
8. Meals and entertainment	47%
9. Advertising	43%
10. Repairs	40%
11. Travel	31%
12. Rent on business property	26%
13. Home office	21%
14. Rent on equipment and machinery	21%
15. Interest	18%

Source: *Information on Expenses Claimed by Small Business Sole Proprietorships,* Government Accounting Office (GAO-04-304; January 2004.)

2.   Current Expense

Only current expenses are deductible as business operating expenses. Current expenses are for items that will benefit your business for less than one year. These are the costs of keeping your business going on a day-to-day basis, including money you spend on items or services that get used up, wear out, or become obsolete in less than one year. A good example of a current expense is your business's monthly phone bill, which benefits your business for one month. In contrast, buying a telephone for your business would be a capital expense (not a current expense) because the phone will benefit your business for more than one year. Other common capital expenses include cars, business equipment, computers, and real estate. (For more on deducting capital expenses, see Chapter 5.)

Current expenses are currently deductible—that is, they are fully deductible in the year when you incur them. Because all business operating expenses are current expenses, they are also all currently deductible. However, your total annual deduction for some operating expenses (notably home office costs) cannot exceed the profits you earn from the business in that year. (See Chapter 6 for more on the home office deduction.)

3.   Business Related

An expenditure must be *directly related to your business* to be deductible as a business operating expense. This means that you cannot deduct personal expenses. For example, the cost of a personal computer is a deductible operating expense only if you use the computer for business purposes; it is not deductible if you use it to pay personal bills or play computer games. If you buy something for both personal and business use, you can deduct only the business portion of the expense. For example, if you buy a cellular phone and use it half of the time for business calls and half of the time for personal calls, you can deduct only half of the cost of the phone as a business expense.

A business expense for one person can be a personal expense for another, and vice versa. For example, a professional screenwriter could probably deduct the cost of going to movies—seeing movies is an essential part of the screenwriting business. But a salesperson could not deduct this type of expense.

Many expenses have both a personal and a business component, which can make it difficult to tell if an expense is business related. Even the most straightforward costs can present difficulties. For example, it's usually easy to tell whether postage is a personal or business expense. If you mail something for your business, it's a business expense; if you mail something unrelated to your business, it's a personal expense. But even here, there can be questions. For example, should a doctor be allowed to deduct the postage for postcards he sends to his patients while he is on vacation in Europe? (The tax court thinks so—it said the doctor's postage was deductible as an advertising expense (*Duncan v Commr*, 30 TC 386 (1958).)

The IRS has created rules and regulations for some operating expenses that commonly involve a crossover of personal and business use. Some of these rules lay out guidelines to help you figure out when an expense is and isn't deductible. Others impose record-keeping and other requirements to prevent abuses by dishonest taxpayers. Most of the complexity in determining whether an expense is deductible as a business operating expense involves understanding and applying these special rules and regulations.

The expenses that present the most common problems (and are therefore subject to the most comprehensive IRS rules and regulations) include:

- home office expenses (see Chapter 6)
- meals and entertainment (see Chapter 7)
- travel (see Chapter 9)
- car and truck expenses (see Chapter 8)
- business gifts (see Chapter 14)
- bad debts (see Chapter 14)
- employee benefits (see Chapter 11)
- interest payments (see Chapter 14)
- health insurance (see Chapter 12)
- casualty losses (see Chapter 14)
- taxes (see Chapter 14), and
- education expenses (see Chapter 14).

Through these rules and regulations, the IRS provides guidance on the following types of questions:

- If you rent an apartment and use part of one room as a business office, should you be allowed to deduct all or a portion of the rent as a business operating expense? How much of the room must you use as an office (and for what period of time) to convince the IRS that you're using the room for business rather than personal purposes? (See Chapter 6 for information on the home office deduction.)

- Can you deduct the money you spend on a nice suit to wear when you visit business clients? (See Chapter 14 for information about deducting business clothing.)
- Can you deduct the cost of going out of town for a business meeting? Does it matter if you spend part of the time sightseeing? (See Chapter 9 for rules about deducting business travel expenses.)
- Can you deduct the cost of lunch with a former client or customer? Does it matter whether you actually talk about business during lunch? (See Chapter 7 for rules about deducting meals and entertainment.)

Writer's Brothel Expenses Not Deductible

Vitale, a retired federal government budget analyst, decided to write a book about two men who travel cross-country to patronize a legal brothel in Nevada. To authenticate the story and develop characters for the book, he visited numerous legal brothels in Nevada by acting as a customer for prostitutes. He kept a detailed journal describing his experiences at the brothels, including the dates (and sometimes the hours) of his visits, the prostitutes he met, and the amount of cash he paid each one. He wrote and published the book, called *Searchlight, Nevada*, and later claimed a deduction of $3,480 on his tax return for cash payments to prostitutes. The tax court denied the deduction for prostitutes, declaring that the expenditures were "so personal in nature as to preclude their deductibility." (*Vitale v Commr*, T.C. Memo 1999-131.)

4.   Reasonable In Amount

Subject to some important exceptions, there is no limit on how much you can deduct, as long as the amount is reasonable and you don't deduct more than you spend. As a rule of thumb, an expense is reasonable unless there are more economical and practical ways to achieve the same result. If the IRS finds that your deductions are unreasonably large, it will disallow them or at least disallow the portion it finds unreasonable.

Certain areas are hot buttons for the IRS—especially entertainment, travel, and meal expenses. The IRS won't allow any lavish expenses here, and you will have to follow strict rules requiring you to fully document these deductions (see Chapters 7 and 9). The reasonableness issue also comes up when a business pays excessive salaries to employees to obtain a large tax deduction. For example, a home business owner might hire his 12 year old son to answer phones and pay him $50 an hour—clearly an excessive wage for this type of work.

For a few types of operating expenses, the IRS limits how much you can deduct. These include:

- the home office deduction, which is limited to the profit from your business (although you can carry over and deduct any excess amount in future years) (see Chapter 6)
- business meals and entertainment, which are only 50% deductible (see Chapter 7)
- travel expenses, which are limited depending on the length of your trip and the time you spend on business while away (see Chapter 9), and
- business gifts, which are subject to a $25 maximum deduction per individual per year (see Chapter 14).

A Deductible Day in the Life of a Home Business Owner

Gina is a full-time suburban mom who runs a part-time baby photography business from her home office. On a particular day, she gets up, makes breakfast, and drives her two kids to school. On the way, she drops off some photos at the home of a client. Later that morning, she drives to the grocery store where she buys food for her family and a box of envelopes for her business. She then drives to a fancy restaurant, where she has lunch with an old friend who recently had a baby. Along with personal chitchat, they arrange a date for Gina to photograph the friend's baby. Gina pays for the lunch. That afternoon, Gina enrolls in a class on photographic printmaking at a local college. She plans to use this skill to expand her photography business. Later that day, the maid comes to clean the house, including Gina's home office (which takes up 20% of her home). That evening, Gina and her husband go to a baby photo exhibition at a local art gallery, where they pay for parking.

Here are her tax deductions for business operating expenses:

Activity	Type of Business Expense	Amount of Business Expense	
Driving to drop off photos to clients	Business transportation	5 miles at 36.5 cents per mile =	$1.82
Driving to grocery store	Business transportation	7 miles at 36.5 cents per mile =	2.55
Buying envelopes	Business supplies		5.00
Lunch	Business meal	50% of cost of lunch =	25.00
Driving to lunch	Business transportation	3 miles at 36.5 cents per mile =	1.09
Registering for photography class	Business-related education		200.00
Cleaning home office	Business operating expense	20% of $75 house-cleaning fee =	15.00
Parking fee to visit photo exhibition	Business-related transportation costs		10
Total Deductions			$260.46

As this example shows, you should get into the habit of looking for possible operating expense deductions whenever you spend money on anything related to your business-

B. Operating Expenses That Are Not Deductible

Even though they might be ordinary and necessary, some types of operating expenses are not deductible under any circumstances. In some cases, this is because Congress has declared that it would be morally wrong or otherwise contrary to sound public policy to allow people to deduct these costs. In other cases, Congress simply doesn't want to allow the deduction. These nondeductible expenses include:

- fines and penalties paid to the government for violation of any law—for example, tax penalties, parking tickets, or fines for violating city housing codes (IRC § 162(f))
- illegal bribes or kickbacks to private parties or government officials (IRC § 162(c))
- lobbying expenses or political contributions; however, a business may deduct up to $2,000 per year in expenses to influence local legislation (state, county, or city), not including the expense of hiring a professional lobbyist (such lobbyist expenses are not deductible)
- two-thirds of any damages paid for violation of the federal anti-trust laws (IRC § 162(g))
- bar or professional examination fees
- charitable donations by any business other than a C corporation (these donations are deductible only as personal expenses; see Chapter 14)
- country club, social club, or athletic club dues (see Chapter 14)
- federal income taxes you pay on your business income (see Chapter 14), and
- certain interest payments (see Chapter 14).

C. How to Report Operating Expense Deductions

It's very easy to deduct operating expenses from your income taxes. Simply keep track of everything you buy (or spend money on) for your business during the year, including the amount you spend on each item. Then, record the expenses on your tax return. If, like the vast majority of home business owners, you are a sole proprietor, you do this on IRS Schedule C, *Profit or Loss from Business*. To make this task easy, Schedule C lists common current expense categories—you just need to fill in the amount for each category. For example, if you spend $1,000 for business advertising during the year, you would fill in this amount in the box for the advertising category. You add up all of your current expenses on Schedule C and deduct the total from your gross business income to determine your net business income—the amount on which you are taxed.

If you are a limited liability company owner, partner in a partnership, or S corporation owner, the process is very similar, except you don't use Schedule C. LLCs and partnerships file IRS Form 1065, *U.S. Partnership Return of Income,* and their owners' share of expenses is reported on Schedule K-1, *Partner's Share of Income, Credits, Deductions, etc.* S corporations use Form 1120S, *U.S. Income Tax Return for an S Corporation.* Regular C corporations file their own corporate tax returns. ■

Deducting Long-Term Assets

D o you like to go shopping? How would you like to get a 45% discount on what you buy? Sound impossible? It's not. Consider this example: Sid and Sally each buy the same $2,000 computer at their local computer store. Sid uses his computer to play games and balance his personal checkbook. Sally uses her computer in her graphic design business. Sid's net cost for his computer—that is, his cost after he pays his taxes for the year—is $2,000. Sally's net cost for her computer is $1,100.

Why the difference in cost? Because Sally uses her computer for business, she is allowed to deduct its cost from her taxable income, which saves her $900 in federal and state taxes. Thanks to tax laws designed to help people who own businesses, Sally gets a 45% discount on the computer.

This chapter explains how you can take advantage of these tax laws whenever you purchase long-term property for your business. You will need to be aware of, and follow, some tax rules that at times may seem complicated. But it's worth the effort. After all, by allowing these deductions, the government is effectively offering to help pay for your equipment and other business assets. All you have to do is take advantage of the offer.

A. Long-Term Assets

This chapter explains how to deduct long-term assets—business property that you reasonably expect to last for more than one year. Long-term assets are also called capital expenses (the terms are used interchangeably in this book). There are three methods for deducting long-term business property:

- Section 179
- regular depreciation, and
- bonus depreciation (currently scheduled to end on 12/31/04).

Each is covered in the sections that follow.

1. Long-Term Assets Versus Current Expenses

Whether an item is a long-term asset (a capital expense) or not depends on its useful life. The useful life of an asset is not its physical life, but rather the period during which it may reasonably be expected to be useful in your business—and the IRS, not you, makes this call. Anything you buy that will benefit your business for *more than one year* is a capital expense. For home businesses, this typically includes items such as computers, office furniture, office equipment such as telephones and copiers, books, vehicles, and software.

> **EXAMPLE:** Doug pays $3,000 for office furniture for his home office. Because furniture can reasonably be expected to be useful for several years, it is a capital expense. The $50 per month that Doug spends on utilities for his home office, however, is a current expense.

Are Paperclips Long-Term Assets?

Are paperclips and other inexpensive items that you buy for your business long-term assets for tax purposes? No. Although paperclips and similar items might be expected to last more than one year, you can treat their cost as a current expense for tax purposes. Most businesses establish a cost threshold for assets—things that cost more are treated like long-term assets, while items that cost less are treated as currently deductible business expenses. The IRS has no rules on the amount of the limit, except that it must be reasonable. For a small home business, a reasonable limit would be $100 to $250. Thus, for example, you could treat a $50 bookcase you buy for your business as an operating expense; a $500 bookcase would be a long-term asset.

2. Deducting Capital Expenses

There are two ways to deduct capital expenses: You can depreciate them, deducting some of the cost each year over the asset's useful life, or you can deduct all or most of the cost in one year under Section 179 of the Internal Revenue Code (IRC). If Doug (from the above example) chose the depreciation method, he would have to deduct the $3,000 cost of his office furniture over its useful life (seven years, according to the IRS), instead of deducting the entire amount in one year. This is usually economically disadvantageous because of the time value of money—the sooner you get your money, the sooner you can start using it to make more money.

Because depreciation forces you to spread out your deduction over several years or more, many small business owners choose to deduct their capital expenses under Section 179 of the IRC instead. Using Section 179, you can currently deduct up to $102,000 in long-term assets purchased each year. Because of the size of the Section 179 deduction (which has increased substantially in recent years), most home businesses no longer need to depreciate long-term business assets. This enormous change in the tax law could greatly benefit you.

3. Repairs and Improvements

When you make repairs or improvements to long-term assets, it can be hard to tell if the cost is a capital or an operating expense. The rule is that ordinary repairs and maintenance for long-term assets are operating expenses that can be currently deducted. However, you must treat a repair or replacement as a capital expense if it:

- increases the value of your property
- makes it more useful, or
- lengthens its useful life.

EXAMPLE 1: Doug spends $100 to repair the carburetor on his car, which he uses for his sales business. This is a current expense because the repair doesn't increase the value of his car or lengthen its useful life. The repair merely allows the car to last for its expected lifespan.

EXAMPLE 2: Doug spends $1,500 on a brand new engine for his car. This is a capital expense because the new engine increases the car's value and useful life.

This rule can be difficult to apply because virtually all repairs increase the value of the property being repaired. A repair becomes a capital improvement when it makes the property *more valuable than it was before the repair.* Individual repairs made as part of a general plan of improvement are also capital expenses.

> **EXAMPLE:** Larry buys an old house and fixes up one of the bedrooms to use as the office for his architecture business. He pays to repaint and replaster the walls and ceilings, repair the floor, put in new wiring, and install an outside door. The plastering, painting, and floor work are repairs. Because they are part of a general plan to alter the home for business use, they are capital expenses.

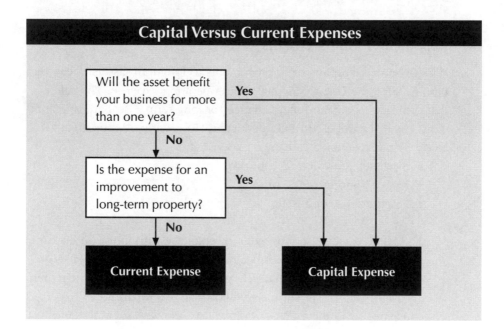

Capital Versus Current Expenses

Inventory is not a business expense. This chapter covers the tax treatment of things you buy *to use* in your business. It does not cover the cost of items you buy or make *to sell* to others. Such items are called inventory. Inventory is neither a current nor a capital expense. Rather, businesses deduct the cost of inventory as it is sold. (See Chapter 10 for information on deducting inventory.)

B. Section 179 Deductions

If you learn only one section number in the tax code, it should be Section 179. This provision is one of the greatest tax boons ever for small business owners. Section 179 doesn't increase the total amount you can deduct, but it allows you to take your entire depreciation deduction in one year, rather than taking it a little at a time over the term of an asset's useful life—which can be up to 39 years. This is called first-year expensing or Section 179 expensing. (Expensing is an accounting term that means currently deducting a long-term asset.)

EXAMPLE: In 2004, Ginger buys a $4,000 photocopy machine for her home business. Under the regular depreciation rules (using the straight-line depreciation method—see Section C6, below), Ginger would have to deduct a portion of the cost each year over its five-year useful life, as follows:

Year	Depreciation Deduction
2004	$500
2005	$1,000
2006	$1,000
2007	$1,000
2008	$500

By using Section 179 instead, Ginger can deduct the entire $4,000 expense from her income taxes in 2004. This is $3,500 more than she could have deducted for the year using depreciation.

You might want to save your deductions for later. Because of inflation and the time value of money, it is often better to use Section 179 if you can, to get the largest possible deduction for the current year. There are some circumstances, however, when it may be more advantageous to use depreciation instead (see Section C1, below).

1.   Property You Can Deduct

You qualify for the Section 179 deduction only if you buy long-term, tangible personal property that you use in your business more than 50% of the time.

a.   Tangible Personal Property

Under Section 179, you can deduct the cost of tangible personal property (new or used) that you buy for your business, if the IRS has determined that the property will last more than one year. Examples of tangible personal property include computers, business equipment, and office furniture. Although it's not really tangible property, computer software can also be deducted under Section 179 (see Section C8, below, for more on deducting software).

You can't use Section 179 to deduct the cost of:

- land
- permanent structures attached to land, including buildings and their structural components, fences, swimming pools, or paved parking areas
- inventory (see Chapter 10)
- intangible property such as patents, copyrights, and trademarks
- property used outside the United States, or
- air conditioning and heating units.

However, nonpermanent property attached to a building is deductible. For example, refrigerators, grocery store counters, printing presses, testing equipment, and signs are all deductible under Section 179. Structures such as barns and greenhouses that are specifically designed and used for agriculture or horticulture are also deductible, as is livestock (including horses). Special rules apply to cars (see Chapter 8).

b.   Property Used Primarily (51%) for Business

To deduct the cost of property under Section 179, you must use the property primarily for your business. The deduction is not available for property you use solely for personal purposes or to manage investments or otherwise produce nonbusiness income.

EXAMPLE: Jill bought a computer for $3,000 in 2005. During that year, she used it to play games, manage her checkbook, and surf the Internet for fun. In other words, she used it only for personal purposes. The computer is not deductible under Section 179.

You can take a Section 179 deduction for property you use for both personal and business purposes, as long as you use it for business *more than half of the time*. The amount of your deduction is reduced by the percentage of your personal use (see Section B2, below). You'll need to keep records showing your business use of the property. If you use an item for business less than half the time, you will have to use regular depreciation instead and deduct the cost of the item over several years.

There is another important limitation regarding the business use of property: You must use the property over half the time for business in *the year in which you buy it*. You can't convert property you previously used for personal use to business use and claim a Section 179 deduction for the cost.

EXAMPLE: In 2002, Kim bought a $1,500 desk and credenza that she used for personal activities—managing her personal checkbook, writing personal letters, and so forth. In 2005, Kim decides to start a home business. She uses her desk and credenza 75% of the time for the business. She may not deduct the cost under Section 179 because she didn't use the furniture for business until two years after she bought it.

You must *actually be in business* to take the Section 179 deduction. Property that you buy before you start your business is not deductible under Section 179. This is one reason why it's a good idea to postpone large purchases until your business is up and running.

EXAMPLE: Andre decides to quit his job as a staff scientist and become a home-based inventor. While still employed and before he actually starts his inventing business, he establishes a home laboratory at a cost of $100,000. This amount is not deductible under Section 179 because he had not yet started his new business.

There are other ways to deduct start-up costs. Business start-up expenses that are not deductible under Section 179 might be deductible under other tax law provisions. See Chapter 3 for information on deducting business start-up expenses.

Special 9/11 Tax Relief for New Yorkers

Congress passed a tax law in March 2002 that gives special tax relief to taxpayers in the Lower Manhattan area of New York City—the area devastated by the 9/11 attacks and collapse of the World Trade Center. People who have their businesses in this area are entitled to increased depreciation, bonus depreciation, and Section 179 deductions, as well as various tax credits. For detailed information, see IRS Publication 3920, *Tax Relief for Victims of Terrorist Attacks*. You can obtain this and all other IRS publications by calling the IRS at 800-TAX-FORM, visiting your local IRS office, or downloading the publication from the IRS website at www.irs.gov.

c.   Property That You Purchase

You can use Section 179 expensing only for property that you purchase—not for leased property or property you inherit or receive as a gift. You also can't use it for property that you buy from a relative or from a corporation or an organization that you control. The property you purchase may be used or new.

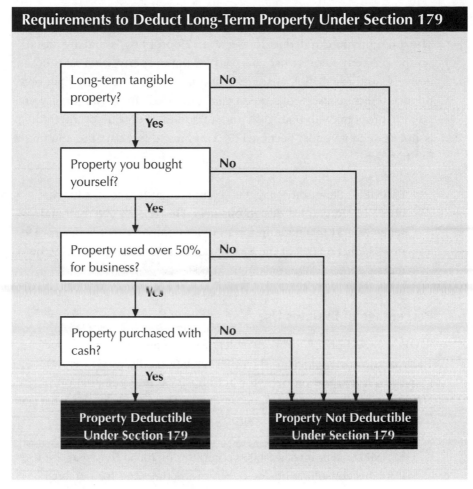

Requirements to Deduct Long-Term Property Under Section 179

Long-term tangible property? — **No**

↓ **Yes**

Property you bought yourself? — **No**

↓ **Yes**

Property used over 50% for business? — **No**

↓ **Yes**

Property purchased with cash? — **No**

↓ **Yes**

Property Deductible Under Section 179

Property Not Deductible Under Section 179

2. Calculating Your Deduction

There are several limitations on the amount you can deduct each year under Section 179. Your total annual deduction will depend on:

- what you paid for the property
- how much you use the property for business
- how much Section 179 property you buy during the year, and
- your annual business income.

a.   Cost of Property

The amount you can deduct for Section 179 property is initially based on the property's cost: what you paid for the property, plus sales tax, delivery, and installation charges. It doesn't matter if you pay cash or finance the purchase with a credit card or bank loan. However, if you pay for property with both cash and a trade-in, the value of the trade-in is not deductible under Section 179. You must depreciate the amount of the trade-in.

> **EXAMPLE:** Stuart buys a $5,000 computer system to use for his home-based graphic design business. He pays $4,000 cash and receives a $1,000 trade-in for an older computer that he owns. He may deduct $4,000 of the $5,000 purchase under Section 179; he must depreciate the remaining $1,000.

b.   Percentage of Business Use

If you use Section 179 property solely for business, you can deduct 100% of the cost (subject to the other limitations discussed below). However, if you use property for both business and personal purposes, you must reduce your deduction by the percentage of the time that you use the property for personal purposes.

> **EXAMPLE:** Max buys a $4,000 computer in 2005. That year, he uses it for his consulting business 75% of the time and for personal purposes 25% of the time. He may currently deduct 75% of the computer's cost ($3,000) under Section 179 for 2005. The remaining $1,000 is not deductible as a business expense.

You must continue to use property that you deduct under Section 179 for business at least 50% of the time for as many years as it would take to depreciate the item under the normal depreciation rules. For example, computers have a five-year depreciation period. If you deduct a computer's cost under Section 179, you must use the computer at least 50% of the time for business for five years.

If you don't meet these rules, you'll have to report as income (and pay tax on) part of the deduction you took under Section 179. This is called recapture, which is discussed in more detail in Section B4, below.

c.   Annual Deduction Limit

There is a limit on the total amount of business property expense you can deduct each year under Section 179. In 2003, the limit was increased from $24,000 to $100,000. For 2004 and 2005, the deduction limit is $102,000—subject to adjustment for inflation in 2005. These whopping increases were enacted by Congress as a temporary measure to jumpstart the faltering U.S. economy.

In 2006, the Section 179 limit is scheduled to go back down to $25,000. Congress could decide to make the higher limit permanent, but at this point no one knows what will happen. If you're planning on buying more than $25,000 worth of property for your business in one year and you want to deduct the whole amount under Section 179, your best bet is to make your purchases before 2006.

The annual deduction limit applies to all of your businesses combined, not to each business you own and run.

> **EXAMPLE:** Britney owns a successful website that provides invest-
> ment advice. She also works as a financial consultant. On the side,
> she works part-time as a boudoir photographer. Because the Section
> 179 limit applies to all her businesses together, in 2004 she may
> expense a total maximum of $102,000 in long-term asset purchases
> for all three businesses.

You don't have to claim the full amount—it's up to you to decide how much to deduct under Section 179. Whatever amount you don't claim under Section 179 must be depreciated instead. (Depreciation *is not* optional—see Section C, below.)

Because Section 179 is intended to help smaller businesses, there is also a limit on the total amount of Section 179 property you can purchase each year. In the highly unlikely event that you purchase long-term assets worth more than $500,000 in 2003, 2004, or 2005, or more than $300,000 in 2006 or later, you cannot use Section 179 to deduct any property for that year. If you buy more than $410,000 (but less than $500,000) of Section 179 property during 2004 or 2005, then you must reduce your deduction by one dollar for every dollar you spend over $410,000. The $410,000 amount is scheduled to go down to $200,000 in 2006 and later years.

Year	Section 179 Deduction Limit	Property Value Limit
2002	$24,000	$200,000
2003	$100,000	$400,000
2004	$102,000	$410,000
2005	$102,000 + inflation adjustment	$410,000 + inflation adjustment
2006 and later	$25,000	$200,000

The Section 179 limit for 2004 and 2005 is so high ($102,000) that few home business owners need worry about ever reaching it. However, if you purchase enough business property in one year to go over the limit, you can divide the deduction among the items you purchase in any way you want, as long as the total deduction doesn't exceed the Section 179 limit. It's usually best to apply Section 179 to property that has the longest useful life—and therefore, the longest depreciation period. This reduces the total time you will have to wait to get your deductions, which usually works to your financial benefit.

Legislation Pending to Extend Section 179 Deduction Increases

As this book went to press, legislation was pending in Congress to extend the $102,000 Section 179 deduction limit beyond 2005, or even make it permanent. It is impossible to predict whether this legislation will be enacted. If you're using this book in 2006 or later, be sure to find out whether the Section 179 limit has been changed. You can find important legal updates like these at Nolo's website, www.nolo.com.

d.   Business Profit Limitation

You can't use Section 179 to deduct more in one year than your total annual business income. Your business income is the total profit you earn from business during the year—whether you have one business or more than one. If you have no business income, you can't take a Section 179 deduction.

This limitation is particularly important to home business owners because many earn very small incomes. A 1999 study sponsored by the Small Business Administration found that 57% of all home businesses earned less than $10,000 in profits per year. Only 16% earned more than $10,000 in profit, while 27% incurred losses. (See *Homebased Business: The Hidden Economy*, by Joanne H. Pratt (Office of Advocacy, United States Small Business Administration, 1999).)

If you are a sole proprietor (like most home business owners), you can count your salary from a regular job as business income, if you work in addition to running your business. If you're a married sole proprietor and file a joint tax return, you can include your spouse's salary and business income in this total as well. You can't count investment income—for example, interest you earn on your personal savings account—as business income. But you can include interest you earn on your business working capital—for example, interest you earn on your business bank account.

You can't use Section 179 to reduce your taxable income below zero. But you can carry over to the next tax year (or any other year in the future) any amount you cannot currently take as a Section 179 deduction.

> **EXAMPLE 1:** In 2004, Amelia earned $5,000 in profit from her engineering consulting business and $10,000 in salary from a part-time job. She spent $17,000 for a computer and office equipment. She can use Section 179 to deduct $15,000 of this expense for 2004. She can deduct the remaining $2,000 the following year.

> **EXAMPLE 2:** In 2004, James purchased $100,000 of recording equipment for his fledgling commercial voiceover business, but earned only $5,000 from the venture. James's wife, however,

earned $75,000 from her job as a college professor. Because James and his wife file a joint return, they may take a Section 179 deduction for up to $80,000 for 2004 ($5,000 + $75,000 = $80,000). Thus, James may deduct $80,000 of his equipment purchases in 2004 under Section 179 and deduct the remaining $20,000 in a future year.

If you're a partner in a partnership, member of a limited liability company (LLC), or shareholder in an S corporation, the Section 179 limit applies both to the business entity and to each owner personally.

EXAMPLE: Dean, a builder, is a partner in the ABC Partnership. He also runs his own part-time home repair business as a sole proprietor. In 2004, ABC purchases $100,000 in construction equipment that it elects to expense under Section 179. Its business income for the year is $120,000, so it can deduct the full $100,000. ABC allocates $50,000 of its purchases and $50,000 of its income to Dean. Dean also purchases $10,000 of equipment for his sole proprietor business that he would like to expense under Section 179. However, Dean's home repair business incurs a $5,000 loss for the year. Dean's total permissible Section 179 deduction for 2004 is $102,000. His purchases for the year total $60,000 ($50,000 from the partnership plus $10,000 for equipment for his home business). His total business income for the year is $45,000 ($50,000 from the partnership minus the $5,000 loss from his home repair business). Thus, Dean may expense only $45,000 of the equipment purchases in 2004. He must carry the remaining $15,000 over to deduct in future years.

e. Date of Purchase

As long as you meet the requirements, you can deduct the cost of Section 179 property up to the limits discussed above, no matter when you place the property in service during the year (that is, when you buy the property and make it available for use in your ongoing business). This differs from regular depreciation rules, by which property bought later in the year may be subject to a smaller deduction for the first year (see Section C5, below). This is yet another advantage of taking a Section 179 deduction rather than using regular depreciation.

EXAMPLE: John buys a $5,000 computer for his home business on January 1, 2004 and $5,000 of office furniture on December 31, 2004. Both purchases are fully deductible under Section 179 in 2004.

Use It or Lose It—Make Your Section 179 Claims

Section 179 deductions are not automatic. You must claim a Section 179 deduction on your tax return by completing Part 1 of IRS Form 4562, *Depreciation and Amortization*, and checking a specific box. If you neglect to do this, you may lose your deduction. If you filed your return for the year without making the election to use Section 179, you can file an amended return within six months after your tax return was due for the year—April 15 plus any extensions you receive. Once this deadline passes, however, you lose your right to a Section 179 deduction forever—you can't file an amended return in a later year to claim the deduction. (See Chapter 16 for detailed guidance on amending tax returns.)

3.   Listed Property

The IRS imposes special rules on certain items that can easily be used for personal as well as business purposes. These items, called listed property, include:

- cars and certain other vehicles
- motorcycles, boats, and airplanes
- computers
- cellular phones, and
- any other property generally used for entertainment, recreation, or amusement—for example, VCRs, cameras, stereos, and camcorders.

The IRS fears that taxpayers might claim a business deduction for listed property but actually use it for personal reasons. To prevent this kind of behavior, the IRS requires you to document your business use of listed property. You can satisfy this requirement by keeping a logbook showing when and how the property is used. (See Chapter 15 for more on record keeping.)

a.   Exception for Computers

You generally have to document your use of listed property even if you use it 100% for business. However, there is an exception to this rule for computers: If you use a computer or computer peripheral (such as a printer) only for business and keep it at your business location, you need not comply with the record-keeping requirement. This includes computers that you keep at your home office, as long as the office qualifies for the home office deduction (see Chapter 6).

> **EXAMPLE:** John, a freelance writer, works full time in his home office that he uses exclusively for writing. The office is clearly his principal place of business and qualifies for the home office deduction. He buys a $4,000 computer for his office and uses it exclusively for his writing business. He does not have to keep records showing how and when he uses the computer.

This exception does not apply to items other than computers and computer peripheral equipment—for example, it doesn't apply to calculators, copiers, fax machines, or typewriters.

b.   Deducting Listed Property

If you use listed property for business more than 50% of the time, you may deduct its cost just like any other long-term business property. For example, you may deduct the cost in one year using Section 179 or depreciate it over several years under the normal depreciation rules. You may also use bonus depreciation.

However, if you use listed property 50% or less of the time for business, you may not deduct the cost under Section 179 or use accelerated depreciation or bonus depreciation (see Section D, below). Instead, you must use the slowest method of depreciation: straight-line depreciation. (See Section C7, below, for more on deducting listed property.)

4.   Recapture Under Section 179

Recapture is a nasty tax trap for unwary business owners. It requires you to give back part of a tax deduction that you took in a previous year. You may have to recapture part of a Section 179 tax deduction if, during the property's recovery period, either:

- your business use of the property drops below 51%, or
- you sell the property.

The recovery period is the property's useful life as determined under IRS rules. The IRS has determined the useful life of all types of property that can be depreciated. The useful life is the time period over which you must depreciate the asset. For personal property that can be expensed under Section 179, the useful life ranges from three years for computer software to seven years for office furniture and business equipment. If you deduct property under Section 179, you must continue to use it in your business at least 51% of the time for each year of its useful life. For example, if you buy office furniture, you must use it more than half of the time for business for at least seven years.

If your business use falls below 51% or you sell the property before the recovery period ends, you become subject to recapture. This means that you have to give back to the IRS all of the accelerated deductions you took under Section 179. You get to keep the amount you would have been entitled to under regular depreciation (using the fastest method available), but you must include the rest of your Section 179 deduction in your ordinary income for the year—and pay tax on it.

> **EXAMPLE:** In 2003, Paul purchases office equipment worth $10,000 and deducts the entire amount under Section 179. He uses the property 100% for business during 2003 and 2004, but in 2005 he uses it only 40% for business. The equipment has a seven-year recovery period, so Paul is subject to recapture. He figures the recapture amount as follows:
>
> First, he figures all the annual depreciation he would have been entitled to during 2003 through 2005 had he depreciated the property under the regular depreciation rules. He calculates this using the fastest depreciation method available—the 200% double declining

balance method. (If he had purchased listed property, he would have had to use the slowest method—straight line depreciation; see Sections C6 and C7, below.)

2003	$1,429	
2004	2,449	
2005	700	($1,749 x 40% business use)
Total	$4,578	

He then deducts this amount from the $10,000 Section 179 deduction he claimed in 2003: $10,000–$4,578 = $5,422.

Thus, Paul's 2005 recapture amount is $5,422. Paul must add $5,422 to his income for 2005. He can continue to depreciate the equipment for the next four years.

You eventually get back through depreciation any recapture amount you have to pay. But recapture can spike your tax bill for the year, so it's best to avoid the problem by making sure that you use property you deduct under Section 179 for business more than half of the time for every year of its recovery period.

You can maximize your Section 179 deduction by keeping your percentage of business use of Section 179 property as high as possible during the year that you buy the property. After the first year, you can reduce your business use—as long as it stays above 50%—and avoid recapture.

EXAMPLE: Paul buys $10,000 of office equipment and uses it 90% for business in 2003. He would have been entitled to currently deduct $9,000 of the cost under Section 179 (90% business use x $10,000 cost = $9,000 deduction). In 2004 and 2005, he uses the equipment for business only 60% of the time. Nevertheless, he need not recapture any of his Section 179 deduction because his business use is still more than 50%.

C. Depreciation

The traditional method of getting back the money you spend on long-term business assets is to deduct the cost a little at a time over several years (exactly how many years is determined by the IRS). This process is called depreciation.

Depreciation is a complicated subject. The IRS instruction booklet on the subject (Publication 946, *How to Depreciate Property*) is over 100 pages long. For a comprehensive discussion of depreciation, read Publication 946 or, better yet, talk to an accountant. This section covers the depreciation basics that all business owners should know.

Depreciation is not optional. Unlike the Section 179 deduction, depreciation is not optional. You *must* take a depreciation deduction if you qualify for it and you don't deduct the property under Section 179. If you fail to take it, the IRS will treat you as if you had taken it. This means that you could be subject to depreciation recapture when you sell the asset—even if you never took a depreciation deduction. This would increase your taxable income by the amount of the deduction you failed to take. (See Section C11, below.) So if you don't expense a depreciable asset under Section 179, be sure to take the proper depreciation deductions for it. If you realize later that you failed to take a depreciation deduction that you should have taken, you may file an amended tax return to claim any deductions that you should have taken in prior years. (See Chapter 16 for guidance about filing amended returns).

1. When to Use Depreciation

Do you ever buy more than $100,000 worth of business equipment in one year? For the vast majority of home businesses, the answer is no. Now that the Section 179 deduction has been increased to $102,000 (at least through the end of 2005), you may never have to use depreciation.

However, you might need to use depreciation to write off the cost of long-term assets that don't qualify for Section 179 expensing. Also, under some circumstances, it may be better to use depreciation and draw out your deduction over several years, instead taking the whole deduction at once under Section 179.

a.   Assets That Don't Qualify Under Section 179

You must meet strict requirements to use Section 179 to currently deduct long-term business property. You will not be able to expense an item under Section 179 if:

- You use the item less than 51% of the time for business.
- You convert personal property to business use.
- The property is a structure, such as a building or building component.
- You financed the purchase with a trade-in (the value of the trade-in must be depreciated).
- The property is an intangible asset such a patent, copyright, or trademark.
- You bought the property from a relative.
- You inherited the property or received it as a gift.
- The property is an air conditioning or heating unit.

For items that fall within one or more of these categories, you will have to use regular depreciation instead of Section 179 to take your deduction.

You will also have to use depreciation instead of Section 179 to the extent that your long-term asset expenses exceed the Section 179 annual limit. This limit is $102,000 in 2004 through 2005, and $25,000 thereafter (unless Congress makes the higher limit permanent). In addition, Section 179 expensing is not available if you spend more than $500,000 in long-term assets in a year during 2003 through 2005, or more than $300,000 in 2006 or later. Very few home businesses purchase enough business assets to exceed these limits.

b.   Expenses That Exceed Your Income

Under Section 179, you may not deduct more than your business income, including your or your spouse's salary income (see Section B, above). If your business is making little or no money and you have little or no income from wages, you may not be able take a Section 179 deduction for the current year; you will have to postpone the entire deduction to a future year, if you want to use Section 179.

In contrast, there is no income limitation on depreciation deductions. You can deduct your entire depreciation from your business income for the year; if this results in a net loss for the year, you can deduct the loss from income taxes you paid in prior years.

> **EXAMPLE:** Marvin made no money from his Internet start-up company in 2004, but incurred $100,000 in expenses for depreciable property. He has no other income for the year, but he earned $100,000 in 2003 from a prior job, on which he paid $25,000 in federal taxes. By depreciating the $100,000 expense, his business ends up with a net loss of $10,000 in 2004. He can file an amended tax return for 2003 and deduct this amount from his income for the year, resulting in a $2,500 tax refund. Had he deducted the $100,000 under Section 179 instead, he would have had to carry forward his $10,000 loss to use in subsequent years.

c.   When Depreciation Offers a Better Deduction

Even if you can deduct an asset under Section 179, you may not always want to. There are some circumstances in which taking a depreciation deduction is more advantageous than using Section 179.

You Expect to Earn More in Future Years

Section 179 expensing lets you take your total deduction up front and in one year, while depreciation requires you to deduct the cost of an asset a little at a time over several years. The slower depreciation method isn't always a bad thing. In some circumstances, you may be better off using depreciation instead of Section 179.

Remember: The value of a deduction depends on your income tax bracket. If you're in the 15% bracket, a $1,000 deduction is worth only $150 of federal income tax savings. If you're in the 28% bracket, it's worth $280. (See Chapter 1 for more calculating on the value of a tax deduction.) If you expect to earn more in future years, it may make sense to spread out your deductions and save some to use in later years when you expect to be in a higher tax bracket.

> **EXAMPLE:** Marie, a self-employed consultant, buys a $5,000 computer system for her business in 2005. She elects to depreciate the computer instead of using the Section 179 deduction. That way, she

can deduct a portion of the cost from her gross income for each of the next six years. Marie is only in the 15% tax bracket in 2005, but expects to be in the 28% bracket by 2008.

The following chart shows how much money Marie saves by using depreciation to deduct a portion of the computer's cost over six years, instead of taking a Section 179 deduction for the entire cost in the first year. Marie is using the straight-line depreciation method, which gives her the same deduction every year, except for the first and last.

Comparison of Deductions: Section 179 and Depreciation			
Year	Marie's Marginal Federal Income Tax Rate	Federal Income Tax Savings Using Section 179 Deduction	Federal Income Tax Savings Using Depreciation Deduction
2003	15%	$750 (15% x $5,000 total cost)	$ 75 (15% x $500 of total $5,000 cost)
2004	25%	0	250 (25% x $1,000)
2005	28%	0	280 (28% x $1,000)
2006	28%	0	280 (28% x $1,000)
2007	28%	0	280 (28% x $1,000)
2008	28%	0	140 (28% x $500)
Total		$750	$1,305

You Want to Show a Profit

You may also prefer to use depreciation instead of Section 179 if you want to puff up your business income for the year. This can help you get a bank loan or help your business show a profit instead of incurring a loss—and, therefore, avoid tempting the IRS to classify your business as a hobby. (See Chapter 2 for more on the hobby loss rule.)

EXAMPLE: Larry began his home design business in 2000. His business expenses exceeded his income in 2001 and 2002. He earned a small profit in 2003 and 2004. In 2005, he purchased $10,000 worth of long-term property with a five-year depreciation period. If he expenses the whole amount under Section 179, his business income for the year will be reduced by $10,000, which will cause him to incur a $2,000 loss for the year. Larry doesn't want to have another losing year for his business, because he will have lost money in three of his first five years. This could cause the IRS to determine that his venture is a hobby, not a real business. So Larry decides to depreciate his 2005 asset purchases using the straight-line depreciation method. This way, he gets only a $1,000 deduction in 2005, instead of the full $10,000. This enables his business to show a profit for the year. He'll be able to deduct the remaining $9,000 over the next five years.

2. Some Depreciation Basics

Depreciation is a tax deduction for the decline in value of long-term property over time due to wear and tear, deterioration, or obsolescence. Unless the Section 179 deduction applies, depreciation is the only way you can deduct the cost of long-term property—that is, property that lasts for more than one year, such as buildings, computers, equipment, machinery, patents, trademarks, copyrights, and furniture. You can also depreciate the cost of major repairs or improvements that increase the value or extend the life of an asset—for example, the cost of a major upgrade to make your computer run faster (see Section A3, above).

a. Property You Cannot Depreciate:

You cannot depreciate:
- property that doesn't wear out, including land (whether developed or not), stocks, securities, gold, or goodwill
- property you use solely for personal purposes
- property purchased and disposed of in the same year inventory, or
- collectibles that appreciate in value over time, such as antiques and artwork.

If you use nondepreciable property in your business, you can't take a tax deduction while you own it. But if you sell it, you can subtract its tax basis (see Section C3, below) from the sales price to calculate your taxable profit. If the basis exceeds the sales price, you'll have a deductible loss on the property. If the price exceeds the basis, you'll have a taxable gain.

You may depreciate only property that you own. For example, you can't take a depreciation deduction for property you lease. The person who owns the property—the lessor—gets to depreciate it. (However, you may deduct your lease payments as current business expenses—see Chapter 4).

Harrah's Craps Out in Tax Court

Harrah's Club in Reno, Nevada has one of the world's greatest collections of antique automobiles. Harrah's tried to depreciate the cost of restoring 94 of its vintage vehicles. Both the IRS and the tax court held that the cars were not depreciable because they didn't wear out or become obsolete. Noting that the vehicles were kept in a humidity-controlled environment and needed remarkably little repair or maintenance beyond occasional mending of a crack in a wood part, the court reasoned that, although the vehicles would not last forever, no definite limit could be put on their use as museum objects. (*Harrah's Club. v. U.S.*, 661 F.2d 203 (9th Cir. 1981).)

b.   When Depreciation Begins and Ends

You begin to depreciate your property when it is placed in service—that is, when it's ready and available for use in your business. As long as it is available for use, you don't have to actually use the property for business during the year to take depreciation.

> **EXAMPLE:** Tom bought a planter for his farm late in 2004, after the harvest was over. Tom may take a depreciation deduction for the planter for 2004, even though he didn't actually use it, because it was ready and available for use.

You stop depreciating property either when you have fully recovered your cost or other basis, or when you retire it from service, whichever occurs first. Property is retired from service when you stop using it for business, sell it, destroy it, or otherwise dispose of it.

> **EXAMPLE:** Tom depreciates the $10,000 cost of his planter a portion at a time over seven years. At the end of that time, he has recovered his $10,000 basis and depreciation ends. He is free to continue using the planter, but he can't take any more depreciation deductions for it.
>
> If Tom depreciates his planter during 2004 and 2005 and then sells it in 2006, he must stop depreciating the property and pay tax on any gain on the sale.

You must *actually be in business* to take depreciation deductions. In other words, you cannot start depreciating an asset until your business is up and running. This is one important reason why it is a good idea to postpone large property purchases until your business has begun. (See Chapter 3 for a detailed discussion of tax deductions for business start-up expenses.)

c.   Calculating Depreciation

How to calculate depreciation is one of the more confusing and tedious aspects of the tax law. In the past, most people had accountants perform the calculations for them. Today, you can use tax preparation software to calculate your depreciation deductions and complete the required IRS forms.

Although a tax preparation program can do the math for you, you still need to make some basic decisions about how you will depreciate your property. To make the best choices, you'll need to have a basic understanding of how depreciation works.

In a nutshell, your depreciation deduction is determined by five factors:
- your basis in the property (usually the asset's cost)
- the depreciation period
- the depreciation convention that determines how much depreciation you get in the first year

- the depreciation method, and
- whether you take bonus depreciation in the first year.

3.   Figuring Out Your Tax Basis in the Property

Depreciation allows you to deduct your total investment in a long-term asset you buy for your business over its useful life. In tax lingo, your investment is called your basis or tax basis. Basis is a word you'll hear over and over again when the subject of depreciation comes up. Don't let it confuse you; it just means the amount of your total investment in the property for depreciation purposes.

Usually, your basis in depreciable property is whatever you paid for it. This includes not only the purchase price, but also sales tax, delivery charges, installation, and testing fees, if any. You may depreciate the entire cost, no matter how you paid for the property—in cash, on a credit card, or with a bank loan.

> **EXAMPLE:** Victor, a home-based inventor, buys an electron micro-scope for his business. He pays $9,000 cash, $500 in sales tax, and $500 for delivery and installation. His basis in the microscope is $10,000.

a.   Adjusted Basis

Your basis in property is not fixed. It changes over time to reflect the true amount of your investment. Each year, you must subtract from the property's basis the amount of depreciation allowed for the property— this is true regardless of whether you actually claimed any depreciation on your tax return. This new basis is called the adjusted basis because it reflects adjustments from your starting basis. Your depreciation deduction for each year is based on the amount of your adjusted basis. Eventually, your adjusted basis will be reduced to zero, and there will be nothing left to depreciate.

> **EXAMPLE:** Victor bought his microscope in 2005. His starting basis was $10,000. He depreciates the cost over the next six years using

the double declining balance method (see Section 6, below). The following chart shows his adjusted basis for each year.

Year	Depreciation Deduction	Adjusted Basis
2005	$2000	$8000
2006	$3200	$4800
2007	$1920	$2880
2008	$1152	$1728
2009	$1152	$576
2010	$576	0

Your starting basis in property will also be reduced by:

- any Section 179 deduction you take for the property
- casualty and theft losses, and
- manufacturer or seller rebates you receive.

If you sell depreciable property, your gain or loss on the sale is determined by subtracting its adjusted basis on the date of sale from the sales price.

> **EXAMPLE:** If Victor sells his microscope for $7,500 in 2007 when its adjusted basis is $2,880, his taxable gain on the sale will be $4,620 ($7,500 − $2,880 = $4,620). If he sells the microscope for $1,000 instead, he will incur a $1,880 loss that he can deduct from his business income.

b. Property Not Bought Entirely With Cash

Of course, not all business property is bought with cash or a cash equivalent (such as a check or credit card). You may also pay for property wholly or partly with a trade-in, inherit it, receive it as a gift, or convert personal property to property used for your business. In these cases, the property's basis is not determined by its cost.

If you buy property with a trade-in, your starting basis is equal to the adjusted basis in the trade-in property plus any cash you pay for the property.

> **EXAMPLE:** Phil creates leather goods at home. He trades in leather-making equipment he already owns, which has a $5,000 basis, and pays $3,000 cash for new equipment. His starting basis in the new equipment is $8,000. This is true even if the list price for the equipment is only $7,500.

If you convert personal property to business use, your starting basis is equal to the property's fair market value when you start using it for your business.

> **EXAMPLE:** In 2004, Miranda decides to start a home business, and converts one of the bedrooms in her home to an office. To furnish the office, she moves in a desk set and office chair she purchased in 2002 and had kept in her den. The fair market value of the desk and chair in 2004 is $400. This is her starting basis when she begins to depreciate the property.

You determine your property's fair market value by figuring out how much someone would be willing to pay for it. Look at classified ads and listings for similar property on EBay, or call people who buy and sell the type of property involved. If you think the property is extremely valuable, get an appraisal from an expert. Keep records of how you calculated the property's value.

Most personal property that you convert to business use probably won't be worth much. You can't claim inflated values for old property just to maximize your depreciation deductions.

> **EXAMPLE:** Kunz, the owner of a cement company, bought out a competitor for $60,000. Included in the purchase were 19 old trucks and cement mixers. Kunz claimed on his tax return that these were worth $32,900 and used this amount as his tax basis to figure out his depreciation deduction. The IRS found that the value Kunz assigned the equipment was "absurd" and "grossly excessive." In reality, the equipment was so old that it had no substantial value except as scrap or junk. In fact, Kunz had resold one of the mixers for only $25. The IRS concluded that the items were worth only

$2,700 total. (*Kunz v Comm'r*, 333 F.2d 556 (6th Cir. 1964), affg TC Memo 1962-276.)

The starting basis of inherited property is its fair market value on the day the owner died. Your starting basis in gifted property is its fair market value at the time of the gift.

c.   Mixed-Use Property

You may take a depreciation deduction for property you use for both business and personal purposes. However, your depreciable basis in the property will be reduced by the percentage of your personal use. This will, of course, reduce the amount you can depreciate.

> **EXAMPLE:** Miranda uses her desk and office chair 75% of the time for business and 25% for personal use. Her depreciable basis in the furniture is reduced by 25%, so her basis is only $300 instead of $400 (75% x $400 = $300). Miranda can depreciate only $300 over the assets' depreciation period. (Miranda won't be entitled to a home office deduction because she doesn't use her office 100% for business, but she can still depreciate her office furniture; see Chapter 6.)

You can take a depreciation deduction even if you use an asset only 1% of the time for business. (However, special rules apply if you use cars and other types of listed property less than 50% of the time for business—see Section C7, below.) This is one advantage of depreciation over the Section 179 deduction, which is available only for property you use more than 50% of the time for business.

If you use property for both business and personal purposes, you must keep a diary or log listing the dates, times, and reasons the property was used to distinguish business from personal use.

4.   Depreciation Period

The depreciation period (also called the recovery period) is the time over which you must take your depreciation deductions for an asset.

Depreciation Periods	
Depreciation Period	**Type of Property**
3 years	Computer software
	Tractor units for over-the-road use
	Any race horse over 2 years old when placed in service
	Any other horse over 12 years old when placed in service
5 years	Automobiles, taxis, buses, and trucks
	Computers and peripheral equipment
	Office machinery (such as typewriters, calculators, and copiers)
	Any property used in research and experimentation
	Breeding cattle and dairy cattle
	Appliances, carpets, furniture, and so on used in a residential rental real estate activity
7 years	Office furniture and fixtures (such as desks, files, and safes)
	Agricultural machinery and equipment
	Any property that does not have a class life and has not been designated by law as being in any other class
10 years	Vessels, barges, tugs, and similar water transportation equipment
	Any single-purpose agricultural or horticultural structure
	Any tree or vine bearing fruits or nuts
15 years	Improvements made directly to land or added to it (such as shrubbery, fences, roads, and bridges)
	Any retail motor fuels outlet, such as a convenience store
20 years	Farm buildings (other than single-purpose agricultural or horticultural structures)
27.5 years	Residential rental property—for example, an apartment building
39 years	Nonresidential real property, such as a home office, office building, store, or warehouse

The tax code has assigned depreciation periods to all types of business assets, ranging from three to 39 years. These periods are somewhat arbitrary. However, property that can be expected to last a long time generally has a longer recovery period than property that has a short life—for example, nonresidential real property has a 39-year recovery period, while software has only a three-year period. Most of the property that you buy for your business will probably have a five- or seven-year depreciation period.

The major depreciation periods are listed above. These periods are also called recovery classes; all property that comes within a period is said to belong to that class. For example, computers have a five-year depreciation period and thus fall within the five-year class, along with automobiles and office equipment.

5. When Property Is Placed in Service

Sid and Sam are identical twins who have competing horse breeding businesses, which they operate from adjoining ranches. Sid buys a horse on January 2, 2005, and Sam buys one on December 30, 2005. How much depreciation should each be allowed for the first year they own their horses? Should Sid get a full year and Sam just a day?

The IRS has established certain rules (called "conventions") that govern how many months of depreciation you can take for the first year that you own an asset.

a.   Half-Year Convention

The basic rule is that, no matter when you buy an asset, you treat it as being placed in service on July 1—the mid-point of the year. This means that you can take half a year of depreciation for the first year that you own an asset.

> EXAMPLE: If Sam buys one horse in January, one in March, and one in December, he treats them all as having been placed in service on July 1.

b.   Mid-Quarter Convention

You are not allowed to use the half-year convention if more than 40% of the long-term personal property you buy during the year is placed in service during the last three months of the year. The 40% figure is determined by adding together the basis of all the depreciable property you bought during the year and comparing that to the basis of all of the property you bought during the fourth quarter.

If you exceed the 40% ceiling, you must use the mid-quarter convention. You must group all of the property that you purchased during the year by quarter (depending on when you bought it) and treat it as if you had placed it in service at the mid-point of that quarter. (A quarter is a three-month period: The first quarter is January through March; the second quarter is April through June; the third quarter is July through September; and the fourth quarter is October through December.)

> **EXAMPLE:** Sam buys one horse in January, one in October, and one in December. Each horse costs $25,000, so the basis for all the horses he bought during the year is $75,000. He paid $50,000 of this amount during the fourth quarter, so more than 40% of his purchases were made in the fourth quarter of the year. Sam must use the mid-quarter convention. He must treat the first horse he bought as being placed in service on February 15—the midpoint of the first quarter. The second and last horses must be treated as being placed in service on November 15—the midpoint of the fourth quarter. As a result, Sam gets very little depreciation that year for the horses he bought in October and December.

It's usually best to avoid having to use the mid-quarter convention, which means you'll want to buy more than 60% of your total depreciable assets before September 30 of the year. Assets you currently deduct using Section 179 do not count toward the 40% limitation, so you can avoid the mid-quarter convention by using Section 179 to deduct most or all of your purchases in the last three months of the year.

6.   Depreciation Methods

There are several ways to calculate depreciation. However, most tangible property is depreciated using the Modified Accelerated Cost Recovery System, or MACRS. (A slightly different system, called ADS, applies to certain listed property (see Section C7, below), property used outside the United States, and certain farm property and imported property.)

You can ordinarily use three different methods to calculate the depreciation deduction under MACRS: straight-line depreciation or one of two accelerated depreciation methods. Once you choose your method, you're stuck with it for the entire life of the asset.

In addition, you must use the same method for all property of the same class that you purchase during the year. For example, if you use the straight-line method to depreciate a computer, you must use that method to depreciate any other property in the same class as computers. Computers fall within the five-year class, so you must use the straight-line method for all other five-year property you buy during the year, such as office equipment.

a.   Straight-Line Method

Using the straight-line depreciation method, you deduct an equal amount each year over the useful life of an asset. However, if the mid-year convention applies (as it often does), you deduct only a half-year's worth of depreciation in the first year. You make up for this by taking an extra one-half year of depreciation at the end. You can use the straight-line method to depreciate any type of depreciable property.

> **EXAMPLE:** Sally buys a $1,000 printer-fax-copy machine for her home business in 2005. It has a useful life of five years. (See "Depreciation Periods" in Section C4, above). Sally bought more than 60% of her depreciable property for the year before September 30, so she can use the mid-year convention. Using the straight-line method, she can depreciate the asset over six years—the five years of the printer's useful life, plus an extra year to allow her to make up for the partial deduction she takes for the first year. Her annual depreciation deductions are as follows:

2005	$100
2006	200
2007	200
2008	200
2009	200
2010	100
Total	$1,000

If the mid-quarter convention applies, you don't get a half year's worth of depreciation the first year. Instead, your first year depreciation amount depends on the month of the year when you bought the property. Whatever you can't depreciate in the first year is tacked on to the last year. For example, if Sally bought her machine in September, she could deduct $75 depreciation in 2005, $200 in 2005 through 2009, and $125 in 2010. If she bought it in December, she would get $25 in 2005 and $175 in 2010. If she bought it in January, she would get $175 in 2005 and $25 in 2010.

b.   Accelerated Depreciation Methods

There is nothing wrong with straight-line depreciation, but the tax law provides an alternative that most businesses prefer: accelerated depreciation. As the name implies, this method provides faster depreciation than the straight-line method. It does not increase your total depreciation deduction, but it permits you to take larger deductions in the first few years after you buy an asset. You make up for this by taking smaller deductions in later years.

The fastest and most commonly used form of accelerated depreciation is the double declining balance method. This is a confusing name, but all it means is that you get double the deduction that you would get for the first full year under the straight-line method. You then get less in later years. However, in later years, you may switch to the straight-line method (which will give you a larger deduction). This is built into the IRS depreciation tables. You may use this method to depreciate all property within the three-, five-, seven-, and ten-year classes, excluding farm property. This covers virtually all of the tangible personal property you might buy for your business.

EXAMPLE: Sally decides to use the double declining balance method to depreciate her $1,000 printer-fax-copier machine. Her annual depreciation deductions are as follows:

2005	$200
2006	320
2007	192
2008	115
2009	115
2010	58
Total	$1,000

Using this method, she takes a $200 deduction in 2005, instead of the $100 deduction she'd get using straight-line depreciation. But starting in 2007, she'll get smaller deductions than she would using the straight-line method.

The following IRS table shows you the percentage of the cost of an asset you may deduct each year using the double declining balance method.

200% Declining Balance Depreciation Method			
Convention: Half-year			
Year / If the recovery period is:			
Year	3-year	5-year	7-year	10-year
---	---	---	---	---
1	33.33%	20.00%	14.29%	10.00%
2	44.45%	32.00%	24.49%	18.00%
3	14.81%	19.20%	17.49%	14.40%
4	7.41%	11.52%	12.49%	11.52%
5		11.52%	8.93%	9.22%
6		5.76%	8.92%	7.37%
7			8.93%	6.55%
8			4.46%	6.55%
9				6.55%
10				6.55%
11				3.28%

An alternative to the double declining method is the 150% declining balance method. This method gives you one-and-one-half times the deduction in the first year that you would otherwise get using the straight-line method. The 150% method may be used for three-, five-, seven-, ten-, 15-, and 20-year personal property, including farm property.

> **EXAMPLE:** Sally decides to use the 150% declining balance method to depreciate her printer-fax-copier. This gives her a smaller deduction in the first year than the double declining balance method, but larger deductions in later years.

2005	$150
2006	255
2007	178
2008	167
2009	167
2010	83
Total	$1,000

Using accelerated depreciation is not necessarily a good idea if you expect your income to go up in future years. There are also some restrictions on when you can use accelerated depreciation. For example, you can't use it for cars, computers, and certain other property that you use for business less than 50% of the time (see Section C7, below).

The following IRS table shows the percentage of the cost of an asset you may deduct each year using the 150% declining balance method.

	150% Declining Balance Depreciation Method Convention: Half-year						
Year	If the recovery period is:						
	3-year	5-year	7-year	10-year	12-year	15-year	20-year
1	25.00%	15.00%	10.71%	7.50%	6.25%	5.00%	3.750%
2	37.50%	25.50%	19.13%	13.88%	11.72%	9.50%	7.219%
3	25.00%	17.85%	15.03%	11.79%	10.25%	8.55%	6.677%
4	12.50%	16.66%	12.25%	10.02%	8.97%	7.70%	6.177%
5		16.66%	12.25%	8.74%	7.85%	6.93%	5.713%
6		8.33%	12.25%	8.74%	7.33%	6.23%	5.285%
7			12.25%	8.74%	7.33%	5.90%	4.888%
8			6.13%	8.74%	7.33%	5.90%	4.522%
9				8.74%	7.33%	5.91%	4.462%
10				4.37%	7.32%	5.90%	4.461%
11					7.33%	5.91%	4.462%
12					3.66%	5.90%	4.461%
13						5.91%	4.462%
14						5.90%	4.461%
15						5.91%	4.462%
16						2.95%	4.461%
17							4.462%
18							4.461%

c.   Depreciation Tables

Figuring out your annual depreciation deduction might seem to require some complicated calculations, but actually it's not that difficult. Of course, if you use a tax preparation computer program, it will do the math for you. However, if you want to do it yourself, you can use depreciation tables prepared by the IRS. These tables factor in the depreciation convention and method. They are all available in IRS Publication 946, *How to Depreciate Property*.

> **EXAMPLE:** In 2004, Joe buys a $9,600 lathe for his machining business. He wants to depreciate it using the double declining balance method so he can get the largest possible deduction during the first year.

He uses the property 100% for business and the mid-year convention applies because he didn't buy more than 40% of his business property during the last three months of 2004. To figure his depreciation, he can use the applicable IRS depreciation table from Publication 946, which is reprinted below:

200% Declining Balance Depreciation Method
Convention: Half-year

Year	If the recovery period is:					
	3-year	5-year	7-year	10-year	15-year	20-year
1	33.33%	20.00%	14.29%	10.00%	5.00%	3.750%
2	44.45%	32.00%	24.49%	18.00%	9.50%	7.219%
3	14.81%	19.20%	17.49%	14.40%	8.55%	6.677%
4	7.41%	11.52%	12.49%	11.52%	7.70%	6.177%
5		11.52%	8.93%	9.22%	6.93%	5.713%
6		5.76%	8.92%	7.37%	6.23%	5.285%
7			8.93%	6.55%	5.90%	4.888%
8			4.46%	6.55%	5.90%	4.522%
9				6.56%	5.91%	4.462%
10				6.55%	5.90%	4.461%
11				3.28%	5.91%	4.462%
12					5.90%	4.461%
13					5.91%	4.462%
14					5.90%	4.461%
15					5.91%	4.462%
16					2.95%	4.461%
17						4.462%
18						4.461%
19						4.462%
20						4.461%
21						2.231%

You can see from the table that for five-year property (like the lathe), Joe gets 20% of his total depreciation deduction in the first year. To figure the deduction for the lathe, Joe multiplies $9,600 by

20%, resulting in a $1,920 deduction in 2004. In 2005, the deduction will be $3,072 (32% x $9,600 = $3,072). For 2004, the deduction is smaller than for 2005 because of the mid-year convention—that is, Joe gets only half of the first year's depreciation because the property is assumed to have been purchased on July 1. This is factored into the table.

Appendix A of Publication 946 contains 18 different depreciation tables—one for each type of depreciation you can take.

7. Listed Property

The IRS imposes special rules on listed property—items that can easily be used for personal as well as business purposes. (See Section B3, above, for a discussion of listed property.) If you use listed property for business more than 50% of the time, you may deduct its cost just like any other long-term business property (under Section 179, using the normal depreciation rules, or using bonus depreciation).

However, if you use listed property 50% or less for business, you may not deduct the cost under Section 179 or use accelerated depreciation or bonus depreciation. Instead, you must use the slowest method of depreciation: straight-line depreciation. In addition, you are not allowed to use the normal depreciation periods allowed under the MACRS depreciation system. Instead, you must use the depreciation periods provided for by the Alternative Depreciation System (ADS for short). These are generally longer than the ordinary MACRS periods. However, you may still depreciate cars, trucks, and computers over five years. The main ADS depreciation periods for listed property are provided in the following chart.

ADS Depreciation Periods	
Property	**Depreciation Period**
Cars and light trucks	5 years
Computers and peripheral equipment	5 years
Communication equipment	10 years
Personal property with no class life	12 years

If you start out using accelerated depreciation and/or bonus depreciation and in a later year your business use drops to 50% or less, you have to switch to the straight-line method and ADS period for that year and subsequent years. In addition, you are subject to depreciation recapture for the prior years—that is, you must calculate how much more depreciation you got in the prior years by using accelerated depreciation and/or bonus depreciation and count that amount as ordinary taxable income for the current year (see Section B4, above). This will, of course, increase your tax bill for the year.

8.   Computer Software

Most businesses buy computer software; some also create it themselves. The tax law favors the latter group.

a.   Software You Buy

The software you buy comes in two basic types for tax purposes: software that comes already installed on a computer that you buy and software you purchase separately and install yourself (often called "off-the-shelf" software).

Software that comes with a computer you buy and is included in the price—for example, your operating system—is depreciated as part of the computer, unless you're billed separately for the software.

You must depreciate off-the-shelf software over three years using the straight-line method. You can also use bonus depreciation for off-the-shelf software.

In the past, Section 179 expensing was not available for computer software. However, Congress temporarily changed the law in 2003 to permit off-the-shelf software to be currently deducted under Section 179. However, this exception applies only to software placed in service from January 1, 2003 through December 31, 2005. Starting in 2006, Section 179 will once again be prohibited for off-the-shelf software (unless, of course, the law is changed again).

If you acquire software that is not off-the-shelf by buying another business or its assets, the rules discussed above don't apply. You must depreciate this software over 15 years using the straight-line method; this type of depreciation is called amortization (see IRC § 197).

b. Software You Create

If you create software yourself, you can currently deduct the cost under Section 174 of the Internal Revenue Code. This provision allows deductions for research and experimentation expenses incurred in developing an invention, patent, process, prototype, formula, technique, or similar product.

You may currently deduct the costs under Section 174 whether you develop the software for your own use, or to sell or license to others. (Rev. Proc. 2000-50.) For a detailed discussion of Section 174, see *The Inventor's Guide to Law, Business and Taxes*, by Stephen Fishman (Nolo).

9. Real Property

As mentioned above, land cannot be depreciated because it never wears out. However, this doesn't mean you never get a tax deduction for land. When you sell it, you may deduct the cost of the land from the sale price to determine your taxable gain, if any. The cost of clearing, grading, landscaping, or demolishing buildings on land are not depreciable. They are added to the tax basis of the land—that is, to its cost— and subtracted from the money you get when you sell the land to calculate your taxable loss or gain.

Unlike land, buildings do wear out over time and therefore may be depreciated. This means that when you buy property with buildings on it, you must separate the cost of the buildings from the total cost of the property to calculate your depreciation.

As you might expect, the depreciation periods for buildings are quite long (after all, buildings usually last a long time). The depreciation period for nonresidential buildings placed in service after May 12, 1993 is 39 years. Nonresidential buildings include office buildings, stores, workshops, and factories. Residential real property—an apartment building, for example—is depreciated over 27.5 years. Different periods apply to property purchased before 1993; see IRS Publication 946, *How to Depreciate Property,* for more information.

You must use the straight-line method to depreciate real property. This means you'll only be able to deduct a small fraction of its value each year—one-39th of its value annually if the 39-year period applies.

If you have an office or other workplace in your home that you use solely for your business, you are entitled to depreciate the business portion of the home. For example, if you use 10% of your home for your business, you may depreciate 10% of the home's cost (excluding the cost of the land). In the unlikely event your home has gone down in value since you bought it, you must use its fair market value on the date you began using your home office as your tax basis. You depreciate a home office over 39 years—the term used for nonresidential property. (A home office is nonresidential property because you don't live in that portion of your home.)

10. Intangible Assets

Tangible things like equipment and computers aren't the only business assets that wear out or get used up. Intangible assets can also get used up or become obsolete. Intangible assets are things you can't see or touch. They include intellectual property—patents, copyrights, trade secrets, and trademarks—and business goodwill.

The cost of intangible assets that get used up may be deducted over the useful life of the asset. This process is called amortization, but it works just like straight-line depreciation. You deduct an equal amount of the cost of the asset each year over its useful life.

If you buy an intangible asset from someone else, you may deduct its cost over its useful life. Except for trademarks, which are amortized over 15 years, the IRS has not established any set time periods for the useful lives of intangible assets. The taxpayer determines the useful life, subject to review by the IRS. The useful life of an invention or copyright for tax purposes can be complex to determine: It could be the entire legal duration of the copyright or patent (at least 70 years for copyrights, and up to 20 years for patents) or a shorter time if the asset will become worthless or obsolete more quickly.

Patents and copyrights that you obtain through the purchase of another business or its assets are depreciated over 15 years using the straight-line method. (IRC Sec. 197.)

Generally, if you create an intangible asset (such as an invention or a copyrighted work of authorship like a book or film) yourself, you may currently deduct the cost. Any costs that you can't currently deduct may be amortized as described above.

⚠️ **Amortization can be tricky.** This is a complex area of taxation. Consult with a knowledgeable tax pro if you need to amortize an intangible asset.

📖 **Need more information on deductions for inventors?** For a detailed discussion of the tax deductions involved in creating inventions, see *The Inventor's Guide to Law, Business and Taxes,* by Stephen Fishman (Nolo).

11. Depreciation Recapture

To currently deduct long-term property under Section 179 or depreciate listed property using accelerated depreciation, you must use the property for your business at least 51% of the time. If your business use falls to 50% or less, you'll have to give back part of the Section 179 or accelerated depreciation deductions you received. This is called "recapture" because the IRS is getting back—recapturing—part of your deduction. (See Section B4, above, for more on recapture.)

Recapture is required for listed property (personal use property) when your business use falls below 51% and for property for which you took a Section 179 deduction. It is not required for nonlisted property for which you took no Section 179 deduction. For example, it is not required for a building or factory machine.

Recapture may be triggered when you sell a long-term asset for a gain—that is, for more than your adjusted basis.

> **EXAMPLE:** Sam buys a computer for $5,000 for his home business in 2003. By 2005, he has taken $3,370 in depreciation deductions, leaving an adjusted basis of $1,630. He resells the computer in 2005 for $2,500. This gives Sam a gain of $870. This $870 gain is taxable as ordinary income.

You can't avoid recapture by not taking a Section 179 or depreciation deduction to which you were entitled. The IRS will treat you as though you took the deduction for recapture purposes, even if you didn't.

EXAMPLE: If Sam fails to depreciate his computer and then sells it in 2005 for $2,500, the IRS will figure that his adjusted basis is $1,630 because he could have taken $3,370 in depreciation for it. So he still has a taxable gain of $870.

D. Bonus Depreciation

In the wake of the 9/11 tragedy and the ensuing recession, Congress revised the tax laws to give businesses the opportunity to take substantial depreciation deductions during the first year they buy long-term property. First, it added a 30% first-year bonus depreciation for long-term business property purchases. Then, in 2003, it increased the bonus to an almost incredible 50%. You can take this bonus in addition to the $102,000 deduction already available under Section 179.

Bonus depreciation is scheduled to end on 12/31/2004. Bonus depreciation was enacted as a temporary measure to help the ailing U.S. economy. It is scheduled to end on December 31, 2004. This means that, unless Congress acts to extend it, you won't be able to use bonus depreciation for business property that you place in service during 2005 or later. If you're using this book to help figure your tax deductions for 2005 or later, be sure to find out whether bonus depreciation is still available. Your first stop should be the legal update page on Nolo's website, www.nolo.com.

Bonus depreciation is optional—you don't have to take it if you don't want to. At first glance, it might seem that very few home business owners would need to use bonus depreciation. After all, you can already deduct up to $102,000 per year in long-term asset purchases under Section 179 (through the end of 2005). Very few home businesses buy this much long-term property in one year.

However, bonus depreciation can actually be a huge boon for home business owners, who often can't use Section 179 because they don't earn enough profits. Unlike the Section 179 deduction, there is no business profit limit for bonus depreciation. You can claim bonus depreciation even if your business shows a loss. There is also no dollar limit on the amount of the first-year bonus.

1. Property That Qualifies for Bonus Depreciation

Bonus depreciation began for property placed in service on September 11, 2001 (the day of the World Trade Center attack) and is scheduled to end on December 31, 2004. Legislation to extend bonus depreciation to future years or even make it permanent was introduced in Congress as this book went to press in 2004, but no one can predict whether it will be enacted.

There are several significant limitations on bonus depreciation. You may take it only for property that:

- is new
- has a useful life of 20 years or less (this includes most types of property other than real property—see Section C4, above), and
- you use over 50% of the time for business.

In contrast, you can take the Section 179 deduction and regular depreciation for both used and new property. Moreover, you can take regular depreciation for property you use less than 51% of the time for business (see Section C, above).

2. The 50% or 30% Bonus

There are two levels of bonus depreciation—50% and 30%. You qualify for 50% bonus depreciation in the first year for property you buy from May 6, 2003 through December 31, 2004. The 30% bonus depreciation applies to property purchased from September 11, 2001 through May 5, 2003. You also have the option of using the 30% bonus instead of the 50% bonus for any property you purchase during the later period. However, most business owners will want to use the 50% bonus if it's available to them.

Type of Bonus Depreciation	When Property Purchased
50%	5/6/03 through 12/31/04
30%	9/11/01 through 5/5/2003

3. Bonus Depreciation Applies Class-Wide

If you use bonus depreciation, you must use it for all assets that fall within the same class. Unlike Section 179 expensing, you may not pick and choose the assets you want to apply it to within a class. For example, if you buy a car and take bonus depreciation, you must take bonus depreciation for any other property you buy that year that falls within the five-year class—for example, computers and office equipment. (See Section C4, above, for a list of the various classes of property.)

4. Calculating the Bonus Amount

You use bonus depreciation to figure out your depreciation deduction for the first year that you own an asset. You depreciate the remaining value of the asset under the regular depreciation rules discussed in Section C, above.

> **EXAMPLE:** Stan purchases and places in service $150,000 worth of new equipment for his home business in 2004. He gets a bonus depreciation deduction of $75,000 in 2004 (50% of $150,000 = $75,000) and depreciates the remaining cost of the equipment— $75,000—in 2004 and later years under the normal depreciation rules.

If you take the Section 179 deduction, you combine it with the 50% bonus depreciation (or the 30% bonus, if applicable) and regular depreciation, in that order. In other words, you must take your Section 179 deduction first, if you choose to take it.

> **EXAMPLE:** Stan purchases and places in service $150,000 worth of equipment for his home business in 2004. First, he may take a $102,000 Section 179 deduction—that is, he may currently deduct this entire amount from his income. Next, he may take a 50% bonus depreciation deduction on the remaining $48,000 of the equipment cost—this amounts to a $24,000 deduction (50% of $48,000). This gives him a total deduction of $126,000 in 2004. He may deduct the remaining $24,000 of the original equipment cost in 2004 and later

under the normal depreciation rules. Using the double declining balance method, he can take an additional $4,800 depreciation deduction in 2004.

Combining the Section 179 deduction with 50% bonus depreciation can result in an enormous tax deduction in the first year for businesses that buy substantial amounts of depreciable property. As the example shows, if you buy $150,000 worth of property, you may take a total deduction of $131,400 in the first year. If you want to take advantage of the bonus, make your purchases before January 1, 2005, when bonus depreciation is currently scheduled to end.

If you purchase business property during the year for an amount equal to or less than the Section 179 deduction ($102,000 in 2004 and 2005) and deduct it all under Section 179, you can't use bonus depreciation because you'll have nothing left to depreciate.

EXAMPLE: Stan purchases $10,000 worth of equipment that he uses 100% for his business in 2004. He may deduct this entire amount in 2004 under Section 179. He therefore has no need for bonus (or regular) depreciation.

On the other hand, bonus depreciation will prove very useful if you don't earn enough profits from your home business (and salary, if any) to deduct your purchases under Section 179. As with regular depreciation, there is no income limitation on bonus depreciation.

EXAMPLE: Stan purchases $10,000 in equipment that he uses 100% for his home business in 2004. However, Stan earned no income from his business that year, and had no salary from an outside job. He can't use Section 179 to deduct the property, but he can still use bonus depreciation. This enables him to deduct $5,000 in 2004, and he can deduct the remaining amount in 2004 and future years using regular depreciation. He can use his bonus depreciation deduction to offset his investment income for 2004 or he can carry it over to use in later years or back to apply to prior years.

5.   Opting Out of the Bonus

The IRS automatically applies the bonus depreciation deduction to all taxpayers who qualify for it. However, the deduction is optional. If you decide not to take it, you must opt out by attaching a note to your tax return. It may be advantageous to do this if you expect your income to go up substantially in future years, which would place you in a higher tax bracket (and therefore, make the tax deductions you take in those years more valuable).

> **EXAMPLE:** Bill Jones, a sole proprietor, purchased $10,000 worth of equipment for his fledgling home business in 2004. He earned no income that year, so he does not want to take bonus depreciation. Instead, he wants to save as much depreciation as possible for future years when he expects to earn a substantial income from his business. He wants to depreciate the property using the slowest method available—straight line depreciation. The equipment has a five-year depreciation period. To opt out of bonus depreciation, he attaches the following note to his 2004 tax return:

> Dear Commissioner:
>
> I hereby elect not to claim any special allowance for qualified five-year property acquired by me after May 5, 2003.
>
> /s/ Bill Jones

When you opt out, you do so for the entire class of assets. If you decide to opt out of the bonus, you must do so for the *entire class* of assets, not just one asset within a class. The same rule applies when you opt in to the bonus.

E.   Tax Reporting and Record Keeping for Section 179 and Depreciation

You must report depreciation and Section 179 deductions on IRS Form 4562, *Depreciation and Amortization*. If you have more than one business for which you're claiming depreciation, you must use a separate Form 4562 for each business. If you're a sole proprietor, you carry over the amount of your depreciation and Section 179 deductions to your Schedule C and subtract them from your gross business income along with your other business expenses.

Let your computer handle the fine print. Form 4562 is one of the most complex and confusing IRS forms. If you want to complete it yourself, do yourself a favor and use a tax preparation program.

You need to keep accurate records for each asset you depreciate or expense under Section 179, showing:

- a description of the asset
- when and how you purchased the property
- the date it was placed in service
- its original cost
- the percentage of time you use it for business
- whether and how much you deducted under Section 179 and/or bonus depreciation
- the amount of depreciation you took for the asset in prior years, if any
- the asset's depreciable basis
- the depreciation method used
- the length of the depreciation period, and
- the amount of depreciation you deducted for the year.

If you use tax preparation software, it should create a worksheet containing this information. Be sure to check these carefully and save them. You can also use an accounting program such as *QuickBooks* to keep track of your depreciating assets. (Simple checkbook programs like *Quicken* and *MSMoney* are not designed to track depreciation.) You may also use a spreadsheet program to create your own depreciation worksheet. Spreadsheet templates are available for this purpose. Of course, you can also do the job by hand.

The Instructions to IRS Form 4562 contain a worksheet you can use. Here's an example of a filled-out worksheet prepared by the IRS:

Description of Property	Date Placed in Service	Cost or Other Basis	Business/Investment Use Percentage	Section 179 Deduction and Special Allowance	Depreciation in Prior Years	Basis for Depreciation	Method/Convention	Recovery Period	Rate or Table Percentage	Depreciation Deduction
Depreciation Worksheet										
Used Equipment —Transmission Jack	1-3	3,000	100%	—	—	3,000	200 DB/HY	7	14.29%	$ 429
Used Pickup Truck	1-3	8,000	100%	—	—	8,000	200 DB/HY	5	20%	1,600
Used Heavy-Duty Tow Truck	1-3	30,000	100%	—	—	30,000	200 DB/HY	5	20%	6,000
Used Equipment —Engine Hoist	1-3	4,000	100%	—	—	4,000	200 DB/HY	7	14.29%	572
										$8,601

For listed property, you'll also have to keep records showing how much time you spend using it for business and personal purposes. You should also keep proof of the amount you paid for the asset—receipts, canceled checks, and purchase documents. You need not file these records with your tax return, but you must have them available to back up your deductions if you're audited. ■

Chapter 6

The Home Office Deduction

The home office deduction allows you to deduct many of the costs associated with running a business from your home. If you're a renter, this may be your single largest tax deduction. It won't save you nearly as much if you own your home, but you'll still be able to recoup some of your business-related costs by using this deduction.

A.   Qualifying for the Home Office Deduction

The federal government helps out home business owners by letting them deduct their home office expenses from their taxable income. This is true whether you own your home or apartment or are a renter. Although this tax deduction is commonly called the home office deduction, it applies not only to space devoted to office work, but also to a workshop, lab, studio, or any other home workspace that you use for your business.

> **EXAMPLE:** Rich, a professional musician and freelance writer, uses the basement of his San Francisco rental home as his writing office and recording studio. He can deduct his home office expenses, including a portion of his rent, from his business income. This saves him over $2,000 per year on his income and self-employment taxes.

If you've heard stories about how difficult it is to qualify for the home office deduction, you can breathe more easily. Changes in the tax law that took effect in 1999 make it much easier for businesspeople to qualify for the deduction. So even if you haven't qualified for the deduction in the past, you may be entitled to take it now.

Some people believe that taking the home office deduction invites an IRS audit. The IRS denies this. But even if taking the deduction increases your audit chances, the risk of an audit is still low (see Chapter 17). Moreover, you have nothing to fear from an audit if you're entitled to take the deduction and you keep good records to prove it.

However, if you plan on taking the deduction, you need to learn how to do it properly. There are strict requirements you must meet in order to qualify for the home office deduction. You are entitled to the home office deduction if you:

- are in business
- use your home office exclusively for business (unless you store inventory or run a day care center in your home—see Section A2, below), and
- use your home office for business on a regular basis.

These are the three threshold requirements that everyone must meet. If you get past this first hurdle, then you must also meet *any one* of the following five requirements:

- your home office is your principal place of business
- you meet clients or customers at home
- you use a separate structure on your property exclusively for business purposes
- you store inventory or product samples at home, or
- you run a day care center at home.

These rules apply whether you are a sole proprietor, partner in a partnership, limited liability company (LLC) owner, or a corporation owner. If you're one of the few home business people who has formed a regular C corporation that you own and operate, and you work as its employee, however, you must meet some additional requirements (see Section B, below).

1. Threshold Requirements: Regular and Exclusive Business Use

To take the home office deduction, you must have a home office—that is, an office or other workplace in your home that you use regularly and exclusively for business. Your "home" may be a house, apartment, condominium, mobile home, or even a boat. You can also take the deduction for separate structures on your property that you use for business, such as an unattached garage, workshop, studio, barn, or greenhouse.

a. You Must Be in Business

You must be in business to take the home office deduction. You can't take the deduction for a hobby or other nonbusiness activity that you conduct out of your home. Nor can you take it if you perform personal investment activities at home—for example, researching the stock

Requirements for Home Office Deduction

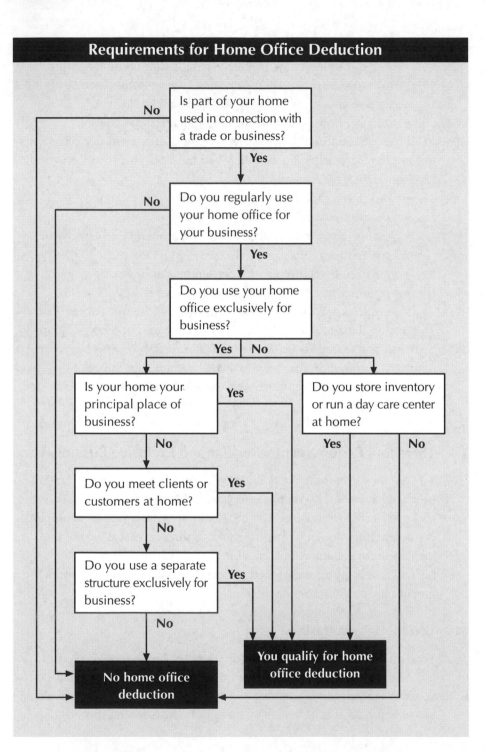

market. (See Chapter 2 for information on what constitutes a business for tax purposes.)

You don't have to work full time in a business to qualify for the home office deduction. If you satisfy the requirements, you can take the deduction for a side business that you run from a home office. However, you must use your home office regularly, and the total amount you deduct cannot exceed your profit from the business. (See Section C2, below, for more on the profit limitation.)

> **EXAMPLE:** Barbara works full time as an editor for a publishing company. An avid bowler, she also spends about 15 hours a week writing and publishing a bowling newsletter. She does all the work on the newsletter from an office in her apartment. Barbara may take the home office deduction, but she can't deduct more than she earns from the newsletter.

If you have more than one business, each business must qualify separately for the home office deduction. Depending on where you do your work, it's possible that one of your businesses will qualify while the other does not.

> **EXAMPLE:** Jim has two businesses: He runs a bookkeeping service and also works as a professional magician, performing at birthdays, conventions, and similar events. He performs all of his bookkeeping work at home, so he can take a home office deduction for his bookkeeping business. However, because he does not work on his magic business at home, he gets no home office deduction for that income.

This rule can be important because of the profit limit on the amount of the home office deduction—that is, your deduction may not exceed the net profit you earn from your home office business or businesses. You'll want to make sure that your most profitable enterprises qualify for the deduction.

b.   You Must Use Your Home Office Exclusively for Business

You can't take the home office deduction unless you use part of your home exclusively for your business. In other words, you must use your home office *only for your business*. The more space you devote exclusively to your business, the more your home office deduction will be worth. (See Section C, below.) This requirement doesn't apply if you store inventory at home or run a home day care center. (See Section A2, below.)

If you use part of your home—such as a room or studio—as your business office, but you also use that space for personal purposes, you won't qualify for the home office deduction.

> **EXAMPLE:** Johnny, a home-based professional fundraiser, has a den at home furnished with a desk, chair, bookshelf, filing cabinet, and a bed for visiting guests. He uses the desk and chair for both business and personal reasons. The bookshelf contains both personal and business books, the filing cabinet contains both personal and business files, and the bed is used only for personal reasons. Johnny can't claim a business deduction for the den because he does not use it, or any part of it, exclusively for business purposes.

The easiest way to meet the exclusive use test is to devote an entire room in your home to your business—for example, by using an extra bedroom as your office. However, not everybody has a room to spare—and the IRS recognizes this. You can still claim the deduction even if you use just part of a room as your office, as long as you devote that portion of the room exclusively to your business.

> **EXAMPLE:** Paul, a software engineer, keeps his desk, chair, bookshelf, computer, and filing cabinet in one part of his den and uses them exclusively for business. The remainder of the room—one-third of the space—is used to store a bed for houseguests. Paul can take a home office deduction for the two-thirds of the room that he uses exclusively as an office.

How Big (or Small) Can Your Home Office Be?

Your home office can be as big or small as you want or need. You are not required to use as small a space as possible. If you like plenty of office space, you can spread out and even use more than one room. But remember, you may use your home office space only for business. You aren't even supposed to use it for personal business, such as writing personal checks.

Although the IRS probably won't be inspecting your home office, your deduction must still make sense in the event you are audited. If you live in a one-bedroom apartment and claim the entire bedroom as a home office, you'll have to have an answer ready when the IRS asks where you sleep.

In one case, for example, a psychologist who lived in San Francisco claimed a home office deduction for one-quarter of her apartment. However, the entire apartment was a 400 square foot studio, consisting of an open area (approximately 13 feet by 15 feet) furnished with a desk and a couch, and a small dining area and kitchen (each approximately seven feet by eight feet). Given the layout of this tiny apartment, neither the IRS nor the tax court bought the psychologist's claim that she used 100 square feet exclusively for her psychology practice. (*Mullin v. Comm'r.*, T.C. Memo 2001-121.) On the other hand, a home-based entrepreneur who lived in a studio apartment in Detroit was allowed to take the home office deduction for a walk-in closet he claimed to use exclusively to store corporate books and records. In this case, it was plausible that he used the closet only for business. (*Hughes v. Comm'r*, T.C. Memo 1981-140.)

If you use the same room (or rooms) for your office and for other purposes, you'll have to arrange your furniture and belongings so that a portion of the room is devoted exclusively to your business. Place only your business furniture and other business items in the office portion of the room. Business furniture includes anything that you use for your business, such as standard office furniture like a desk and chair. Depending on your business, it could include other items as well—for example, a psychologist might need a couch, an artist might need work tables and easels, and a consultant might need a seating area to meet with clients. One court held that a financial planner was entitled to have a television in his home office because he used it to keep up on financial news. Be careful what you put in this space, however. In another case, the IRS disallowed the deduction for a doctor because he had a television in the part of his living room that he claimed as his home office. The court wouldn't buy the doctor's claim that he used the TV only to watch medical programs.

The IRS does not require you to physically separate the space you use for business from the rest of the room. However, doing so will help you satisfy the exclusive use test. For example, if you use part of your living room as an office, you could separate it from the rest of the room with folding screens or bookcases.

Although you must use your home office exclusively for business, you and other family members or visitors may walk through it to get to other rooms in your residence.

As a practical matter, the IRS doesn't have spies checking to see whether you're using your home office just for business. However, complying with the rules from the beginning means you won't have to worry if you are audited.

When the IRS Can Enter Your Home

IRS auditors may not enter your home unless you or another lawful occupant gives them permission. The only exception is if the IRS obtains a court order to enter your home, which is very rare. In the absence of such a court order, an IRS auditor must ask permission to come to your home to verify your home office deduction. You don't have to grant permission for the visit—but if you don't, the auditor will probably disallow your deduction.

c.   You Must Use Your Home Office Regularly

It's not enough to use a part of your home exclusively for business; you must also use it regularly. For example, you can't place a desk in a corner of a room and claim the home office deduction if you almost never use the desk for your business.

Unfortunately, the IRS doesn't offer a clear definition of regular use. The agency has stated only that you must use a portion of your home for business on a continuing basis—not just for occasional or incidental business. One court has held that 12 hours of use a week is sufficient. (*Green v. Comm'r.*, 79 TC 428 (1982).) You might be able to qualify with less use—for example, an hour a day—but no one knows for sure.

2.   Additional Requirements

Using a home office exclusively and regularly for business is not enough to qualify for the home office deduction. You also must satisfy at least one of the additional five tests described below.

a.   Home as Principal Place of Business

The most common way to satisfy the additional home office deduction requirement is to show that you use your home as your principal place of business. How you accomplish this depends on where you do most of your work and what type of work you do at home.

If you only work at home

If, like many home business owners, you do all or almost all of your work in your home office, your home is clearly your principal place of business, and you'll have no trouble qualifying for the home office deduction. This would be the case, for example, for a writer who writes only at home or a salesperson who sells by phone and makes sales calls from home.

If you work in multiple locations

If you work in more than one location, your home office still qualifies as your principal place of business if you perform your most important business activities—those activities that most directly generate your income—at home.

EXAMPLE: Charles is a self-employed author who uses a home office to write. He spends 30 to 35 hours per week in his home office writing and another ten to 15 hours a week at other locations conducting research, meeting with publishers, and attending promotional events. The essence of Charles's business is writing— this is how he generates his income. Therefore, his home qualifies as his principal place of business because that's where he writes.

If you perform equally important business activities in several locations, your principal place of business is where you spend more than half of your time. If there is no such location, you don't have a principal place of business.

EXAMPLE: Sue sells costume jewelry over EBay from her home office, at crafts fairs, and through consignments to craft shops. She spends 25 hours per week in her home office and 15 hours at fairs and crafts shops. Her home office qualifies as her principal place of business.

If you do only administrative work at home

Of course, many businesspeople spend the bulk of their time working away from home. This is the case, for example, for:

- building contractors who work primarily on building sites
- doctors who work primarily in hospitals
- traveling salespeople who visit clients at their places of business, and
- house painters, gardeners, and home repair people who work primarily in their customers' homes.

Fortunately, legal changes that took effect in 1999 make it possible for these people to qualify for the home office deduction. Under the rules, your home office qualifies as your principal place of business, even if you work primarily outside your home, if:

- you use the office to conduct administrative or management activities for your business, and
- there is no other fixed location where you conduct these activities.

This means that you can qualify for the home office deduction even if your home office is not where you generate most of your business income. It's sufficient that you regularly use your office to administer or manage your business—for example, to keep your books, schedule appointments, do research, write reports, forward orders, or order supplies. As long as you have no other fixed location where you do these things—for example, an outside office—you'll get the deduction.

Because of these rules, almost any business owner can qualify for the home office deduction. All you have to do is set up a home office that you regularly and exclusively use to manage or administer your business. Even people who spend most of their work time away from home can usually find plenty of business-related work to do in a home office.

> **EXAMPLE:** Sally, a self-employed handyperson, performs home repair work for clients in their homes. She also has a home office that she uses regularly and exclusively to keep her books, arrange appointments, and order supplies. Sally is entitled to a home office deduction.

Under these rules, you may have an outside office or workplace and still qualify for the home office deduction as long as you use your home office to perform administrative or management tasks and you don't perform substantial administrative tasks at your outside office.

> **EXAMPLE:** Bill, a self-employed goldsmith, maintains a workshop in an industrial park where he performs his goldsmithing. He also has a home office where he takes care of all the administrative functions for his business, including taking orders and record keeping. Bill may take the home office deduction.

You may also perform some administrative tasks in a place other than a fixed location, such as your car or clients' offices (a client's office is a fixed location only for the client, not for you).

> **EXAMPLE:** Millie sells Bibles door-to-door. She stores order forms and keeps tracks of appointments in her car. She regularly uses her

home office to forward orders and perform other administrative tasks. Millie is entitled to take a home office deduction.

b.   Meeting Clients or Customers at Home

Even if your home office is not your principal place of business, you may deduct your expenses for any part of your home that you use exclusively to meet with clients, customers, or patients. You must physically meet with others in this home location; phoning them from there is not sufficient. And the meetings must be a regular part of your business; occasional meetings don't qualify.

It's not entirely clear how often you must meet clients at home for those meetings to be considered regular. However, the IRS has indicated that meeting clients one or two days a week is sufficient. Exclusive use means you use the space where you meet clients only for business. You are free to use the space for business purposes other than meeting clients—for example, doing your business bookkeeping or other paper-work. But you cannot use the space for personal purposes, such as watching television.

> **EXAMPLE:** June, an attorney, works three days a week in her city office and two days in her home office, which she uses only for business. She meets clients at her home office at least once a week. Because she regularly meets clients at her home office, she qualifies for the home office deduction even though her city office is her principal place of business.

If you want to qualify under this part of the rule, encourage clients or customers to visit you at home and keep a log or appointment book showing all of their visits.

c.   Using a Separate Structure for Business

You can also deduct expenses for a separate freestanding structure, such as a studio, garage, or barn, if you use it exclusively and regularly for your business. The structure does not have to be your principal place of business, and you do not have to meet patients, clients, or customers there.

Exclusive use means that you use the structure only for business—for example, you can't use it to store gardening equipment or as a guesthouse. Regular use is not precisely defined, but it's probably sufficient to use the structure ten or 15 hours a week.

> **EXAMPLE:** Deborah is a freelance graphic designer. She has her main office in a downtown office building, but also works every weekend in a small studio in her back yard. Because she uses the studio regularly and exclusively for her design work, she qualifies for the home office deduction.

d. Storing Inventory or Product Samples at Home

You can also take the home office deduction if you are in the business of selling retail or wholesale products and you store inventory or product samples at home. To qualify, you can't have an office or other business location outside your home. And you must store your inventory in a particular place in your home—for example, a garage, closet, or bedroom. You can't move your inventory from one room to the other. You don't have to use the storage space exclusively to store your inventory to take the deduction—you just have to regularly use it for that purpose.

> **EXAMPLE:** Lisa sells costume jewelry door to door. She rents a home and regularly uses half of her attached garage to store her jewelry inventory; she also parks her Harley Davidson motorcycle there. Lisa can deduct the expenses for the storage space even though she does not use her entire garage exclusively to store inventory.

e. Operating a Day Care Center at Home

You're also entitled to a home office deduction if you operate a day care center at home. This is a place where you care for children, people who are at least 65 years old, or people who are physically or mentally unable to care for themselves. Your day care must be licensed by the appropriate licensing agency, unless it's exempt. You must regularly use part of your home for day care, but your day care use need not be exclusive—for example, you could use your living room for day care during the day and for personal reasons at night.

B. C Corporation Employees

If you form a regular C corporation to own and operate your business, you'll probably work as its employee. You'll be entitled to deduct your home office expenses only if you meet the requirements discussed above and you maintain your home office for the convenience of your employer—that is, your corporation. An employee's home office is deemed to be for an employer's convenience if it is:

- a condition of employment
- necessary for the employer's business to properly function, or
- needed to allow the employee to properly perform his or her duties.

When you own the business that employs you, you ordinarily won't be able to successfully claim that a home office is a condition of your employment—after all, as the owner of the business, you're the person who sets the conditions for employees, including yourself. If there is no other office where you do your work, however, you should be able to establish that your home office is necessary for your business to properly function and/or for you to perform your employee duties.

It will be more difficult to establish convenience if you have separate corporate offices. Nevertheless, business owners in this situation have successfully argued that their home offices were necessary—for example, because their corporate offices were not open or not useable during evenings, weekends, or other nonbusiness hours, or were too far from home to use during off-hours.

Some clever taxpayers have tried to get around this rule by renting a portion of their home to their corporate employer (their own corporation), and then claiming to use the space for work as the corporation's employee. This won't fly with the IRS: You can't claim a home office deduction for space that you rent out. And you would have to pay personal income tax on any rent that you receive from your corporation for the office space.

C.   Calculating the Home Office Deduction

This is the fun part—figuring out how much the home office deduction will save you in taxes.

1.   How Much of Your Home Is Used for Business?

To calculate your home office deduction, you need to determine what percentage of your home you use for business. The law says you can use "any reasonable method" to do this. Obviously, you want to use the method that will give you the largest home office deduction. To do this, you want to maximize the percentage of your home that you claim as your office. There is no single way to do this for every home office. Try both methods described below and use the one that gives you the largest deduction.

Some tax experts advise not to claim more than 20% to 25% of your home as an office unless you store inventory at home. However, home business owners have successfully claimed much more. In one case, for example, an interior decorator claimed 74% of his apartment (850 of 1150 square feet) as a home office. He was audited by the IRS, but the Service did not object to the amount of space he claimed for his office. (*Visin v. Comm'r*, T.C. Memo 2003-246.) And a professional violinist successfully claimed a home office deduction for her entire living room, which took up 40% of her one-bedroom apartment. She used the room solely for violin practice. (*Popov v. Comm'r*, 246 F.3d 1190 (9th Cir. 2002).) It is probably true, though, that the larger your home office deduction, the greater your chances of being audited.

The day care center deduction amount is calculated differently. If you operate a day care center at home but you don't devote a portion of your home exclusively to day care, your home office deduction is calculated differently than described here. You need to compare the time you use the space for day care with the time you use it for personal purposes—for example, if you use 50% of your house as a day care center for 25% of the hours in a year, you can claim a deduction for 12.5% of your housing costs (50% x 25% = 12.5%). See IRS Publication 587, *Business Use of Your Home*, for more information.

When Is an Office Part of a Home?

Kenneth Burkhart, a professional photographer, purchased a two-story building with a full basement. The building was originally constructed and used as a three-flat apartment building with a separate apartment in the basement and on each of the two upper floors. Burkhart converted the upper two floors into a single residence for his use and converted the basement into a studio and darkroom for his photography business.

Was the studio part of his residence or a separate apartment? This was not an idle question. The home office deduction rules apply only to offices or other workspaces that are part of a business owner's "dwelling."

Courts faced with this issue look at whether the area used for business is physically and functionally part of the business owner's residence. In this case, the court noted that Burkhart had removed the basement's outside entrance, kitchen, bathroom, and sleeping area. Because the basement could only be reached from the upper floors of the building, the court reasoned that the upper floors and the basement had become a single "house," similar to millions of other family homes with two upper floors and a basement. Thus, Burkhart's studio was part of his dwelling and was subject to the home office deduction rules. (*Burkhart v. Comm'r*, T.C. Memo 1989-417.)

a.   Square Footage Method

The most precise method of measuring your office space is to divide the square footage of your home office by the total square footage of your home. For example, if your home is 1,600 square feet and you use 400 square feet for your home office, 25% of the total area is used for business. Of course, you must know the square footage of your entire home and your office to make this calculation. Your home's total square footage may be listed on real estate documents or plans; you'll have to measure your office space yourself. You don't need to use a tape measure; you can just pace off the measurements.

You are allowed to subtract the square footage of common areas— such as hallways, entries, stairs, and landings—from the total area that you are measuring. You can also exclude attics and garages from your total space if you don't use them for business purposes. You aren't required to measure this way, but doing so will give you a larger deduction because your overall percentage of business use will be higher.

b.   Room Method

Another way to measure is the room method. You can use this method only if all of the rooms in your home are about the same size. Using this method, you divide the number of rooms used for business by the total number of rooms in the home. Don't include bathrooms, closets, or other storage areas. You may also leave out garages and attics if you don't use them for business. For example, if you use one room in a five-room house for business, your office takes up 20% of your home.

The room method often yields a larger deduction. Even though IRS Form 8829, *Expenses for Business Use of Your Home* (the form sole proprietors file to claim the home office deduction), seems to require you to use the square footage method, this isn't the case. As long as all of the rooms in your home are about the same size, you can use the room method. Using the room method will often result in a larger deduction.

> **EXAMPLE:** Rich rents a six-room house in San Francisco and uses one bedroom as his home office. Using the square footage method, Rich measures his entire house and finds it is 2,000 square feet. His home office is 250 square feet. Using these figures, his home office percentage is 12.5% (250 divided by 2,000 = 12.5%). However, he wants to do better than this, so he measures his common areas, such as hallways and stairways, which amount to 200 square feet. He subtracts this amount from the 2,000 total square feet, which leaves 1,800 square feet. This gives him a home office percentage of 14% (250 divided by 1,800 = 14%.)
>
> Rich then tries the room method to see whether this provides a better result. His house has six rooms—three bedrooms, a living room, a dining room, and a kitchen. He doesn't count the bathroom, garage, or attic. Because he uses one entire room as his home office, he divides one by six, leaving 16.7% as his home office percentage. Rich uses this amount to figure his home office deduction.

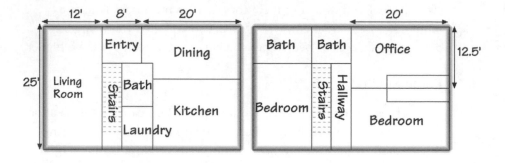

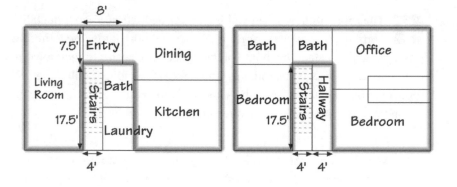

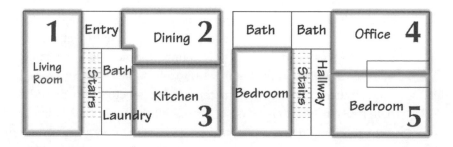

2. What Expenses Can You Deduct?

The home office deduction is not one deduction, but many. Most costs associated with maintaining and running your home office are deductible. However, because your office is in your home, some of the money you spend also benefits you personally. For example, your utility bill pays to heat your home office, but it also keeps the rest of your living space warm. The IRS deals with this issue by dividing home office expenses into two categories: direct expenses, which benefit only your home office; and indirect expenses, which benefit both your office and the rest of your home.

a. Direct Expenses

You have a direct home office expense when you pay for something just for the home office portion of your home. This includes, for example, the cost of painting your home office, carpeting it, or hiring someone to clean it. The entire amount of a direct home office expense is deductible.

> **EXAMPLE:** Jean pays a housepainter $400 to paint her home office. She may deduct this entire amount as a home office deduction.

Virtually anything you buy for your office is deductible. However, you may have to depreciate permanent improvements to your home over 39 years, rather than deduct them in the year when you pay for them. Permanent improvements are changes that go beyond simple repairs, such as adding a new room to your home to serve as your office. (See Chapter 5 for more information.)

b. Indirect Expenses

An indirect expense is a payment for something that benefits your *entire home*, including both the home office portion and your personal space. You may deduct only a portion of this expense—the home office percentage of the total.

You Can Deduct Business Expenses Even If You Don't Qualify for the Home Office Deduction

Many business owners believe that they can't deduct any expenses they incur while working at home unless they qualify for the home office deduction. This is a myth that has cost many taxpayers valuable deductions. Even if you don't qualify for or take the home office deduction, you can still take tax deductions for expenses you incur while doing business at home. These are expenses that arise from the fact that you are doing business, not from your use of the home itself.

These include:

- **Telephone expenses:** You can't deduct the basic cost of a single telephone line into your home, but you can deduct the cost of long-distance business calls and special phone services that you use for your business (such as call waiting or message center). You can also deduct the entire cost of a second phone line that you use just for business.

- **Business equipment and furniture:** The cost of office furniture, copiers, fax machines, and other personal property you use for your business and keep at home is deductible, whether or not you qualify for the home office deduction. If you purchase these items specifically for your home business, you can expense them (deduct them in one year) under Section 179 or depreciate them over several years. If you convert personal property you already own to business use, you may depreciate the fair market value. If you're a sole proprietor, you deduct these costs directly on Schedule C, *Profit or Loss From Business*. You don't have to list them on the special tax form used for the home office deduction. If you use the property for both business and personal reasons, the IRS requires you to keep records showing when the item was used for business or personal reasons—for example, a diary or log with the dates, times, and reasons the item was used. See Chapter 5 for a detailed discussion of these rules.

- **Supplies:** Supplies for your business are currently deductible as an operating expense if they have a useful life of less than one year (see Chapter 4). Otherwise, you must depreciate them or expense them under Section 179, as explained in Chapter 5.

EXAMPLE: Instead of just painting her home office, Jean decides to paint her entire home for $1,600. She uses 25% of her home as an office, so she may deduct 25% of the cost, or $400.

Most of your home office expenses will be indirect expenses, including:

- **Rent:** If you rent your home or apartment, you can use the home office deduction to deduct part of your rent—a substantial expense that is ordinarily not deductible. Your tax savings will be particularly great if you live in a high-rent area.

  EXAMPLE: Sam uses 20% of his one-bedroom Manhattan apartment as a home office for his consulting business. He pays $2,000 per month in rent, and may therefore deduct $400 of his rent per month ($4,800 per year) as a home office expense. This saves him over $2,000 in federal, state, and self-employment taxes.

- **Mortgage interest and property taxes:** Whether or not you have a home office, you can deduct your monthly mortgage interest and property tax payments as a personal itemized income tax deduction on your Schedule A, *Itemized Deductions* (the tax form where you list your personal income tax deductions). But if you have a home office, you have the option of deducting the home office percentage of your mortgage interest and property tax payments as part of your home office deduction. If you do this, you may not deduct this amount on your Schedule A (you can't deduct the same item twice). The advantage of deducting the home office percentage of your monthly mortgage interest and real estate tax payments as part of your home office deduction is that it is a business deduction, not a personal deduction; as such, it reduces the amount of your business income subject to self-employment taxes, as well as reducing your income taxes. The self-employment tax is 15.3%, so you save $153 in self-employment taxes for every $1,000 in mortgage interest and property taxes you deduct as part of your home office deduction.

EXAMPLE: Suzy, a self-employed medical record transcriber, uses 20% of her three-bedroom Tulsa home as a home office. She pays $10,000 per year in mortgage interest and property taxes. When she does her taxes for the year, she may deduct $2,000 of her interest and taxes as part of her home office deduction (20% of $10,000). She adds this amount to her other home office expenses and decreases her business income for both income tax and self-employment tax purposes. The extra $2,000 business deduction saves her $306 in self-employment tax (15.3% x $2,000). She may deduct the remaining $8,000 of mortgage interest and property tax as a personal deduction on her Schedule A.

- **Depreciation:** If you own your home, you're also entitled to a depreciation deduction for the office portion of your home. See Chapter 5 for a detailed discussion of depreciation.
- **Utilities:** You may deduct your home office percentage of your utility bills for your entire home, including electricity, gas, water, heating oil, and trash removal. If you use a disproportionately large amount of electricity for your home office, you may be able to deduct more.

EXAMPLE: Sheila, a pottery maker, works out of a home workshop that takes up 25% of the space in her home. Her work requires a substantial amount of electricity. About 50% of her monthly electricity bill is for her home workshop. She may deduct 50% of her electricity costs as a home office expense, instead of just 25%. However, to prove that she isn't deducting too much, she should keep electricity bills for her home before she began using the workshop, or for periods when she doesn't use the workshop, to show that her bills for these months are about 50% lower than the bills for her working months.

- **Insurance:** Both homeowner's and renter's insurance are partly deductible as indirect home office expenses. However, special insurance coverage you buy just for your home office—for example, insurance for your computer or other business equipment—is fully deductible as a direct expense.

- **Home maintenance:** You can deduct the home office percentage of home maintenance expenses that benefit your entire home, such as housecleaning of your entire house, roof and furnace repairs, and exterior painting. These costs are deductible whether you hire someone or do them yourself. If you do the work yourself, however, you can only deduct the cost of materials, not the cost of your own labor. Termite inspection, pest extermination fees, and snow removal costs are also deductible. However, the IRS won't let you deduct lawn care unless you regularly use your home to meet clients or customers. Home maintenance costs that don't benefit your home office—for example, painting your kitchen—are not deductible at all.

- **Casualty losses:** Casualty losses are damage to your home caused by such things as fire, floods, or theft. Casualty losses that affect your entire house—for example, a leak that floods your entire home—are deductible in the amount of your home office percentage. Casualty losses that affect only your home office—for example, a leak that floods only the home office area of the house—are fully deductible direct expenses. Casualty losses that don't affect your home office—for example, if only your kitchen floods—are not deductible as business expenses. However, they may be deductible as itemized personal deductions. (See Chapter 14 for a detailed discussion of casualty losses.)

- **Condominium association fees:** These fees (often substantial) are partly deductible as an indirect expense if you have a home office.

- **Security system costs:** Security system costs are partly deductible as an indirect expense if your security system protects your entire home. If you have a security system that protects only your home office, the cost is a fully deductible direct expense.

Mileage Deductions for Leaving the House

If your home office is your principal place of business, you can deduct the cost of traveling from your home to other work locations for your business. For example, you can deduct the cost of driving to perform work at a client's or customer's office. If you don't have a home office, these costs are not deductible. See Chapter 8 for a detailed discussion of the business mileage deduction.

- **Computer equipment:** Computers and peripheral equipment (such as printers) are deductible whether or not you qualify for the home office deduction. However, if you don't qualify for the home office deduction, you must prove that you use your computer more than half of the time for business by keeping a log of your usage. (See Chapter 5 for more information on this requirement.) If you qualify for the home office deduction, you don't need to keep track of how much time you spend using your computer for business.
- **Supplies and materials:** Office supplies and materials you use for your home business are not part of the home office deduction. They are deductible whether or not you qualify for the home office deduction.

Types of Home Expenses

Expense	Description	Deductibility
Direct	Things you buy only for your home office	Deductible in full
Indirect	Things you buy to keep your entire home up and running	Deductible based on the percentage of your home used as a business office
Unrelated	Things you buy only for parts of your home that are not used for business	Not deductible

Sam Creates a Home Office

Sam starts a part-time home business to help people repair bad credit. He converts one of the bedrooms of his two-bedroom condominium into a home office. He goes on something of a shopping spree, purchasing the following items:

- carpeting for his office and living room
- a separate telephone for the office
- office supplies, such as stapler and paper
- a new desk for his office, and
- a new computer for his office (and one for his family).

He also moves a fancy chair he already owns to his office and uses it solely for his business. In the meantime, Sam's wife has their kitchen repainted and hires a maid to clean the entire condo twice a month. Sam and his wife pay $2,000 each month on mortgage interest, real estate taxes, and homeowner's insurance.

The chart below shows which of these expenses are direct and indirect home office expenses, business operating expenses that are deductible whether or not Sam qualifies for the home office deduction, long-term asset expenses that are also deductible without regard to the home office deduction, and expenses that are not deductible.

Direct Home Office Expenses (100% Deductible)	Indirect Home Office Expense (Deductible in Amount of Home Office Percentage)	Business Operating Expenses	Long-Term Asset Expenses	Not Deductible
Carpet for home office	Mortgage interest and real estate taxes	Office supplies	Office desk	Carpet for living room
	Utilities (electricity and heat)	Business telephone	Office chair	Computer for children
	Maid service		Computer for business	
	Homeowner's insurance			

c.   Profit Limit on Deductions

Gilbert Parker worked full time for a large accounting firm, but in his spare time he was writing a book. Parker set aside a portion of his home as an office he used exclusively for writing. Like many beginning authors, he earned no money from writing. But he thought that he could at least get a tax deduction for his writing efforts by deducting his home office expenses, totaling $6,571, $4,904, and $5,444 over three years. He used these deductions to reduce the income tax he had to pay on his salary from his day job. However, both the IRS and the tax court held he could not deduct these expenses. Although he had a legitimate home office, Parker wasn't entitled to a home office deduction because he earned no money from writing. (*Parker v. Comm'r.*, TC Memo 1984-233.)

Gilbert Parker ran afoul of the most significant limitation on the home office deduction: You cannot deduct more than the net profit you earn from your home office. If you run a successful business out of your home office, this won't pose a problem. But if your business earns very little or loses money, the limitation could prevent you from deducting part or even all of your home office expenses in the current year.

If your deductions exceed your profits, you can deduct the excess in the following year and in each succeeding year until you deduct the entire amount. There is no limit on how far into the future you can deduct these expenses; you can claim them even if you are no longer living in the home where they were incurred.

So, whether or not your business is making money, you should keep track of your home office expenses and claim the deduction on your tax return. You do this by filing IRS Form 8829, *Expenses for Business Use of Your Home* (see Section D, below). When you complete the form by plugging in the figures for your business income and home office expenses, it will show you how much you can deduct in the current year and how much you must carry over to the next year.

The profit limitation applies only to the home office deduction. It does not apply to business expenses that you can deduct under other provisions of the tax code.

For these purposes, your profit is the gross income you earn from your business minus your business deductions other than your home office deduction. You must also subtract the home office portion of your mortgage interest, real estate taxes, and casualty losses.

Tax preparation software can calculate your profit for home office deduction purposes, but it's a good idea to understand how it works. First, start with your gross income from your business—if you sell goods, this is the total sales of your business minus the cost of goods sold; if you sell services, it's all the money you earn. You must list this amount on line 7 of your Schedule C. Next, figure out how much money you earn from using your home office. If you do all of your work at home, this will be 100% of your business income. But if you work in several locations, you must determine the portion of your gross income that comes from working in your home office. To do this, consider how much time you spend working in your home office and the type of work you do at home.

Then, subtract from this amount:

- the business percentage of your mortgage interest and real estate taxes (you'll have these expenses only if you own your home), plus any casualty losses, and

- all of your business expenses that are not part of the home office deduction; these are all the deductions listed in Part II of your Schedule C—for example, car expenses, travel, insurance, depreciation of business equipment, business phone, supplies, or salaries. You must deduct these separately from the home office deduction, even if you incurred them while doing business at home.

The remainder is your net profit—the most you can deduct for using your home office.

> **EXAMPLE:** Sam runs a part-time consulting business out of his home office, which occupies 20% of his home. In one year, his gross income from the business was $4,000 and he had $1,000 in expenses separate from his home office deduction. He paid $10,000 in mortgage interest and real estate taxes for the year. His home office deduction for the year is limited to $1,000. He calculates this as follows:

Gross income from business		$4,000
Minus business portion of mortgage		
interest and taxes ($10,000 x 20%)	–	2,000
Balance	=	2,000
Minus direct business expenses	–	1,000
Home office deduction limit	=	$1,000

Sam's total home office expenses for the year amount to $4,000; this includes $2,000 in mortgage interest and real estate taxes, plus $2,000 in other expenses, such as utilities and depreciation of his home. Sam first deducts those home office expenses that are not deductible as personal itemized deductions—everything other than mortgage interest, real estate taxes, and casualty losses. These expenses were $2,000; he may deduct only $1,000 of this amount because his home office deduction profit limit is $1,000. Because he has reached his profit limit, Sam can't deduct as a home office deduction any portion of his $2,000 mortgage interest and real estate tax expenses. However, he may deduct these amounts as personal itemized deductions on Schedule A. Sam may deduct the $1,000 in unused home office expenses the following year, if he has sufficient income from his business.

d.   Special Concerns for Homeowners

Until recently, homeowners who took the home office deduction were subject to a special tax trap: If they took a home office deduction for more than three of the five years before they sold their house, they had to pay capital gains taxes on the profit from the home office portion of their home. For example, if you made a $50,000 profit on the sale of your house, but your home office took up 20% of the space, you would have had to pay a tax on $10,000 of your profit (20% x $50,000 = $10,000).

Fortunately, IRS rules no longer require this. As long as you live in your home for at least two out of the five years before you sell it, the profit you make on the sale—up to $250,000 for single taxpayers and $500,000 for married taxpayers filing jointly—is not taxable. (See IRS Publication 523, *Selling Your Home.*) If you sold your house after May 6,

1997 and paid capital gains tax on the home office portion, you may be entitled to amend your return for the year you sold the house and receive a tax refund from the IRS. (See Chapter 16 for information on amending tax returns for prior years.)

However, you will have to pay a capital gains tax on the depreciation deductions you took after May 6, 1997 for your home office. This is the deduction you are allowed for the yearly decline in value due to wear and tear of the portion of the building that contains your home office. (See Chapter 5 for more information on depreciation deductions.) These "recaptured" deductions are taxed at a 25% rate (unless your income tax bracket is lower than 25%).

> **EXAMPLE:** Sally bought a $200,000 home in the year 2000 and used one of her bedrooms as her home office. She sold her home in 2004 for $300,000, realizing a $100,000 gain (profit). Her depreciation deductions for her home office from 2000 through 2004 totaled $2,000. She must pay a tax of 25% of $2,000, or $500.

Having to pay a 25% tax on the depreciation deductions you took in the years before you sold your house is actually not a bad deal. This is probably no more—and is often less—tax than you would have had to pay if you hadn't taken the deductions in the first place and instead paid tax on your additional taxable income at ordinary income tax rates.

e.   Additional Limitations for C Corporation Employees

If you form a regular C corporation to own and operate your business, you will probably be its employee. In this event, you can take home office deductions only as miscellaneous itemized deductions on Schedule A of your tax return. This means you may deduct home office expenses only to the extent that they, along with your other miscellaneous deductions (if any), exceed 2% of your adjusted gross income (AGI). For example, if your AGI was $100,000, you would get a tax benefit only on the amount of your miscellaneous deductions that exceed $2,000. This rule greatly reduces the value of the home office deduction for C corporation employees.

Make Your Corporation Reimburse You

There is a better way to recoup your office expenses if you're a corporate employee. Instead of claiming these expenses as miscellaneous itemized deductions, get your C corporation to reimburse you directly for your home office expenses. The corporation can then deduct this amount as an ordinary business expense.

The reimbursement will not be taxable to you personally if:

• you keep careful track of your home office expenses and can prove them with receipts or other records

• your corporation formally approves reimbursement of your home office expenses and the approval is documented in its corporate minutes, and

• you have an "accountable reimbursement plan"—a written agreement in which the corporation agrees to reimburse you if you provide proper substantiation for your expenses. (Reimbursement plans are covered in Chapter 11.)

For more information, see *The Corporate Minutes Book*, by Anthony Mancuso (Nolo), and IRS Publication 334, *Tax Guide for Small Business*.

D. IRS Reporting Requirements

If, like the vast majority of home business owners, you are a sole proprietor, you deduct your business operating expenses by listing them on IRS Schedule C, *Profit or Loss from Business*. You must list your home office deduction on Schedule C, but you also have to file a special tax form to show how you calculated the home office deduction: Form 8829, *Expenses for Business Use of Your Home*. This form tells the IRS that you're taking the deduction and shows how you calculated it. You should file this form even if you can't currently deduct your home office expenses because your business has no profits. By filing, you can apply the deduction to a future year in which you earn a profit. For detailed guidance on how to fill out Form 8829, see IRS Publication 587, *Business Use of Your Home*.

If you organize your business as a partnership, multimember LLC, or S corporation, you don't have to file Form 8829. If you are a partner in a partnership or an LLC member, you must list your unreimbursed home office expenses along with other partnership expenses on the partnership or LLC tax return, IRS Form 1065, *U.S. Partnership Return of Income.* These deductions pass through to you along with other partnership deductions. However, you must have a written partnership or LLC agreement stating that you are required to pay these expenses. S corporations list home office expenses, along with all their other expenses, on IRS Form 1120S, *Income Tax Return for an S Corporation.*

If you're a renter and take the home office deduction, you should file an IRS Form 1099-MISC each year, reporting the amount of your rental payments attributable to your home office.

> **EXAMPLE:** Bill rents a house and takes the home office deduction. He spends $12,000 per year on rent and uses 25% of his house as a home office. He should file Form 1099, reporting $3,000 of his rental payments.

You should file three copies of Form 1099:
- file one copy with the IRS by February 28
- give one copy to your landlord by January 31, and
- file one copy with your state tax department, if your state imposes income taxes.

Your landlord may not appreciate receiving a Form 1099 from you, but it will definitely be helpful if you're audited by the IRS and your home office deduction is questioned. It helps to show that you really were conducting a business out of your home.

You don't have to file Form 1099 if your landlord is a corporation. Form 1099 is also not required in the unlikely event that your rental payments for your home office total less than $600 for the year.

E. Audit-Proofing Your Home Office Deduction

If you are audited by the IRS and your home office deduction is questioned, you want to be able to prove that you:

- qualify for the deduction, and
- have correctly reported the amount of your home office expenses.

If you can do both those things, you should be home free.

1. Prove That You Are Following the Rules

Here are some ways to convince the IRS that you qualify for the home office deduction.

- Take a picture of your home office and draw up a diagram showing your home office as a portion of your home. Do not send the photo or diagram to the IRS. Just keep it in your files to use in case you're audited. The picture should have a date on it—this can be done with a digital camera, or you can have your film date-stamped by a developer.
- Have all of your business mail sent to your home office.
- Use your home office address on all of your business cards, stationery, and advertising.
- Obtain a separate phone line for your business and keep that phone in your home office.
- Encourage clients or customers to regularly visit your home office, and keep a log of their visits.
- To make the most of the time you spend in your home office, communicate with clients by phone, fax, or electronic mail instead of going to their offices. Use a mail or messenger service to deliver your work to customers.
- Keep a log of the time you spend working in your home office. This doesn't have to be fancy; notes on your calendar will do.

2. Keep Good Expense Records

Be sure to keep copies of your bills and receipts for home office expenses, including:

- IRS Form 1098, *Mortgage Interest Statement* (sent by whoever holds your mortgage), showing the interest you paid on your mortgage for the year
- property tax bills and your canceled checks as proof of payment

- utility bills, insurance bills, and receipts for payments for repairs to your office area, along with your canceled checks paying for these items, and
- a copy of your lease and your canceled rent checks, if you're a renter. ■

Chapter 7

Meal and Entertainment Expenses

E ven though you don't have an outside office, you probably do a significant amount of work away from home. Some of your most important
business meetings, client contacts, and marketing efforts may take place
at restaurants, golf courses, or sporting events. The tax law recognizes that
much business is mixed with pleasure—in the form of meals and social events—
and permits you to deduct part of the cost of business-related entertainment.
However, because many taxpayers have abused this deduction in the past,
the IRS has imposed strict rules limiting the types of entertainment expenses
you can deduct and the size of the deduction.

A. What Is Business Entertainment?

You may deduct only half of the total amount you spend on business
entertainment activities. Because ordinary and necessary business
activities are usually fully deductible, you'll need to know how the IRS
distinguishes between regular business activities and entertainment.

The basic rule is that entertainment involves something fun, such as:
- dining out
- going to a nightclub
- attending a sporting event
- going to a concert, movie, or the theater
- visiting a vacation spot (a ski area or beach resort, for example),
or
- taking a hunting, yachting, or fishing trip.

Although eating out might fall into other categories of business
operating expenses (depending on the circumstances), it is by far the
number one business entertainment expense—that is, it is claimed more
often than any other entertainment expense and makes up the largest
dollar portion of most taxpayers' entertainment deductions

1. Activities That Aren't Entertainment

Anything you do as a regular part of your business does not count as
entertainment. This is true even though these same activities might
constitute entertainment for others. For example, the cost of going to
the theater would not be an entertainment expense for a professional

theater critic. But if a salesperson invited a client to the theater following an important business meeting, the outing would constitute entertainment. The critic could deduct the entire cost of the theater tickets as a business operating expense (see Chapter 4), while the salesperson could deduct only 50% of the cost as an entertainment expense.

Entertainment does not include activities that are for business purposes only and don't involve any fun or amusement, such as:

- the cost of a hotel room used while traveling on business
- automobile expenses incurred while conducting business, or
- supper money paid to an employee working overtime.

In addition, meals or other entertainment expenses related to advertising or promotions are not considered entertainment. As a rule, an expense for a meal or other entertainment item will qualify as advertising if you make it available to the general public—for example, if a wine importer holds wine tastings where he provides customers with free wine and food to promote his business, the costs of the events would not be considered entertainment expenses. These kinds of advertising and promotion costs are fully deductible as business operating expenses. (See Chapter 14 for more on deducting advertising costs.)

2. Meals Can Be Travel or Entertainment

A meal can be a travel expense, an entertainment expense, or both. The distinction won't affect how much you can deduct—both travel (overnight) and entertainment expenses are only 50% deductible. But different rules apply to the two categories.

A meal is a travel expense if you eat out of necessity while away on a business trip. For example, any meal you eat alone while on the road for business is a travel expense. On the other hand, a meal is an entertainment expense if you treat a client, customer, or other business associate, and the purpose of the meal is to benefit your business. A meal is both a travel and an entertainment expense if you treat a client or other business associate to a meal while on the road. However, you may only deduct this cost once—whether you choose to do it as an entertainment or a travel expense, only 50% of the cost is deductible (see Section D, below).

B.   Who You Can Entertain

You must be with at least one person who can benefit your business in some way to claim an entertainment expense. This could include current or potential:

- customers
- clients
- suppliers
- employees (see Chapter 11 for special tax rules for employees)
- independent contractors
- agents
- partners, or
- professional advisors.

This list includes almost anyone you're likely to meet for business reasons. Although you can invite family members or friends along, you can't deduct the costs of entertaining them, except in certain limited situations (see Section D, below).

C.   Deducting Entertainment Expenses

Entertainment expenses, like all business operating expenses, are deductible only if they are ordinary and necessary. This means that the entertainment expense must be common, helpful, and appropriate for your business. Taxpayers used to have to show only that the entertainment wasn't purely for fun, and that it benefited their business in some way. This standard was so easy to satisfy that the IRS came up with a few additional requirements.

Before the IRS made the standard tougher, you could deduct ordinary and necessary entertainment expenses even if business was never discussed. For example, you could deduct the cost of taking a client to a restaurant, even if you spent the whole time drinking martinis and talking about sports (the infamous "three-martini lunch"). This is no longer the case—now you must discuss business with one or more business associates either before, during, or after a social activity if you want to claim an entertainment deduction (subject to one exception: see Section C4, below).

Who's going to know? The IRS doesn't have spies lurking in restaurants, theaters, or other places of entertainment, so it has no way of knowing whether you really discuss business with a client or other business associate. You're pretty much on the honor system here. However, be aware that if you're audited, the IRS closely scrutinizes this deduction because many taxpayers cheat when they take it. You'll also have to comply with stringent record-keeping requirements. (See Chapter 15 for tips on record keeping.)

1. Business Discussions Before or After Entertainment

The easiest way to get a deduction for entertainment is to discuss business before or after the activity. To meet this requirement, the discussion must be "associated" with your business—that is, it must have a clear business purpose, such as developing new business or encouraging existing business relationships. You don't, however, have to expect to get a specific business benefit from the discussion. Your business discussion can involve planning, advice, or simply exchanging useful information with a business associate.

You automatically satisfy the business discussion requirement if you attend a business-related convention or meeting to further your business. Business activities—not socializing—must be the main purpose for the convention. Save a copy of the program or agenda to prove this.

Generally, the entertainment should occur on the same day as the business discussion. However, if your business guests are from out of town, the entertainment can occur the day before or the day after the business talk.

> **EXAMPLE:** Mary, a home-based architect who lives in Los Angeles, has been hired to design a large home for Wayne, who lives in Las Vegas. Wayne travels to Los Angeles to discuss his ideas for the house and look at some preliminary drawings prepared by Mary. Wayne arrives on Tuesday evening and Mary treats him to dinner at a nice restaurant that night. The following morning, Wayne goes to Mary's home office to discuss the home building project. Mary can deduct half of the cost of the dinner they had the night before as an entertainment expense.

You can get a deduction even if the entertainment occurs in a place like a nightclub, theater, or loud sports arena, where it's difficult or impossible to talk business. Because your business discussions can take place before or after the entertainment, the IRS won't be scrutinizing whether or not you actually could have talked business during your entertainment activity.

> **EXAMPLE:** Following lengthy contract negotiations at a prospective client's office, you take the client to a baseball game to unwind. You can deduct half of the cost of the tickets as a business expense.

The entertainment can last longer than your business discussions, as long as you don't spend just a small fraction of your total time on business. In other words, you can't simply ask an associate "How's business?" You must have a substantial discussion. Also, your business-related discussions don't have to be face-to-face—they can occur over the telephone or even by email.

2.   Business Discussions During Entertainment

Another way to make your entertainment expenses deductible is to discuss business during an entertainment activity. To get the deduction, you must show that:

- the main purpose of the combined business discussion and entertainment was the active conduct of business—you don't have to spend the entire time talking business, but the main character of the entertainment must be business
- you did in fact have a business meeting, negotiation, discussion, or other bona fide business transaction with your guest or guests during the entertainment, and
- you expect to get income or some other *specific business benefit* in the future from your discussions during the entertainment— thus, for example, a casual conversation in which the subject of business comes up won't do; you must have a specific business goal in mind.

EXAMPLE: Ivan, a home-based consultant, has had ongoing email discussions with a prospective client who is interested in hiring him. Ivan thinks he'll be able to close the deal and get a contract signed in a face-to-face meeting. He chooses a lunch meeting because it's more informal and the prospective client will like getting a free lunch. He treats the client to a $40 lunch at a nice restaurant. During the lunch, they finalize the terms of a contract for Ivan's consulting services and come to a handshake agreement. This meal clearly led to a specific business benefit for Ivan, so he can deduct half of the cost as an entertainment expense.

You don't necessarily have to close a deal, sign a contract, or otherwise obtain a specific business benefit to get a deduction. But you do have to have a *reasonable expectation* that you can get some specific business benefit through your discussions during the entertainment—for example, to make progress toward new business, sales of your product, or investment in your business.

With the possible exception of some types of home entertainment (see Section B3, below), this deduction is limited to business discussions held during meals. In the IRS's view, it's usually not possible to engage in serious business discussions at other types of entertainment activities because of the distractions. Examples of places the IRS would probably find not conducive to serious talk include:

- nightclubs, theaters, or sporting events
- cocktail parties or other large social gatherings
- hunting or fishing trips
- yachting or other pleasure boat outings, or
- group gatherings at a cocktail lounge, golf club, athletic club, or vacation resort that includes people who are not business associates.

This means, for example, that you usually can't claim that you discussed business *during* a golf game, even if your foursome consists of you and three business associates. In the IRS's view, golfers are unable to play and talk business at the same time. On the other hand, you could have a business discussion *before or after* a golf game—for example, in the clubhouse. This might seem ridiculous, but it is the rule.

3.   Entertaining at Home

Home business owners don't just work at home; they may entertain business associates there as well. The cost of entertaining at your home is deductible if it meets either of the above two tests. You cannot, however, deduct the costs of inviting nonbusiness guests to your house, with the possible exception of a business associate's spouse (see Section D3, below).

a.   Business Discussed During Home Entertainment

You are most likely to qualify for a deduction for home entertainment if you discuss business during the activity.

> **EXAMPLE:** Jack, a home-based venture capital entrepreneur, invites Thomas, an inventor, and his wife to his house for dinner to discuss investing in Thomas's latest invention. They have a lengthy discussion that helps Jack decide to make the investment. The dinner qualifies as a deductible entertainment expense

However, the IRS probably won't believe that you discussed business during home entertainment if large numbers of people are involved.

> **EXAMPLE:** Arthur invited 40 people to his house for a celebratory party after he passed the bar exam. He served a catered, buffet-style dinner and hired a bartender to serve drinks. Both the IRS and the tax court ruled that the party was not a deductible business entertainment expense. They both concluded that the party was primarily a social event at which Arthur engaged in no substantial business-related conversations. (*Ryman v. Comm'r.*, 51 T.C. 799.)

A quiet dinner party at home is more likely to qualify as an entertainment expense.

> **EXAMPLE:** Jack Howard, president and managing editor of a large newspaper chain, held monthly dinner parties to which he invited eight to ten guests who were prominent in politics, business, the arts, and other fields. The tax court held that the gatherings were a

deductible entertainment expense. The court believed Howard when he said that he held the dinner parties at his home to have "off the record" conversations that helped his media business. The court noted in particular that the gatherings were small and were held on weeknights. (*Howard v. Comm'r.*, TC Memo 98-250.)

b. Business Discussed Before or After Home Entertainment

A large home gathering (such as a cocktail party) will probably qualify as an entertainment expense only if you have business discussions before or after the event. Of course, small gatherings could qualify on this basis as well.

> **EXAMPLE:** Sheila, a home based public relations consultant, signs a new contract to represent the raisin growers' trade association. To celebrate and help cement her new business relationship, she invites the association's president and board of directors to her house for a catered dinner party that evening. The party is a deductible business entertainment expense.

4. Entertainment in Business Settings

An exception to the general rule that you must discuss business before, during, or after entertainment applies when the entertainment occurs in a clear business setting. For example, you can deduct half of the following costs as entertainment expenses:

- the price of renting a hospitality room at a convention where you display or discuss your business products
- entertainment that is mainly a price rebate on the sale of your products—for example, when a restaurant owner provides a free meal to a loyal customer, or
- entertainment that occurs under circumstances where there is no meaningful personal relationship between you and the people you entertained—for example, you entertain local business or civic leaders at the opening of a new hotel to get business publicity, rather than to form business relationships with them.

D. Calculating Your Deduction

Most expenses you incur for business entertainment are deductible, including meals (with beverages, tax, and tips), your transportation expenses (including parking), tickets to entertainment or sporting events, catering costs for parties, cover charges for admission to night clubs, and rent you pay for a room in which to hold a dinner or cocktail party.

You are allowed to deduct only *50%* of your entertainment expenses. For example, if you spend $50 for a meal in a restaurant, you can deduct $25. (Even though you can deduct only half of the expense, you must keep track of everything you spend and report the entire amount on your tax return.) The only exception to the 50% rule is for transportation expenses, which are 100% deductible.

If you have a single bill or receipt that includes some business entertainment and some other expenses (such as lodging or transportation), you must allocate the expense between the cost of the entertainment and the cost of the other services. For example, if your hotel bill covers meals as well as lodging, you'll have to make a reasonable estimate of the portion that covers meals. It's best to avoid this hassle by getting a separate bill for your deductible entertainment.

1. Expenses Must Be Reasonable

Your entertainment expenses must be reasonable—the IRS won't let you deduct entertainment expenses that it considers lavish or extravagant. There is no dollar limit on what is reasonable, nor are you necessarily barred from entertaining at deluxe restaurants, hotels, nightclubs, or resorts.

Whether your expenses will be considered reasonable depends on the particular facts and circumstances—for example, a $250 expense for dinner with a client and two business associates at a fancy restaurant would probably be considered reasonable if you closed a substantial business deal during the meal. Because there are no concrete guidelines, you have to use your common sense.

2.   Going "Dutch"

You can deduct entertainment expenses only if you pay for the activity. If a client picks up the tab, you obviously get no deduction. If you split the expense, you must subtract what it would ordinarily cost you for the meal from the amount you actually paid, and then deduct 50% of that total. For example, if you pay $20 for lunch and you usually pay only $5, you can deduct 50% of $15, or $7.50.

If you split a lot of tabs and are worried that the IRS might challenge your deductions, you can save your grocery bills or receipts from eating out for a month to show what you usually spend. You don't need to keep track of which grocery items you eat for each meal. Instead, the IRS assumes that 50% of your total grocery receipts are for dinner, 30% for lunch, and 20% for breakfast.

3.   Expenses You Can't Deduct

There are certain expenses that you are prohibited from deducting as entertainment.

a.   Entertainment Facilities

You may not deduct the cost of buying, leasing, or maintaining an entertainment facility, such as a yacht, swimming pool, tennis court, hunting camp, fishing lodge, bowling alley, car, airplane, hotel suite, apartment, or home in a vacation resort. These entertainment facilities are not considered deductible business assets.

> **EXAMPLE:** Sue, a home-based salesperson, takes a customer for a day of fishing at a nature resort. The expenses of the outing, such as fishing licenses, bait and tackle, and boat rental are deductible if the requirements are met. However, if Sue and her customer stay overnight at a fishing lodge at the resort, the cost of the lodging is not deductible.

This rule also applies to your home if you use it for business-related entertaining. Thus, for example, you can't take a business entertainment deduction for your normal home maintenance costs just because you do business entertaining at home. You may deduct only expenses that are directly attributable to the entertainment—for example, the cost of food, liquor, caterers, bartenders, and so on.

b.   Expenses of Nonbusiness Guests

You may not deduct the cost of entertaining people who are not business associates. If you entertain business and personal guests at an event, you must divide your entertainment expenses between the two and deduct only the business part.

> **EXAMPLE:** You take three business associates and six friends to dinner. Because there were ten people at dinner (including you), and only four were business related, 40% of this expense qualifies as business entertainment. If you spend $200 for the dinner, only $80 would be deductible. And because you can deduct only half of your entertainment expenses, your total deduction for the event is $40.

Ordinarily, you cannot deduct the cost of entertaining your spouse or the spouse of a business associate. However, there is an exception: You can deduct these costs if you can show that you had a clear business purpose (rather than a personal or social purpose) for bringing the spouse or spouses along.

> **EXAMPLE:** You take a client who is visiting from out of town to dinner with his wife. The client's wife joins you because it's impractical (not to mention impolite) to have dinner with the client and not include his wife. Your spouse joins the party because the client's spouse is present. You may deduct half of the cost of dinner for both spouses.

c.   Club Dues and Membership Fees

In the good old days, you could deduct dues for belonging to a country club or similar private facility where business associates gathered. This is no longer possible. The IRS says you cannot deduct dues (including initiation fees) for membership in any club if one of the principal purposes of the club is to:

- conduct entertainment activities for members, or
- provide entertainment facilities for members to use.

Thus, you cannot deduct dues paid to country clubs, golf and athletic clubs, yacht clubs, airline clubs, hotel clubs, or clubs operated to provide members with meals. However, you can deduct the direct expenses you incur to entertain a business associate at a club.

> **EXAMPLE:** Jack, a home-based salesperson, is a member of the Golden Bear Golf Club in Columbus, Ohio. His annual membership dues are $10,000. One night, Jack invites a client to dinner at the club's dining room where they discuss whether Jack should buy the client out. Jack pays $100 for the dinner. Jack's $10,000 annual dues are not deductible, but his costs for the dinner are. Because of the 50% limitation on entertainment expenses, Jack can deduct $50 for the meal.

You can deduct dues you pay to join a business-related tax-exempt organization or civic organization as long as the organization's primary purpose isn't to provide entertainment. Examples include organizations like the Kiwanis or Rotary Club, business leagues, chambers of commerce, real estate boards, trade associations, and professional associations such as a medical or bar association.

4. Entertainment Tickets

You can deduct only the face value of an entertainment ticket, even if you paid a higher price for it. For example, you cannot deduct service fees that you pay to ticket agencies or brokers, or any amount over the face value of tickets that you buy from scalpers. However, you can deduct the entire amount you pay for a ticket to an amateur sporting event run by volunteers to benefit a charity.

Ordinarily, you or an employee must be present at an entertainment activity to claim it as a business entertainment expense. This is not the case, however, for entertainment tickets. You can give tickets to clients or other business associates rather than attending the event yourself, and still take a deduction. If you don't go to the event, you have the option of treating the tickets as a gift. You can get a bigger deduction this way sometimes. Gifts of up to $25 are 100% deductible (see Chapter 14), so you get a bigger deduction for tickets that cost less than $50 if you treat them as a gift. If they cost more, treat them as an entertainment expense to maximize your deduction.

> **EXAMPLE:** You pay $40 to a scalper for a ticket to a college basketball game; the ticket has a face value of only $30. You give the ticket to a client, but don't attend the game yourself. By treating the ticket as a gift, you may deduct $25 of the expense. If you treated it as an entertainment expense, your deduction would be limited to 50% of the face value of the ticket ($30), or $15. However, if you paid $100 for a ticket with a $60 face value, you would be better off treating it as an entertainment expense. This way you would be able to deduct 50% of $60 or $30. If you treated the ticket as a gift, your deduction would still be limited to $25.

You may also deduct the cost of season tickets at a sports arena or theater. But if you rent a skybox or other private luxury box, your deduction is limited to the cost of a regular nonluxury box seat. The cost of season tickets must be allocated to each separate event.

> **EXAMPLE:** Jim, an investment counselor, spends $5,000 for two season tickets to his local professional football team. The tickets entitle him and a guest to attend 16 games. He must allocate the cost game by game. If, during the course of the football season, he gives tickets for half of the games to clients and uses the others for himself and his wife, half of the total cost of the season tickets is a business entertainment expense. Because entertainment expenses are only 50% deductible, Jim may deduct $1,250 (half of the cost of half of the games).

5. Reimbursed Expenses

If a client reimburses you for entertainment expenses, you get no deduction. This actually works out great for you because you don't have to count the reimbursement that you receive as income. So, the client gets to deduct 50% of the expenses and you get 100% of your expenses paid by somebody else. This is a lot better than getting only a 50% entertainment expense deduction.

> **EXAMPLE:** Philip, a home-based private detective, takes several people out to lunch to discuss the theft of trade secrets from a biotechnology firm. He bills his client $200 for the lunches and provides all the proper documentation. The client reimburses Philip $200. Philip gets no deduction for the lunches, but he also doesn't have to include the $200 reimbursement in his income for the year; his client may deduct $100 (50% of the expense) as a business entertainment expense.

On the other hand, if you don't properly document your expenses and obtain reimbursement from your client, you can still deduct the cost as a business entertainment expense, although your deduction will be subject to the 50% limit. The moral is that you should try to get your clients to reimburse you for entertainment expenses whenever possible— and keep careful track of your costs. ■

Chapter 8

Car and Local Travel Expenses

That expensive car parked in your garage doesn't just look great—it could also give you a great tax deduction. If, for example, you drive 10,000 miles per year for business, you can take a deduction of at least $3,750 (based on 2004 rates). You might be able to deduct even more, depending on how you choose to deduct your car expenses.

This chapter shows you how to deduct expenses for *local transportation*—that is, business trips that don't require you to stay away from home overnight. These rules apply to local business trips using any means of transportation, but this chapter focuses primarily on car expenses, the most common type of deduction for local business travel. Overnight trips (whether by car or other means) are covered in Chapter 9.

Different rules apply to corporate employees. This chapter covers local transportation deductions by business owners—sole proprietors, partners in partnerships, or LLC members—not by corporate employees. If you have incorporated your business and work as its employee, you must follow special rules to deduct local transportation expenses. Those rules are covered in Chapter 11.

Transportation expenses are a red flag for the IRS. Transportation expenses are the number one item that IRS auditors look at when they examine small business tax returns. These expenses can be substantial—and it is easy to overstate them—so the IRS will look very carefully to make sure that you're not bending the rules. Your first line of defense against an audit is to keep good records to back up your deductions. This is something no tax preparation program or accountant can do for you—you must develop good record-keeping habits and follow them faithfully to stay out of trouble with the IRS. You can find information on record keeping in Chapter 15.

A. Deductible Local Transportation Expenses

Local transportation costs are deductible as business operating expenses if they are ordinary and necessary for your business, trade, or profession. The cost must be common, helpful, and appropriate for your business. (See Chapter 4 for a detailed discussion of the ordinary and necessary requirement.) It makes no difference what type of transportation you use to make the local trips—car, van, pickup, truck, motorcycle, taxi, bus, or train—or whether the vehicle you use is owned or leased. You can deduct these costs as long as they are ordinary and necessary and meet the other requirements discussed below.

1.   Travel Must Be for Business

You can only deduct local trips that are for business—that is, travel to a business location. Personal trips—for example, to the supermarket or the gym—are not deductible as business travel expenses. A business location is any place where you perform business-related tasks, such as:

- the place where you have your principal place of business, including a home office
- other places where you work, including temporary job sites
- places where you meet with clients or customers
- the bank where you do business banking
- a local college where you take work-related classes
- the store where you buy business supplies, or
- the warehouse or other place where you keep business inventory.

Starting a New Business

The cost of local travel before you start your business, such as travel to investigate starting a new business, is not a currently deductible business operating expense. It is a start-up expense that you must deduct over the first 60 months that you are in business. (See Chapter 3 for information on deducting start-up costs.)

As explained below, you can take the largest deduction for local business trip expenses if you have a home office.

2.   Trips From Your Home Office

If, like most home business people, you have a home office that qualifies as your principal place of business, you can deduct the cost of any trips you make from home to another business location. You can get a lot of travel deductions this way. For example, you can deduct the cost of driving from home to a client's office or to attend a business-related seminar.

Your home office will qualify as your principal place of business if it is the place where you earn most of your income or perform adminis- trative or management tasks. Virtually all home businesses should be able to qualify under either or both of these criteria.

> **EXAMPLE:** Kim, a personal trainer, spends most of her time work- ing with her clients at their homes or gyms. But she maintains a home office where she does administrative work for her business, such as billing, scheduling appointments, and creating written exercise programs for her clients. She may deduct the cost of driving from home to meet with clients and back home again.

3.   If You Have No Regular Workplace

If you have no regular office—whether inside or outside your home— the location of your first business contact of the day is considered your office for tax purposes. Transportation expenses from your home to this first business contact are commuting expenses, which are not deductible. The same is true for your last business contact of the day—your trip home is nondeductible commute travel. You can deduct the cost of all your other trips during the day between clients or customers.

> **EXAMPLE:** Jim is an encyclopedia salesman who works in the Houston metropolitan area. He works out of his car, with no office at home or anywhere else. One day, he makes ten sales calls by car. His trip from home to his first sales contact of the day is a non- deductible commuting expense. His next nine trips are deductible, and his trip home from his last sales contact is a nondeductible personal commuting expense.

There is an easy way to get around this rule about the first and last trip of the day: Open a home office. That way, all of your trips are deductible.

EXAMPLE: Jim creates an office at home where he performs administrative tasks for his sales business, such as bookkeeping. He may
now deduct the cost of all of his business trips during the day,
including driving from home to his first business contact and back
home from his last contact of the day.

B.   The Standard Mileage Rate

If you drive a car, panel truck, van, pickup, or an SUV for business (as
most people do), you have two options for deducting your vehicle
expenses: You can use the standard mileage rate or you can deduct
your actual expenses.

Let's start with the easy one—the standard mileage rate. This method
works best for people who don't want to bother with a lot of record
keeping or calculations. But this ease comes at a price—it often results
in a lower deduction than you might be entitled to if you used the
actual expense method.

1.   How the Standard Mileage Rate Works

To use the standard mileage rate, you deduct a specified number of
cents for every business mile you drive. The IRS sets the standard mileage rate each year—in 2004, the rate was 37.5 cents per mile. (The rate
should be substantially higher in 2005 to reflect the large increase in gas
prices in 2004.)

To figure out your deduction, simply multiply your business miles by
the standard mileage rate for the year. The rate is the same whether you
own or lease your car.

EXAMPLE: Ed, a self-employed salesperson, drove his car 10,000
miles for business in 2004. To determine his car expense deduction,
he simply multiplies the total business miles he drove by 37.5 cents.
This gives him a $3,750 deduction (37.5 cents x 10,000 = $3,750).

The big advantage of the standard mileage rate is that it requires very little record keeping. You only need to keep track of how many business miles you drive, not the actual expenses for your car, such as gas, maintenance, or repairs. However, the standard mileage rate will often give you a smaller deduction than the actual expense method.

If you choose the standard mileage rate, you cannot deduct actual car operating expenses—for example, maintenance and repairs, gasoline and its taxes, oil, insurance, and vehicle registration fees. All of these items are factored into the rate set by the IRS. And you can't deduct the cost of the car through depreciation or Section 179 expensing because the car's depreciation is also factored into the standard mileage rate (as are lease payments for a leased car).

The only actual expenses you can deduct (because these costs aren't included in the standard mileage rate) are:

- parking fees and tolls for business trips (but you can't deduct parking ticket fines or the cost of parking your car at your place of work)
- interest on a car loan, and
- personal property tax you paid when you bought the vehicle, based on its value—this is often included as part of your auto registration fee.

If you use your car for both business and personal trips, you can deduct only the business use percentage of the above-mentioned interest and taxes.

> **EXAMPLE:** Ralph uses his car 50% for his home business and 50% for personal trips. He uses the standard mileage rate to deduct his car expenses. He pays $3,000 a year in interest on his car loan. He may deduct 50% of this amount, or $1,500, as a business operating expense in addition to his business mileage deduction.

2. Requirements to Use the Standard Mileage Rate

Not everyone can use the standard mileage rate. You won't be able to use it (and will have to use the actual expense method instead) if you can't meet the following requirements.

a.   First-Year Rule

You must use the standard mileage rate in the first year you use a car for business or you are forever foreclosed from using that method for that car. Therefore, when you first use a car for business, you have to decide whether or not you want to use the standard mileage rate. If you lease your car, you must use the standard mileage rate for the entire lease period if you use it in the first year.

   If you own your car and choose the standard mileage rate in the first year, you are then free to switch back and forth in later years between the standard mileage rate and the actual expense method as often as you want. However, you may only use the straight line method of depreciation during the years you use the actual expense method. This method gives you equal depreciation deductions every year, rather than the larger deductions in the early years available by using accelerated depreciation methods (See Chapter 5 for more on depreciation.) More-over, when you use the actual expense method, you'll have to reduce the tax basis of your car by a portion of the standard mileage rate deductions you already received. This will reduce your depreciation deduction.

b.   Five-Car Rule

You can't use the standard mileage rate if you have five or more cars that you use for business simultaneously. (Before 2004, the IRS didn't allow business owners who used more than one car at the same time to use the standard mileage rate. The change to five or more cars allows an additional 800,000 businesses to use the standard mileage rate.)

> **EXAMPLE:** Maureen owns a car and five vans that are used in her housecleaning business. Her employees use the five vans and she uses the car to travel to customers' houses. Maureen can't use the standard mileage rate for her vehicles because all six cars are used in her business at the same time.

Stop That Cab!

Taxi drivers and others who hire out their vehicles for business can't use the standard mileage rate. They must use the actual expense method as described in the following section.

C. The Actual Expense Method

Instead of using the standard mileage rate, you can deduct the actual cost of using your car for business. This requires more record keeping, but usually results in a higher deduction.

Business Travel By Motorcycle

You must use the actual expense method if you ride a motorcycle—the standard mileage rate is only for passenger vehicles. However, the limits on depreciation for passenger automobiles (discussed in Section C3, below) do not apply to bicycles or motorcycles. You may depreciate these items just like any other business property. Or, if you wish, you can deduct the full cost of a motorcycle or bicycle in the year that you purchase it under Section 179. (See Chapter 5 for more on depreciation and Section 179.)

1.   How the Actual Expense Method Works

As the name implies, under the actual expense method, you deduct the actual costs you incur each year to operate your car, plus depreciation. If you use this method, you must keep careful track of all of your car expenses during the year, including:

- gas and oil
- repairs and maintenance

- depreciation of your original vehicle and improvements (see Section C3, below)
- car repair tools
- license fees
- parking fees for business trips
- registration fees
- tires
- insurance
- garage rent
- tolls for business trips
- car washing
- lease payments
- interest on car loans
- towing charges, and
- auto club dues.

Watch Those Tickets

You may not deduct the cost of driving violations or parking tickets, even if you were on business when you got the ticket. Government fines and penalties are never deductible as a matter of public policy.

When you do your taxes, add up the cost of all these items. For everything but parking fees and tolls, multiply the total cost of each item by the percentage of time you use your car for business. For parking fees and tolls that are business related, include (and deduct) the full cost. The total is your deductible transportation expense for the year.

EXAMPLE: In one recent year, Laura, a salesperson, drove her car 8,000 miles for her business and 8,000 miles for personal purposes. She can deduct 50% of the actual costs of operating her car, plus the full cost of any business-related tolls and parking fees. Her expenses amount to $10,000 for the year, so she gets a $5,000 deduction, plus $500 in tolls and parking for business.

If you have a car that you use only for business, you may deduct 100% of your actual car costs. Be careful here. If you own just one car, it's hard to successfully claim that you use it only for business. The IRS is not likely to believe that you walk or take public transportation everywhere, except when you're on business. Your argument might be more persuasive if you live in a city with a developed transportation system, such as Chicago, New York City, or San Francisco, and drive your car only when you go out of town on business. But be prepared for the IRS to question your deduction. (If you're a sole proprietor, the IRS will know how many cars you own; sole proprietors who claim transportation expenses must provide this information on their tax returns—see Section F, below).

2.   Record-Keeping Requirements

When you deduct actual car expenses, you must keep records of all the costs of owning and operating your car. This includes not only the number of business miles and total miles you drive, but also gas, repair, parking, insurance, tolls, and any other car expenses. (You'll find more information on record-keeping requirements in Chapter 15.)

3.   Vehicle Depreciation Deductions

Using the actual expense method, you can deduct the cost of your vehicle. However, you can't deduct the entire cost in the year when you purchase your car. Instead, you must deduct the cost a portion at a time over several years, using a process called depreciation. (For more on depreciation generally, see Chapter 5). Although the general concept of depreciation is the same for every type of property, special rules apply to depreciation deductions for cars. These rules give you a lower deduction for cars than you'd be entitled to using the normal depreciation rules.

This section focuses on the depreciation rules for passenger automobiles, as defined by the IRS. This category of vehicles includes almost all automobiles and other passenger vehicles—cars, trucks, pickups, vans, and SUVs. To understand the depreciation rules discussed in this section, you will need to be familiar with the general depreciation rules covered in Chapter 5.

a.   Is Your Vehicle a Passenger Automobile?

First, you must figure out whether your vehicle is a passenger automobile as defined by the IRS. A passenger automobile is any four-wheeled vehicle made primarily for use on public streets and highways that has an unloaded gross weight of 6,000 pounds or less. This definition includes virtually all automobiles.

However, if your vehicle is a truck or van, or has a truck base (as do most SUVs), it is a passenger automobile only if it has a gross loaded vehicle weight of 6,000 pounds or less. The gross loaded weight is based on how much the manufacturer says the vehicle can carry and is different from unloaded weight—that is, the vehicle's weight without any passengers or cargo.

You can find out your vehicle's gross loaded and unloaded weight by looking at the metal plate in the driver's side door jamb, looking at your owner's manual, checking the manufacturer's website or sales brochure, or asking an auto dealer. The gross loaded weight is usually called the Gross Vehicle Weight Rating (GVWR for short). The gross unloaded weight is often called the "curb weight."

Trucks that weigh 14,000 pounds or less when fully loaded are subject to the same rules as passenger automobiles, unless the vehicle is not likely to be used for personal purposes (as is true of taxis, moving vans, construction vehicles, hearses, tractors, and utility repair trucks). In that case, the vehicles are not considered passenger automobiles, and the limitations on depreciation discussed in this section don't apply.

b.   Passenger Automobiles Are Listed Property

All passenger automobiles are "listed property"—property that is often used for personal purposes. As explained in Chapter 5, the IRS imposes more stringent requirements on deductions for listed property to discourage fraudulent deduction claims. Because passenger automobiles are listed property, you must keep mileage records showing how much you use your car for business and personal purposes. You must also file IRS Form 4562, *Depreciation and Amortization*, with your annual tax return.

c.   What You Can Depreciate

You can depreciate your entire investment in a car (also called your basis). If you buy a passenger automobile and use it for business that same year, your basis is its cost. You may depreciate the entire cost, even if you financed part of the purchase with a car loan. The cost also includes sales taxes, destination charges, and other fees the seller charges. It does not, however, include auto license and registration fees.

If you trade in your old car to a dealer to purchase a new car, your basis in the car you purchase is the adjusted basis of the trade-in car, plus the cash you pay (whether out of your own pocket or financed with a car loan).

> **EXAMPLE:** Brenda buys a new pickup for her construction business. The pickup has a $20,000 sticker price. She trades in her old pickup and pays the dealer $15,000, all of which she finances with a car loan from her bank. Her trade-in has an adjusted basis of $7,000. Her basis in the new pickup is $22,000 ($7,000 + $15,000), even though the sticker price on the new pickup was only $20,000.

If you convert a car that you previously owned for personal use to a business car, your basis is the lower of what you originally paid for it (when you purchased it for personal use) or its fair market value at the time you convert it to business use. Your basis will usually be its fair market value, as this is usually the lower number.

You can determine the fair market value of your car on the date of conversion by checking used car value guides, such as the Kelley Blue Book. These guides often give more than one value—for example, the Kelley Blue Book gives a private party value and a retail value. Using the highest value will give you the largest deduction. The best known used car price guides (available free on the Internet) are:

- Kelley Blue Book: www.kbb.com
- Edmunds: www.edmunds.com
- NADA guides: www.nadaguides.com

Look at more than one guide, because the prices can vary.

⚠ **You can't use Section 179 and bonus depreciation when you convert a personal car to business use.** If you use a car for personal travel, then later decide to convert it to a business vehicle, you cannot use the Section 179 deduction or bonus depreciation. Instead, you must use regular depreciation (described in Chapter 5).

d.   Depreciation Limits For Passenger Automobiles

There are three different ways to deduct the cost of a passenger automobile that you use for business:

- regular depreciation
- first-year bonus depreciation (available only for new cars and scheduled to end on 1/1/05), and
- Section 179 expensing.

These three methods are discussed in detail in Chapter 5. You can use regular depreciation and Section 179 expensing for both new and used cars. Bonus depreciation, however, can be used only for new cars.

Cars Used Primarily for Personal Purposes

If you use a passenger automobile for business less than 50% of the time, you must depreciate it using the straight-line method. In addition, if you start out using a car more than 50% for business and your business use falls below 50% in a later year, you must give back any extra depreciation you received using accelerated depreciation in the prior years. In other words, you must recalculate all of your deductions for the car using the straight-line method, and repay any difference between this amount and the deductions you actually took using another method.

You can combine these deduction methods to give yourself the maximum possible annual deduction. But, unlike other assets, there are rules limiting the size of the annual deduction you can take for passenger automobiles. These limits are adjusted each year for inflation.

Starting in 2003, the IRS established two different sets of deduction limits for passenger automobiles: one for passenger automobiles other than trucks and vans; and one for trucks and vans that qualify as passenger automobiles (based on their weight) and are built on a truck chassis. This includes minivans and many sports utility vehicles (as long as they meet the weight limit).

The first chart below shows the maximum annual deduction allowed for passenger automobiles (not including trucks and vans), adjusted for inflation through 2004. (You can triple these limits if you buy an electric car after May 6, 2003.) The second chart shows the limits for passenger automobiles that are trucks and vans as defined above. Both charts assume 100% business use of the vehicle. You can find the current deduction limits in IRS Publication 946, *How to Depreciate Property,* and Publication 463, *Travel, Entertainment, Gift, and Car Expenses.*

> **EXAMPLE:** Mario pays $50,000 for a new passenger automobile on June 1, 2004 and uses it only for his sales business. He may deduct a maximum of $10,610 in 2004, $4,800 in 2005, $2,850 in 2006, and $1,675 each year thereafter.

The first year deduction limit is so large (compared to the other years) because of first-year bonus depreciation. (See Chapter 5 for more on depreciation.) For passenger automobiles other than trucks and vans, the first-year bonus allows you to add $7,650 to the regular depreciation limit of $2,960 for 2004. However, if you don't qualify for bonus depreciation or decide not to take it (it isn't required), your first year deduction limit will be reduced to the regular $2,960 level. To take bonus depreciation, you must buy a new car and use it more than 50% of the time for your business during the period from September 11, 2001 through December 31, 2004.

> **EXAMPLE:** Mario buys a used car in 2004 instead of a new one. He may not take first year bonus depreciation for the car, so his first year deduction is limited to $2,960.

Maximum Depreciation Deductions for Passenger Automobiles (100% Business Use)

Year Placed in Service	1st Year (regardless of month car placed in service)	2nd Year	3rd Year	4th Year and Later
2004	$10,610 ($2,960 + $7,650 bonus depreciation)	$4,800	$2,850	$1,675
5/6/2003- 12/31/03	$10,710 ($3,060 + $7,650 bonus depreciation)	$4,900	$2,950	$1,775
9/11/2001- 5/5/2003	$7,660 ($3,060 + $4,600 bonus depreciation)	$4,900	$2,950	$1,775
1/1/2001- 9/10/2001	$3,060	$4,900	$2,950	$1,775
2000	$3,060	$4,900	$2,950	$1,775
1999	$3,060	$5,000	$2,950	$1,775
1998	$3,060	$5,000	$2,950	$1,775
1997	$3,060	$5,000	$3,050	$1,775
1995-1996	$3,060	$4,900	$2,950	$1,775

Maximum Depreciation Deductions for Passenger Automobiles That Are Trucks and Vans (100% Business Use)

Year Placed in Service	1st Year (regardless of month vehicle placed in service)	2nd Year	3rd Year	4th Year and Later
2004	$10,910 ($3,160 + $7,650 bonus depreciation)	$5,300	$3,150	$1,875
5/6/2003- 12/31/03	$11,010 ($3,360 + $7,650 bonus depreciation)	$5,400	$3,250	$1,975
1/1/2003- 5/5/2003	$7,960 ($3,360 + $4,600 bonus depreciation)	$5,400	$3,250	$1,975
9/11/2001- 12/31/2002	$7,660 ($3,060 + $4,600 bonus depreciation)	$4,900	$2,950	$1,775
1/1/2001- 9/10/2001	$3,060	$4,900	$2,950	$1,775
2000	$3,060	$4,900	$2,950	$1,775
1999	$3,060	$5,000	$2,950	$1,775
1998	$3,060	$5,000	$2,950	$1,775
1997	$3,060	$5,000	$3,050	$1,775
1995-1996	$3,060	$4,900	$2,950	$1,775

These figures are the maximum amount you can deduct each year, regardless of what depreciation method you use or whether you use first-year bonus depreciation or Section 179 expensing.

The deduction limits in the above tables are based on 100% business use of the vehicle. If you don't use your car solely for business, the limits are reduced based on your percentage of personal use.

> **EXAMPLE:** Mario uses his new car 60% for business. His first-year deduction is limited to $6,366 (60% x $10,610 = $6,366).

You may combine Section 179 expensing with bonus and regular depreciation, in that order. However, your total deduction cannot exceed the annual limits listed in the charts above.

> **EXAMPLE:** In February 2004, Mario spends $15,000 on a new car, which he uses 100% for business. He may deduct a maximum of $10,610 of the cost for 2004. He decides to deduct $5,000 of the cost the first year using Section 179. This leaves him with a depreciable basis of $10,000 and a remaining $5,610 to deduct within the first year limit ($10,610–$5,000 = $5,610). He may use 50% bonus depreciation to deduct half of his remaining basis, which is $5,000. This leaves $610 within the first year limit, which he can depreciate in the first year using regular depreciation.

As this example shows, you may use Section 179 expensing to write off all or only a portion of the cost of an asset. It's up to you to decide how much. Mario could have used Section 179 to deduct the entire $10,610 in his first year. But combining Section 179 with your available depreciation deduction is often a good idea. That way, you save part of your Section 179 deduction for other assets. You might also want to combine Section 179 with depreciation if your income for the year will be low. Unlike depreciation, Section 179 deductions are subject to an income limit—if you don't have enough income, your deduction for the year might be reduced (see Chapter 5). You can use depreciation to make up the difference.

e.   Depreciation Beyond the Five-Year Limit

Because of the annual limits on depreciation deductions for passenger automobiles, you won't be able to deduct the entire cost of a car you buy in 2004 for more than $21,600 over the five-year depreciation period. Don't worry—as long as you continue to use your car for business, you can keep taking annual deductions after the five-year depreciation period ends, until you recover your full basis in the car. The maximum amount you can deduct each year is determined by the date you placed the car in service and your business use percentage.

> **EXAMPLE:** In 2004, Kim pays $30,000 for a car she uses only for business. Her depreciable basis in the car is $30,000. Her maximum depreciation deductions for the car over the next five years are as follows:

2004	$10,610
2005	4,800
2006	2,850
2007	1,675
2008	1,675
Total	$21,610

At the end of the five-year depreciation period, she has $8,390 in unrecovered basis. Even though the depreciation period is over, she may continue to deduct $1,675 each year until she recovers the remaining money (assuming she continues to use the car 100% for business). This will take another five years.

f.   Heavy Deductions for Heavy Metal: Expensing SUVs and Other Weighty Vehicles

The limits discussed above apply only to passenger automobiles (including trucks and vans that fall within the definition of a passenger automobile because of their weight). They don't apply to trucks, pick-ups, RVs, vans, SUVs, and other vehicles that don't come within the passenger automobile definition—that is, vehicles with a gross loaded weight of more than 6,000 pounds (see Section C3a, above). This means that you could buy an SUV (or a van, truck, pickup, or RV) weighing more than 6,000 pounds for your business and deduct all or almost all of the cost in the first year.

⚠️ **Congress may limit or eliminate tax exemptions for SUVs.** As this book went to press in late 2004, Congress was seriously considering legislation to limit the Section 179 deduction for SUVs to $25,000. It's impossible to predict whether this legislation will be enacted. Make sure to check the current status of the law before buying an SUV that you intend to use for business driving. You can find legal updates at the Nolo website (www.nolo.com).

Weight Is the Deciding Factor

The exception that often applies to SUVs is based solely on the vehicle's weight. There is no blanket exception for all SUVs, although media stories on the subject may have led you to believe otherwise. Your vehicle must weigh more than 6,000 pounds to qualify for the exception; not all SUVs are this hefty.

EXAMPLE: In 2004, Terry pays $150,000 for a 7,000 lb. SUV that she uses only for her travel guide business. She may deduct the following amounts for 2004:

Section 179 Deduction		$100,000
50% bonus depreciation (50% of $50,000)	+	25,000
Regular depreciation (200% declining balance method)	+	5,000
Total	=	$130,000

Terry can depreciate the remaining $20,000 of the $150,000 purchase price over the next several years.

This seems like a great deal for people who want to buy heavy (and expensive) SUVs. But keep in mind that the deduction is reduced by the proportion of time you use the vehicle for personal purposes. If Terry used her SUV 40% of the time for personal pursuits, she would receive only a $78,000 deduction for the year. Moreover, to qualify for

Section 179 expensing and bonus depreciation, the vehicle must be used more than 50% of the time for business for the full five-year period. You can't get around this rule by using it more than 50% for business in the first year and less in subsequent years. If your use falls below 50% during any year in the five-year period, you'll have to repay the extra money you saved by taking Section 179 and bonus depreciation deductions to the IRS. (This process is called recapture—see Chapter 5 for more information.)

g.   Auto Repairs and Improvements

Auto repairs and maintenance costs are fully deductible in the year they are incurred. You add these costs to your other annual expenses when you use the actual expense method. (You get no extra deduction for repairs when you use the standard mileage rate.) If you fix your car yourself, you may deduct the cost of parts and depreciate or deduct tools, but you can't take a deduction for your time or labor.

Unlike repairs, improvements to your car must be depreciated over several years, not deducted all in the year when you pay for them. What's the difference between a repair and an improvement? Unlike a repair, an improvement:

- increases the value of your car
- makes the car more useful, or
- lengthens your car's useful life.

EXAMPLE 1: Doug spends $100 to repair his car's carburetor. This is a current expense because the repair doesn't increase the value of his car or lengthen its useful life. The repair merely allows the car to last for a normal time.

EXAMPLE 2: Doug spends $2,000 on a brand new engine for his car. This is a capital expense because the new engine increases the car's value and useful life.

This rule can be difficult to apply because virtually all repairs increase the value of the property being repaired. Just remember that an improvement makes your vehicle *more valuable than it was before it was worked on*, while a repair simply restores the car's value to what it was worth before it broke down.

Improvements must be depreciated separately from the vehicle itself—that is, they are treated as separate items of depreciable property. The same rules, however, apply to depreciating improvements as to regular auto depreciation. The cost of the original vehicle and the improvements are combined for purposes of the annual automobile depreciation limit. The recovery period begins when the improvement is placed in service.

EXAMPLE: Doug spends $2,000 for a new engine for his car in April of 2004 and starts using the car 100% for business that same month. Using the fastest form of depreciation (accelerated instead of straight-line), he can depreciate the $2,000 expense over five years (the car's useful life) as follows:

2004	$400
2005	640
2006	385
2007	230
2008	230
2009	$115
Total	2,000

Alternatively, Doug could deduct the entire $2,000 in 2004 using his Section 179 deduction.

Deduct Your Car Repair Tools

If you work on your car yourself, you may deduct the cost of your car repair tools. You must deduct your tools separately from your auto expenses. If they are worth only $100 or so, you can currently deduct them as a business operating expense. If they are worth more, you must depreciate them or expense them under Section 179. If your tools are older or you haven't kept your receipts for tools you bought this year, you'll have to estimate their fair market value. Take a look in your garage and see what you have to deduct.

4.   Leasing a Car

If you lease a car that you use in your business, you can use the actual expense method to deduct the portion of each lease payment that reflects the business percentage use of the car. You cannot deduct any part of a lease payment that is for commuting or personal use of the car.

> **EXAMPLE:** John pays $400 a month to lease a Lexus. He uses it 50% for his dental tool sales business and 50% for personal purposes. He may deduct half of his lease payments ($200 a month) as a local transportation expense for his sales business.

Leasing companies typically require you to make an advance or down payment to lease a car. You can deduct this cost as well, but you must spread the deduction out equally over the entire lease period.

You may use either the actual expense method or the standard mileage rate when you lease a car for business. However, if you want to use the standard mileage rate, you must use it the first year you lease the car and continue to use it for the entire lease term. If you use the standard mileage method, you can't deduct any portion of your lease payments. Instead, this cost is covered by the standard mileage rate set by the IRS. (See Section B, above).

a.   Is It Really a Lease?

Some transactions that are called "auto leases" are really not leases at all. Instead, they are installment purchases—that is, you pay for the car over time, and by the end of the lease term you own all or part of the car. You cannot deduct any payments you make to buy a car, even if the payments are called lease payments. Instead, you have to depreciate the cost of the car as described in Section C3, above.

b.   Leasing Luxury Cars

If you lease what the IRS considers to be a luxury car for more than 30 days, you may have to reduce your lease deduction. The purpose of this rule is to prevent people from leasing very expensive cars to get around the limitations on depreciation deductions for cars that are purchased (see Section C3, above). A luxury car is currently defined as one with a fair market value of more than $17,500.

The amount by which you must reduce your deduction (called an "inclusion amount") is based on the fair market value of your car and the percentage of time that you use it for business. The IRS recalculates it each year. You can find the inclusion amount for the current year in the tables published in IRS Publication 463, *Travel, Entertainment, Gift & Car Expenses*. The amount is usually fairly modest. For example, if you leased a $40,000 car in 2004 and used it solely for business that year, you would have to reduce your car expense deduction by $90 for the year. If you used the car only 50% for business, the reduction would be $45. The inclusion amount for the first year is prorated based on the month when you start using the car for business.

Should You Lease or Buy Your Car?

When you lease a car, you are paying rent for it—a set fee each month for the use of the car. At the end of the lease term, you give the car back to the leasing company and own nothing. As a general rule, leasing a car instead of buying it makes economic sense only if you absolutely must have a new car every two or three years and drive no more than 12,000 to 15,000 miles per year. If you drive more than 15,000 miles a year, leasing becomes an economic disaster because most leases penalize you for higher mileage.

There are numerous financial calculators available on the Internet that can help you determine how much it will cost to lease a car rather than buying one. You can find one at www.financenter.com/consumertool. Be careful when you use these calculators—they are designed based on certain assumptions, and different calculators can give different answers. For a detailed consumer guide to auto leasing created by the Federal Reserve Board, go to the Board's website at www.federalreserve.gov/pubs/leasing.

D. How to Maximize Your Car Expense Deduction

Sam and Sue both drive their cars 10,000 miles for business each year. This year, Sam got a $3,750 auto deduction, while Sue got $5,500. Why the difference? Sue took some simple steps to maximize her deduction. You can follow her lead—and get the largest deduction possible—by following these tips.

1. Use the Method That Gives the Largest Deduction

Many taxpayers choose the standard mileage rate because it's easier—it requires much less record keeping than the actual expense method. However, you'll often get a larger deduction if you use the actual expense method. The American Automobile Association estimated that the average cost of owning a car in 2003 was 51.7 cents per mile. This is substantially more than the 37.5 cents per mile the IRS allows you to deduct under the standard mileage rate in 2004. Of course, this is just an average; your expenses could be lower, depending on the value of your car and how much you spend on repairs, gas, and other operating costs. The only way to know for sure which method gives you the largest deduction is to do the numbers.

> **EXAMPLE:** In January 2004, Vicky buys a $20,000 car. During the year, she drives it 10,000 miles for her sales business and 5,000 miles for personal purposes. She keeps track of all of her car expenses during the year. When she does her taxes, she compares the deduction she would receive using the actual expense method and the standard mileage rate. To do so, she completes the following table:

Actual Expense Method Worksheet

Business/Personal Use		
Total Mileage for Business		10,000
Total Mileage for Year		÷ 15,000
Business %	=	67%
Actual Annual Expenses		
Gas and Oil		$2,400
Insurance	+	1,500
Repairs and Maintenance	+	500
Registration	+	50
Wash and Wax	+	200
Other	+	50
Total Actual Expenses	=	$4,700
Business %	X	67%
Business Total	=	$3,149
Depreciation Deduction (67% x $10,710)	+	7,109
Interest (total x business %)	+	500
Personal Property Taxes (total x business %)	+	350
Parking and Tolls	+	1,800
Total Auto Deduction	=	$12,908

Standard Mileage Rate Worksheet

Total Business Mileage		10,000
Total Mileage for Year		÷ 15,000
Business %	=	67%
Standard Mileage Rate Deduction (37.5 x 10,000 x 67%)	=	$2,512
Interest (total x business %)	+	500
Personal Property Taxes (total x business %)	+	350
Parking and Tolls	+	1,800
Total Auto Deduction	=	$5,162

The standard mileage rate is a particularly bad deal if you purchase a new car between September 11, 2001 and December 31, 2004. Why? Because you don't get the bonus depreciation that you would be able to take if you used the actual expense method. Bonus depreciation can be used only for new cars and greatly increases the amount you can deduct the first year (when you purchase the item). (See Chapter 5 for more about bonus depreciation.)

> **EXAMPLE:** Slim buys a new business car for $30,000 in January of 2004. He uses the car solely for business, driving 15,000 miles during the year. If Slim uses the standard mileage rate, his 2004 deduction will be $5,625 (37.5 cents x 15,000 = $5,625). If he uses the actual expense method, his bonus depreciation alone comes to $15,000—this is $9,375 more than his total depreciation using the standard mileage rate. He can't use the entire bonus depreciation deduction because it exceeds the $10,610 maximum passenger automobile depreciation limit. But he can also deduct all of his other car-related expenses for the year, which amount to $5,000. So he has a total auto deduction of $15,610 (the $10,610 depreciation limit plus $5,000 for other expenses)—almost three times what he would get using the standard mileage rate.

There are circumstances when the standard mileage rate might give you a larger deduction than the actual expense method. If you drive a car that's not worth much (because it's old or an inexpensive model), you might come out ahead. Why? Because you get the same fixed deduction rate no matter how much the car is worth. Fifteen cents of the 37.5-cent rate for 2004 is for depreciation. The owner of an inexpensive car might benefit from using the standard mileage rate, because the car's actual depreciation will be far less than the 15-cent fixed amount.

> **EXAMPLE:** Max pays $1,000 for a used car in January 2004 and uses it exclusively in his photocopier repair business. He drives it 20,000 miles in 2004. Using the standard mileage rate, he gets a $7,500 deduction (20,000 x 37.5 cents = $7,500). Using the actual expense rate, he could get a $1,000 deduction for depreciation the first year (assuming he used Section 179 to deduct the entire purchase price of the car). This is $2,000 less than the $3,000 depreciation deduction

he can get using the standard mileage rate (15 cents x 20,000 miles = $3,000). Because his other actual expenses are less than $6,500, he's better off using the standard mileage rate. He'll do even better in 2005 and later—he would get no depreciation at all under the actual expense method, but he still gets 15 cents a mile using the standard mileage rate.

2. Use Two Cars for Business

If you use the actual expense method, you might think you would always get a larger deduction by using one car 100% of the time for business rather than using two cars less than 100% for business. This is not the case, however—two cars are usually better than one.

EXAMPLE: Biff owns two cars. He needs to drive 20,000 miles for business during the year and 10,000 miles for personal purposes. Let's compare the deduction he could take using one car to the deduction he could take using two.

One Business Car

	Car 1	Car 2
Total Miles	20,000	10,000
Business Miles	20,000	0
Business %	100%	0
Total Costs	$6,500	$5,000
Total Auto Deduction	$6,500	0

Two Business Cars

	Car 1	Car 2
Total Miles	20,000	10,000
Business Miles	15,000	5,000
Business %	75%	50%
Total Costs	$6,500	$5,000
Total Auto Deduction	$4,875	$2,500

By driving the same total number of miles but using two cars instead of one, Biff gets a $7,375 deduction, compared with only a $6,500 deduction for one car.

The IRS requires you to have a good reason for using two cars instead of one for your business. It shouldn't be hard to come up with one—for example, you don't want to put too many miles on each car, or one car carries more cargo and the other gets better gas mileage.

Of course, if you use the standard mileage rate, it makes no difference how many cars you drive—your deduction is based solely on your total business mileage.

3.   Keep Good Records

More than anything else, keeping good records is the key to the local transportation deduction. The IRS knows that many people don't keep good records. When they do their taxes, they make wild guesses abut how many business miles they drove the previous year. This is why IRS auditors are more suspicious of this deduction than almost any other.

Record keeping for the transportation deduction doesn't have to be too burdensome. If keeping records of gas, oil, repairs, and all your other car expenses is too much trouble (and it can be a pain in the neck), use the standard mileage rate (assuming you qualify for it). That way, you'll only need to keep track of how many miles you drive for business. Indeed, you might not even have to keep track of your business miles for the entire year; instead you may be able to use a sample period of thee months or one week a month. Remember that keeping track of your actual expenses often gives you a larger deduction. It's up to you to decide which is more important: your time or your money.

See Chapter 15 for a detailed discussion of how to keep car and mileage records.

E.   Other Local Transportation Expenses

You don't have to drive a car or other vehicle to get a tax deduction for local business trips. You can deduct the cost of travel by bus or other public transit, taxi, train, ferry, motorcycle, bicycle, or any other means.

However, all the rules limiting deductions for travel by car (discussed in Section A, above) also apply to other transportation methods. This means, for example, that you can't deduct the cost of commuting from your home to your office or other permanent work location. The same record-keeping requirements apply as well.

F. Reporting Transportation Expenses on Your Tax Return

How you report transportation expenses on your tax return will depend on how your business is organized. The IRS reporting requirements differ depending on what type of business you have.

1. Sole Proprietors

If, like most home businesspeople, you're a sole proprietor, you will list your car expenses on Schedule C, *Profit or Loss From Business*. Schedule C asks more questions about this deduction than almost any other deduction (reflecting the IRS's general suspicion about auto deductions). In Part IV of the form, you must provide the total number of business, commuting, and personal miles you drove during the year. Then you must answer several more questions.

Schedule C asks whether you or your spouse had another vehicle available for personal use during the year. If you answer no, you will have a tough time claiming that you used your only car 100% for business.

You are also asked whether your vehicle was available for "off-duty hours"—that is, whether you could use it before and after work. If not, you should only have business miles for the vehicle.

Finally, you must state whether you have evidence to support your deduction, and whether it's written. If your answer is no, you won't qualify for the deduction. This is why good record keeping is so important.

You must also file IRS Form 4562, *Depreciation and Amortization*, to report your Section 179 and depreciation deductions for the vehicle.

2. Partners and LLCs

Partners in partnerships and LLC members may directly deduct their transportation expenses by filing Schedule E, *Supplemental Income or Loss*, with their annual tax return. The car deduction amount must be listed in the schedule, but the form does not contain all of the questions that Schedule C does. The deductions listed on Schedule E are considered additional partnership or LLC deductions, not personal deductions.

Alternatively, partners or LLC members may be reimbursed for their transportation expenses by the partnership or LLC. This relieves the partners or members of having to claim the deduction on their individual tax returns. If you go this route, the amount of the expense must be included on the partnership or LLC information return filed with the IRS and will be factored into whether the business earned a profit or incurred a loss for the year. The partners or LLC members receive IRS Schedule K-1, *Shareholder's Share of Income, Credits, Deductions, etc.,* which shows their share of the business's annual profits or losses. (See Chapter 1 for more information on tax reporting requirements.)

3. Corporations

If your business is incorporated, you will ordinarily be its employee. You can deduct any transportation expenses for which the corporation does not reimburse you as miscellaneous itemized expenses on Schedule A. However, these deductions are subject to special limitations. (See Chapter 11, Section D, for more on working for your corporation.) ■

Chapter 9

Business Travel

I f you travel overnight for business, you can deduct your airfare, hotel bills, and other expenses. If you plan your trip carefully, you can even mix business with pleasure and still take a deduction. However, IRS auditors closely scrutinize deductions for overnight business travel—and many taxpayers get caught claiming these deductions without proper records to back them up. To stay within the law (and avoid unwanted attention from the IRS), you need to know how this deduction works and how to properly document your travel expenses.

A.   What Is Business Travel?

For tax purposes, business travel occurs when you travel away from your tax home overnight for business. You don't have to travel any set distance to take a travel expense deduction. However, you can't take this deduction if you just spend the night in a motel across town. You must travel outside your city limits. If you don't live in a city, you must go outside the general area where your business is located.

You must stay away overnight or at least long enough to require a stop for sleep or rest. You cannot satisfy the rest requirement by merely napping in your car.

> **EXAMPLE:** Phyllis, a home-based salesperson who lives in Los Angeles, flies to San Francisco to meet potential clients, spends the night in a hotel, and returns home the following day. Her trip is a deductible travel expense.

If you don't stay overnight, your trip will not qualify as business travel. However, this does not necessarily mean that you can't take a tax deduction. Local business trips are also deductible (see Chapter 8), but you are entitled to deduct only your transportation expenses—the cost of driving or using some other means of transportation. You may not deduct meals or other expenses like you can when you travel for business and stay overnight.

> **EXAMPLE:** Philip drives from his home office in Los Angeles to a business meeting in San Diego and returns the same day. His 200-

mile round trip is a deductible local business trip. He may deduct his expenses for the 200 business miles he drove, but he can't deduct the breakfast he bought on the way to San Diego.

 How to deduct local travel. For a detailed discussion of tax deductions for local business travel, see Chapter 8.

1.   Where Is Your Tax Home?

Your tax home is the entire city or general area where your principal place of business is located. If you run your business out of your residence, your tax home is the city or area where you live.

The IRS doesn't care how far you travel for business. You'll get a deduction as long as you travel outside your tax home's city limits and stay overnight. Thus, even if you're just traveling across town, you'll qualify for a deduction if you manage to stay outside your city limits.

> **EXAMPLE:** Pete, a tax advisor, works from his home in San Francisco. He travels to Oakland for an all day meeting with a client. At the end of the meeting, he decides to spend the night in an Oakland hotel rather than brave the traffic back to San Francisco. Pete's stay qualifies as a business trip even though the distance between his San Francisco office and the Oakland business meeting is only eight miles. Pete can deduct his hotel and meal expenses.

If you don't live in a city, your tax home covers the general area where you reside—typically, the area within about 40 miles of your home.

a.   No Main Place of Business

Some people have no main place of business—for example, a salesperson who is always on the road, traveling from sales contact to sales contact. In this situation, your home (main residence) can qualify as your tax home, as long as you:

- perform part of your business there and live at home while doing business in that area

- have living expenses at your home that you must duplicate because your business requires you to travel away from home, and
- satisfy one of the following three requirements:
  - you have not abandoned the area where your home is located— that is, you work in the area or have other contacts there
  - you have family living in the home, or
  - you often live in the home yourself.

EXAMPLE: Ruth is a liquor salesperson whose territory includes the entire southern United States. She has a home in Miami, Florida where her mother lives. Ruth's sales territory includes Florida. She uses her home for her business when she is in the Miami area and lives in it when making sales calls in the area. She spends about 12 weeks a year at home and is on the road the rest of the time. Ruth's Miami home is her tax home because she satisfies all three factors listed above: (1) She does business in the Miami area and stays in her Miami home when doing so; (2) she has duplicate living expenses; and (3) she has family living at the home.

Even if you satisfy only two of the three factors, your home may still qualify as your tax home, depending on all the facts and circumstances.

EXAMPLE: Assume that Ruth's sales territory is the Northeast, and she does no work in the Miami area where her home is located. She fails the first factor, but satisfies the second two. Her Miami home would still probably qualify as her tax home.

If you can't satisfy at least two of the three factors, you have no tax home. You are a transient for tax purposes. This means you cannot deduct any travel expenses, because you are never considered to be traveling away from home. Obviously, this is not a good situation to find yourself in, tax-wise.

EXAMPLE: James Henderson was a stage hand for a travelling ice skating show. He spent most of his time on the road, but spent two to three months a year living rent-free in his parents' home in Boise, Idaho. Both the IRS and the courts found that he was a transient for tax purposes because he failed to satisfy the first two of the three criteria listed above: (1) He did no work in Boise, and (2) because he paid no rent to live in his parents' house, he had no home living expenses that he had to duplicate while on the road. Thus, Henderson was not entitled to a tax deduction for his travel expenses. (*Henderson v. Comm'r*, 143 F.3d 497 (9th Cir. 1998).)

If you travel a lot for business, you should do everything you can to avoid being classified as a transient. This means you must take steps to satisfy at least two of the three factors listed above. For example, Henderson might have avoided his transient status if he had paid his parents for his room (thereby resulting in duplicate expenses).

b. Temporary Work Locations

You may regularly work both at your tax home and at another location, such as a client's office or a temporary job site. It may not always be practical to return from this other worksite to your tax home at the end of each workday. Your overnight stays at these temporary work locations qualify as business travel as long as your work there is truly temporary— that is, it is reasonably expected to last no more than one year. In this situation, your tax home does not change, and you are considered to be traveling away from home for the entire period you spend at the temporary work location.

> **EXAMPLE:** Betty is a self-employed sexual harassment educator. She works out of her home office in Chicago, Illinois. She is hired to conduct sexual harassment training and counseling for a large company in Indianapolis, Indiana. The job is expected to last three months. Betty's assignment is temporary and Chicago remains her tax home. She may deduct the expenses she incurs traveling to and staying in Indianapolis.

On the other hand, if you reasonably expect your work at the other location to last more than one year, that location becomes your new tax home and you cannot deduct your travel expenses while there.

EXAMPLE: Carl is a Seattle-based plumbing contractor. He is hired to install the plumbing in a new subdivision in Boise, Idaho, and the job is expected to take 18 months. Boise is now Carl's tax home, and he may not deduct his travel expenses while staying there.

If you return to your tax home from a temporary work location on your days off, you are not considered away from home while you are in your hometown. You cannot deduct the cost of meals and lodging there. However, you can deduct your expenses, including meals and lodging, for travel between your temporary work location and your tax home. You can claim these expenses up to the amount it would have cost you to stay at your temporary work location. In addition, if you continue to pay for your hotel room during your visit home, you can deduct that cost.

2.   Your Trip Must Be for Business

Your trip must be primarily for business to be deductible. This means that you must have a business purpose in mind before leaving on the trip, and you must actually do some business while you're away.

You have a business purpose if the trip is intended to benefit your business in some way. Examples of business purposes include:

- finding new customers or markets for your products or services
- dealing with existing customers or clients
- learning new skills to help in your business
- contacting people who could help your business, such as potential investors, or
- checking out what the competition is doing.

EXAMPLE: A taxpayer who manufactured and sold weightlifting equipment was entitled to deduct the cost of attending the summer Olympics in Rome because the purpose of the trip was to find new customers for his product line. (*Hoffman v. Comm'r.*, 798 F2d 784 (3d Cir. 1962).)

It's not enough to claim that you had a business purpose for your trip. You must also be able to show that you actually spent some time on business activities while at your destination. Acceptable business activities include:

- visiting or working with existing or potential clients or customers
- attending trade shows or conventions, or
- attending professional seminars or business conventions that are clearly connected to your business.

On the other hand, business activities do not include:

- sightseeing
- recreational activities that you attend by yourself or with family or friends, or
- attending personal investment seminars or political events.

Use common sense when deciding whether to claim that a trip is for business. If you're audited, the IRS is likely to question any trip that doesn't have some logical connection to your existing business.

A. Travel for a New Business or Location

You must actually be in business to have deductible business trips. Trips you take to investigate a potential new business or to actually start or acquire a new business are not currently deductible business travel expenses. However, they may be deductible as business start-up expenses, which means that you can deduct them over the first 60 months you're in business. (See Chapter 3 for more on deducting start-up costs.)

That Trip to Europe Was Not for Business

In 1984, Oliver Bentley and his foster son spent approximately $7,500 for an extensive European trip. When they got back, they tried to make money off their travel by attempting to arrange student tours to Europe. They contacted travel agents and distributed flyers, but the business never got off the ground. When Bentley did his taxes for the year, he took a $5,127 tax deduction for the trip, claiming it was primarily for this business. The IRS and the tax court both disagreed. Bentley could not claim a business travel deduction because he did not have an existing business when he took the trip, and the costs of investigating a new business venture are not currently deductible. (*Bentley v. Comm.'s.*, T.C. Memo 1988-444.)

b.   Travel as an Education Expense

You may deduct the cost of traveling to an educational activity directly related to your business. For example, a French translator can deduct the cost of traveling to France to attend formal French language classes. However, you can't take a trip and claim that the travel itself constitutes a form of education and is therefore deductible. For example, a French translator who travels to France may not take a business travel deduction if the purpose of the trip is to see the sights and become familiar with French language and culture. (See Chapter 14 for more on education expenses.)

c.   Visiting Business Colleagues

Visiting business colleagues or competitors may be a legitimate business purpose for a trip. But you can't just socialize with them—you must use your visit to learn new skills, check out what your competitors are doing, seek investors, or attempt to get new customers or clients.

B.   Deductible Travel Expenses

Subject to the limits covered in Section C, below, virtually all of your business travel expenses are deductible. These costs fall into two broad categories: your transportation expenses and the expenses you incur at your destination.

Transportation expenses are the costs of getting to and from your destination—for example:

- fares for airplanes, trains, or buses
- driving expenses, including car rentals
- shipping costs for your personal luggage or samples, displays, or other things you need for your business, and
- meals, beverages, and lodging expenses you incur while en route to your final destination.

If you drive your own car to your destination, you may deduct your costs by using the standard mileage rate or deduct your actual expenses. You may also deduct your mileage while at your destination. (See Chapter 8 for more on mileage deductions.)

You may also deduct the expenses you incur to stay alive (food and lodging) and do business while at your destination. Destination expenses include:

- hotel or other lodging expenses for business days
- 50% of meal and beverage expenses (see Section C, below)
- taxi, public transportation, and car rental expenses at your destination
- telephone, Internet, and fax expenses
- computer rental fees
- laundry and dry cleaning expenses, and
- tips you pay on any of the other costs.

You may deduct 50% of your entertainment expenses if you incur them for business purposes. You can't deduct entertainment expenses for activities that you attend alone; this solo entertainment obviously wouldn't be for business purposes. If you want to deduct the cost of a nightclub or ball game while on the road, be sure to take a business associate along. (See Chapter 7 for a detailed discussion of the special rules that apply to deductions for entertainment expenses.)

1. Traveling First Class or Steerage

To be deductible, business travel expenses must be ordinary and necessary. This means that the trip and the expenses you incur must be helpful and appropriate for your business, not necessarily indispensable. You may not deduct lavish or extravagant expenses, but the IRS gives you a great deal of leeway here. You may, if you wish, travel first class, stay at four-star hotels, and eat at expensive restaurants. On the other hand, you're also entitled to be a cheapskate—for example, you could stay with a friend or relative at your destination to save on hotel charges and still deduct your meals and other expenses.

2. Taking People With You

You may deduct the expenses you pay for a person who travels with you only if he or she:

- is your employee

- has a genuine business reason for going on the trip with you, and
- would otherwise be allowed to deduct the travel expenses.

These rules apply to your family as well. This means you can deduct the expense of taking your spouse, child, or other relative only if the person is your employee and has a genuine business reason for going on a trip with you. Typing notes or assisting in entertaining customers is not enough to warrant a deduction; the work must be essential to your business. For example, if you hire your son as a salesperson for your product or service and he calls on prospective customers during the trip, both your expenses and his are deductible.

If you bring your family along simply to enjoy the trip, you may still deduct your own business expenses as if you were traveling alone—and you don't have to reduce your deductions, even if others get a free ride with you. For example, if you drive to your destination, you can deduct the entire cost of the drive, even if your family rides along with you. Similarly, you can deduct the full cost of a single hotel room even if you obtain a larger, more expensive room for your whole family.

> **EXAMPLE:** Yamiko travels from New Orleans to Sydney, Australia, for her landscape design business. She takes her husband and young son with her. The total airfare expense for her and her family is $2,500. She may deduct the cost of a single ticket—$1,000. She spends $250 per night for a two-bedroom hotel suite in Sydney. She may deduct the cost of a single room for one person—$100 per night.

C. How Much You Can Deduct

If you spend all of your time at your destination on business, you may deduct 100% of your expenses (except meal expenses, which are only 50% deductible—see Section C6, below). However, things get more complicated if you mix business and pleasure. Different rules apply to your transportation expenses and the expenses you incur while at your destination ("destination expenses"). The rules also depend on whether you travel to another country or remain in the United States.

Reimbursement for Business Travel Expenses

If a client or customer reimburses you for all or part of your business travel expenses, you get no deduction for the amount of the reimbursement—the client gets the deduction. However, you don't have to count the reimbursed amounts as business income.

> **EXAMPLE:** Clarence, a documents examiner, travels from Philadelphia to Nashville, Tennessee, to testify in a case for a client, Acme Corporation. He stays in Nashville for two weeks and incurs $5,000 in travel expenses. He bills Acme for this amount and receives the reimbursement. Clarence may not deduct the cost of the trip, but he also doesn't have to report the $5,000 reimbursement from Acme as business income. Acme may deduct the $5,000 as a business expense.

1. Travel Within the United States

Business travel within the United States is subject to an all or nothing rule: You may deduct 100% of your transportation expenses only if you spend *more than half of your time* on business activities while at your destination. In other words, your business days must outnumber your personal days. If you spend more time on personal activities than on business, you get no transportation deduction.

You may also deduct the destination expenses you incur on days when you do business. Expenses incurred on personal days at your destination are nondeductible personal expenses. (See Section C5, below, for the rules used to determine what constitutes a business day.)

> **EXAMPLE:** Tom works out of his Atlanta home. He takes the train for a business trip to New Orleans. He spends six days in New Orleans, where he spends all of his time on business, and spends $400 for his hotel, meals, and other living expenses. On the way home, he stops in Mobile for three days to visit his parents and spends $100 for lodging and meals there. His round-trip train fare is $250. Tom's trip consisted of six business days and three personal days, so he spent more than half of the trip on business. He can

deduct 100% of his train fare and the entire $400 he spent while on business in New Orleans. He may not, however, deduct the $100 he spent while visiting his parents.

If your trip is primarily a vacation—that is, you spend more than half of your time on personal activities—the entire cost of the trip is a nondeductible personal expense. However, you may deduct destination expenses that are directly related to your business. This includes things like phone calls or faxes to your office, or the cost of renting a computer for business work. It doesn't include transportation, lodging, or food.

> **EXAMPLE:** Tom (from the above example) spends two days in New Orleans on business and seven days visiting his parents in Mobile. His entire trip is a nondeductible personal expense. However, while in New Orleans he spends $50 on long distance phone calls to his office; this expense is deductible.

As long as your trip is primarily for business, you can add a vacation to the end of the trip, make a side trip purely for fun, or enjoy evenings at the theater or ballet, and still deduct your entire airfare. What you spend while having fun is not deductible, but you can deduct all of your business and transportation expenses.

> **EXAMPLE:** Bill flies to Miami for a four-day business meeting. He spends three extra days in Miami swimming and enjoying the sights. Because he spent over half his time on business—four days out of seven—the cost of his flight is entirely deductible, as are his hotel and meal costs during the business meeting. He may not deduct his hotel, meal, or other expenses during his vacation days.

2. Travel Outside the United States

Travel outside the United States is subject to more flexible rules than travel within the country. The rules for deducting your transportation expenses depend on how long you stay at your destination.

a. Trips for Up to Seven Days

If you travel outside the United States for *no more than seven days,* you can deduct 100% of your airfare or other transportation expenses, as long as you spend part of the time on business. You can spend a majority of your time on personal activities, as long as you spend at least some time on business. Seven days means seven consecutive days, not counting the day you leave but counting the day you return to the United States. You may also deduct the destination expenses you incur on the days you do business. (See Section C5, below, for the rules used to determine what constitutes a business day.)

> **EXAMPLE:** Billie flies from Portland, Oregon, to Vancouver, Canada. She spends four days sightseeing in Vancouver and one day visiting suppliers for her import-export business. She may deduct 100% of her airfare, but she can deduct her lodging, meal, and other expenses from her stay in Vancouver only for the one day when she did business.

b. Trips for More Than Seven Days

The IRS does not want to subsidize foreign vacations, so more stringent rules apply if your foreign trip lasts more than one week. For these longer trips, the magic number is 75%: If you spend more than 75% of your time on business at your foreign destination, you can deduct what it would have cost to make the trip if you had not engaged in any personal activities. This means you may deduct 100% of your airfare or other transportation expenses, plus your living expenses while you were on business and any other business-related expenses:

> **EXAMPLE:** Sean flies from Boston to Dublin, Ireland. He spends one day sightseeing and nine days in business meetings. He has spent 90% of his time on business, so he may deduct 100% of his airfare to Dublin and all of the living and other expenses he incurred during the nine days he spent on business. He may not deduct any of his expenses (including hotel charges) for the day he spent sightseeing.

If you spend more than 50%—but less than 75%—of your time on business, you can deduct only the business percentage of your transportation and other costs. You figure out this percentage by counting the number of business days and the number of personal days to come up with a fraction. The number of business days is the numerator (top number) and the total number of days away from home is the denominator (bottom number). For ease in determining the dollar amount of your deduction, you can convert this fraction into a percentage.

> **EXAMPLE:** Sam flies from Las Vegas to London, where he spends six days on business and four days sightseeing. He spent 6/10 of his total time away from home on business. The fraction 6/10 converts to 60% (6 ÷ 10 = 0.60). He therefore spent 60% of his time on business. He can deduct 60% of his travel costs—that is, 60% of his round-trip airfare, hotel, and other expenses. The trip cost him $3,000, so he gets an $1,800 deduction.

If you spend 50% or less of your time doing business on foreign trip that lasts more than seven days, you cannot deduct any of your costs.

c.   Side Trips

You may not deduct expenses you incur if you stop at a nonbusiness (personal) destination en route to, or returning from, your business destination. For example, if you stop for three vacation days in Paris on your way to a weeklong business meeting in Bangladesh, you may not deduct your expenses from your Paris stay.

To determine how much of your airfare or other transportation costs are deductible when you make side trips, follow this three-step process:

1. Determine the percentage of the time you spent on vacation.
2. Multiply this vacation percentage by what it would have cost you to fly round trip from your vacation destination to the United States.
3. Subtract this amount from your total airfare expense to arrive at your deductible airfare expense.

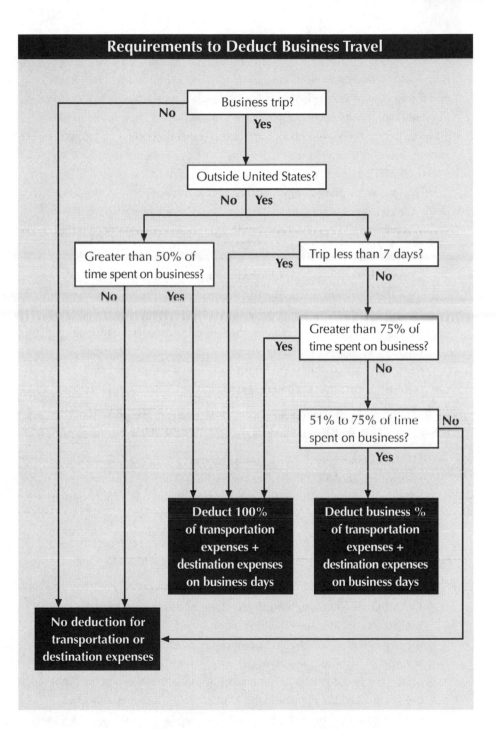

Requirements to Deduct Business Travel

Business trip?

No →

Yes ↓

Outside United States?

No | Yes

No branch:
Greater than 50% of time spent on business?

No | Yes

Yes branch:
Trip less than 7 days?

Yes →

No ↓

Greater than 75% of time spent on business?

Yes →

No ↓

51% to 75% of time spent on business?

No →

Yes ↓

Deduct 100% of transportation expenses + destination expenses on business days

Deduct business % of transportation expenses + destination expenses on business days

No deduction for transportation or destination expenses

What Is Foreign Travel?

Because different deduction rules apply to travel within the United States and foreign travel, it's important to know which is which. For IRS purposes, foreign travel means travel outside of the United States. Thus, for example, a trip to Puerto Rico would be a foreign trip, even though it is a United States possession. Travel outside the United States does not include travel from one point in the United States to another point in the United States.

If you travel by plane, train, or other public transportation, any place in the United States where your plane or other means of transportation makes a scheduled stop is a point in the United States. Your foreign trip begins at the last scheduled stop in the United States.

> **EXAMPLE:** Ben flies from Chicago to Miami, changes planes, and then flies to Puerto Rico. The flight from Chicago to Miami is within the United States, so the domestic travel rules apply. The flight from Miami to Puerto Rico is outside the United States, so the foreign travel rules apply. Ben then returns to Chicago on a nonstop flight from Puerto Rico. All of the return trip counts as foreign travel because there are no scheduled stops in the United States.

If you travel by private car to a foreign destination, the portion of the trip that is within the United States is governed by the domestic travel rules.

> **EXAMPLE:** Bart travels by car from Denver to Mexico City and returns. His travel between Denver and the United States border is travel within the United States. The foreign travel rules apply only to the portion of his trip within Mexico.

If you travel by private airplane, any flight (or portion thereof) that both takes off and lands in the United States is travel within the United States, even if the plane flies over a foreign country.

> **EXAMPLE:** Brenda flies her private plane nonstop from Seattle to Juneau, Alaska. Because she took off and landed in the United States, the trip is within the United States for tax purposes—even though she had to fly over Canada on the way to Juneau. However, if she makes a scheduled stop in Vancouver, Canada, both legs of the flight are considered travel outside the United States, and are subject to the foreign travel rules.

EXAMPLE: Jason lives in New York. On May 5, he flew to Paris to attend a business conference that began that same day. The conference ended on May 14. That evening, he flew from Paris to Dublin to visit friends until May 21, when he flew directly home to New York. The entire trip lasted 18 days—11 business days (the nine days in Paris and the two travel days) and seven vacation days. He spent 39% of his time on vacation (7/18 = 39%). His total airfare was $2,000. Round trip airfare from New York to Dublin would have been $1,000. To determine his deductible airfare, he multiplies $1,000 by 39% and then subtracts this amount from his $2,000 airfare expense: $1,000 x 39% = $390; $2,000–$390 = $1,610. His deductible airfare expense is $1,610.

3. Conventions

The cost of traveling to, and staying at, a convention are deductible just like the cost of any other business trip, as long as you satisfy the following rules.

a. Conventions Within North America

You may deduct the expense of attending a convention in North America if your attendance benefits your business. You may not, however, deduct any expenses for your family.

How do you know if a convention benefits your business? Look at the convention agenda or program (and be sure to save a copy). The agenda does not have to specifically address what you do in your business, but it must be sufficiently related to show that your attendance was for business purposes. Examples of conventions that don't benefit your business include those for investment, political, or social purposes.

You probably learned in school that North America consists of the United States, Canada, and Mexico. However, for convention expense purposes, North America includes much of the Caribbean and many other great vacation destinations, including:

- American Samoa
- Baker Island
- Barbados

- Bermuda
- Canada
- Costa Rica
- Dominica
- Dominican Republic
- Grenada
- Guam
- Guyana
- Honduras
- Howland Island
- Jamaica
- Jarvis Island
- Johnston Island
- Kingman Reef
- Marshall Islands
- Mexico
- Micronesia
- Midway Islands
- Northern Mariana Islands
- Palau
- Palmyra
- Puerto Rico
- Saint Lucia
- Trinidad and Tobago
- United States (the 50 states and Washington, D.C.)
- U.S. Virgin Islands, and
- Wake Island

b.   Foreign Conventions

More stringent rules apply if you attend a convention outside of North America (as defined above). You can take a deduction for a foreign convention only if:

- the convention is directly related to your business (rather than merely benefiting it), and
- it's as reasonable for the convention to be held outside of North America as in North America.

To determine whether it's reasonable to hold the convention outside of North America, the IRS looks at the purposes of the meeting and the sponsoring group, the activities at the convention, where the sponsors live, and where other meetings have been or will be held.

As a general rule, if you want a tax deduction, avoid attending a convention outside of North America unless there is a darn good reason for holding it there. For example, it would be hard to justify holding a convention for New York court reporters in Tahiti. On the other hand, it would probably be okay for a meeting of American travel writers to be held in Paris.

4.   Travel by Ship

You can deduct travel by ship if a convention or other business event is conducted on board, or if you use a ship as a means of transportation to a business destination. The following additional rules apply to sea travel.

a.   Shipboard Conventions and Seminars

Forget about taking a tax deduction for a pure pleasure cruise. You may, however, be able to deduct part of the cost of a cruise if you attend a business convention, seminars, or similar meetings directly related to your business while on board. (Personal investment or financial planning seminars don't qualify.)

But there is a major restriction: You must travel on a U.S.-registered ship that stops only in ports in the United States or its possessions, such as Puerto Rico or the U.S. Virgin Islands. If a cruise sponsor promises you'll be able to deduct your trip, investigate carefully to make sure it meets these requirements.

To deduct your business-related cruise expenses, you must file a signed note with your tax return from the meeting or seminar sponsor listing the business meetings scheduled each day aboard ship and certifying how many hours you spent in attendance. Make sure to get this statement from the meeting sponsor. Your annual deduction for attending conventions, seminars, or similar meetings on ships cannot exceed $2,000.

b. Transportation by Ship

You can get a deduction if you use an ocean liner, cruise ship, or other vessel solely as a means of transportation to a business destination. This isn't very common these days, but it can be done. In this situation, your deduction for each travel day is limited to twice the highest amount federal workers are paid each day (called the per diem rate) for their living expenses while traveling inside the U.S. on government business. You can find the latest rates at www.policyworks.gov/org/main/mt/homepage/mtt/perdiem/travel.shtml (you want the rates listed in the column entitled "Maximum per diem rate").

> **EXAMPLE:** In 2004, Caroline, a home-based art restorer, travels by ocean liner from New York to England to perform work at a museum in London. She pays $5,000 for the six-day cruise. However, she may deduct only up to twice the highest federal per diem amount for each day of the cruise. This amount is $259, so she can deduct up to $518 per day. Caroline's deduction for the cruise cannot exceed $3,108 (6 days x $518 = $3,108).

In addition, if your bill includes separately stated amounts for meals and entertainment while on the ship, you can deduct only 50% of these expenses. And the expenses you deduct for food and entertainment count towards your total per diem deduction.

> **EXAMPLE:** Assume Caroline found a cheaper cruise line, and paid $2,500 for her six-day cruise fare, plus another $1,500 for separately billed food and entertainment aboard ship. Caroline can deduct only half of her meals and entertainment expenses, or $750. Caroline's total daily deduction still cannot exceed twice the highest federal per diem amount, or $518 per day. Her total deduction for the trip is $3,108. Once she deducts her meal and entertainment expenses, she may deduct only $2,358 of her fare ($3,108–$750 = $2,358). She can't deduct the remaining $142.

Does this mean you can take a long pleasure cruise to a business destination and take a deduction for each day? The answer is no—the regular foreign travel rules apply to ship travel. A foreign trip that lasts more than 14 days is deductible only if you spend more than half of the time on business.

> **EXAMPLE:** Marcia embarks on a 30-day cruise from Los Angeles to Tokyo, where she attends a three-day business conference. She then flies back to Los Angeles. Her entire trip took 34 days, three of which were for business. Because she spent less than 50% of her time on business, the entire trip is a nondeductible personal expense.

5. Calculating Time Spent on Business

To calculate how much time you spend on business while on a trip, you must compare the number of days you spend on business to the number of days you spend on personal activities. A day is considered a business day if you:

- work for more than four hours
- must be at a particular place for your business—for example, to attend a business meeting—even if you spend most of the day on personal activities
- spend more than four hours on business travel (business travel time begins when you leave home and ends when you reach your hotel, or vice versa)
- drive at least 300 miles for business, you can average your mileage—for example, if you drive 600 miles to your destination in two days, you may claim two 300-mile days, even if you drove 500 miles on one day and 100 miles on the other
- spend more than four hours on some combination of travel and work
- are prevented from working because of circumstances beyond your control, such as a transit strike or terrorist act
- stay at your destination between work days, if it would have cost more to go home and return than to remain where you are (this "sandwich" rule allows you to count weekends as business days, if you work at your travel destination during the previous and following week; see Section D, below).

EXAMPLE: Mike, a home-based inventor who hates flying, travels by car from his home in Reno, Nevada, to Cleveland, Ohio, for a meeting with a potential investor concerning his latest invention: diapers for pet birds. He makes the 2,100-mile drive in six days, arriving in Cleveland on Saturday night. He has his meeting with the investor for one hour on Monday. The investor is intrigued with his idea, but wants him to flesh out his business plan. Mike works on this for five hours on Tuesday and three hours on Wednesday, spending the rest of his time resting and sightseeing. He has his second investor meeting on Thursday, which lasts two hours. He spends the rest of the day sightseeing and then drives straight home on Friday. Mike's trip consisted of 15 business days: 11 travel days, one sandwiched day (the Sunday before his first meeting), two meeting days, and one day when he worked more than four hours. He had one personal day—the day when he spent only three hours working.

Be sure to keep track of your time while you're away. You can do this by taking notes on your calendar or travel diary. (See Chapter 15 for a detailed discussion of record keeping while traveling.)

6.   Fifty Percent Limit on Meal Expenses

The IRS figures that you have to eat, whether you're at home or away on a business trip. Because meals you eat at home ordinarily aren't deductible, the IRS won't let you deduct all of your food expenses while traveling. Instead, you can deduct only 50% of your meal expenses while on a business trip. There are two ways to calculate your meal expense deduction: You can keep track of your actual expenses or use a daily rate set by the federal government.

a.   Deducting Actual Meal Expenses

If you use the actual expense method, you must keep track of what you spend on meals (including tips and tax) while traveling and at your business destination. When you do your taxes, you add these amounts together and deduct half of the total.

EXAMPLE: Frank goes on a business trip from Santa Fe, New Mexico, to Reno, Nevada. He gets there by car. While on the road, he spends $200 for meals. In Reno, he spends another $200. His total meal expense for the trip is $400. He may deduct half of this amount, or $200.

If you combine a business trip with a vacation, you may deduct only those meals you eat while on business—for example, meals you eat while attending business meetings or doing other business-related work. Meals that constitute business entertainment (for example, if you take a client out to a business lunch) are subject to the rules on entertainment expenses covered in Chapter 7.

You do not necessarily have to keep every receipt for your business meals, but you need to keep careful track of what you spend, and you should be able to prove that the meal was for business. See Chapter 15 for a detailed discussion of record keeping for meal expenses.

b.   Using the Standard Meal Allowance

When you use the actual expense method, you must keep track of what you spend for each meal. This can be a lot of work, so the IRS provides an alternative method of deducting meals: Instead of deducting your actual expenses, you can deduct a set amount for each day of your business trip. This amount is called the standard meal allowance. It covers your expenses for business meals, beverages, tax, and tips. The amount of the allowance depends on where and when you travel.

The advantage of using the standard meal allowance is that you don't have to keep track of how much you spend on meals and tips. However, you have to keep records to prove the time, place, and business purpose of your travel. (See Chapter 15 for more on record keeping.)

The disadvantage is that the standard meal allowance is one-half of what federal workers are allowed to charge for meals while traveling, and is therefore relatively modest. In 2004, the full rate federal workers could charge for domestic travel ranged from $34 per day for travel in the least expensive areas to up to $51 for high-cost areas, which includes most major cities. And because you can generally deduct only half of your meal and entertainment expenses, your deduction is limited to one half of the federal meal allowance. While it is possible to eat on $25 per day in places like New York City or San Francisco, you probably won't be enjoying the finest culinary experience. If you use the standard meal allowance and spend more than the allowance, you get no deduction for the overage.

The rates are generally higher for travel outside the continental United States—that is, Alaska, Hawaii, and foreign countries. For example, in 2004 the allowance was $138 for London and $144 for Tokyo. In contrast, travelers to rural Afghanistan were permitted only $15 per day.

The standard meal allowance includes $3 per day for incidental expenses—tips you pay to porters, bellhops, maids, and transportation workers. If you wish, you can use the actual expense method for your meal costs and the $3 incidental expense rate for your tips. However, you'd have to be a pretty stingy tipper for this amount to be adequate.

The standard meal allowance is revised each year. You can find the current rates for travel within the United States on the Internet at www.policyworks.gov/perdiem, or in IRS Publication 1542, *Per Diem Rates (for Travel Within the Continental United States)*. The rates for foreign travel are set by the U.S. State Department, and can be found at www.state.gov/m/a/als/prdm. When you look at these rate listings, you'll see several categories of numbers. You want the "M & IE Rate"—short for meals and incidental expenses. Rates are also provided for lodging, but these don't apply to nongovernmental travelers.

You can claim the standard meal allowance only for business days. If you travel to more than one location in one day, use the rate in effect for the area where you spend the night. Remember, you are allowed to deduct only 50% of the federal worker rate as a business expense.

> **EXAMPLE:** Art travels from Los Angeles to Chicago for a five-day business conference. Chicago is a high-cost locality, so the daily meal and incidental expense rate (M & IE) is $51. Art figures his deduction by multiplying the daily rate by five and dividing this in half: 5 days x $51 = $255; $255 x 50% = $127.50.

If you use the standard meal allowance, you must use it for *all of the business trips you take during the year*. You can't use it for some trips and use the actual expense method for others. For example, you can't use the standard allowance when you go to an inexpensive destination and the actual expense method when you go to a pricey one.

Because the standard meal allowance is relatively small, it's better to use it only if you travel exclusively to low cost areas, or if you are simply unable or unwilling to keep track of what you actually spend for meals.

You Don't Have to Spend Your Whole Allowance

When you use the standard meal allowance, you get to deduct the whole amount, regardless of what you spend. If you spend more than the daily allowance, you are limited to the allowance amount. But if you spend less, you still get to deduct the full allowance amount. For example, if you travel to New York City and live on bread and water, you may still deduct $25.50 (half of the $51 per diem rate) for each business day. This strategy will not only save you money; you'll lose weight as well.

D. Maximizing Your Business Travel Deductions

Here are some simple strategies you can use to maximize your business travel deductions.

1. Plan Ahead

Plan your itinerary carefully before you leave to make sure your trip qualifies as a business trip. For example, if you're traveling within the United States, you must spend more than half of your time on business for your transportation to be deductible. If you know you're going to spend three days on business, arrange to spend no more than two days on personal activities so that your trip meets the requirements. If you're traveling overseas for more than 14 days, you'll have to spend at least 75% of your time on business to deduct your transportation—you may be able to do this by using strategies to maximize your business days (see Section D3, below).

2.   Make a Paper Trail

If you are audited by the IRS, you will probably be questioned about business travel deductions. Of course, you'll need to have records showing what you spent for your trips (see Chapter 15 for a detailed discussion). However, you'll also need documents proving that your trip was for your existing business. You can do this by:

- making a note in your calendar or daily planner of every business meeting you attend or other business-related work you do—be sure to note the time you spend on each business activity
- obtaining and saving business cards from anyone you meet while on business
- noting in your calendar or daily planner the names of all the people you meet for business on your trip
- keeping the programs or agendas from any conventions or training seminars you attend, as well as any notes you made
- keeping copies of thank you notes you send to the business contacts you met on your trips, and
- keeping copies of business-related correspondence or e-mails you sent or received before the trip.

3.   Maximize Your Business Days

If you mix business with pleasure on your trip, you have to make sure that you have enough business days to deduct your transportation costs. You'll need to spend more than 50% of your days on business on domestic trips and more than 75% for foreign trips of more than 14 days.

You don't have to work all day for that day to count as a business day: Any day in which you work at least four hours is a business day, even if you goof off the rest of time. The day will count as a business day for purposes of determining whether your transportation expenses are deductible, and you can deduct your lodging, meal, and other expenses during the day, even though you only worked four hours.

You can easily maximize your business days by taking advantage of this rule. For example, you can:

- work no more than four hours in any one day whenever possible

- spread your business over several days—for example, if you need to be present at three meetings, try to spread them over two or three days instead of one, and
- avoid using the fastest form of transportation to your business destination—travel days count as business days, so you'll add business days to your trip if you drive instead of fly. Remember, there's no law that says you have to take the quickest means of transportation to your destination.

4.   Take Advantage of the Sandwich Day Rule

Days when you do no business-related work still count as business days if they are sandwiched between workdays, as long as it was cheaper to spend that day away than to go back home for the off days. If you work on Friday and Monday, this rule allows you to count Saturday and Sunday as business days, even if you don't do any work.

> **EXAMPLE:** Kim flies from Houston to Honolulu, Hawaii, for a business convention. She arrives on Wednesday and returns the following Wednesday. She does not attend any convention activities during the weekend and goes to the beach instead. Nevertheless, because it was cheaper for her to stay in Hawaii than to fly back to Houston for the weekend and return to Hawaii, she may count Saturday and Sunday as business days. This means she can deduct her lodging and meal expenses for those days (but not the cost of renting a surfboard). ■

Chapter 10

Inventory

B arbee owns a home-based crafts business—she makes her own crafts and buys finished products from others, which she then sells at crafts fairs and on her website. This year, she spent $28,000 on inventory. You might think that she would be able to deduct all of these costs because she is a business owner. Well, think again—Barbee can deduct only a portion of her expenses because of the way the tax code treats inventories.

This chapter covers inventory, including how to determine which of your purchases constitute inventory, how to value your inventory, and how to calculate your deduction for inventory costs.

Service providers can skip ahead. If your home business involves making or buying goods to sell to customers—even if your primary business is to provide services—you need to read this chapter and learn about inventories. If you only provide services to your clients or customers, then you don't need to worry about inventories. You can skip ahead to Chapter 11.

A.   What Is Inventory?

Inventory (also called merchandise) is the goods and products that a business owns to sell to customers in the ordinary course of business. It includes almost anything a business offers for sale, except for real estate. It makes no difference whether you manufacture the goods yourself or buy finished goods to resell to customers. Inventory includes not only finished merchandise, but also unfinished work in progress, as well as the raw materials and supplies that will become part of the finished merchandise.

Only things to which you hold title—that is, things you own—constitute inventory. Inventory includes items you haven't yet received or paid for, as long as you own them. For example, an item you buy with a credit card counts as inventory, even if you haven't paid the bill yet. However, if you buy merchandise that is sent C.O.D., you acquire ownership only after the goods are delivered and paid for. Similarly, goods that you hold on consignment are not part of your inventory because you don't own them.

EXAMPLE: Barbee's inventory consists of the finished crafts she has for sale, the unfinished crafts she is working on, and the raw material she will eventually use to create finished crafts. Raw materials that she has on order (but has not paid for) are not inventory. Neither are Barbee's craft-making equipment, such as her leather hole punch and jewelry tools, nor the computer she uses to keep track of sales and maintain her website. These items are part of her business assets, not merchandise that she is offering for sale to customers. Jewelry pieces that Barbee is selling in her store on consignment also don't count as inventory because they still belong to the craftspeople who made them, not to Barbee.

1.   Supplies Are Not Inventory

Materials and supplies that do not physically become part of the merchandise a business sells are not included in inventory. Unless they are incidental supplies (as described in Section A2, below), the cost of these supplies must be deducted *in the year in which they are used or consumed*, which is not necessarily the year when you purchase them. This means that you must keep track of how much material you use each year.

EXAMPLE: Barbee decides to tan her own leather, which she will use to create leather pouches to sell to customers. She orders large amounts of various expensive chemicals needed for the tanning process. In 2005, she spent $5,000 for the tanning chemicals, but used only half of them. She may deduct $2,500 of the cost of the chemicals for 2005. She may not deduct the cost of the remaining chemicals until she uses them.

2.   Incidental Supplies

There is an important exception to the rule that the cost of materials and supplies may be deducted only as they are used or consumed. You may deduct the entire cost of supplies that are *incidental* to your business in the year when you purchase them. Supplies are incidental if:

- they are of minor or secondary importance to your business (see Section B, below)—if you treat the cost of supplies on hand as an asset for financial reporting purposes, they are not incidental (IRS Private Letter Ruling 9209007)
- you do *not* keep a record of when you use the supplies
- you do not take a physical inventory of the supplies at the beginning and end of the tax year (Private Letter Ruling 8630003 and 9209007), and
- deducting the cost of supplies in the year you purchase them does not distort your taxable income (§1.162-3; Private Letter Ruling 9209007).

EXAMPLE: In 2005, Barbee purchases $100 worth of light bulbs to light her home workspace. She does not keep a record of how many light bulbs she uses each year or take a physical inventory of how many she has on hand at year's end. The light bulbs are incidental supplies. Barbee may deduct the entire $100 in 2005, regardless of how many light bulbs she actually used that year.

3.   Long-Term Assets

Long-term assets are things that last for more than one year—for example, equipment, tools, office furniture, vehicles, and buildings. Long-term assets that you purchase to use in your business are not a part of your inventory. They are deductible capital expenses that you may depreciate over several years or, in many cases, deduct in a single year under Section 179. (See Chapter 5 for more on deducting long-term assets.)

EXAMPLE: Barbee buys a new computer to help her keep track of her sales. The computer is not part of Barbee's inventory because she bought it to use in her business, not to resell to customers. Because it will last for more than one year, it's a long-term asset, which she must either depreciate or expense under Section 179.

Merchandise to Include in Inventory	
Include the following merchandise in inventory:	**Do not include the following items in inventory:**
Purchased merchandise if title has passed to you, even if the merchandise is in transit or you do not have physical possession of it for some other reason.	Goods you have sold, if title has passed to the buyer.
	Goods consigned to you.
Merchandise you've agreed to sell but have not separated from other similar merchandise you own to supply to the buyer.	Goods ordered for future delivery, if you do not yet have title.
Goods you have placed with another person or business to sell on consignment.	Assets such as land, buildings, and equipment used in your business.
Goods held for sale in display rooms, merchandise mart rooms, or booths located away from your place of business.	Supplies that do not physically become part of the item intended for sale.

B. Maintaining an Inventory

A business is said to maintain or carry an inventory when it must include unsold inventory items as assets on its books, to be deducted only when the items are sold or become worthless. A business is required to carry an inventory if the production, purchase, or sale of merchandise produces income for the business—that is, if these activities account for a substantial amount of the business's revenues. And any business that wants to take an inventory deduction must carry an inventory and account to the IRS on inventory costs and sales.

How big is "substantial"? You must carry an inventory if buying, selling, or producing merchandise accounts for a substantial amount of your company's revenue. So how much is substantial? There's no exact figure, but many tax experts believe that a business that derives 8% or less of its revenue from the sale or production of merchandise need not maintain an inventory. A business that makes at least 15% of its money from selling or producing merchandise probably has to maintain an inventory, and a business that earns 9% to 14% of its money from merchandise is in a gray area.

Often, it's perfectly obvious when a business must carry an inventory. Barbee's crafts business is a perfect example. Barbee obtains all of her income from the manufacture and sale of crafts to customers, so she must maintain an inventory. On the other hand, a taxpayer who only provides a service to customers ordinarily doesn't have to maintain an inventory. For example, a bookkeeper who provides bookkeeping services to clients need not maintain an inventory of the paper he uses, nor does he need to compute the cost of goods sold each year for his taxes.

1.   When You Provide Services and Sell Merchandise

Some home businesses provide services to customers and also sell merchandise. For example, a home-based plumbing contractor who provides plumbing services to customers may also supply various plumbing fixtures and materials. If the customer is separately billed for this merchandise, the service provider must always maintain an inventory. Even if the merchandise is included in the price of the service, the IRS generally requires this type of business to carry an inventory, unless the merchandise does not account for a substantial amount of the business's gross income.

The standards are far from clear in this area. If you sell services and goods, talk to a tax professional for advice on dealing with inventory.

2.   Supplies for Providing a Service

Merchandise includes only items that are sold or otherwise furnished to customers, clients, or patients. Items used in the course of providing a service are supplies, not merchandise that must be included in inventory. Thus, for example, the IRS has held that medicines, serums, and bandages provided to patients by a medical clinic were merchandise, whereas disposable syringes and rubber gloves used by doctors and nurses to provide medical services were materials and supplies.

The same item can constitute supplies for one business and inventory for another. It all depends on whether the item is furnished to the customer or consumed in performing a service. For example, the paper and ink used to prepare blueprints are inventory in the hands of a paper and ink manufacturer, but supplies in the hands of an architect.

C. Deducting Inventory Costs

You cannot deduct inventory costs in the same way as other costs of doing business, such as your office rent or employee salaries. A business may deduct only the cost of goods it actually sells during a tax year—not the cost of its entire inventory. Inventory that remains unsold at the end of the year is a business asset, not a deductible expense.

You may deduct unsold inventory when you sell it in later years or in the year it becomes worthless (as a business loss). In contrast, you may deduct business expenses (such as home office expenses) entirely in the year when you incur them—in other words, they are currently deductible.

To figure out how much you can deduct for inventory, you must calculate the cost (to you) of the goods you sold during the year. You can then deduct this amount from your gross income when you do your taxes.

1. Computing the Cost of Goods Sold

The easiest way to calculate your inventory costs is to work backwards. Rather than trying to add up everything they sold during the year, most business owners figure out how much inventory they had available for sale during the year and how much they have left at the end of the year. The difference between these two numbers is the inventory sold that year.

To figure out the cost of goods sold, start with the cost of any inventory on hand at the beginning of your tax year. Add the cost of inventory that you purchased or manufactured during the year. Subtract the cost of any merchandise you withdrew for personal use. The sum of all this addition and subtraction is the cost of all goods available for sale during the tax year. Subtract from this amount the value of your inventory at the end of your tax year. (See Section C2, below, for information on how to calculate this value.) The cost of all goods sold during the year—and therefore, the amount you can deduct for inventory expenses on your taxes—is the remainder. This can be stated by the following equation:

	Inventory at beginning of year
Plus:	Purchases or additions during the year
Minus:	Goods withdrawn from sale for personal use
Equals:	Cost of goods available for sale
Minus:	Inventory at end of year
Equals:	Cost of goods sold

EXAMPLE: Barbee had $1,000 in inventory at the beginning of the year and purchased another $28,000 of inventory during the year. She removed $500 of inventory for her own personal use (to give away as Christmas presents). The cost of the inventory she had left at the end of the year is $10,500. She would calculate her cost of goods sold as follows:

Inventory at beginning of year	$ 1,000
Purchases or additions during the year	+ 28,000
Goods withdrawn from sale for personal use	– 500
Cost of goods available for sale	= 28,500
Inventory at end of year	– 10,500
Cost of goods sold	= $18,000

Note that all of these costs are based on what Barbee paid for her inventory, not what she sold it for (which was substantially greater).

2. Determining the Value of Inventory

To use the equation in Section C1, above, you must be able to calculate the value of the inventory you have left at the end of the year. There is no single way to do this—standard methods for tracking inventory vary according to the type and size of business involved. As long as your inventory methods are consistent from year to year, the IRS doesn't care which method you use.

Need more information on how to value your inventory? This section provides only a small overview of a large subject. For more information on valuing inventory, refer to:

- *The Accounting Game*, by Darrell Mullis and Judith Orloff (Sourcebooks, Inc.)
- *Small Time Operator*, by Bernard B. Kamoroff (Bell Springs Publishing)
- IRS Publication 334, *Tax Guide for Small Businesses* (Chapter 7), and
- IRS Publication 538, *Accounting Periods and Methods*.

a. Taking Physical Inventory

You need to know how much inventory you have at the beginning and end of each tax year to figure your cost of goods sold. If, like most businesses, you use the calendar year as your tax year, this means that you need to figure out your inventory each December 31. Unless you hold a New Year's Eve sale, your inventory on January 1 will usually be the same as the prior year's ending inventory—your inventory on December 31. Any differences must be explained in a schedule attached to your tax return.

Until recently, the IRS required all businesses that sold or manufactured goods to make a physical inventory of the merchandise they owned—that is, to actually count it. This process, often called "taking inventory," is usually done at the end of the year, although it doesn't have to be. Nor is it necessary to count every single item in stock. Businesses can make a physical inventory of a portion of their total merchandise, then extrapolate their total inventory from the sample.

The IRS no longer requires small businesses to take physical inventories. (Small businesses are those that earn less than $1 million in gross receipts per year, and service businesses that earn up to $10 million per year.) But even small businesses must keep track of how much inventory they buy and sell to determine their cost of goods sold for the year. With modern inventory software, it is possible for a business to keep a continuous record of the goods on hand during the year. Keep copies of your invoices and receipts to prove to the IRS that you correctly accounted for your inventory, in case you are audited.

b. Identifying Inventory Items Sold During the Year

The second step in figuring out your cost of goods sold is to identify which inventory items were sold during the year. There are several ways to do this. You can specifically track each item that is sold during the year. This is generally done only by businesses that sell a relatively small number of high-cost items each year, such as automobile dealers or jewelers.

If you don't want to identify specific items by their invoices, you must make an assumption about which items were sold during the year and which items remain in stock. Small businesses ordinarily use the first-in, first-out (FIFO) method. The FIFO method assumes that the first items you purchased or produced are the first items that you sold, consumed, or otherwise disposed of.

> **EXAMPLE:** Barbee purchased three leather pouches to sell to customers during 2005. She bought the first pouch on February 1 for $5, the second on March 1 for $6, and the third on April 1 for $7. At the end of the year, Barbee finds that she only has one of these pouches left in stock. Using the FIFO method, she assumes that the first two pouches that she bought were the first ones sold. This means that in 2005, she sold two pouches that cost her $11 and has one pouch left in her inventory that cost $7.

Another method of identifying inventory makes the opposite assumption. Under the last-in, first-out (LIFO) method, you assume that the last items purchased or produced were the first to sell. This method is not favored by the IRS. You may use it only if you use the accrual method of accounting (see Chapter 15) and take physical inventory. To use the

LIFO method, you must file IRS Form 970, *Application to Use LIFO Inventory Method*, and follow some very complex tax rules.

c.   Valuing Your Inventory

You must also determine the value of the inventory you sold during the year. The value of your inventory is a major factor in figuring out your taxable income, so the method that you use is very important. The two most common methods are the cost method and the lower of cost or market method. A new business that doesn't use LIFO to determine which goods were sold (see above) may choose either method to value its inventory. You must use the same method to value your entire inventory, and you cannot change the method from year to year without first obtaining IRS approval.

Cost Method

As the name indicates, when you use the cost method, your inventory cost is the amount that you paid for the merchandise. Note that this is not the same as what you sold it for, which will (hopefully!) be higher.

Using the cost method is relatively easy when you purchase goods to resell. To calculate the value of each item, start with the invoice price. Add the cost of transportation, shipping, and other money you had to spend to acquire the items. Subtract any discounts you received.

Things get much more complicated if you manufacture goods to sell. In this situation, you must include all direct and indirect costs associated with the goods. This includes:

- the cost of products or raw materials, including the cost of having them shipped to you
- the cost of storing the products you sell, and
- direct labor costs (including contributions to pension or annuity plans) for workers who produce the products; this does not include your own salary unless you are a corporate employee.

In addition, larger businesses (those with more than $10 million in gross receipts) must include an amount for depreciation on machinery used to produce the products and factory overhead expenses. If your home business makes this much money, obtain an accountant's help.

Lower of Cost or Market Method

What if the retail value of your inventory goes down during the year? This could happen, for example, if your inventory becomes obsolete or falls out of fashion. In this event, you may use the lower of cost or market method to value your inventory. Under this method, you compare the market (retail) value of each item on hand on the inventory date with its cost, and use the lower value as its inventory value. By using the lower of these two numbers, your inventory will be worth less and your deductible expenses will be greater, thereby reducing your taxable income.

> **EXAMPLE:** Barbee purchased a jeweled belt in 2005 for $1,000. Due to a change in fashion, Barbee finds she can sell the belt for only $500. Using the lower of cost or market method, she may value the belt at $500.

However, you can't simply make up an inventory item's market value. You must establish the market value of your inventory through objective evidence, such as actual sales price for similar items.

Consider donating excess inventory to charity. One way to get rid of inventory you can't sell is to donate it to charity. You'll benefit a worthwhile charity and, by removing the items from your shelves, generate a tax deduction as well.

D. IRS Reporting

You must report the cost of goods sold on your tax return. If you're a sole proprietor, the amount goes directly on your Schedule C. Part III of Schedule C tracks the cost of goods equation provided in Section C, above. LLCs and partnerships report their cost of goods sold on Schedule A of IRS Form 1065, *U.S. Partnership Return of Income*. S corporations report cost of goods sold on Schedule A of Form 1120, *U.S. Income Tax Return for an S Corporation*. C corporations report this information on Schedule A of Form 1020, *U.S. Corporation Income Tax Return*.

Technically speaking, the cost of goods sold is not a business expense. Rather, it is subtracted from a business's gross income to determine its gross profit for the year. Business expenses are then subtracted from the gross profit to determine the business's taxable net profit, as shown by the following formula:

	Gross income
Minus:	Cost of goods sold
Equals:	Gross profit
Minus:	Deductible business expenses
Equals:	**Net profit**

As a practical matter, this is a distinction without a difference—both the cost of goods sold and business expenses are subtracted from your business income to calculate your taxable profit. However, you cannot deduct the cost of goods sold to determine your gross profit and then deduct it again as a business expense—this would result in a double deduction.

EXAMPLE: Barbee subtracts her $18,000 cost of goods sold from her gross income (all the money she earned from selling her crafts) to determine her gross profit. She earned $50,000 in total sales for the year and had $10,000 in business expenses, including rent, advertising costs, and business mileage. She calculates her net profit as follows:

Gross income		$ 50,000
Cost of goods sold	–	18,000
Gross profit	=	32,000
Business expenses	–	10,000
Net profit	=	$ 22,000

Barbee has to pay tax only on her $22,000 in net profit.

Obviously, the larger the cost of goods sold, the smaller your taxable income will be and the less tax you'll have to pay. ∎

Chapter 11

Hiring Workers

A nne has a highly successful home business selling used clothing on eBay. In fact, business is so good that she needs help keeping up with all of her orders. She hires John, a high school kid who lives next door, to help her with fulfillment. John works ten hours per week, and Anne is delighted with his work. But she has a problem: How does she treat John—and the money she pays him—for tax purposes?

This chapter is about the host of tax rules that apply to home business owners like Anne who hire people to help them, whether as employees or independent contractors. These rules apply when you hire strangers or family members, or when your incorporated business hires you.

A. Employees Versus Independent Contractors

As far as the IRS is concerned, there are only two types of people you can hire to help in your home business: employees and independent contractors. It's very important to understand the difference between these two categories because the tax rules are very different for each. If you hire an employee, you become subject to a wide array of state and federal tax requirements. You must withhold taxes from your employee's earnings, and pay other taxes yourself. You must also comply with complex and burdensome bookkeeping and reporting requirements. If you hire an independent contractor, none of these requirements apply. Tax deductions for businesses that hire employees and independent contractors differ as well. Independent contractors (ICs) go by a variety of names: self-employed, freelancers, free agents, consultants, entrepreneurs, or business owners. What they all have in common is that they are people who are in business for themselves. In contrast, employees work for someone else's business.

Initially, it's up to you to determine whether any person you hire is an employee or an IC. However, your decision about how to classify a worker is subject to review by various government agencies, including:

- the IRS
- your state's tax department
- your state's unemployment compensation insurance agency, and
- your state's workers' compensation insurance agency.

These agencies are mostly interested in whether you have classified workers as independent contractors when you should have classified them as employees. The reason is that you must pay money to each of these agencies for employees, but not for independent contractors. The more workers that are classified as employees, the more money flows into the agencies' coffers. In the case of taxing agencies, employers must withhold tax from employees' paychecks and hand it over to the government; ICs pay their own taxes, which means the government must wait longer to get its money and faces the possibility that ICs won't declare their income or will otherwise cheat on their taxes. If an agency determines that you misclassified an employee as an IC, you may have to pay back taxes, fines, and penalties.

Scrutinizing agencies use various tests to determine whether a worker is an IC or an employee. The determining factor is usually whether you have the right to control the worker. If you have the right to *direct and control* the way a worker performs—both the final results of the job and the details of when, where, and how the work is done—then the worker is your employee. On the other hand, if you have only the right to accept or reject the final results the worker achieves, then that person is an IC.

An employer may not always exercise its right of control. For example, if an employee is experienced and well trained, the employer may not feel the need to closely supervise him or her. But the employer still has the right to step in at any time, which distinguishes an employment relationship from an IC arrangement.

> **EXAMPLE:** Anne hires John to help her fill orders and ship her clothing items to customers. John works ten hours per week in Anne's home office and warehouse (which is located in her garage). Anne carefully trains John, a 17-year-old, in how to take orders and ship the ordered items. When John first starts work, Anne closely supervises how he does his job. Virtually every aspect of John's behavior on the job is under Anne's control, including what time he arrives at and leaves work, when he takes a lunch break, and the sequence of tasks he must perform. If John proves to be an able and conscientious worker, Anne may choose not to look over

his shoulder very often. But Anne has the right to do so at any time. John is Anne's employee.

In contrast, a worker is an independent contractor if the hiring business does not have the right to control the person on the job. Because the worker is an independent businessperson not solely dependent on you (the hiring party) for a living, your control is limited to accepting or rejecting the final results the IC achieves.

> **EXAMPLE:** Anne hires Mary, a bookkeeper, to keep her business's books. Anne is only one of Mary's many clients. Anne doesn't tell Mary how to do her bookkeeping tasks; Mary is a professional who already knows how to do her work. Mary sets her own hours, provides her own equipment, and works from her own home office. Mary is an independent contractor.
>
> Because Mary is clearly running her own business, it's virtually certain that Anne does not have the right to control the way Mary performs her bookkeeping services. Anne's control is limited to accepting or rejecting the final result. If Anne doesn't like the work Mary has done, she can refuse to pay her.

There's no clear cut way for auditors to figure out whether you have the right to control a worker you hire. After all, they can't look into your mind to see whether you are controlling a worker (or whether you believe that you have the right to do so). They rely instead on indirect or circumstantial evidence indicating control or lack of it—for example, whether you provide a worker with tools and equipment, where the work is performed, how the worker is paid, and whether you can fire the worker. The following chart shows the primary factors used by the IRS and most other government agencies to determine if you have the right to control a worker.

⚠ **Part-time workers and temps can be employees.** Don't assume that a person you hire to work part time or for a short period automatically qualifies as an IC. People who work for you only temporarily or part time are your employees if you have the right to control the way they work.

IRS Test for Worker Status		
Behavioral Control	Workers will more likely be considered ICs if you: • do not give them instructions • do not provide them with training	Workers will more likely be considered employees if you: • give them instructions they must follow about how to do the work • give them detailed training
Financial Control	Workers will more likely be considered ICs if they: • have a significant investment in equipment and facilities • pay business or travel expenses themselves • make their services available to the public • are paid by the job • have opportunity for profit or loss	Workers will more likely be considered employees if: • you provide them with equipment and facilities free of charge • you reimburse their business or travel expenses • they make no effort to market their services to the public • you pay them by the hour or other unit of time • they have no opportunity for profit or loss—for example, because they're paid by the hour and have all expenses reimbursed
Relationship Between You and the Worker	Workers will more likely be considered ICs if: • they don't receive employee benefits such as health insurance • they sign a client agreement with the hiring firm • they can't quit or be fired at will • they perform services that are not part of your regular business activities	Workers will more likely be considered employees if they: • receive employee benefits • have no written client agreement • can quit at any time without incurring any liability to you • can be fired at any time • perform services that are part of your core business

Need more information about independent contractors? For a detailed discussion of the practical and legal issues business owners face when hiring ICs, see *Hiring Independent Contractors: The Employer's Legal Guide*, by Stephen Fishman (Nolo).

B. Tax Deductions for Employee Pay and Benefits

Only nine percent of home businesses hire employees, according to a study sponsored by the Small Business Administration. However, the tax law provides valuable deductions for those who do have employees. You may deduct most or all of what you pay an employee as a business expense. Thus, for example, if you pay an employee $25,000 per year in salary and benefits, you'll ordinarily get a $25,000 tax deduction. You should factor this into your calculations whenever you're thinking about hiring employees or deciding how much to pay them.

1. Employee Pay

You may pay your employees in the form of salaries, sales commissions, bonuses, vacation allowances, sick pay (as long as it's not covered by insurance), or fringe benefits. For tax deduction purposes, it doesn't really matter how you measure or make the payments. The amounts you pay an employee may fall into any of the four basic categories of deductible business expenses:

- business operating expenses
- business start-up expenses
- long-term asset purchase expenses, or
- inventory costs.

The general rules for each of these types of expenses are discussed in earlier chapters; this section explains how employee pay can fall into each category.

a. Operating Expenses

Most of the time, amounts you pay employees to work in your business will be business operating expenses. These expenses are currently deductible as long as they are:

- ordinary and necessary
- reasonable in amount
- paid for services actually performed, and
- actually paid or incurred in the year the deduction is claimed (as shown by your payroll records).

(See Chapter 4 for more on business operating expenses.)

An employee's services are ordinary and necessary if they are common, accepted, helpful, and appropriate for your business; they don't have to be indispensable. An employee's pay is reasonable if the amount is within the range that other businesses pay for similar services. These requirements usually won't pose a problem when you hire an employee to perform any legitimate business function.

> **EXAMPLE:** Ken, a lawyer who works from home, hires Kim to work as a paralegal and pays her $2,500 per month—what such workers are typically paid in the area. Ken can deduct Kim's $2,500 monthly salary as a business operating expense. If Kim works a full year, Ken will get a $30,000 deduction.

Payments to employees for personal services are not deductible as business expenses.

> **EXAMPLE:** Ken hires Samantha to work as a live-in nanny for his three children. Samantha is Ken's employee, but her services are personal, not related to his business. Thus, Ken may not deduct her pay as a business expense.

Special rules (described in Section D, below) apply if you hire family members to work in your business or hire yourself as an employee.

b.   Start-Up Expenses

Anything you pay employees for services performed during the start-up phase of your business is a start-up expense. These expenses are not currently deductible, but you may deduct them over the first 60 months you're in business. (See Chapter 3 for more information on deducting business start-up costs.)

> **EXAMPLE:** Michelle hires Benjamin to work as her full-time personal assistant while she works to start up a Web-based home-schooling service. Benjamin helps Michelle deal with myriad details involved in starting the business. Benjamin worked for Michelle for four months before the website went online. His salary during this start-up phase—$15,000—is a business start-up expense that Michelle may deduct a little at a time, over the first 60 months she is in business.

c.   Long-Term Asset Expenses

If you pay an employee to help purchase, transport, install, or improve a long-term asset, the payments are not business operating expenses. Instead, they are added to the basis (cost) of the asset. As such, you may either depreciate them over several years or (in most situations) currently deduct them under Section 179. (See Chapter 5 for more on deducting long-term assets.)

> **EXAMPLE:** John owns a fleet of 50 used delivery trucks. He employs Martha, a mechanic, to install new engines in the trucks. The engines are long-term asset purchases. What John pays Martha to install the engines is added to their purchase price to arrive at their value for tax purposes (their taxable basis). John can depreciate this amount over five years or deduct the entire amount in one year under Section 179.

d.   Inventory Costs

If you hire an employee to help you manufacture products for sale to customers, the employee's compensation is not a regular business expense. Instead, it is considered part of the cost of the products. These products are inventory, the cost of which may be deducted only as each item is sold. (See Chapter 10 for more on deducting inventory.)

> **EXAMPLE:** Richard owns a home pottery studio that manufactures pottery for sale to collectors. He pays Jean, his employee assistant, $25,000 a year. He adds this cost to the other costs he incurs to produce the pottery (materials, equipment, electricity, and so forth) to figure his total cost of goods sold. He deducts this amount from his gross income to determine his business's gross profit.

2.   Payroll Taxes

Whenever you hire an employee, you become an unpaid tax collector for the government. You are required to withhold and pay both federal and state taxes for the worker. These taxes are called payroll taxes or employment taxes. Federal payroll taxes consist of:

- Social Security and Medicare taxes—also known as FICA
- unemployment taxes—also known as FUTA, and
- federal income taxes—also known as FITW.

You must periodically pay FICA, FUTA, and FITW to the IRS, either electronically or by making federal tax deposits at specified banks, which then transmit the money to the IRS. You are entitled to deduct as a business expense payroll taxes that you pay yourself. You get no deductions for taxes you withhold from employees' pay.

Every year, employers must file IRS Form W-2, *Wage and Tax Statement*, for each of their workers. The form shows the IRS how much the worker was paid and how much tax was withheld.

Find out more about payroll taxes. IRS Circular E, *Employer's Tax Guide*, provides detailed information on payroll tax requirements. You can a get free copy by calling the IRS at 800-TAX-FORM, by calling or visiting your local IRS office, or by downloading it from the IRS website, www.irs.gov.

a.   Employer's FICA Contributions

FICA is an acronym for Federal Income Contributions Act, the law requiring employers and employees to pay Social Security and Medicare taxes. FICA consists of:

- a 12.4% Social Security tax on an employee's wages up to an annual wage ceiling or cap—in 2004, the cap was $87,900 per year, and
- a 2.9% Medicare tax on all employee wages paid.

This adds up to a 15.3% tax, up to the Social Security tax ceiling. Employers must pay half of this—7.65%—out of their own pockets. They must withhold the other half from their employees' pay. You are entitled to deduct (as a business operating expense) the portion of the tax that you pay yourself.

The ceiling for the Social Security tax changes annually. You can find out what the Social Security tax ceiling is for the current year from IRS Circular E, *Employer's Tax Guide*; the amount is printed right on the first page.

b.   FUTA

FUTA is an acronym for the Federal Unemployment Tax Act, the law that establishes federal unemployment taxes. Most employers must pay both state and federal unemployment taxes. Even if you're exempt from the state tax, you may still have to pay the federal tax. Employers alone are responsible for FUTA—you may not collect or deduct it from employees' wages.

You must pay FUTA taxes if:

- you pay $1,500 or more to employees during any calendar quarter—that is, any three month period beginning with January, April, July, or October, or
- you had one or more employees for at least some part of a day in any 20 or more different weeks during the year. The weeks don't have to be consecutive, nor does it have to be the same employee each week.

Technically, the FUTA tax rate is 6.2%, but in practice, you rarely pay this much. You are given a credit of 5.4% if you pay the applicable state unemployment tax in full and on time. This means that the actual FUTA tax rate is usually 0.8%. In 2004, the FUTA tax was assessed on only the first $7,000 of an employee's annual wages. Therefore, the full amount of the tax is $56 per year per employee. This amount is a deductible business expense.

c.   FITW

FITW is an acronym for federal income tax withholding. You must calculate and withhold federal income tax from your employees' paychecks. Employees are solely responsible for paying federal income tax. Your only responsibility is to withhold the funds and remit them to the government. You get no deductions for FITW; it wasn't your money to begin with.

d.   State Payroll Taxes

Employers in every state are required to pay and withhold state payroll taxes. These taxes include:

- state unemployment compensation taxes in all states
- state income tax withholding in most states, and
- state disability taxes in a few states.

Employers in every state are required to contribute to a state unemployment insurance fund. Employees make no contributions, except in Alaska, New Jersey, Pennsylvania, and Rhode Island, where employers must withhold small employee contributions from employees' paychecks. The employer contributions are a deductible business expense.

If your payroll is very small—less than $1,500 per calendar quarter—you probably won't have to pay unemployment compensation taxes. In most states, you must pay state unemployment taxes for employees if you're paying federal FUTA taxes. However, some states have stricter requirements. Contact your state labor department for the exact rules and payroll amounts.

All states except Alaska, Florida, Nevada, South Dakota, Texas, Washington, and Wyoming have income taxation. If your state has income taxes, you must withhold the applicable amount from your employees' paychecks and pay it to the state taxing authority. Each state has its own income tax withholding forms and procedures. Contact your state tax department for information. Of course, employers get no deductions for withholding their employees' state income taxes.

California, Hawaii, New Jersey, New York, and Rhode Island have state disability insurance programs that provide employees with coverage for injuries or illnesses that are not related to work. Employers in these states must withhold their employees' disability insurance contributions from their pay. Employers must also make their own contributions in Hawaii, New Jersey, and New York—these employer contributions are deductible.

In addition, subject to some important exceptions, employers in all states must provide their employees with workers' compensation insurance to cover work-related injuries. Workers' compensation is not a payroll tax. Employers must purchase a workers' compensation policy from a private insurer or the state workers' compensation fund. Your workers' compensation insurance premiums are deductible as a business insurance expense (see Chapter 14).

⚠️ **Employers in California must withhold for parental leave.** California recently became the first state to require paid family leave. Employers in California must withhold money from their employees' paychecks (as part of the state's disability insurance program) to fund this leave program. For more information on the program, go to www.edd.ca.gov/direp/pflind.asp.

EXAMPLE: Isaac, a photographer, hires Vendela to work as his assistant at a salary of $2,000 per month. Isaac may deduct this amount as a business operating expense. In addition, he may deduct his payroll tax contributions on her behalf. These consist of a monthly $153 FICA contribution (7.65% x $2,000 = $153), $56 annual FUTA contribution, and a $1,200 annual Washington state unemployment contribution. Isaac must withhold $300 from Vendela's pay each month to cover her FICA and FITW taxes, and send it to the IRS. He need not withhold state income taxes because Washington has no income tax. He gets no deduction for these withheld amounts. So Isaac's annual tax deduction for Vendela is $27,092 ($24,000 salary + $1,836 FICA contribution + $1,200 state unemployment insurance + $56 FUTA = $27,092).

Bookkeeping expenses are deductible. Figuring out how much to withhold, doing the necessary record keeping, and filling out the required forms can be complicated. If you have a computer, software programs such as QuickBooks can help with all the calculations and print out your employees' checks and IRS forms. You can also hire a bookkeeper or payroll tax service to do the work. Amounts you pay a bookkeeper or payroll tax service are deductible business operating expenses. Moreover, the cost will be quite small if you only have a few employees.

3. Employee Fringe Benefits

You don't have to provide any fringe benefits to your employees—not even health insurance, sick pay, or vacation. However, the tax law encourages you to provide employee benefits by allowing you to deduct the cost as a business expense. (You should deduct these expenses as employee benefits, not employee compensation.) Moreover, your employees do not have to treat the value of their fringe benefits as taxable income. So you get a deduction and your employees get tax free goodies. Tax-free employee fringe benefits include:

- health insurance
- accident insurance
- Health Savings Accounts (see Chapter 12)
- dependent care assistance
- educational assistance
- group term life insurance coverage—limits apply based on the policy value
- qualified employee benefits plans, including profit sharing plans, stock bonus plans, and money purchase plans
- employee stock options
- lodging on your business premises
- moving expense reimbursements
- achievement awards
- commuting benefits
- employee discounts on the goods or services you sell
- supplemental unemployment benefits

- de minimis (low-cost) fringe benefits such as low-value birthday or holiday gifts, event tickets, traditional awards (such as a retirement gift), other special occasion gifts, and coffee and soft drinks, and
- cafeteria plans that allow employees to choose among two or more of the tax-qualified benefits listed above, or receive reimbursement for specified expenses.

Health insurance is by far the most important tax-free employee fringe benefit; it is discussed in detail in Chapter 12. See IRS Publication 15-B, *Employer's Guide to Fringe Benefits*, for more information on the other types of benefits.

Other types of fringe benefits are not tax-free to the employee, though the employer can still deduct them. For example, if you supply an employee with a company-owned car that the employee uses part or all of the time for personal purposes, the value of that personal use must be added to the employee's income. There are various ways to calculate this value; a special valuation rule applies if you allow an employee to use a company car to commute to work. See IRS Publication 463, *Travel, Entertainment, Gift, and Car Expenses*, for a detailed discussion.

In contrast, if you're a business owner (a sole proprietor, partner in a partnership, or an LLC member), you must include in your income—and pay tax on—the value of any fringe benefits your company provides to you. The only exception is for de minimis fringes.

C. Reimbursing Employees for Business-Related Expenditures

When you own a business, you generally pay all of your business expenses yourself, including the cost of things you buy to enable your employees to do their work—for example, tools and equipment. However, there may be times when an employee must pay for a work-related expense. Most commonly, this occurs when an employee is traveling or entertaining while on the job. However, depending on the circumstances, an employee could end up paying for almost any work-related expense—for example, an employee might pay for office supplies or parking at a client's office.

These employee payments have important tax consequences, no matter what form they take. The rules discussed below apply whether the expenses are incurred by an employee who is not related to you or by an employee who is your spouse or child. They also apply to a business owner who has incorporated the business and works as its employee.

1. Accountable Plans

The best way to reimburse or otherwise pay your employees for work-related expenses is to use an accountable plan, as defined by the IRS (see Subsection C1a, below). When you pay employees for their expenses under an accountable plan, two great things happen:

- you don't have to pay payroll taxes on the payments, and
- the employees won't have to include the payments in their taxable income.

Moreover, your business can deduct the amounts you pay, just like your other business expenses, subject to the same rules.

> **EXAMPLE:** Ken works as an employee for Amy's home-based wedding planning company. Amy decides that Ken should attend the Wonderful World of Weddings convention in Las Vegas. Ken pays his convention expenses out of his own pocket. When he gets back, he documents his expenses as required by Amy's accountable plan. He paid $2,000 for transportation and hotel, and $1,000 in meal and entertainment expenses. Amy reimburses Ken $3,000. Amy may deduct the entire $2,000 cost of Ken's flight and hotel and deduct 50% of the cost of the meals and entertainment. Ken doesn't have to count the $3,000 reimbursement as income (or pay taxes on it), and Amy doesn't have to report that amount to the IRS on the W-2 form she files for Ken. Moreover, Amy need not withhold income tax or pay any Social Security or Medicare taxes on the $3,000.

Deductions for Employee Meals and Entertainment

Ordinarily, your employees' meal and entertainment expenses are only 50% deductible, just like your own meal and entertainment expenses. (Chapter 7 covers deductions for meals and entertainment.) However, you may take a 100% deduction for employee meals:

- provided as part of a company recreational or social activity—for example, a company picnic
- provided on company premises for your convenience—for example, if you provide lunch because your employees must remain in the office to be available to work, or
- if the cost is included as part of the employee's compensation and reported as such on his or her W-2.

a.   Requirements for an Accountable Plan

An accountable plan is an arrangement by which you agree to reimburse or advance employee expenses only if the employee:

- pays or incurs expenses that qualify as deductible business expenses for your business while performing services as your employee
- adequately accounts to you for the expenses within a reasonable period of time, and
- returns to you (within a reasonable time) any amounts received in excess of the actual expenses incurred.

You can pay your employees' expenses in a variety of ways. For example, you can provide a cash advance the employee uses to pay expenses as they occur; you can have the employee pay the expenses out of his or her own pocket and then provide reimbursement; you can give the employee a company credit card; or, instead of the employee paying the expenses, you can have the bills sent directly to you for payment.

These strict rules are imposed to prevent employees from seeking reimbursement for personal expenses (or phony expenses) under the guise that they were business expenses. Employees used to do this all

the time to avoid paying income tax on the reimbursed amounts
(employees must count employer reimbursements for their personal
expenses as income, but not reimbursements for the employer's
business expenses).

An accountable plan need not be in writing (although it's not a bad
idea). All you need to do is set up procedures for your employees to
follow that meet these requirements.

b.   Employees Must Document Expenses

Your employees must give you the same documentation for a work-
related expense that the IRS requires of you when you claim that expense
for your business. The employee should provide this documentation
within 60 days after incurring the expense.

You need thorough documentation for car, travel, entertainment, and
meal expenses—these are the expenses the IRS is really concerned
about (see Chapters 7, 8, and 9). However, you can ease up on the
documentation requirements if you pay employees a per diem (per day)
allowance equal to or less than the per diem rates the federal government pays its workers while traveling. You can find these rates at
www.policyworks.gov/perdiem or in IRS Publication 1542, *Per Diem
Rates*. If you use this method, the IRS will assume that the amounts
claimed for lodging, meals, and incidental expenses are accurate without any further documentation. The employee need only substantiate
the time, place, and business purpose of the expense. The same is true
if you pay the standard mileage rate for an employee who uses a
personal car for business (see Chapter 8).

The documentation requirements are less onerous for other types of
expenses. Nevertheless, the employee still has to document the amount
of money spent and show that it was for your business. For example,
an employee who pays for a repair to his workplace computer out of
his own pocket should save the receipt and write "repair of office
computer" or something similar to show the business purpose of the
payment. It's not sufficient for an employee to submit an expense report
with vague categories or descriptions such as "travel" or "miscellaneous
business expenses."

c.   Returning Excess Payments

Employees who are advanced or reimbursed more than they actually spent for business expenses must return the excess to the employer within a reasonable time. The IRS says a reasonable time is within 120 days after an expense is incurred. Any amounts not returned are treated as taxable wages for the employee and must be added to the employee's income for tax purposes. This means that you, the employer, must pay payroll tax on those amounts.

> **EXAMPLE:** You give your employee a $1,000 advance to cover her expenses for a short business trip. When she gets back, she gives you an expense report and documentation showing she only spent $900 for business while on the trip. If she doesn't return the extra $100 within 120 days, it will be considered wages for tax purposes. The employee will have to report this extra money on her tax return, and you'll have to pay payroll tax on the $100.

2.   Unaccountable Plans

If you don't comply with the accountable plan rule, any reimbursements you pay to employees for business-related expenses are deemed to be made under an unaccountable plan. These payments are treated as employee wages, which means that all of the following are true:

- The employee must report the payments as income on his or her tax return and pay tax on them.
- The employee may deduct the expenses—but only as a miscellaneous itemized deduction (see Section C3, below).
- You may deduct the payments as wages paid to an employee
- You must withhold income taxes and the employee's share of Social Security and Medicare taxes from the payments.
- You must pay the employer's 7.65% share of the employee's Social Security and Medicare taxes on the payments.

This is a tax disaster for the employee—and a pretty lousy result for the employer as well—because you will have to pay Social Security and Medicare tax that you could have avoided if the payments had been made under an accountable plan.

3. Unreimbursed Employee Expenses

Employees are entitled to deduct from their own income ordinary and necessary expenses arising from their employment that are not reimbursed by their employers. In this event, you (the employer) get no deduction, because you haven't paid for the expense.

! **Some states require reimbursement.** Check with your state's labor department to find out the rules for reimbursing employee expenses. You might find that you are legally required to repay employees, rather than letting your employees deduct the expenses on their own tax returns. In California, for example, employers must reimburse employees for all expenses or losses they incur as a direct consequence of carrying out their job duties. (Cal. Labor Code § 2802.)

Employees may deduct essentially the same expenses as business owners, subject to some special rules. For example, there are special deduction rules for employee home office expenses (see Chapter 6), and employees who use the actual expense method for car expenses may not deduct car loan interest.

However, it's much better for the employees to be reimbursed by the employer under an accountable plan and let the employer take the deduction. Why? Because an employee can deduct unreimbursed employee expenses only if the employee itemizes deductions and only to the extent these deductions, along with the employee's other miscellaneous deductions, exceed 2% of his or her adjusted gross income. Adjusted gross income (AGI) is the employee's total income, minus deductions for IRA and pension contributions and a few other deductions (shown on Form 1040, line 35). Moreover, if an employee's AGI is more than $139,500, the deductible amount is reduced by 3% of the excess (this figure is adjusted each year for inflation).

These rules apply to all employees, including family members who work as your employees, and to you, if you've incorporated your business and work as its employee.

EXAMPLE: Eric has formed a regular C corporation for his political consulting business. He is its president and employee. He travels to Boston to attend a political convention for his business, incurring $3,500 in expenses. He pays these expenses out of his own pocket and does not seek reimbursement from his corporation. $1,000 of his expenses were for meals and entertainment, so they are only 50% deductible. This gives him a $500 deduction. The remaining $2,500 in expenses are fully deductible. Thus, his deductible expenses for the trip total $3,000. However, he may deduct this amount only as an unreimbursed business expense, and only to the extent that it, along with his other miscellaneous deductions, exceeds 2% of his adjusted gross income. Eric's AGI for the year was $100,000, and he had no other miscellaneous deductions, so he may deduct only that portion of his expenses that exceeds $2,000 (2% x $100,000 = $2,000). He therefore may deduct only $1,500 of his $3,500 total convention expenses ($3,500 – $2,000 = $1,500).

An employee's unreimbursed expenses must be listed on IRS Schedule A, Form 1040 as a miscellaneous itemized deduction. Employees must also file IRS Form 2106, *Employee Business Expenses,* reporting the amount of the expenses.

D. Employing Your Family or Yourself

Whoever said "never hire your relatives" must never have read the tax code. The tax law promotes family togetherness by making it highly advantageous for home business owners to hire family members. And when you have a home business, hiring your spouse, children, or other relatives can be very convenient for everyone (and eliminate the commute!)

1.   Employing Your Children

Believe it or not, your children can be a great tax savings device. If you hire your children as employees to do legitimate work in your business, you may deduct their salaries from your business income as a business expense. Your child will have to pay tax on his or her salary only to the extent it exceeds the standard deduction amount for the year—$4,850 in 2004. Moreover, if your child is under the age of 18, you won't have to withhold or pay any FICA (Social Security or Medicare) tax on the salary (subject to a couple of exceptions).

These rules allow you to shift part of your business income from your own tax bracket to your child's bracket, which should be much lower than yours (unless you earn little or no income). This can result in substantial tax savings.

The following chart shows the federal income tax brackets for 2004. A child need only pay a 10% tax on taxable income up to $7,150 taxable income means total income minus the standard deduction. Thus, a child could earn up to $12,000 and pay only a 10% income tax. In contrast, if you were married and earned just $58,101, you'd have to pay a 25% federal income tax on that money. You'd also have to pay a 15.3% Social Security and Medicare tax (up to an annual ceiling), which your child under the age of 18 need not pay.

2004 Federal Personal Income Tax Brackets

Tax Bracket	Income If Single	Income If Married Filing Jointly
10%	Up to $7,150	Up to $14,300
15%	From $7,151 to $29,950	$14,301 to $58,100
25%	$29,951 to $70,350	$58,101 to $117,250
28%	$70,351 to $146,750	$117,251 to $178,650
33%	$146,751 to $319,100	$178,651 to $319,100
35%	All over $319,100	All over $319,100

EXAMPLE: Carol hires Mark, her 16-year-old son, to perform computer inputting services for her medical record transcription business, which she owns as a sole proprietor. He works ten hours per week and she pays him $20 per hour (the going rate for such work). Over the course of a year, she pays him a total of $9,000. She need not pay FICA tax for Mark because he's not yet 18. When she does her taxes for the year, she may deduct his $9,000 salary from her business income as a business expense. Mark pays tax only on the portion of his income that exceeds the $4,750 standard deduction—so he pays federal income tax only on $4,250 of his $9,000 salary. With such a small amount of income, he is in the lowest federal income tax bracket—10%. He pays $425 in federal income tax for the year. Had Carol not hired Mark, she would have lost her $9,000 deduction and had to pay income tax and self-employment taxes on this amount—a 40% tax in her tax bracket (25% federal income tax + 15.3% self-employment tax = 40%). Thus, she would have had to pay an additional $3,600 in federal taxes. Depending on the state where Carol lives, she likely would have had to pay a state income tax as well.

What About Child Labor Laws?

You're probably aware that certain types of child labor are illegal under federal and state law. However, these laws generally don't apply to children under the age of 16 who are employed by their parents, unless the child is employed in mining, manufacturing, or a hazardous occupation. Hazardous occupations include driving a motor vehicle; being an outside helper on a motor vehicle; operating various power-driven machines, including machines for woodworking, metal forming, sawing, and baking; or roofing, wrecking, excavation, demolition, and shipbreaking operations.

A child who is at least 16 may be employed in any nonhazardous occupation. Children at least 17 years of age may spend up to 20% of their time driving cars and trucks weighing less than 6,000 pounds as part of their job if they have licenses and no tickets, drive only in daylight hours, and go no more than 30 miles from home. They may not perform dangerous driving maneuvers (such as towing) or do regular route deliveries. For detailed information, see the Department of Labor website, www.dol.gov.

a.   No Payroll Taxes

One of the advantages of hiring your child is that you need not pay FICA taxes for your child under the age of 18 who works in your trade or business, or your partnership, if it's owned solely by you and your spouse.

> **EXAMPLE:** Lisa, a 16-year-old, makes deliveries for her mother's mail order business, which is operated as a sole proprietorship. Although Lisa is her mother's employee, her mother need not pay FICA taxes on her salary until she turns 18.

Moreover, you need not pay federal unemployment (FUTA) taxes for services performed by your child who is under 21 years old.

However, these rules do not apply—and you must pay both FICA and FUTA—if you hire your child to work for:

- your corporation, or
- your partnership, unless all the partners are parents of the child.

> **EXAMPLE:** Ron works in a home-based computer repair business that is co-owned by his mother and her partner, Ralph, who is no relation to the family. The business must pay FICA and FUTA taxes for Ron because he is working for a partnership and not all of the partners are his parents.

b.   No Withholding

In addition, if your child has no unearned income (for example, interest or dividend income), you must withhold income taxes from your child's pay only if it exceeds the standard deduction for the year. The standard deduction was $4,850 in 2004 and is adjusted every year for inflation. Children who are paid less than this amount need not pay any income taxes on their earnings. However, you must withhold income taxes if your child has more than $250 in unearned income for the year and his or her total income exceeds $750.

EXAMPLE: Connie, a 15-year-old girl, is paid $4,000 a year to help out in her parents' home business. She has no income from interest or any other unearned income. Her parents need not withhold income taxes from Connie's salary.

If Connie is paid $4,000 in salary and has $500 in interest income, her parents must withhold income taxes from her salary because she has more than $250 in unearned income and her total income for the year was more than $750.

2.   Employing Your Spouse

You don't get the benefits of income shifting when you employ your spouse in your business because your income is combined when you file a joint tax return. You'll also have to pay FICA taxes on your spouse's wages, so you get no savings there either. However, you need not pay FUTA tax if you employ your spouse in your unincorporated business. This tax is usually only $56 per year, so this is not much of a savings.

The real advantage of hiring your spouse is in the realm of employee benefits. You can provide your spouse with any or all of the employee benefits discussed in Section B, above. You can take a tax deduction for the cost of the benefit and your spouse doesn't have to declare the benefit as income, provided the IRS requirements are satisfied. This is a particularly valuable tool for health insurance—you can give your spouse health insurance coverage as an employee benefit. (See Chapter 12 for a detailed discussion.)

Another benefit of hiring your spouse is that you can take business trips together and deduct the cost as a business expense, as long as your spouse's presence was necessary (for your business, not for you, personally).

3. Rules to Follow When Employing Your Family

The IRS is well aware of the tax benefits of hiring a child or spouse, so it's on the lookout for taxpayers who claim the benefit without meeting the requirements. If the IRS concludes that your children or spouse aren't really employees, you'll lose your tax deductions for their salary and benefits. And they'll have to pay tax on their benefits. To avoid this, you should follow these simple rules:

a. Rule 1: Your Child or Spouse Must Be a Real Employee

First of all, your child or spouse must be a bona fide employee. Their work must be ordinary and necessary for your business, and their pay must be compensation for services actually performed. Their services don't have to be indispensable, but they must be common, accepted, helpful, and appropriate for your business. Any real work for your business can qualify—for example, you could employ your child or spouse to clean your office, answer the phone, stuff envelopes, input data, or make deliveries. You get no business deductions when you pay your child for personal services, such as babysitting or mowing your lawn at home. On the other hand, money you pay for yard work performed on business property could be deductible as a business expense.

The IRS won't believe that an extremely young child is a legitimate employee. How young is too young? The IRS has accepted that a seven-year-old child may be an employee (see "Hardworking Seven-Year-Old Was Parents' Employee," below), but probably won't believe that children younger than seven are performing any useful work for your business.

You should keep track of the work and hours your children or spouse perform by having them fill out time sheets or timecards. You can find these in stationery stores or you can create a timesheet yourself. It should list the date, the services performed, and the time spent performing the services.

Hardworking Seven-Year-Old Was Parents' Employee

Walt and Dorothy Eller owned three trailer parks and a small strip mall in Northern California. They hired their three children, ages seven, 11, and 12, to perform various services for their businesses including pool maintenance, landscaping, reading gas and electric meters, delivering leaflets and messages to tenants, answering phones, doing minor repairs, and sweeping and cleaning trailer pads and parking lots. The children worked after school, on weekends, and during their summer vacations. The Ellers paid their children a total of $17,800 over a three-year period and deducted the amounts as business expenses. The IRS tried to disallow the deductions, claiming that the children's pay was excessive. The court allowed most of the deductions, noting that these hardworking children performed essential services for their parents' businesses. The court found that the seven-year old was a bona fide employee, but ruled that he should earn somewhat less than his older brother and sister because 11- and 12-year-old children can generally handle greater responsibility and do more work than seven-year-old children. Thus, while the older siblings could be paid $5,700 for their services over the three years in question, the seven-year-old could reasonably be paid only $4,000. (*Eller v. Comm'r.*, 77 T.C. 934 (1981).)

b.   Rule 2: Compensation Must Be Reasonable

When you hire your children, it is advantageous (tax-wise) to pay them as much as possible. That way, you can shift more of your income to your children, who are probably in a much lower income tax bracket. Conversely, you want to pay your spouse as little as possible, because you get no benefits from income shifting; you and your spouse are in the same income tax bracket (assuming you file a joint return, as the vast majority of married people do). Moreover, your spouse will have to pay a 7.65% Social Security tax on his or her salary—an amount that is not tax deductible. (As your spouse's employer, you'll have to pay employment taxes on your spouse's salary as well, but these taxes are deductible business expenses.)

However, you can't just pay whatever amount will result in the lowest tax bill: Your spouse's or child's wages must be reasonably related to the value of the services performed. You shouldn't have a problem as long as you don't pay more than you'd pay a stranger for the same work. In other words, don't try paying your child $100 per hour for office cleaning just to get a big tax deduction. Find out what workers who perform similar services in your area are being paid. For example, if you plan to hire your teenager to do computer inputting, call an employment agency or temp agency in your area to see what these workers are being paid.

To prove how much you paid (and that you actually paid it), you should pay your child or spouse by check, not cash. Do this once or twice a month, just as you would for any other employee. The funds should be deposited in a bank account in your child's or spouse's name. Your child's bank account may be a trust account.

c.   Rule 3: Comply With Legal Requirements for Employers

You must comply with most of the same legal requirements when you hire a child or spouse as you do when you hire a stranger.

- **At the time you hire:** When you first hire your child or spouse, you must fill out IRS Form W-4. You (the employer) use it to determine how much tax you must withhold from the employee's salary. A child who is exempt from withholding should write "exempt" in the space provided and complete and sign the rest of the form. You must also complete U.S. Citizenship and Immi- gration Services Form I-9, *Employment Eligibility Verification*, verifying that the employee is a U.S. citizen or is otherwise eligible to work in the U.S. Keep both forms. You must also record your employee's Social Security number. If your child doesn't have a number, you must apply for one. In addition, you must have an Employer Identification Number (EIN). If you don't have one, you may obtain it by filing IRS Form SS-4.
- **Every payday:** You'll need to withhold income tax from your child's pay only if exceeds a specified amount (see Section D1, above). You don't have to withhold FICA taxes for children younger than 18. You must withhold income tax and FICA for

your spouse, but not FUTA tax. If the amounts withheld, plus the employer's share of payroll taxes, exceed $2,500 during a calendar quarter, you must deposit the amounts monthly by making federal tax deposits at specified banks or electronically depositing them with the IRS.

- **Every calendar quarter:** If you withhold tax from your child's or spouse's pay, every calendar quarter (every three months starting with January) you must file Form 941, *Employer's Quarterly Federal Tax Return*, with the IRS, showing how much the employee was paid during the quarter and how much tax you withheld and deposited. If you need to deposit less than $2,500 during a calendar quarter, you can make your payment along with the Form 941, instead of paying monthly. Starting in 2006, the IRS will allow employers that deposit less than $2,500 per quarter in payroll taxes to file Form 941 once a year. To qualify, a business will need an on-time payment record for at least two years.

- **Each year:** By January 31 of each year, you must complete and give your employee a copy of IRS Form W-2, *Wage and Tax Statement*, showing how much you paid the employee and how much tax was withheld. You must also file copies with the IRS and Social Security Administration by February 28. You must include IRS Form W-3, *Transmittal of Wage and Tax Statements*, with the copy you file with the Social Security Administration. If your child is exempt from withholding, a new W-4 form must be completed each year.

Need more information on employing family members? IRS Circular E, *Employer's Tax Guide* and Publication 929, *Tax Rules for Children and Dependents*, provide detailed information on these requirements. You can get free copies by calling the IRS at 800-TAX-FORM, by calling or visiting your local IRS office, or by downloading them from the IRS website, www.irs.gov.

4. Employing Yourself

If, like the vast majority of home business owners, you are a sole proprietor, partner in a partnership, or member of a limited liability company (LLC) taxed as a partnership, you are *not* an employee of your business. You are a business owner. However, if you have incorporated your business, whether as a regular C corporation or an S corporation, you are an employee of your corporation if you actively work in the business. In effect, you will be employing yourself. This has important tax consequences.

a. Your Company Must Pay Payroll Taxes

Your incorporated business must treat you just like any other employee for tax purposes. This means it must withhold income and FICA taxes from your pay, and pay half of your FICA tax itself. It must also pay FUTA taxes for you. It gets a tax deduction for its contributions, just like any other employer (see Section B, above). Your corporation—not you personally—must pay these payroll taxes.

You can't avoid these payroll taxes by working for free. The corporation must pay you at least a reasonable salary—what similar companies pay for the same services.

b. Tax Deductions for Your Salary and Benefits

When you're an employee, your incorporated business can deduct your salary as a business expense. However, you will have to pay income tax on your salary, so you won't realize a net tax savings.

But being an employee can have a significant up side. You'll be eligible for all of the tax-advantaged employee benefits discussed in Section B, above. This means that your corporation can provide you with benefits, like health insurance, and deduct the expense (see Chapter 12). If your corporation is a regular C corporation, you won't have to pay income tax on the value of your employee benefits. However, most employees of S corporations must pay tax on their employee benefits, so you probably won't get an overall tax savings. Employees of an S corporation who own less than 2% of the corporate stock don't have to pay tax on benefits, but it's unlikely you'll have this little stock in your own S corporation.

You Can't Deduct Your Draw

If you're a sole proprietor, partner, or LLC member, you do not pay your-self a salary. If you want money from your business, you simply withdraw it from your business bank account. This is called a "draw." Because you are not an employee of your business, your draws are not employee compensation and are not deductible as business expenses.

c.   Your Employee Expenses

You have a couple of options for dealing with expenses you incur while working for your corporation—for example, when you travel on company business.

From a tax standpoint, the best option is to have your corporation reimburse you for your expenses. Whether you've formed a C or an S corporation, the rules regarding reimbursement of employee expenses (discussed in Section C, above) apply to you. If you comply with the requirements for an accountable plan, your corporation gets to deduct the expense and you don't have to count the reimbursement as income to you. If you fail to follow the rules, you must treat any reimbursements as employee income subject to tax.

Another option is simply to pay the expenses yourself and forego reimbursement from your corporation. This is not a good idea, how-ever—as an employee, you may deduct work-related expenses only to the extent they exceed 2% of your adjusted gross income (see Section C3, above).

E.   Tax Deductions When You Hire Independent Contractors

Anyone you hire to help in your home business who does not qualify as an employee is an independent contractor for tax purposes. As far as tax deductions are concerned, hiring independent contractors is very simple. Most of the time, the money you pay to an IC to perform services for your business will be deductible as a business operating expense. These expenses are deductible as long as they are ordinary, necessary, and reasonable in amount.

> **EXAMPLE:** Emily, a graphic designer, hires Don, an attorney, to sue a client who failed to pay her. He collects $5,000 and she pays him $1,500 of this amount. The $1,500 is an ordinary and necessary business operating expense—Emily may deduct it from her business income for the year.

Of course, you get no business deduction if you hire an IC to perform personal services.

> **EXAMPLE:** Emily pays Lawyer Don $2,000 to write her personal will. Because this is a personal expense, Emily cannot deduct the $2,000 from her business income.

If you hire an IC to perform services during the start-up phase of your business, to manufacture inventory, or as part of a long-term asset purchase, you can't deduct payments to the IC as operating expenses. Instead, you must follow the rules to deduct these amounts as start-up expenses, inventory, or long-term assets, respectively. (See Section B, above, for more on this rule.)

1. No Deductions for ICs' Taxes

When you hire an independent contractor, you don't have to withhold or pay any state or federal payroll taxes on the IC's behalf. Therefore, you get no deductions for the IC's taxes; the IC is responsible for paying them.

However, if you pay an unincorporated IC $600 or more during the year for business-related services, you must:

- file IRS Form 1099-MISC, *Miscellaneous Income,* telling the IRS how much you paid the IC, and
- obtain the IC's taxpayer identification number.

The IRS may impose a $100 fine if you fail to file a Form 1099 when required. You could also be subject to more severe penalties if the IRS later audits you and determines that you misclassified the worker.

If you're not sure whether you must file a Form 1099-MISC for a worker, go ahead and file one. You lose nothing by doing so—and you'll save yourself the consequences of failing to file if you were legally required to do so.

Need more information on reporting requirements for ICs? For a detailed discussion of how to file a 1099 form—and the consequences of not filing one—see *Hiring Independent Contractors: The Employer's Legal Guide*, by Stephen Fishman (Nolo).

2.   Paying Independent Contractors' Expenses

Independent contractors often incur expenses while performing services for their clients—for example, for travel, photocopying, phone calls, or materials. Although many ICs want their clients to separately reimburse them for such expenses, it's better for you not to do so. ICs who pay their own expenses are less likely to be viewed as your employees by the IRS or other government agencies. Instead of reimbursing expenses, pay ICs enough so they can cover their own expenses.

However, it's customary in some businesses and professions for the client to reimburse the IC for expenses. For example, a lawyer who handles a business lawsuit will usually seek reimbursement for expenses such as photocopying, court reporters, and travel. If this is the case, you may pay these reimbursements without too much concern about misclassification problems.

When you reimburse an IC for a business-related expense, you get the deduction for the expense, not the IC. You should not include the amount of the reimbursement on the 1099 form you file with the IRS reporting how much you paid the IC, because the reimbursement is not considered income for the IC. Make sure to require ICs to document expenses with receipts and save them in case the IRS questions the payments.

The IRS is particularly suspicious of travel, meal, and entertainment expenses, so special requirements apply to these costs. The rules differ depending on whether the IC provides you with an "adequate accounting."

a.   Adequate Accounting for Travel and Entertainment Expenses

To make an adequate accounting of travel and entertainment expenses, an IC must comply with all the record-keeping rules applicable to business owners and employees. You must document the date, amount, place, and business purpose of the expense, and show the business relationship of the people at a business meal or entertainment event. (See Chapter 7.) You are required to save these records. You may deduct the IC's travel, entertainment, and meal expenses as your own business expenses for these items. (But remember that meal and entertainment expenses are only 50% deductible.) You do not include the amount of the reimbursement you pay the IC on the Form 1099 you file with the IRS reporting how much you paid the IC.

> **EXAMPLE:** Tim, a writer, hires Mary, a self-employed book publicity consultant to help him promote his latest book. In the course of her work, Mary incurs $1,000 in meal and entertainment expenses while meeting potential contacts. She makes an adequate accounting of these expenses and Tim reimburses her the $1,000. Tim may deduct 50% of the $1,000 as a meal and entertainment expense for his business; Mary gets no deduction. When Tim fills out the 1099 form telling the IRS how much he paid Mary, he does not include the $1,000.

b.   No Adequate Accounting for Travel and Entertainment Expenses

If an IC doesn't properly document travel, meal, or entertainment expenses, you do not have to keep records of these items. You may reimburse the IC for the expenses and deduct the full amount as IC payments, provided these expenses are ordinary, necessary, and reasonable in amount. You are not deducting these expenses as travel, meal, or entertainment expenses, so the 50% limit on these deductions does not apply. However, you must include the amount of the reimbursement as income paid to the IC on the IC's 1099 form. Clearly, you are better off if the IC doesn't adequately account for travel, meal, and entertainment expenses; but the IC is worse off because he or she will have to pay tax on the reimbursements.

EXAMPLE: Mary (from the example above) incurs $1,000 in meal and entertainment expenses, but fails to adequately account to Tim. Tim reimburses her the $1,000 anyway. Tim may deduct the full $1,000 as a payment to Mary for her IC services. Tim must include the $1,000 as a payment to Mary when he fills out her 1099 form, and Mary must pay tax on the money. ∎

Chapter 12

Medical Expenses

I f you own a home business or are thinking about starting one, one of the most important problems you face is how you'll pay for your health insurance and other medical expenses. There are at least three possibilities:

- If you have a job that provides health insurance coverage, you can keep it (and your coverage).
- If your spouse has a job that provides health coverage, you can obtain coverage through him or her (one-third of all home business owners obtain their health coverage this way).
- You can purchase your own health insurance.

The last alternative is the most costly, but it will be your only choice if you don't have (or want to keep) your day job, or you don't have the benefit of a spouse's coverage. Fortunately, the tax law provides several deductions intended to help business owners pay their medical expenses. In addition, an entirely new tax-advantaged method of paying for medical expenses is now available: the Health Savings Account.

A. The Personal Deduction for Medical Expenses

All taxpayers—whether or not they own a business—are entitled to a personal income tax deduction for medical and dental expenses for themselves and their dependents. Eligible expenses include both health insurance premiums and out-of-pocket expenses not covered by insurance (see Section D4c, below, for a list of eligible expenses). However, there are two significant limitations on the deduction, which make it difficult to use for most taxpayers.

To take the personal deduction, you must comply with both of the following requirements:

- You must itemize your deductions on IRS Schedule A. (You can itemize deductions only if all of your itemized deductions exceed the standard deduction for the year—$9,700 for joint returns and $4,850 for single returns in 2004.)
- You can deduct only the amount of your medical and dental expenses that exceeds 7.5% of your adjusted gross income (AGI). Your AGI is your net business income and other taxable income, minus deductions for retirement contributions and one-half of your self-employment taxes, plus a few other items (as shown at the bottom of your Form 1040).

EXAMPLE: Al is a self-employed interior decorator whose adjusted gross income for 2004 is $80,000. He pays $350 per month for health insurance for himself and his wife. He spends another $2,000 in out-of-pocket medical and dental expenses for the year. Al may deduct his medical expenses only if all of his itemized deductions exceed the $9,700 standard deductions for the year. If they do exceed the standard deduction, his personal medical expense deduction is limited to the amount he paid that exceeds $6,000 (7.5% x $80,000 = $6,000). Because he paid a total of $6,200 in medical expenses for the year, he may deduct only $200.

As you can see, unless your medical expenses are substantial, the 7.5% limitation eats up most or all of your deduction. The more money you make, the less you can deduct. For this reason, most home business owners need to look elsewhere for meaningful medical expense deductions.

B. Deducting Health Insurance Premiums

Health insurance premiums are the largest medical expense most people pay. There are several ways that home business owners can deduct these premiums.

1. Personal Income Tax Deduction for the Self-Employed

Self-employed people, whether or not they work at home, are allowed to deduct health insurance premiums (including dental and long-term care coverage) for themselves, their spouses, and their dependents. Sole proprietors, partners in partnerships, LLC members, and S Corporation shareholders who own more than 2% of the company stock can use this deduction. Only owners of regular C corporations may not take this deduction. And you get the deduction whether you purchase your health insurance policy as an individual or have your business obtain it for you. However, this is not a business deduction. It is a special personal deduction for the self-employed. The deduction applies to your federal, state, and local income taxes, but not to self-employment taxes.

Self-Employment Tax Primer

Self-employment taxes are the Social Security and Medicare taxes that business owners must pay. They consist of a 12.4% Social Security tax and a 2.9% Medicare tax, for a total tax of 15.3%. You must pay the tax on self-employment income, which is your net income from your business, less deductions for retirement contributions. The Social Security tax is subject to an income ceiling that is adjusted each year for inflation. In 2004, the ceiling was $87,900 in self-employment income. Self-employed people who earn more than the ceiling amount pay only the 2.9% Medicare tax on the excess. If you earn more than the ceiling, deducting your health insurance costs from your self-employment income will not give you a very significant tax savings, because you would have had to pay only a 2.9% tax on that income.

EXAMPLE: Kim is a sole proprietor who pays $10,000 each year for health insurance for herself, her husband, and her three children. Her business earned a $70,000 profit for the year. She may deduct her $10,000 annual health insurance expense from her gross income for federal and state income tax purposes. Her combined federal and state income tax rate is 30%, so she saves $3,000 in income taxes (30% x $10,000 = $3,000). She may not deduct her premiums from her income when she figures her self-employment taxes—in other words, she must pay the 15.3% self-employment tax on her full $70,000 business profit.

a.   Business Income Limitation

There is a significant limitation on the health insurance deduction for the self-employed: You may deduct only as much as you earn from your business. If your business earns no money or incurs a loss, you get no deduction. Thus, if Kim from the above example earned only $3,000 in profit from her business, her self-employed deduction would be limited to that amount; she wouldn't be able to deduct the remaining $7,000 in premiums she paid for the year.

If your business is organized as an S corporation, your deduction is limited to the amount of wages you are paid by your corporation.

b.   No Other Health Insurance Coverage

You may not take the self-employed health insurance deduction if you are eligible to participate in a subsidized health insurance plan maintained by your employer or your spouse's employer. This is so even if the plan requires copayments, or you have to pay additional premiums to obtain all the coverage you need.

> **EXAMPLE:** Rich works as an employee editor at a publishing company and also has a part-time home business. He obtains insurance coverage for himself and his wife through his employer. However, he must pay $500 per month for his wife's coverage. This amount is not deductible under the self-employed health insurance deduction.

This rule applies separately to plans that provide long term care insurance and those that do not. Thus, for example, if your spouse has employer-provided health insurance that does not include long-term care, you may purchase your own long-term care policy and deduct the premiums.

c.   Tax Reporting

Because the self-employed health insurance deduction is a personal deduction, you take this deduction directly on your Form 1040 (it does not go on your Schedule C if you're a sole proprietor). If you itemize your deductions and do not claim 100% of your self-employed health insurance costs on your Form 1040, you may include the rest with your other medical expenses on Schedule A, subject to the 7.5% threshold. You would have to do this, for example, if your health insurance premiums exceed your business income.

2.   Deducting Health Insurance as a Business Expense

You can deduct health insurance costs as a currently deductible business expense if your business pays them on behalf of an employee. The benefit to treating these costs as a business expense is that you can deduct them from your business income for tax purposes. The premiums are an employee fringe benefit and are not taxable income for the employee. Thus, if you are an employee of your business, you can have your business pay your health insurance premiums and then deduct the cost as a business expense, reducing both your income and your self-employment taxes.

> **EXAMPLE:** Mona, a sole proprietor data miner, hires Milt to work as an employee in her business. She pays $250 per month to provide Milt with health insurance. The payments are a business expense that she can deduct from her business income. Milt need not count the value of the insurance as income or pay any tax on it. Mona deducts her $3,000 annual payments for Milt's insurance from her business income for both income tax and self-employment tax purposes. The $3,000 deduction saves her $750 in income taxes (she's in the 25% income tax bracket; 25% x $3,000 = $750). She also saves $459 in self-employment taxes (15.3% x $3,000 = $459).

Unfortunately, if (like the vast majority of home business owners) you are a sole proprietor, partner in a partnership, LLC member, or S corporation shareholder with more than 2% of the company stock, you *cannot* be an employee of your own business for these purposes. Thus, you cannot have your business provide you with health insurance and deduct the cost as a business expense.

a.   Form a C Corporation and Hire Yourself

If you want to convert your own health insurance premiums to a business expense, you must form a C corporation to run your business and have the corporation hire you as its employee. You can do this even if you're running a one-person home business.

As an employee of a C corporation, your corporation must pay you a salary, as well as the employer's share of Social Security and Medicare taxes. Your corporation deducts your health insurance premiums from its taxes—you don't deduct them from your personal taxes. Because you own the corporation, you get the benefit of the deduction.

There are disadvantages to incorporating, however: Incorporating costs money, you'll have to comply with more burdensome bookkeeping requirements, and you will have a more complex tax return. You'll also have to pay state and federal unemployment taxes for yourself—a tax you don't have to pay if you're not an employee of your business. And, depending on your state's requirements, you may have to provide yourself with workers' compensation coverage.

Because your health insurance is 100% deductible from your income taxes, it may not be worthwhile to incorporate just to save on Social Security and Medicare taxes. This is particularly true if your employee income would substantially exceed the 12.4% Social Security tax ceiling—$87,900 in 2004. If you're in this situation, think about obtaining a Health Savings Account instead (see Section D, below).

Disability Insurance

Disability insurance pays a monthly benefit to employees who are unable to work due to sickness or injury. You may provide disability Insurance as an employee benefit to your workers, including your spouse, and deduct the premiums as a business expense. If your business is a C corporation, it may deduct disability payments made for you, its employee. However, any employees who collect disability benefits must include them in their taxable income.

b. Employing Your Spouse

If, like 90% of home business owners, you're a sole proprietor (or have formed a C corporation to run your business), there's another way you can deduct health insurance costs as a business expense: Hire your spouse to work in your business as an employee and provide him or her with health insurance. The policy can cover your spouse, you, your children, and other dependents as well (your spouse should be the primary insured, however). Then you can deduct the cost of the health insurance as a business expense.

> **EXAMPLE:** Joe, a successful home-based financial consultant, hires his wife, Martha, to work as his employee assistant. He pays her $25,000 per year and provides her with a health insurance policy covering both of them and their two children. The annual policy premiums are $5,000. Joe may deduct the $5,000 as a business expense for his consulting practice, listing it as an expense on his Schedule C. He may deduct the $5,000 not only from his $80,000 income for income tax purposes, but also from his self-employment income. His federal and state income tax rate is 40%, so he saves $2,000 in income tax. The self-employment tax is a 15.3% tax (up to the Social Security tax ceiling—$87,900 in 2004), so Joe saves $765 in self-employment taxes.

There are a couple of catches to this deduction. Only sole proprietors and C corporations can use this method—it doesn't work if you have a partnership, LLC, or an S corporation. In addition, your spouse must be a bona fide employee. In other words, he or she must do real work in your business, you must pay applicable payroll taxes, and you must otherwise treat your spouse like any other employee. (See Chapter 11 for a detailed discussion of your obligations to workers.)

You'll probably want to pay your spouse as low a salary as possible, because both of you will have to pay Social Security and Medicare taxes on that salary (but not on employee benefits like health insurance and medical expense reimbursements). You should, however, regularly pay your spouse at least some cash wages or the IRS could claim that your spouse is not a real employee. However, you can make the cash wages a relatively small part of your spouse's total compensation—wages plus fringe benefits like your medical reimbursement plan.

> **EXAMPLE:** Tina's husband, Tim, works part-time as a helper in her home-based wedding photography business. She provides Tim, her employee, with health insurance coverage that covers him and his

family (including Tina) and a medical reimbursement plan to pay for uninsured medical expenses. The reasonable value of his services this year is about $6,000. The value of Tim's fringe benefits—his health insurance and medical reimbursements—is $5,000. Tina should pay Tim at least $1,000 in employee salary. Tina and Tim must pay a 15.3% tax on his $1,000 in wages. But Tina gets to deduct the wages and the $5,000 in health insurance and medical reimbursement costs as a business expense. This saves her (and Tim) $2,000 in federal and state taxes for the year.

Of course, if you're single, you won't be able to hire a spouse to take advantage of this method for turning health insurance costs into a business expense. However, if you're a single parent, you could hire your child and deduct the cost of your child's health insurance as a business expense. But your child's policy cannot cover you or other family members.

C. Medical Reimbursement Plans

Health insurance usually doesn't cover all of your medical expenses. For example, it doesn't cover preexisting conditions, or deductibles or copayments—that is, amounts you must pay yourself before your insurance coverage kicks in. Many costs aren't covered by insurance at all, including ongoing physical therapy, fertility treatment, and optometric care. As a result, the average American pays about $900 a year in out-of-pocket health-related expenses. One way to deduct these expenses is to establish a medical reimbursement plan. Another way is to use a Health Savings Account (see Section D, below).

Few home business owners take advantage of medical reimbursement plans. But you should definitely consider adopting one if you must obtain your own health insurance coverage, are married, and need or want your spouse to work as an employee in your home business. The potential tax benefits are substantial.

1.   What Is a Medical Reimbursement Plan?

A medical reimbursement plan is an arrangement under which an employer reimburses its employees for uninsured health or dental expenses. These plans are usually self-funded—that is, the employer pays the expenses out of its own pocket, not through insurance.

Why would an employer do this? One good reason is that the reimbursements are deductible business expenses for the employer. Also, the employee doesn't have to include the reimbursements as taxable income (as long as the employee has not taken a deduction for these amounts as a personal medical expense).

So how does this help you? Again, your spouse (if you have one) comes to the rescue. You can hire your spouse as your employee and provide him or her with a medical reimbursement plan. The plan may cover not only your spouse, but also you, your children, and other dependents. This allows your business to reimburse you and your family for out-of-pocket medical expenses and deduct the amounts as a business expense. And you don't have to include the reimbursements in your own taxable income. The IRS has ruled that this is perfectly legal. (Tax Advice Memo 9409006—see Chapter 18 for information on finding tax advice memoranda and other tax authorities).

> **EXAMPLE:** Jennifer has her own home-based public relations business. She hires her husband Paul to work as her employee assistant. She establishes a medical reimbursement plan covering Paul, her, and their young child. During the year, Paul spends $4,000 for family medical expenses not covered by their insurance. Jennifer reimburses Paul for the $4,000 as provided by their plan. Jennifer may deduct the $4,000 from her business income for the year, which means that she won't have to pay income or self-employment taxes on it. Paul need not include the $4,000 in his income—it's tax free to him. The $4,000 deduction saves Jennifer and Paul $1,600 in taxes for the year.

Lawyer's Wife Is Not Really an Employee

Mr. Haeder, a sole proprietor attorney who practiced law from his home, claimed that he hired his wife as his employee to answer the telephone, greet visitors, type legal papers, and clean his office. Mrs. Haeder had no employment contract or set work schedule, did not keep track of her hours, and did not directly or regularly receive a salary. Instead, Mr. Haeder paid her the maximum amount she could deduct as an IRA contribution. Annually, he transferred money in his brokerage account to an IRA in his wife's name. For all but one of the years eventually audited by the IRS, no W-2 was issued to Mrs. Haeder. Mr. Haeder sponsored a medical reimbursement plan that covered out-of-pocket expenses for his wife, her children, and her spouse—that is, himself. Mrs. Haeder submitted bills for out-of-pocket medical expenses to her husband, which he reimbursed and attempted to deduct as business expenses. The IRS determined Mr. Haeder was not entitled to deduct the reimbursements under the medical reimbursement plan because Mrs. Haeder was not a bona fide employee. The tax court agreed, finding that there was no credible evidence that Mrs. Haeder performed any services other than those reasonably expected of a family member. (*Haeder v. Comm'r.*, T.C. Memo 2001-7 (2001).)

The medical expense reimbursement plan deduction is available only to your employees, not to you (the business owner). The only way you can qualify as an employee is if your business is a C corporation (see Section B2, above). If you don't have a spouse to employ, you could employ your child and provide him or her with a reimbursement plan. But the plan may not cover you or any other family members.

2.   What Expenses May Be Reimbursed?

One of the great things about medical reimbursement plans is that they can be used to reimburse employees for a wide variety of health-related expenses. Deductible medical expenses include any expense for the diagnosis, cure, mitigation, treatment, or prevention of disease; or any expense paid to affect the structure or function of the human body. (IRS Reg. 1.213.1(e).)

This includes, of course, health insurance deductibles and copayments. But it also includes expenses for acupuncture, chiropractors, eyeglasses and contact lenses, dental treatment, laser eye surgery, psychiatric care, and treatment for learning disabilities. (See Section D4, below, for a list of expenses that can and cannot be deducted.) You can draft your plan to include only those expenses you wish to reimburse. Presumably, though, you'd want to include as many expenses as possible if the plan covers only your spouse, yourself, and your family.

In addition, the IRS ruled in 2003 that a medical expense reimbursement plan may include reimbursements for employee expenses for nonprescription medicines and drugs. (Rev. Rul. 2003-102.) Any over-the-counter drug or medicine is covered except for dietary supplements and other items that are used only for general health, not for specific medical problems. Thus, for example, reimbursements may be provided for nonprescription antacids, allergy medicines, pain relievers, and cold medicines. So, if you have a medical reimbursement plan, you can even take a tax deduction for aspirin! (You can't deduct nonprescription drugs under the personal medical expense deduction discussed in Section A.)

3. Plan Requirements

If you decide to adopt a medical expense reimbursement plan, the plan must be in writing, it may not discriminate in favor of highly compensated employees, and it must reimburse employees only for medical expenses that are not paid for by insurance.

The nondiscrimination rule will affect you only if you have employees other than your spouse or children. If you do, a medical reimbursement plan may be too expensive for you, because you'll have to provide coverage to nonfamily members as well. A plan is nondiscriminatory under IRS rules if it:

- covers at least 70% of all employees
- covers at least 80% of all employees eligible to benefit from the plan, provided that 70% or more of all employees are eligible, or
- is found to be nondiscriminatory by the IRS based on the facts and circumstances.

However, the plan may exclude employees who:
- work fewer than 25 hours a week
- are not yet 25 years old
- work for you fewer than seven months in a year, or
- have worked for you less than three years.

EXAMPLE: Jim employs six people in his home-based crafts company. One works only 20 hours per week, while the other five work full-time. To be nondiscriminatory, Jim's medical expense reimbursement plan must cover 80% of his five employees eligible to participate—in other words, he must cover four of his five full-time employees.

If a plan is found to be discriminatory by the IRS, all or part of the medical benefits paid to highly compensated employees under the plan will be taxable to the employee. Highly compensated employees include:
- anyone among the top 25% highest paid employees
- the five highest paid corporate officers (if your business is incorporated), and
- shareholders who own more than 10% of the corporation stock.

4. How to Establish a Plan

If a medical expense reimbursement plan sounds attractive to you, you should establish one as early in the year as possible because it applies only to medical expenses incurred *after* the date the plan is adopted. (Rev. Rul. 2002-58.) Forget about using a plan to reimburse your spouse or yourself for expenses you have already incurred.

A written medical reimbursement plan must be drawn up and adopted by your business. If your business is incorporated, the plan should be adopted by a corporate resolution approved by the corporation's board of directors. You can find a form for this purpose in *The Corporate Minutes Book*, by Anthony Mancuso (Nolo).

You should require your spouse to periodically submit medical expenses for reimbursement—for example, monthly, quarterly, or at least twice a year. Reimburse your spouse by check, never cash. The checks should be drawn from your business checking account. Make a notation on the check that the payment is being made pursuant to your medical reimbursement plan. Keep copies of your family's medical expense receipts to show that you didn't reimburse your spouse too much and that the payments were for legitimate medical expenses.

5. Sample Plan

A sample medical expense reimbursement plan is provided below. To fill in the blanks, you will need to decide:

- whether to place a limit on the dollar amount of the annual reimbursements you'll make—if your spouse is your only employee, you probably will not want a limit (but if you have other employees, you probably will), and
- how often the employee will submit claims for reimbursement— twice a year is fine, but you might prefer a more frequent schedule.

D. Health Savings Accounts

On January 1, 2004, a new era in health insurance began with the inauguration of the Health Savings Account (HSA). HSAs represent the most radical change in health care financing in the last 50 years and can be a real boon for many home business owners.

Need more information on Health Savings Accounts? The IRS has set up an email address at hsainfo@do.treas.gov, and a voice mailbox at 202-622-4HSA, to answer questions about HSAs. You can also find HSA information on the IRS website at www.irs.gov/formspubs/article/ 0,,id=109876,00.html#hsa_2004. An informative private website is www.hsainsider.com.

1. What Are Health Savings Accounts?

The HSA concept is very simple: Instead of relying on health insurance to pay small or routine medical expenses, you pay them yourself. To help you do this, you establish a Health Savings Account with a health

Medical Expense Reimbursement Plan

Effective _____[date], _____[your business name] ("Employer") will reimburse all eligible employees for medical expenses incurred by themselves and their dependents, subject to the conditions and limitations set forth below.

1. Uninsured Expenses

Employer will reimburse eligible employees and their dependents only for medical expenses that are not covered by health or accident insurance.

2. Medical Expenses Defined

Medical expenses are those expenses defined by Internal Revenue Code Sec. 213(d). They consist of any expense for the diagnosis, cure, mitigation, treatment, or prevention of disease; or any expense paid to affect the structure or function of the human body. Medical expenses include both prescription and nonprescription drugs and medicines.

3. Dependent Defined

Dependent is defined by IRC Sec. 152. It includes any member of an eligible employee's family for whom the employee and his or her spouse provides more than half of the financial support.

4. Eligibility

The Plan shall be open to all employees who:
- work more than 25 hours per week
- are at least 25 years of age, and
- have completed three years of service with Employer.

At its option, Employer may cover any employee who doesn't meet the above requirements.

5. Limitation (*Optional*)

Employer shall reimburse any eligible employee no more than _____ [dollar amount] in any calendar year for medical expenses.

6. Submission of Claims

Any eligible employee seeking reimbursement under this Plan shall submit to Employer, [monthly], [quarterly], or [at least twice a year] (choose one) on _____ [date] and _____ [date], all bills for medical care, including those for accident or health insurance. Such bills and other claims for reimbursement shall be verified by Employer prior to reimbursement. Employer, in its sole discretion, may terminate the employee's right to reimbursement if the employee fails to comply.

7. Direct Payments

At its option, Employer may pay all or part of a covered employee's medical expenses directly, instead of making reimbursements to the employee. Such a direct payment shall relieve Employer of all further liability for the expense.

8. Termination

Employer may terminate this Plan at any time. Medical expenses incurred prior to the date of termination shall be reimbursed by Employer. Employer is under no obligation to provide advance notice of termination.

9. Benefits Not Taxable

Employer intends that the benefits under this Plan shall qualify under IRC Sec. 105 so as to be excludable from the gross income of the employees covered by the Plan.

Employer's Signature: _____

Date: _____

Employee's Signature: _____

Date: _____

insurance company, bank, or other financial institution. Your contributions to the account are tax deductible and you don't have to pay tax on the interest or other money you earn on the money in your account. You can withdraw the money in your HSA to pay almost any kind of health-related expense, and you don't have to pay any tax on these withdrawals.

In case you or a family member develops a serious health problem, you must also obtain a health insurance policy with a high deductible— at least $1,000 for individuals and $2,000 for families. You can use the money in your HSA to pay this large deductible and any copayments you're required to make.

Using an HSA can save you money in two ways:

- you'll get a tax deduction for the money you deposit in your account, and
- the premiums for your high-deductible health insurance policy should be much less than those for traditional comprehensive coverage policies or HMO coverage (you may save as much as 40%).

2. Establishing Your HSA

To participate in the HSA program, you need two things:

- a high-deductible health plan that qualifies under the HSA rules, and
- an HSA account.

a. HSA-Qualified Plans

You can't have an HSA if you're covered by health insurance other than a high-deductible HSA plan—for example, if your spouse has family coverage for you from his or her job. So you may have to change your existing coverage to qualify for an HSA. In addition, people eligible to receive Medicare may not participate in the HSA program.

You need to obtain a bare-bones high deductible health plan that meets the HSA criteria (is "HSA-qualified"). You may obtain coverage from an HMO, PPO, or traditional plan. If the coverage is for yourself only, your plan must have a $1,000 minimum annual deductible. If the coverage is for yourself and your family, your plan must have a $2,000 minimum deductible.

If you get an HSA for your family, the deductible must apply to the whole family, not to each family member separately. With such a per-family deductible, expenses incurred by each family member accumulate and are credited towards the family deductible—for example, a family of four would meet the $2,000 deductible if each family member paid $500 during the year (4 x $500 = $2,000). The family deductible is a unique feature of the HSA program.

You can have a deductible that is larger than the minimum amount if you wish. However, keep in mind that there are limits on how much money you can contribute to your HSA account each year. To be on the safe side, you don't want your deductible to exceed these limits, or your account may not have enough money in it to cover the deductible if you become seriously ill—particularly if you develop a chronic illness that will require payments year after year. In 2004, the maximum annual contribution to an HSA is $2,250 for individuals and $4,500 for families. These amounts will be adjusted each year for inflation.

Special Rule for Preventative Care

A special rule permits high-deductible health plans to provide coverage for preventative health care without the insured first satisfying the minimum annual deductible. Preventative care includes, but is not limited to:

- periodic health evaluations, including tests and diagnostic procedures ordered in connection with routine examinations, such as annual physicals
- routine prenatal and well-child care
- child and adult immunizations
- tobacco cessation programs
- obesity weight-loss programs, and
- health screening services. (IRS Notice 2004-23.)

For example, your plan can pay for your annual physical even though you have not met the annual deductible. Insurers are not required to provide such coverage, however.

Your plan must also have a cap on the annual out-of-pocket payments you can be required to make each year. Out-of-pocket payments include deductibles, copayments, and other amounts (other than insurance premiums) you must pay for covered benefits under your health plan. As you can see from the following chart, the maximum annual out-of-pocket payments that your insurer can require are $5,000 for individuals and $10,000 for families.

HSA Deductibles and Out-of-Pocket Caps		
Type of Coverage	Minimum Annual Deductible	Maximum Annual Out-of-Pocket Payments
Self-only	$1,000	$5,000
Family	$2,000	$10,000

In addition, your health insurance plan must be "HSA-qualified." To become qualified, the insurer must agree to participate in the HSA program and give the roster of enrolled participants to the IRS. If your insurer fails to report to the IRS that you are enrolled in an HSA-qualified insurance plan, the IRS will not permit you to deduct your HSA contributions.

HSA-qualified health insurance policies will be clearly labeled as such on the cover page or declaration page of the policy. It might be possible to convert a high-deductible health insurance policy you already have to an HSA-qualified health insurance policy; ask your health insurer for details.

You'll be able to obtain an HSA-qualified health plan from health insurers that decide to participate in the program. Experts anticipate that many will participate. One way to find participating health insurers is to do an Internet search—use the search terms "Health Savings Account" and "HSA" on an Internet search engine such as Google. Several websites provide detailed information about HSAs—for example, www.healthsavingsaccount-hsa.com. You can also contact your present health insurer to find out if it offers an HSA-qualified plan.

The premiums you pay for an HSA-qualified health plan are deductible to the same extent as any other health insurance premiums. This means that, if you're self-employed, you may deduct your entire premium from your federal income tax as a special personal deduction. (See Section B1, above.)

b.   HSA Account

Once you have an HSA-qualified health insurance policy, you may open your HSA account. You must establish your HSA with a trustee. The HSA trustee keeps track of your deposits and withdrawals, produces annual statements, and reports your HSA deposits to the IRS.

Any person, insurance company, bank, or financial institution already approved by the IRS to be a trustee or custodian of an IRA is automatically approved to serve as an HSA trustee. Others may apply for approval under IRS procedures for HSAs.

It's expected that health insurers will typically administer both the health plan and the HSA. However, you don't have to have your HSA administered by your insurer. You'll also be able to establish an HSA with banks, insurance companies, mutual funds, or other financial institutions offering HSA products.

Whoever administers your account will usually give you a checkbook or debit card to use to withdraw funds from the account. You can also make withdrawals by mail or in person.

Look at the plans offered by several companies to see which offers the best deal. Compare the fees charged to set up the account, as well as any other charges (some companies may charge an annual service fee, for example). Ask about special promotions and discounts, and find out how the account is invested.

c.   HSA Benefits May Be Retroactive for 2004

HSAs are just getting off the ground. Not all insurers offer them, and many people have been unable to locate HSA trustees or custodians. Recognizing this, IRS rules allow your insurer to reimburse you for expenses incurred after January 1, 2004, as long as you establish your HSA by April 15, 2005 (assuming you were eligible to participate in the HSA program in 2004). (IRS Notice 2004-25.) Insurers are not required to do this, however; be sure to ask about it when you choose your HSA insurer.

3.   Making Contributions to Your HSA

Once you set up your HSA-qualified health plan and HSA account, you can start making contributions to your account. There is no minimum amount you are required to contribute each year; you may contribute nothing if you wish. But there are maximum limits on how much you may contribute each year:

- If you have individual coverage, the maximum you may contribute to your HSA each year is the amount of your annual deductible or $2,250, whichever is *less*.
- If you have family coverage, the maximum you may contribute to your HSA each year is the amount of your annual deductible or $4,500, whichever is *less*.

These maximums will be adjusted for inflation each year.

> **EXAMPLE 1:** Elvira has an individual HSA-qualified policy with a $1,500 deductible. She may contribute up to $1,500 each year to her HSA account.

> **EXAMPLE 2:** Jim has a family health policy with a $5,000 deductible. He may contribute up to $4,500 each year.

a.   Catch-Up Contributions

Individuals who are 55 to 65 years old have the option of making additional tax-free catch-up contributions to their HSA accounts of up to $500 in 2004, gradually increasing to $1,000 by 2009. This rule is intended to compensate for the fact that older folks won't have as many years to fund their accounts as younger taxpayers. If you're in this age group, it's wise to make these contributions if you can afford them, so your HSA account will have enough money to pay for future health expenses.

Year	Maximum Annual Catch-Up Contribution
2004	$500
2005	$600
2006	$700
2007	$800
2008	$900
2009 and later	$1,000

b.   Deducting HSA Contributions

The amounts you contribute each year to your HSA account, up to the annual limit, are deductible from your federal income taxes. This is a personal deduction you take on the first page of your IRS Form 1040. You deduct it from your gross income, just like a business deduction. This means you get the full deduction, whether or not you itemize your personal deductions.

> **EXAMPLE:** Martin, a self-employed blacksmith, establishes an HSA for himself and his family with a $2,000 deductible. Every year, he contributes the maximum amount to his HSA account—$2,000. Because he is in the 25% federal income tax bracket, this saves him $500 in federal income tax each year.

c.   Where To Invest Your HSA Contributions

The contributions you make to your HSA account may be invested just like IRA contributions. You can invest in almost anything—money market accounts, bank certificates of deposit, stocks, bonds, mutual funds, Treasury bills, and notes. However, you can't invest in collectibles such as art, antiques, postage stamps, or other personal property. Most HSA funds will likely be invested in money market accounts and certificates of deposit.

Every year, you may roll over up to $500 of unused funds in your HSA into an Individual Retirement Account (IRA), without paying tax on the money.

4. Withdrawing HSA Funds

If you or a family member needs health care, you can withdraw money from your HSA to pay your deductible or any other medical expenses. You pay no federal tax on HSA withdrawals used to pay qualified medical expenses. Qualified medical expenses are broadly defined to include many types of expenses ordinarily not covered by health insurance—for example, dental or optometric care. This is one of the great advantages of the HSA program over traditional health insurance.

a. No Approval Required

HSA participants don't have to obtain advance approval from their HSA trustee (whether their insurer or someone else) that an expense is a qualified medical expense before they withdraw funds from their accounts. You make that determination yourself. You should keep records of your medical expenses to show that your withdrawals were for qualified medical expenses and are therefore excludable from your gross income.

> **EXAMPLE:** Jane, a home-based consultant and single mother, obtains family health insurance coverage with a $2,000 deductible. She sets up an HSA at her bank and deposits $2,000 every year for three years. She deducts each contribution from her gross income for the year for income tax purposes. Jane pays no taxes on the interest she earns on the money in her account, which is invested in a money market fund. By the end of three years, she has $6,600 in the account. Jane becomes ill after the third year and is hospitalized. She withdraws $2,000 from her HSA to pay her deductible. She also withdraws $3,000 to pay for speech therapy for her son, which is not covered by her health insurance. She pays no federal tax on these withdrawals.

However, you may not use HSA funds to purchase nonprescription medications. The only way to deduct these is to hire your spouse and establish a medical reimbursement plan. (See Section C, above.)

b.   Tax-Free Withdrawals

If you withdraw funds from your HSA to use for something other than qualified medical expenses, you must pay regular income tax on the withdrawal plus a 10% penalty. For example, if you were in the 25% federal income tax bracket, you'd have to pay a 35% tax on your nonqualified withdrawals.

Once you reach the age of 65 or become disabled, you can withdraw your HSA funds for any reason without penalty. If you use the money for nonmedical expenses, you will have to pay regular income tax on the withdrawals. When you die, the money in your HSA account is transferred to the beneficiary you've named for the account. The transfer is tax free if the beneficiary is your surviving spouse. Other transfers are taxable.

If you elect to leave the HSA program, you can keep your HSA account and withdraw money from it tax free for health care expenses. However, you won't be able to make any additional contributions to the account.

c.   What HSA Funds Can Be Used For

Ordinarily, you may not use HSA funds to purchase health insurance. However, there are three exceptions to this general rule. You can use HSA funds to pay for:

- a health plan during any period of continuation coverage required under any federal law—for example, when you are terminated from your job and purchase continuing health insurance coverage from your employer's health insurer, which the insurer is legally required to make available to you under COBRA
- long-term health care insurance, or
- health insurance premiums you pay while you are receiving unemployment compensation.

You can use HSA funds to pay for the following:

- abdominal supports
- abortion
- acupuncture
- air conditioner (when necessary for relief from an allergy or for difficulty in breathing)

- alcoholism treatment
- ambulance
- arch supports
- artificial limbs
- birth control pills (by prescription)
- blood tests
- blood transfusions
- braces
- breast reconstruction surgery
- cardiographs
- chiropractor
- Christian Science Practitioner
- contact lenses
- contraceptive devices (by prescription)
- convalescent home (for medical treatment only)
- crutches
- dental treatment
- dentures
- dermatologist
- diagnostic fees
- diathermy
- drug addiction therapy
- elastic hosiery (by prescription)
- eyeglasses
- fees paid to health institute prescribed by a doctor
- fertility treatment
- fluoridation unit
- guide dog
- healing services
- hearing aids and batteries
- hospital bills
- hydrotherapy
- insulin treatments
- lab tests
- laser eye surgery
- lead paint removal
- legal fees to authorize treatment for mental illness

- lodging while away from home for outpatient care
- medical conference expenses (only if the conference concerns the chronic illness of yourself, your spouse, or a dependent)
- metabolism tests
- neurologist
- nursing (including board and meals)
- nursing home
- obstetrician
- operating room costs
- ophthalmologist
- optician
- optometrist
- oral surgery
- organ transplant (including donor's expenses)
- orthopedic shoes
- orthopedist
- osteopath
- oxygen and oxygen equipment
- pediatrician
- physician
- physiotherapist
- podiatrist
- postnatal treatments
- practical nurse for medical services
- prenatal care
- prescription medicines
- psychiatrist
- psychoanalyst
- psychologist
- radium therapy
- sex therapy
- special education costs for the handicapped
- splints
- sterilization
- stop-smoking programs (not including nonprescription drugs)
- surgeon
- telephone or TV equipment to assist the hard-of-hearing

- therapy equipment
- transportation expenses to obtain health care
- ultraviolet ray treatment
- vaccines
- vitamins (if prescribed)
- weight-loss program (only as a treatment for a specific disease diagnosed by a doctor, such as obesity; the cost of reduced calorie foods is not deductible)
- wheelchair, and
- x-rays.

HSA funds cannot be used to pay for the following health-related expenses:

- advance payment for services to be rendered the following year
- athletic club membership
- bottled water
- childcare for a healthy child
- commuting expenses of a disabled person
- cosmetic surgery and procedures
- cosmetics, hygiene products, and similar items
- diaper service
- domestic help
- funeral, cremation, or burial expenses
- health programs offered by resort hotels, health clubs, and gyms
- illegal operations and treatments
- illegally procured drugs
- maternity clothes
- nutritional supplements (unless recommended by a medical practitioner to treat a specific illness diagnosed by a doctor)
- nonprescription medication
- premiums for life insurance, income protection, disability, loss of limbs or sight, or similar benefits
- Scientology counseling
- social activities
- specially designed car for the handicapped (other than an autoette) or special equipment
- swimming pool or swimming lessons
- travel for general health improvement

- tuition and travel expenses to send a child to a particular school, or
- veterinary fees.

5.   Are HSAs a Good Deal?

Should you get an HSA? It depends. HSAs are a very good deal if you're young or in good health, and you don't go to the doctor often or take many expensive medications. You can purchase a health plan with a high deductible, pay substantially lower premiums, and have the security of knowing that you can dip into your HSA if you get sick and have to pay the deductible or other uncovered medical expenses.

If you don't tap into the money, it will keep accumulating free of taxes. You also get the benefit of deducting your HSA contributions from your income taxes. And you can use your HSA funds to pay for many health-related expenses that aren't covered by traditional health insurance.

If you enjoy good health while you have your HSA, you may end up with a substantial amount in your account that you can withdraw without penalty for any purpose once you turn 65. Unlike all other existing tax-advantaged savings or retirement accounts, HSAs provide a tax break when funds are deposited *and* when they are withdrawn. No other account provides both a "front end" and "back end" tax break. With IRAs, for example, you must pay tax either when you deposit or when you withdraw your money. This feature can make your HSA an extremely lucrative tax shelter—a kind of super IRA.

On the other hand, HSAs are not for everybody. You'll probably be better off with traditional comprehensive health insurance if your health care expenses usually exceed $2,000 per year ($1,000 if you don't have a family). In addition, depending on your medical history and where you live, the cost of an HSA-qualified health plan may be too high to make the program cost-effective for you.

Comparing Health Costs for a Typical Family

The Joneses are a family of three whose health care costs are equal to the national average. They pay $650 per month for traditional health insurance. Their policy has a $500 per person deductible and an out-of-pocket expense cap of $1,500. They incur $1,200 in uninsured medical and dental expenses each year.

Let's compare their annual health expenses if they switch to an HSA-qualified insurance plan with a $4,500 family deductible. Let's assume their high-deductible policy costs $400 per month and they put the $250 they save on insurance premiums each month into their HSA account. They use the money in their HSA account to pay their annual $1,200 in uninsured health expenses. Let's also assume that the breadwinner in this family is self-employed and qualifies for the self-employed health insurance deduction and that the family is in the 25% federal income tax bracket.

	Traditional Health Plan	HSA Health Plan
Annual health insurance premiums	$7,800	$4,800
Annual HSA contribution	0	3,000
Annual amount spent on uninsured health costs	1,200	1,200
Total annual expenses	9,000	9,000
HSA account balance on December 31	0	1,800
Tax savings from HSA contribution	0	750
Tax savings from self-employed health insurance deduction	1,950	1,200
Net cost	$7,050	$5,250

6.   HSAs for Employees

Employers may provide HSAs to their employees. Any business, no matter how small, may participate in the HSA program. The employer purchases an HSA-qualified health plan for its employees, who establish their own individual HSA accounts. The employer may pay all or part of its employees' insurance premiums and make contributions to their HSA accounts. Employees may also make their own contributions to their individual accounts. The combined annual contributions of the employer and employee may not exceed the limits listed in Section D3, above.

HSAs are portable when an employee changes employers. Contributions and earnings belong to the account holder, not the employer. Employers are required to report amounts contributed to an HSA on the employee's Form W-2.

Health insurance payments and HSA contributions made by a business on behalf of its employees are currently deductible business expenses. The employees do not have to report employer contributions to their HSA accounts as income.

a.   Hiring Your Spouse

If you're a sole proprietor or have formed a regular C corporation, you may hire your spouse as your employee and have your business pay for an HSA-qualified family health plan for your spouse, you, and your children and other dependents. Your spouse then establishes an HSA, which your business may fully fund each year. The money your business spends for your spouse's health insurance premiums and to fund the HSA is a fully deductible business expense. This allows you to reduce both your income and self-employment taxes. (See Section B1, above.)

b.   Nondiscrimination Rules

If you have employees other than your spouse or other family members, you'll need to comply with nondiscrimination rules—that is, you'll have to make comparable HSA contributions for all employees with HSA-qualified health coverage during the year. Contributions are considered comparable if they are either of the same amount or the same percentage of the deductible under the plan. The rule is applied separately to employees who work fewer than 30 hours per week. Employers who do not comply with these nondiscrimination rules are subject to a 35% excise tax.

Archer Medical Savings Accounts

Starting in 1997, Congress began a pilot program that allowed self-employed people and companies with up to 50 employees to establish Archer Medical Savings Accounts (MSAs). Archer MSAs were very similar to HSAs; they were a way for Congress to try out the health savings account concept. However, very few self-employed people and businesses elected to establish MSAs—fewer than 70,000 were created during the seven years the program was in place.

If you are one of the few with an Archer MSA, you may roll it over into an HSA without paying taxes on the money. Ask your insurer or Archer MSA trustee about this. Although not required, it's a good idea to do this because HSAs offer more advantages than Archer MSAs: You may contribute more each year to an HSA, your annual deductible doesn't have to be as high, HSAs are portable, and both employees and employers may make contributions to HSAs.

7.   Tax Reporting for HSAs

You'll need to report to the IRS how much you deposit to and withdraw from your HSA each year. The IRS will establish a special tax form for this purpose (it was not available as this book went to press; check www.irs.gov for the latest information). You'll also have to keep a record of the name and address of each person or company you pay with funds from your HSA. ■

Retirement Deductions

When you own your own business, it's up to you to establish and fund your own pension plan to supplement the Social Security benefits you'll receive when you retire. The tax law helps you do this by providing tax deductions and other income tax benefits for your retirement account contributions and earnings.

This chapter provides a general overview of the retirement plan choices you have as a small business owner. Deciding what type of account to establish is just as important as deciding how to invest your money once you open your account—if not more so. Once you set up your retirement account, you can always change your investments within the account with little or no difficulty. But changing the type of retirement account you have may prove difficult and costly. So it's best to spend some time up front learning about your choices and deciding which type of plan will best meet your needs.

Need detailed information on retirement plans? For a thorough discussion of retirement plans for self-employed people, see *Creating Your Own Retirement Plan: IRAs and Keoghs for the Self-Employed*, by Twila Slesnick and John Suttle (Nolo). For additional information on the tax aspects of retirement, check out these IRS guides (both are available from the IRS website, at www.irs.gov):
  • IRS Publication 560, *Retirement Plans for the Small Business*, and
  • IRS Publication 590, *Individual Retirement Arrangements*.
Two easy-to-understand guides on retirement investing are:
  • *Get a Life: You Don't Need a Million to Retire Well*, by Ralph Warner (Nolo), and
  • *Investing for Dummies*, by Eric Tyson (IDG Books).

Get professional help if you have employees (other than your spouse). Having employees makes it much more complicated to set up a retirement plan (see "Having Employees Complicates Matters Tremendously," in Section A, below). Because of the many complex issues that come up when you have employees, any business owner with employees should turn to a professional consultant for help in choosing, establishing, and administering a retirement plan.

A. Why You Need a Retirement Plan (or Plans)

In all likelihood, you will receive Social Security benefits when you retire. However, Social Security will probably cover only half of your needs when you retire—possibly less depending upon your retirement lifestyle. You'll need to make up this shortfall with your own retirement investments.

When it comes to saving for retirement, small business owners are better off than employees of most companies. This is because the federal government has created several types of retirement accounts specifically designed for small business owners. These accounts provide enormous tax benefits that are intended to maximize the amount of money you can save during your working years for your retirement years. The amount you are allowed to contribute each year to your retirement account depends upon the type of account you establish and how much money you earn. If your business doesn't earn money, you won't be able to make any contributions—you must have income to fund retirement accounts.

The two biggest benefits that most of these plans provide—tax deductions for plan contributions and tax deferral on investment earnings —are discussed in more detail below.

How Much Money Will You Need When You Retire?

The amount of money you'll need to live on when you retire depends on many factors, including your lifestyle. You could need anywhere from 50% to 100% of the amount you were earning while you were employed. On average, retirees need about 70% to 80% of their pre-retirement earnings.

1. Tax Deduction

Retirement accounts that comply with IRS requirements are called "tax qualified." You can deduct the amount you contribute to a tax-qualified retirement account from your income taxes (except for Roth IRAs—see

Section B2, below). If you are a sole proprietor, partner in a partnership, or an LLC member, you can deduct from your personal income all contributions you make to a retirement account. If you have incorporated your business, the corporation can deduct as a business expense contributions that it makes on your behalf. Either way, you or your business get a substantial income tax savings.

> **EXAMPLE:** Art, a sole proprietor, contributes $10,000 this year to a qualified retirement account. He can deduct the entire amount from his personal income taxes. Because Art is in the 28% tax bracket, he saves $2,800 in income taxes for the year (28% x $10,000) and has also put away $10,000 toward his retirement.

2.   Tax Deferral

In addition to the tax deduction you receive for putting money into a retirement account, there is another tremendous tax benefit to retirement accounts: tax deferral on earnings. When you earn money on an investment, you usually must pay taxes on those earnings in the year when you earn the money. For example, you must pay taxes on the interest you earn on a savings account or certificate of deposit in the year when the interest accrues. And when you sell an investment at a profit, you must pay income tax in that year on the gain you realize from the sale. For example, you must pay tax on the profit you earn from selling stock in the year when you sell the stock.

A different rule applies, however, for earnings you receive from a tax-qualified retirement account. You do not pay taxes on investment earnings from retirement accounts until you withdraw the funds. Most people withdraw these funds at retirement, so they are usually in a lower income tax bracket when they pay tax on these earnings. This results in substantial tax savings for most people, who would have had to pay much higher taxes on these earnings if they had paid as the earnings accumulated.

> **EXAMPLE:** Bill and Brian both invest in municipal bonds and treasury bills. Bill has a taxable individual account, while Brian invests

through a tax-deferred retirement account. They each invest $5,000 per year. They earn 8% on their investments each year and pay income tax at the 28% rate. At the end of 30 years, Brian has $566,416. Bill only has $272,869. Reason: Bill had to pay income taxes on the interest his investments earned each year, while Brian's interest accrued tax-free because he invested through a retirement account. Brian must pay tax on his earnings only when he withdraws the money (but he'll have to pay a penalty tax if he makes withdrawals before age 59½, subject to certain exceptions; see Section D3).

The following chart compares the annual growth of a tax-deferred account and a taxable account.

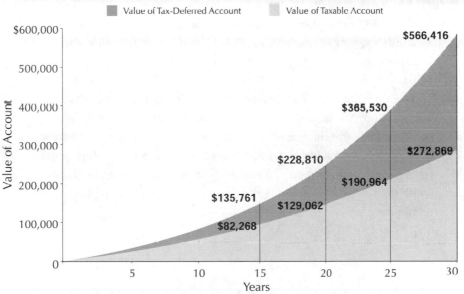

Assumptions:
- Investments earn 8% annually
- $5,000 is invested annually in the tax-deferred account
- $3,600 (what's left after $5,000 is taxed at 28%) is invested annually in the non-tax-deferred account
- Income on the nontax-deferred account is taxed annually at 28%, and recipient does not pay state income tax

Having Employees Complicates Matters Tremendously

If you own your own business and have no employees (other than your spouse), you can probably choose, establish, and administer your own retirement plan with little or no assistance. The instant you add employees to the mix, however, virtually every aspect of your plan becomes more complex. This is primarily due to legal requirements called nondiscrimination rules. These rules are designed to ensure that your retirement plan benefits all employees, not just you. In general, the laws prohibit you from doing the following:

- making disproportionately large contributions for some plan participants (like yourself) and not for others
- unfairly excluding certain employees from participating in the plan, and
- unfairly withholding benefits from former employees or their beneficiaries.

If the IRS finds a plan to be discriminatory at any time (usually during an audit), the plan could be disqualified—that is, determined not to satisfy IRS rules. If this happens, you and your employees will owe income tax and probably penalties, as well.

Having employees also increases the plan's reporting requirements. You must provide employees with a summary of the terms of the plan, notification of any changes you make, and an annual report of contributions. And you must file an annual tax return. Because of all the complex issues raised by having employees, any business owner with employees (other than a spouse) should seek professional help when creating a retirement plan.

B. Individual Retirement Arrangements (IRAs)

The simplest type of tax-deferred retirement account is the individual retirement arrangement (IRA). An IRA is a retirement account established by an individual, not a business. You can have an IRA whether you're a business owner or an employee in someone else's business. Moreover, you can establish an IRA for yourself as an individual and also set up one or more of the other types of retirement plans discussed in Sections C and D below, which are just for businesses.

An IRA is a trust or custodial account set up for the benefit of an individual or his or her beneficiaries. The trustee or custodian administers the account. The trustee can be a bank, mutual fund, brokerage firm, or other financial institution (such as an insurance company).

IRAs are extremely easy to set up and administer. You need a written IRA agreement, but you don't have to file any tax forms with the IRS. The financial institution you use to set up your account will usually ask you to complete IRS Form 5305, *Traditional Individual Retirement Trust Account*, which serves as an IRA agreement and meets all of the IRS requirements. Keep the form in your records— you don't file it with the IRS.

Most financial institutions offer an array of IRA accounts that provide for different types of investments. You can invest your IRA money in just about anything—stocks, bonds, mutual funds, treasury bills and notes, and bank certificates of deposit. However, you can't invest in collectibles like art, antiques, stamps, or other personal property.

You can establish as many IRA accounts as you want, but there is a maximum combined amount of money you can contribute to all of your IRA accounts each year. This amount goes up every year through 2008 as shown in the chart below. After 2008, the limit will be adjusted each year for inflation in $500 increments.

There are different limits for workers who are at least 50 years old. Anyone who is at least 50 years old at the end of the year can make increased annual contributions of $500 per year during 2002 through 2005, and $1,000 per year thereafter. This rule is intended to allow older people to catch up with younger folks who will have more years to make contributions at the higher levels.

Annual IRA Contribution Limits		
Tax Year	Under Age 50	Aged 50 or Over
2002-2004	$3,000	$3,500
2005	$4,000	$4,500
2006-2007	$4,000	$5,000
2008 and later	$5,000	$6,000

If you are married, you can double the contribution limits. For example, a married couple in 2004 can contribute up to $3,000 per spouse into their IRAs, or a total of $6,000. This is true even if one spouse isn't working. To take advantage of doubling, you must file a joint tax return, and the working spouse must earn at least as much as the combined IRA contribution.

1.   Traditional IRAs

There are two different types of IRAs that you can choose from:
- traditional IRAs, and
- Roth IRAs.

Traditional IRAs have been around since 1974. The principal feature of these IRAs is that you receive an income tax deduction for the amount you contribute each year to your account. Once you've made a contribution, your earnings accumulate in the account tax-free until you withdraw them.

There are time restrictions on when you can (and when you must) withdraw money from your IRA. You are not supposed to withdraw any money from your IRA until you reach age 59½, unless you die or become disabled. And you must begin to withdraw your money by April 1 of the year after the year you turn 70. Once you start withdrawing money from your IRA, the amount you withdraw will be included in your regular income for income tax purposes.

As a general rule, if you make early withdrawals, you must pay regular income tax on the amount you take out, plus a 10% federal tax penalty. There are some exceptions to this early withdrawal penalty; for example, if you withdraw money to purchase a first home or pay educational expenses, the penalty doesn't apply to withdrawals up to a specified dollar limit. To learn about these and other exceptions in detail, see *IRAs, 401(k)s & Other Retirement Plans: Taking Your Money Out*, by Twila Slesnick and John Suttle (Nolo).

2. Roth IRAs

Like traditional IRAs, Roth IRAs are tax deferred and allow your retirement savings to grow without any tax burden. Unlike traditional IRAs, however, your contributions to Roth IRAs are *not* tax deductible. Instead, you get to withdraw your money from the account tax-free when you retire.

Once you have established your account, your ability to contribute to it will be affected by changes in your income level. If you are single and your income reaches $95,000, your ability to contribute to your Roth IRA will begin to phase out. Once your income reaches $110,000, you will no longer be able to make contributions. If you are married and filing a joint return with your spouse, your ability to contribute to your account will start to phase out when your income reaches $150,000, and you will be prohibited from making any contributions at all when your income reaches $160,000.

Roth IRAs have the same restrictions on early withdrawals as traditional IRAs. You are not, however, required to make withdrawals when you reach age 70½. Because Roth IRA withdrawals are tax free, the government doesn't care if you leave your money in your account indefinitely. However, your money will be tax free on withdrawal only if you leave it in your Roth IRA for at least five years.

C. Employer IRAs

You can establish an employer IRA as long as you are in business and earn a profit. You don't have to have any employees, and it doesn't matter how your business is organized: you can be a sole proprietor, partner in a partnership, member of a limited liability company, or an owner of a regular or S corporation.

The great advantage of employer IRAs is that you can contribute more than you can to traditional IRAs and Roth IRAs. And as long as you meet the requirements for establishing an employer IRA, you can have one in addition to one or more individual IRAs.

There are two kinds of employer IRAs to choose from: SEP-IRAs and SIMPLE IRAs.

1.   SEP-IRAs

SEP-IRAs are designed for the self-employed. Any person who receives self-employment income from providing a service can establish a SEP-IRA. It doesn't matter whether you work full time or part time. You can have a SEP-IRA even if you are also covered by a retirement plan at a full-time employee job.

A SEP-IRA is a simplified employee pension. It's very similar to an IRA except that you can contribute more money under this type of plan. Instead of a $3,000 to $5,000 annual contribution limit (see the chart in Section B, above), you can invest up to 13.04% of your net profit from self-employment every year, up to a maximum of $30,000 a year in 2004. You don't have to make contributions every year, and your contributions can vary from year to year. As with IRAs, you can invest your money in almost anything (stocks, bonds, notes, mutual funds, and so on).

You can deduct your contributions to SEP-IRAs from your income taxes, and the interest on your SEP-IRA investments accrues tax free until you withdraw the money. Withdrawals from SEP-IRAs are subject to the same rules that apply to traditional IRAs. If you withdraw money from your SEP-IRA before you reach age 59½, you'll have to pay a 10% tax penalty, plus regular income taxes on your withdrawal, unless an exception applies. And you must begin to withdraw your money by April 1 of the year after the year you turn 70.

2.   SIMPLE IRAs

Self-employed people and companies with fewer than 100 employees can set up SIMPLE IRAs. If you establish a SIMPLE IRA, you are not allowed to have any other retirement plans for your business (although you may still have your own individual IRA). SIMPLE IRAs are easy to set up and administer, and you will be able to make larger annual contributions than you could to a SEP or Keogh plan if you earn less than $10,000 per year from your business.

SIMPLE IRAs may be established only by an employer on behalf of its employees. If you are a sole proprietor, you are deemed to employ yourself for purposes of this rule, and you may establish a SIMPLE IRA in your own name as the employer. If you are a partner in a partnership, an LLC member, or the owner of an incorporated business, the SIMPLE IRA must be established by your business, not by you personally.

Contributions to SIMPLE IRAs are divided into two parts. You may contribute:

- up to 100% of your net income from your business up to an annual limit—the contribution limit is $9,000 for 2004 ($10,500 if you were born before 1955), $10,000 for 2005, and will be indexed to inflation in future years, and
- a matching contribution of up to 3% of your net business income, as long as this amount does not exceed your first contribution.

If you're an employee of your incorporated business, your first contribution (called a salary reduction contribution) comes out of your salary, and the matching contribution is paid by your business.

The money in a SIMPLE IRA can be invested like any other IRA. Withdrawals from SIMPLE IRAs are subject to the same rules as traditional IRAs with one big exception: Early withdrawals from SIMPLE IRAs are subject to a 25% tax penalty if you make the withdrawal within two years after the date you first contributed to your account. Other early withdrawals are subject to a 10% penalty, as with traditional IRAs, unless an exception applies.

D. Keogh Plans

Keogh plans—named after the Congressman who sponsored the legislation that created them—are only for business owners who are sole proprietors, partners in partnerships, or LLC members. You can't have a Keogh if you incorporate your business.

Keoghs require more paperwork to set up than employer IRAs, but they also offer more options: You can contribute more to these plans and still get an income tax deduction for your contributions.

1.   Types of Keogh Plans

There are two basic types of Keogh plans:
- defined contribution plans, in which the amount you receive on retirement is based on how much you contribute to—and how much accumulates in—the plan, and
- defined benefit plans, which provide for payment of a set amount of money upon retirement.

There are two types of defined contribution plans: profit-sharing plans and money purchase plans. These plans can be used separately or in tandem with one other.

a.   Profit-Sharing Plans

You can contribute up to 20% of your net self-employment income to a profit sharing Keogh plan, up to a maximum of $ 41,000 per year. You can contribute any amount up to the limit each year or contribute nothing at all.

b.   Money Purchase Plans

In a money purchase plan, you contribute a fixed percentage of your net self-employment earnings every year. You decide on the percentage when you establish your plan. Make sure you will be able to afford the contributions each year because you can't skip them, even if your business earns no profit for the year. In return for giving up flexibility, you can contribute a higher percentage of your earnings with a money purchase plan—up to 25% of your net self-employment earnings, with a maximum of $41,000 per year (the same maximum amount applies to profit-sharing plans).

2.   Setting Up a Keogh Plan

As with individual IRAs and employer IRAs, you can set up a Keogh plan at most banks, brokerage houses, mutual funds, other financial institutions, and trade or professional organizations. You can also choose among a huge array of investments for your money.

To set up your plan, you must adopt a written Keogh plan and establish a trust or custodial account with your plan provider to invest your funds. Your provider should have an IRS-approved master or prototype Keogh plan for you to sign. You can also have a special plan drawn up for you, but this is expensive and unnecessary for most small business owners.

3.   Withdrawing Your Money

You may begin to withdraw money from your Keogh plan after you reach the age of 59½. If you have a profit-sharing plan, early withdrawals are permitted without penalty if you suffer financial hardship, become disabled, or have to pay health expenses in excess of 7.5% of your adjusted gross income. If you have a money purchase plan, early withdrawals are permitted if you become disabled, leave your business after you turn 55, or make child support or alimony payments from the plan under a court order. Otherwise, early withdrawals from profit-sharing and money purchase Keogh plans are subject to a 10% penalty.

E.   Solo 401(k) Plans

Most people have heard of 401(k) plans—they are retirement plans established by businesses for their employees. 401(k)s are a type of profit-sharing plan in which a business's employees make plan contributions from their salaries and the business makes a matching contribution. These plans are complex to establish and administer and are generally used only by larger businesses. Until recently, self-employed people and businesses without employees rarely used 401(k) plans, because they offered no benefit over other profit-sharing plans that are much easier to set up and run.

However, things have changed. Now, any business owner who has no employees (other than a spouse) can establish a solo self-employed 401(k) plan (also called a one-person or individual 401(k)). Solo 401(k) plans are designed specifically for business owners without employees.

Solo 401(k) plans have the following advantages over other retirement plans:

- You can make very large contributions—as much as 25% of your net profit from self-employment, plus an elective deferral contribution of up to $13,000 in 2004. The maximum contribution per year is $41,000 (the same maximum amount that applies to the Keogh plans discussed in Section D, above). Business owners who are at least 50 years old may make additional contributions of up to $3,000 per year; these catch-up contributions don't count towards the $41,000 annual limit.

- You can borrow up to $50,000 from your solo 401(k) plan penalty-free, as long as you repay the loan within five years (you cannot borrow from a traditional IRA, Roth IRA, SEP-IRA, or SIMPLE IRA).

As with other plans, you must pay a 10% penalty tax on withdrawals you make before the age of 59½, but you may make penalty-free early withdrawals for reasons of personal hardship (defined as an "immediate financial need" that you can't meet any other way).

You can set up a solo 401(k) plan at most banks, brokerage houses, mutual funds, and other financial institutions, and you can invest the money in a variety of ways. You must adopt a written plan and set up a trust or custodial account with your plan provider to invest your funds. Financial institutions that offer solo 401(k) plans have pre-approved plans that you can use.

Beware of retirement account deadlines. If you want to establish any of the retirement accounts discussed in this chapter and take a tax deduction for the year, you must meet specific deadlines. The deadlines vary according to the type of account you set up, as shown in the following chart. Once you establish your account, you have until the due date of your tax return for the year (April 15 of the following year, or later if you receive a filing extension) to contribute to your account and take a deduction.

Retirement Account Deadlines	
Plan Type	**Deadline for Establishing Plan**
Traditional IRA	Due date of tax return (April 15 plus extensions)
Roth IRA	Due date of tax return (April 15 plus extensions)
SEP-IRA	Due date of tax return (April 15 plus extensions)
Simple IRA	October 1
Keogh Profit Sharing Plan	December 31
Keogh Money Purchase Plan	December 31
Keogh Defined Benefit Plan	December 31
401(k) Plan	December 31

Chapter 14

Additional Home Business Deductions

This chapter looks at some of the most common deductible operating expenses that you are likely to incur in the normal course of running your home business, such as advertising expenses, insurance, and legal fees. You can deduct these costs as business operating expenses as long as they are ordinary, necessary, and reasonable in amount, and meet the additional requirements discussed below.

A. Advertising

Almost any type of business-related advertising is a currently deductible business operating expense. You can deduct advertising to sell a particular product or service, to help establish goodwill for your business, or just to get your business known. Advertising costs include what you pay for:

- business cards
- brochures
- advertisements in the local Yellow Pages
- newspaper and magazine advertisements
- trade publication advertisements
- catalogs
- advertisements on the Internet
- fees you pay to advertising and public relations agencies
- package design costs, and
- signs and display racks.

However, advertising to influence government legislation is never deductible. And help-wanted ads you place to recruit workers are not advertising costs, but you can still deduct them as ordinary and necessary business operating expenses.

1. Goodwill Advertising

You can usually deduct the cost of "goodwill" advertising—ads intended to keep your name before the public—if it relates to business you reasonably expect to gain in the future. Examples of goodwill advertising include:

- advertisements that encourage people to contribute to charities, such as the Red Cross or similar causes
- sponsoring a little league baseball team, bowling team, or golf tournament
- giving away product samples, and
- holding contests and giving away prizes.

However, you can't deduct time and labor that you give away as an advertising expense, even though doing so often promotes goodwill. You must actually spend money to have an advertising expense. For example, a lawyer who does pro bono work for indigent clients to gain exposure for his law practice may not deduct the cost of his services as an advertising expense.

2. Giveaway Items

The cost of giveaway items that you use to publicize your business (such as pens, coffee cups, tee-shirts, refrigerator magnets, calendars, tote bags, and key chains) are deductible. However, you are not allowed to deduct more than $25 in business gifts to any one person each year (see Section G, below). This limitation applies to advertising giveaway items unless they:

- cost $4 or less
- have your name clearly and permanently imprinted on them, and
- are one of a number of identical items you distribute widely.

EXAMPLE 1: Jay has a home business selling rare wines. He orders 1,000 ballpoint pens with his name and contact information printed on them and distributes them at wine tastings and gourmet food and wine fairs. Each pen costs Jay $1. The pens do not count toward the $25 gift limit. Jay may deduct the entire $1,000 expense for the pens.

EXAMPLE 2: Jay buys a $200 fountain pen and gives it to his best customer. The pen is a business gift to an individual, so Jay can deduct only $25 of the cost.

Signs, display racks, and other promotional materials that you give to other businesses to use on their premises do not count as gifts.

3. Business Websites

The cost of a business website is a deductible business expense. You can use the site to take orders from customers or just to publicize the products or services your business sells. You can deduct the cost of designing the site and maintaining it—for example, the monthly charge you pay to an Internet access provider.

4. Permanent Signs

Signs that have a useful life of less than one year—for example, paper or cardboard signs—are currently deductible as business operating expenses. However, a permanent metal or plastic sign that has a useful life of more than one year is a long-term business asset, which you cannot currently deduct as a business operating expense. Instead, you must either depreciate the cost over several years or deduct it in one year under Section 179. (See Chapter 5 for more on deducting long-term assets.)

B. Business Bad Debts

Business bad debts are debts that won't be fully repaid and arise from your business activities. Examples include:
- money you lend for a business purpose
- sales you make on credit, or
- guaranteed business-related loans.

You can currently deduct business bad debts as business operating expenses when they become wholly or partly worthless. However, to claim the deduction, you must incur an actual loss of money or have previously included the amount of the debt as income on your tax return. Because of this limitation, many small businesses are unable to deduct bad debts.

1.   Requirements to Deduct Bad Debts

You must meet three requirements to deduct a business bad debt as a business operating expense:

- you must have a bona fide business debt
- the debt must be wholly or partly worthless, and
- you must have suffered an economic loss from the debt.

a.   A Bona Fide Business Debt

A bona fide debt exists when someone has a legal obligation to pay you a sum of money—for example, you sell goods or merchandise to a customer on credit. You will generally need some written evidence of the debt—for example, a signed promissory note or other writing stating the amount of the debt, when it is due, and the interest rate (if any)—in order to claim this deduction. An oral promise to pay may also be legally enforceable, but would be looked upon with suspicion by the IRS.

A business debt is a debt that is created or acquired in the course of your business or becomes worthless as part of your business. Your primary motive for incurring the debt must be related to your business. Debts you take on for personal or investment purposes are not business debts. (Remember, investing is not a business; see Chapter 2.)

> **EXAMPLE 1:** Mark, an advertising agent, loans $10,000 to his brother-in-law, Scott, to help him develop his bird diaper invention. Mark will get 25% of the profits if the invention proves successful. This is an investment, not a business debt.

> **EXAMPLE 2:** Mark loans $10,000 to one of his best business clients to keep the client's business running. Because the main reason for the loan is business related (to keep his client in business so he will continue as a client), the debt is a business debt.

b.   A Worthless Debt

You may deduct a debt only if it is wholly or partly worthless. A debt becomes worthless when there is no longer any chance that it will be repaid. You don't have to wait until a debt is due to determine that it is worthless, nor do you have to go to court to try to collect it. You just have to be able to show that you have taken reasonable steps to try to collect the debt or that collection efforts would be futile. For example:

- you've made repeated collection efforts that have proven unsuccessful
- the debtor has filed for bankruptcy or has already been through bankruptcy and had all or part of the debt discharged (forgiven) by the bankruptcy court, or
- the debtor has gone out of business, gone broke, died, or disappeared.

Keep all documentation that shows a debt is worthless, such as copies of unpaid invoices, collection letters you've sent the debtor, logs of collection calls you've made, bankruptcy notices, and credit reports.

You must deduct the entire amount of a bad debt in the year it becomes totally worthless. If only part of a business debt becomes worthless—for example, you received a partial payment before the debt became uncollectible—you can deduct the unpaid portion that year or you can wait until the following year to deduct it. For example, if you think you might get paid more the next year, you can wait and see what your final bad debt amount is before you deduct it.

c.   An Economic Loss

You are not automatically entitled to deduct a debt simply because the obligation has become worthless. To get a deduction, you must have suffered an economic loss. According to the IRS, you have suffered a loss only if you:

- already reported as business income the amount you were supposed to be paid
- paid out cash, or

- made credit sales of inventory for which you were not paid.

These rules make it impossible to deduct some types of business debts.

2.   Types of Bad Debts

There are many different types of business debts that small businesses can incur. The sections that follow discuss some of the more common ones.

a.   Sales of Services

Unfortunately, if you're a cash basis taxpayer who sells services to your clients (like many home businesses), you can't claim a bad debt deduction if a client fails to pay you. Cash basis taxpayers report income only when they actually receive it, not when they perform the services the client ordered. As a result, cash basis taxpayers don't have an economic loss (in the eyes of the IRS) when a client fails to pay.

> **EXAMPLE:** Bill, a home-based dog walker, works 20 hours walking a client's dogs and bills the client $250. The client never pays. Bill is a cash basis taxpayer, so he doesn't report the $250 as income because he never received it. As far as the IRS is concerned, Bill has no economic loss and cannot deduct the $250 the client failed to pay.

The IRS strictly enforces this rule (harsh as it may seem). Absent the rule, the IRS fears that businesses will inflate the value of their services in order to get a larger deduction.

Accrual basis taxpayers, on the other hand, report sales as income in the year the sales are made—not the year payment is received. These taxpayers can take a bad debt deduction if a client fails to pay for services rendered, because they have already reported the money due as income. Therefore, accrual taxpayers have an economic loss when they are not paid for their services.

EXAMPLE: Andrea, a home-based financial consultant, bills a client $10,000 for consulting services she performed in 2005. Andrea is an accrual basis taxpayer, so she characterizes the $10,000 as income on her books and includes this amount in her gross income for 2005, even though she hasn't actually received payment. The client later files for bankruptcy, and the debt becomes worthless. Andrea may take a business bad debt deduction to wipe out the $10,000 in income she previously charged on her books.

There's no point in switching from cash basis to the accrual method to deduct bad debts. The accrual method doesn't result in lower taxes— the bad debt deduction merely wipes out a sale that was already reported as income and taxed.

Cash or accrual? Read all about it in Chapter 15, which includes a detailed discussion of the cash basis and accrual accounting methods.

b.   Credit Sales of Inventory

Most deductible business bad debts result from credit sales of inventory to customers. If you sell goods on credit to a customer and are not paid, you can take a deduction whether you are an accrual or cash basis taxpayer. You deduct the cost of the inventory at the end of the year to determine the cost of goods sold for the year. (See Chapter 10 for more on inventory deductions.)

c.   Cash Loans

Whether you are a cash basis or an accrual taxpayer, cash loans you make for a business purpose are deductible as bad debts in the year they become worthless.

EXAMPLE: John, an advertising agent, loaned $10,000 to one of his best clients to keep the client's business running. The client later went bankrupt and could not repay the loan. John may deduct the $10,000 as a business bad debt.

d.   Business Loan Guarantees

If you guarantee a debt that becomes worthless, it qualifies as a business bad debt only if you:
- made the guarantee in the course of your business
- have a legal duty to pay the debt
- made the guarantee before the debt became worthless, and
- received reasonable consideration (compensation) for the guarantee—you meet this requirement if you make the guarantee for a good faith business purpose or according to normal business practices.

EXAMPLE: Jane has a home business selling gourmet coffee and teas. She guaranteed payment of a $20,000 note for Pete's Coffee Bar, one of Jane's largest clients. Pete's later filed for bankruptcy and defaulted on the loan. Jane had to make full payment to the bank. She can take a business bad debt deduction because her guarantee was made for a good faith business purpose—her desire to retain one of her better clients and keep a sales outlet.

e.   Loans or Guarantees to Your Corporation

If your business is incorporated, you cannot take a bad debt deduction for a loan to your corporation if the loan is actually a contribution to capital—that is, the money is part of your investment in the business. You must be careful to treat a loan to your corporation just as you would treat a loan made to a business in which you have no ownership interest. You should have a signed promissory note from your corporation setting forth:
- the loan amount
- the interest rate—which should be reasonable
- the due date, and
- a repayment schedule.

If you are a principal shareholder in a small corporation, you'll often be asked to personally guarantee corporate loans and other extensions of credit. Creditors demand these guarantees because they want to be able to go after your personal assets if they can't collect from your corporation. If you end up having to make good on your guarantee and can't get repaid from your corporation, you will have a bad debt. You can deduct this bad debt as a business debt if your dominant motive for making the loan or guarantee was to protect your employment status and ensure your continuing receipt of a salary. If your primary motive was to protect your investment in the corporation, the debt is a personal debt. The IRS is more likely to think you are protecting your investment if you receive little or no salary from the corporation or your salary is not a major source of your overall income.

f.   Personal Debts

The fact that a debt doesn't arise from your business doesn't mean it's not deductible. Bona fide personal debts that become worthless are deductible as *short-term capital losses.* This means you can deduct them only as an offset to any capital gains you received from the sale of capital assets during the year. (Capital assets include items such as real estate, stocks, and bonds.) Your total deduction for personal debts is limited to $3,000 per year. Any loss in excess of this limit may be carried over to future years to offset future capital gains. Unlike business bad debts, personal debts are deductible only if they become wholly worthless.

C.   Casualty Losses

Casualty losses are damage to property caused by fire, theft, vandalism, earthquake, storm, flood, terrorism, or some other "sudden, unexpected, or unusual event." There must be some external force involved in a casualty loss. Thus, you get no deduction if you simply lose property or it breaks or wears out over time.

You may take a deduction for casualty losses to business property only if—and only to the extent that—the loss is not covered by insurance. If the loss is fully covered, you can't take a deduction.

1.   Amount of Deduction

How much you may deduct depends on whether the property involved was stolen, completely destroyed, or partially destroyed. However, you must always reduce your casualty losses by the amount of any insurance proceeds you receive (or reasonably expect to receive). If more than one item was stolen or destroyed, you must figure your deduction separately for each.

a.   Total Loss

If the property is stolen or completely destroyed, your deduction is calculated as follows:

> Adjusted Basis
> – Salvage Value
> – Insurance Proceeds
> = Casualty Loss

(Your adjusted basis is the property's original cost, plus the value of any improvements, minus any deductions you took for depreciation or Section 179 expensing—see Chapter 5.) Obviously, if an item is stolen, there will be no salvage value.

> EXAMPLE: Sean's home computer is stolen by a burglar. The computer cost $2,000. Sean has taken no tax deductions for it because he purchased it only two months ago, so his adjusted basis is $2,000. Sean is a renter and has no insurance covering the loss. Sean's casualty loss is $2,000. ($2,000 Adjusted Basis – $0 Salvage Value – $0 Insurance Proceeds = $2,000.)

b.   Partial Loss

If the property is only partly destroyed, your casualty loss deduction is the lesser of the decrease in the property's fair market value or its adjusted basis, reduced by any insurance you receive or expect to receive.

EXAMPLE: Assume that Sean's computer from the example above is partly destroyed due to a small fire in his home. Its fair market value in its damaged state is $500. Because he spent $2,000 for the computer, the decrease in its fair market value is $1,500. The computer's adjusted basis is $2,000. He received no insurance proceeds. Thus, his casualty loss is $1,500.

c.   Inventory

You don't have to treat damage to or loss of inventory as a casualty loss. Instead, you may deduct it on your Schedule C as part of the cost of your goods sold. (See Chapter 10 for more information on deducting inventory costs.) This is advantageous because it reduces your income for self-employment tax purposes, which casualty losses do not. However, if you do this, you must include any insurance proceeds you receive for the inventory loss in your gross income for the year.

d.   Personal Property

You can deduct casualty losses to personal property—that is, property you don't use for your home business—from your income tax as an itemized personal deduction, but the deduction is severely limited: You can deduct only the amount of the loss that exceeds 10% of your adjusted gross income for the year. This greatly limits or eliminates many casualty loss deductions. To add insult to injury, you must also subtract $100 from each casualty or theft you suffered during the year.

EXAMPLE: Ken's suffers $5,000 in losses to his personal property when a fire strikes his home. His adjusted gross income for the year is $75,000. He can deduct only that portion of his loss that exceeds $7,500 (10% x $75,000 = $7,500). He lost $5,000, so he gets no deduction.

Casualty Gains

In some cases, the insurance reimbursement you receive will exceed the value of the property that is stolen or destroyed. In this event, you have a casualty gain, not a deductible loss.

> **EXAMPLE:** Jeanette's laptop computer is stolen from her car. She has computer insurance covering the loss. Her insurer pays her $1,500. Jeanette paid $2,500 for the computer, but deducted the entire amount in one year under Section 179; thus, her adjusted basis is $0. As a result, she has a $1,500 gain ($0 Adjusted Basis – $1,500 Insurance Proceeds = $1,500 casualty gain).

If you have a gain, you might have to pay tax on it. If you owned the property one year or more, the gain is a capital gain taxed at capital gains rates. Gains on property owned less than one year are taxed at ordinary income tax rates. (Ordinary rates are higher than capital gains rates for everyone but for taxpayers in the lowest tax brackets.) However, you can defer any taxes you owe to a later year (or even indefinitely) by buying property to replace your loss within certain time limits. For more information, see IRS Publication 547, *Casualties, Disasters, and Thefts*. You can download it from www.irs.gov or by calling 800 TAX-FORM.

2. Damage to Your Home Office

You may deduct losses due to damage to or destruction of your home office as part of your home office deduction. However, your loss is reduced by any insurance proceeds you receive or expect to receive.

You can deduct casualty losses that affect your entire house as an indirect home office expense. The amount of your deduction is based on your home office use percentage.

> **EXAMPLE:** Dana's home, valued at $500,000, is completely destroyed by a fire. Her fire insurance covered only 80% of her loss, or $400,000, leaving her with a $100,000 loss. Her home office took up 20% of her home. She can deduct 20% of her $100,000 loss, or $20,000, as an indirect home office deduction.

You can fully deduct casualty losses that affect only your home office—for example, if only your home office is burned in a fire—as direct home office expenses. However, you can't take a business expense deduction for casualty losses that don't affect your home office at all—for example, if your kitchen is destroyed by fire. See Chapter 6 for a detailed discussion of the home office deduction.

If the loss involves business property that is in your home office but is not part of your home—for example, a burglar steals your home office computer—you can deduct the entire value of that loss directly, rather than as part of the home office deduction.

3.   Tax Reporting

You report casualty losses to business property on part B of IRS Form 4684, *Casualties and Thefts*, and then transfer the deductible casualty loss to Form 4797, *Sales of Business Property*, and the first page of your Form 1040. The amount of your deductible casualty loss is subtracted from your adjusted gross income for the year. However, casualty losses are not deducted from your self-employment income for purposes of calculating your Social Security and Medicare tax. These reporting requirements differ from those for other deductions covered in this chapter, which are reported on IRS Schedule C, Form 1040.

Partnerships, S corporations, and LLCs must also fill out Form 4797. The amount of the loss is subtracted when calculating the entity's total business income for the year. This amount is reported on the entity's information tax return (Form 1065 for partnerships and LLCs; Form 1120S for S corporations). C corporations deduct their casualty losses on their own tax returns (Form 1120).

If you take a casualty loss as part of your home office deduction, you must include the loss on Form 8829, *Expenses for Business Use of Your Home* (see Chapter 6.)

D.   Charitable Contributions

If, like the vast majority of home business owners, you are a sole proprietor, partner in a partnership, LLC member, or S corporation shareholder, the IRS treats any charitable contributions your business makes as a personal contribution by you (and your co-owners, if any). As such, the contributions are not business expenses—you can deduct them only as a personal charitable contribution. You may deduct these contributions only if you itemize deductions on your tax personal tax return; they are subject to certain income limitations. The deduction is limited to the fair market value of the inventory on the date it is donated, reduced by any gain you would have realized had you sold the property at its fair market value instead of donating it.

> **EXAMPLE:** Barbee, who runs a crafts business out of her home, donates unsold inventory to a nursing home. The fair market value of the inventory is $1,000. Barbee spent $500 to acquire the inventory, so she would have had a $500 gain had she sold it at its fair market value. Her charitable deduction must be reduced by the amount of this gain, so she gets only a $500 deduction.

E. Dues and Subscriptions

Dues you pay to professional, business, and civic organizations are deductible business expenses, as long as the organization's main purpose is not to provide entertainment facilities to members. You can deduct dues paid to:

- bar associations, medical associations, and other professional organizations
- trade associations, local chambers of commerce, real estate boards, and business leagues, and
- civic or public service organizations, such as a Rotary or Lions club.

You get no deduction for dues you pay to belong to other types of social, business, or recreational clubs—for example, country clubs or athletic clubs (see Chapter 7). For this reason, it's best not to use the word "dues" on your tax return because the IRS may question the expense. Use other words to describe the deduction—for example, if you're deducting membership dues for a trade organization, list the expense as "trade association membership fees."

You may also deduct subscriptions to professional, technical, and trade journals that deal with your business field as a business expense.

F. Education Expenses

You may deduct your expenses for business-related education—for example, a college course or seminar. You may also deduct the cost of attending a convention or professional meeting as an education expense. To qualify for an education deduction, you must be able to show that the education:

- maintains or improves skills required in your business, or
- is required by law or regulation to maintain your professional status.

EXAMPLE 1: Herb has a part-time home-based business repairing computers. To keep up with the latest technology, he takes a computer repair course at a local trade school. Because the course maintains and improves skills required in his business, he can deduct the cost of the course.

EXAMPLE 2: Sue is a self-employed attorney who works from home. Every year, she is required by law to attend 12 hours of continuing legal education to maintain her status as an active member of the state bar. The legal seminars she attends to satisfy this requirement are deductible education expenses.

Deductible education expenses include tuition, fees, books, and other learning materials. They also include transportation and travel (see below). You may also deduct expenses you pay to educate or train your employees.

1.   Starting a New Business

You cannot currently deduct education expenses you incur to qualify for a *new* business or profession. For example, courts have held that IRS agents could not deduct the cost of going to law school, because a law degree would qualify them for a new business—being a lawyer (*Jeffrey L. Weiler*, 54 T.C. 398 (1970)). On the other hand, a practicing dentist was allowed to deduct the cost of being educated in orthodontia, because becoming an orthodontist did not constitute the practice of a new business or profession for a dentist. (Rev. Rul. 74-78.)

2.   Minimum Educational Requirements

You cannot deduct the cost required to meet the minimum or basic level educational requirements for a business or profession. Thus, for example, you can't deduct the expense of going to law school or medical school.

3.   Traveling For Education

Local transportation expenses you pay to travel to and from a deductible educational activity are deductible. This includes transportation between either your home or business and the educational activity. Going to or from home to an educational activity does not constitute nondeductible commuting. If you drive, you may deduct your actual expenses or use the standard mileage rate. (See Chapter 8 for more on deducting the cost of local travel.)

There's no law that says you must take your education courses as close to home as possible. You may travel outside your geographic area for education, even if the same or a similar educational activity is available near your home or place of business. Companies and groups that sponsor educational events are well aware of this rule and take advantage of it by offering courses and seminars at resorts and other enjoyable vacation spots such as Hawaii and California. Deductible travel expenses may include airfare or other transportation, lodging, and meals. (See Chapter 9 for more on business travel deductions.)

You cannot claim travel itself as an education deduction. You must travel *to* some sort of educational activity. For example, an architect could not deduct the cost of a trip to Paris because he studied the local architecture while he was there—but he could deduct a trip to Paris to attend a seminar on French architecture.

G. Gifts

If you give someone a gift for business purposes, your business expense deduction is limited to $25 per person per year. Any amount over the $25 limit is not deductible. If this amount seems low, that's because it was established in 1954!

> **EXAMPLE:** Lisa, a self-employed marketing consultant, gives a $200 Christmas gift to her best client. She may deduct $25 of the cost.

A gift to a member of a customer's family is treated as a gift to the customer, unless you have a legitimate nonbusiness connection to the family member. If you and your spouse both give gifts, you are treated as one taxpayer—it doesn't matter if you work together or have separate businesses.

The $25 limit applies only to gifts to individuals. It doesn't apply if you give a gift to an entire company. Such companywide gifts are deductible in any amount, as long as they are reasonable. However, the $25 limit does apply if the gift is intended for a particular person or group of people within the company.

> **EXAMPLE:** Bob sells products to the Acme Company. Just before Christmas, he drops off a $100 cheese basket at the company's reception area for use by all Acme employees. He also delivers an identical basket to Acme's president. The first basket left in the reception area is a companywide gift, not subject to the $25 limit. The basket for Acme's president is a personal gift and therefore is subject to the limit.

H. Insurance for Your Business

You can deduct the premiums you pay for any insurance you buy for your business as a business operating expense. This includes:
- fire, theft, and flood insurance for business property
- liability insurance
- medical insurance for your employees (see Chapter 12)
- professional malpractice insurance—for example, medical or legal malpractice insurance
- credit insurance that covers losses from business debts
- workers' compensation insurance you are required by state law to provide your employees (if you are an employee of an S corporation, the corporation can deduct worker's compensation payments made on your behalf, but you must report them as part of your employee wages)
- business interruption insurance
- life insurance covering a corporation's officers and directors (unless you are a direct beneficiary under the policy), and
- unemployment insurance contributions (you deduct these either as insurance costs or as business taxes, depending on how they are characterized by your state's laws).

1. Homeowner's Insurance for Your Home Office

If you have a home office and qualify for the home office deduction, you may deduct the home office percentage of your homeowner's or renter's insurance premiums. For example, if your home office takes up 20% of your home, you may deduct 20% of the premiums. You can deduct 100% of any coverage that you add to your homeowner's or renter's policy specifically for your home office and/or business property. For example, if you add an endorsement to your policy to cover business property, you can deduct 100% of the cost.

2. Car Insurance

If you use the actual expense method to deduct your car expenses, you can deduct the cost of insurance that covers liability, damages, and other losses for vehicles used in your business as a business expense. If you use a vehicle only for business, you can deduct 100% of your insurance costs. If you operate a vehicle for both business and personal use, you can deduct only the part of the insurance premiums that applies to the business use of your vehicle. For example, if you use a car 60% for business and 40% for personal reasons, you can deduct 60% of your insurance costs.

If you use the standard mileage rate to deduct your car expenses, you can't take a separate deduction for insurance. The standard rate is intended to cover your insurance costs. (See Chapter 8 for more on vehicle deductions.)

I. Interest on Business Loans

Interest you pay on business loans is usually a currently deductible business expense. It makes no difference whether you pay the interest on a bank loan, personal loan, credit card, line of credit, car loan, or real estate mortgage. Nor does it matter whether the collateral you used to get the loan was business or personal property. If you use the money for business, the interest you pay to get that money is a deductible business expense. It's how you use the money that counts, not how you get it. Borrowed money is used for business when you buy something with the money that's deductible as a business expense.

> **EXAMPLE:** Max, the sole proprietor owner of a small construction company, borrows $50,000 from the bank to buy new construction equipment. He pays 6% interest on the loan. His annual interest expense is deductible.

Your deduction begins only when you spend the borrowed funds for business purposes. You get no business deduction for interest you pay on money that you keep in the bank. Money in the bank is considered an investment—at best, you might be able to deduct the interest you pay on the money as an investment expense.

How to Eliminate Nondeductible Personal Interest

Because interest on money you borrow for personal purposes—like buying clothes or taking vacations—is not deductible, you should avoid paying this type of interest whenever possible. If you own a business, you can do this by borrowing money to pay your business expenses, and then using the money your business earns to pay off your personal debt. By doing this, you "replace" your nondeductible personal interest expense with deductible business expenses.

1.   Home Offices

If you are a homeowner and take the home office deduction, you can deduct the home office percentage of your home mortgage interest as a business expense. (See Chapter 6 for more on the home office deduction.)

2.   Car Loans

If you use your car for business, you can deduct the interest that you pay on your car loan as an interest expense. You can take this deduction whether you deduct your car expenses using the actual expense method or the standard mileage rate, because the standard mileage rate was not intended to encompass interest on a car loan.

If you use your car only for business, you can deduct all of the interest you pay. If you use it for both business and personal reasons, you can deduct the business percentage of the interest. For example, if you use your car 60% of the time for business, you can deduct 60% of the interest you pay on your car loan.

3.   Loans from Relatives and Friends

If you borrow money from a relative or friend and use it for business purposes, you may deduct the interest you pay on the loan as a business expense. However, the IRS is very suspicious of loans between family members and friends. You need to carefully document these transactions.

Treat the loan like any other business loan: Sign a promissory note, pay a reasonable rate of interest, and follow a repayment schedule. Keep your cancelled loan payment checks to prove you really paid the interest.

4.   Loans to Buy a Business

If you borrow money to buy an interest in an S corporation, a partnership, or an LLC, it's wise to seek an accountant's help to figure out how to deduct the interest on your loan. You must allocate the money among the company's assets. Depending on what assets the business owns, the interest might be deductible as a business expense or as an investment expense, which is more limited (see Section I, below).

Interest on money you borrow to buy stock in a C corporation is always treated as investment interest. This is true even if the corporation is small (also called "closely held"), and its stock is not publicly traded.

5.   Interest You Can't Deduct

You can't deduct interest:
- on loans used for personal purposes
- on debts your business doesn't owe
- on overdue taxes (only C corporations can deduct this interest)
- that you pay with funds borrowed from the original lender through a second loan (but you can deduct interest on the new loan once you start making payments)
- that you prepay if you're a cash basis taxpayer (but you may deduct it the next year)
- on money borrowed to pay taxes or fund retirement plans, and
- on loans of more than $50,000 that are borrowed on a life insurance policy on yourself or another owner or employee of your business.

Points and other loan origination fees that you pay to get a mortgage on business property are not deductible business expenses. You must add these amounts to the cost of the building and deduct them over time using depreciation. The same is true for interest on construction loans if you are in the business of building houses or other real property.

6.   Deducting Investment Interest

Investing is not a business, so you can't take a business expense deduction for interest that you pay on money borrowed to make personal investments. You may take a personal deduction for investment interest, but you may not deduct more than your net annual income from your investments. Any amount that you can't deduct in the current year can be carried over to the next year and deducted then.

> **EXAMPLE:** Donald borrows $10,000 on his credit card to invest in the stock market. The interest he pays on the debt is deductible as an itemized personal deduction on Schedule A, Form 1040. He cannot deduct more than he earns during the year from his investments.

7.   Keeping Track of Borrowed Money

As mentioned above, you may deduct interest on borrowed money only if you use the money for business purposes. But if you deposit the money in a bank account that you use to pay both business and personal bills, how do you know what you spent the money on?

> **EXAMPLE:** Linda borrows $10,000 from the bank and deposits it in her checking account. The account already contains $5,000. Over the next several months, she writes checks to pay for food, her mortgage, personal clothing, office furniture, and a computer for her business. How does Linda know whether the money she borrowed was used for her business expenses or personal expenses?

As you might expect, the IRS has plenty of rules to deal with this problem.

Get Separate Credit Cards for Your Business and Car Expenses

If you use the same credit card for your business and nonbusiness expenses, you are theoretically entitled to a business deduction for the credit card interest on your business expenses. However, you'll have a very difficult time calculating exactly how much of the interest you pay is for business expenses. To avoid this problem, use a separate credit card for business. This can be a special business credit card, but it doesn't have to be. You can simply designate one of your ordinary credit cards for business use. If you drive for business and use the actual expense method to take your deduction, it's a good idea to use another credit card just for car expenses. This will make it much easier to keep track of what you spend on your car.

Always pay your personal credit cards first, because you can't deduct the interest you pay on those cards.

a.   30-Day Rule

If you buy something for your business within 30 days of borrowing money, the IRS presumes that the payment was made from those loan proceeds (up to the amount of the loan). This is true regardless of the method or bank account you use to pay the business expense. If you receive the loan proceeds in cash, you can treat the payment as made on the date you receive the cash instead of the date you actually make the payment.

EXAMPLE: Frank gets a loan of $1,000 on August 4 and receives the proceeds in cash. Frank deposits $1,500 in his bank account on August 18 and on August 28 writes a check on the account for a business expense. Also, Frank deposits his paycheck and other loan proceeds into the account, and pays his personal bills from the account during the same period. Regardless of these other transactions, Frank can treat $1,000 of the deposit he made on August 18 as being paid on August 4 from the loan proceeds. In addition, Frank can treat the business expense he paid on August 28 as made from the $1,000 loan proceeds deposited in the account.

b.   Allocation Rules

If you don't satisfy the 30-day rule, special allocation rules determine how loan proceeds deposited in a bank account were spent for tax purposes. Generally, the IRS will assume that loan proceeds were used (spent) before:

- any unborrowed amounts held in the same account, and
- any amounts deposited after the loan proceeds.

EXAMPLE: On January 9, Edith opened a checking account, depositing a $5,000 bank loan and $1,000 in unborrowed money. On February 13, Edith takes $1,000 from the account for personal purposes. On February 15, she takes out $5,000 to buy equipment for her business. Edith must treat the $1,000 used for personal purposes as made from the loan proceeds, leaving only $4,000 of the loan in the account for tax purposes. As a result, she may deduct as a business expense the interest she pays on only $4,000 of the $5,000 she used to buy the business equipment.

It's easy to avoid having to deal with these complex allocation rules: If you think you'll need to keep borrowed money in the bank for more than 30 days before you spend it on your business, place it in a separate account.

J.   Legal and Professional Services

You can deduct fees that you pay to attorneys, accountants, consultants, and other professionals as business expenses if the fees are paid for work related to your business.

EXAMPLE: Ira, a freelance writer, hires attorney Jake to represent him in a libel suit. The legal fees Ira pays Jake are a deductible business expense.

Legal and professional fees that you pay for personal purposes generally are not deductible. For example, you can't deduct the legal fees you incur if you get divorced or you sue someone for a traffic accident injury. Nor are the fees that you pay to write your will deductible, even if the will covers business property that you own.

1. Buying Long-Term Property

If you pay legal or other fees in the course of buying long-term business property, you must add the amount of the fee to the tax basis (cost) of the property. You may deduct this cost over several years through depreciation or deduct it in one year under IRC Section 179. (See Chapter 5 for more on deducting long-term property.)

2. Starting a Business

Legal and accounting fees that you pay to start a business are deductible only as business start-up expenses. You may deduct them over the first 60 months you are in business. The same holds true for incorporation fees or fees that you pay to form a partnership or an LLC. (See Chapter 3 for more on deducting start-up costs.)

3. Accounting Fees

You can deduct any accounting fees that you pay for your business as a deductible business expense—for example, fees you pay an accountant to set up or keep your business books, prepare your business tax return, or give you tax advice for your business.

Self-employed taxpayers may deduct the cost of having an accountant or other tax professional complete the business portion of their tax returns—Schedule C and other business tax forms—but they cannot deduct the time the preparer spends on the personal part of their returns. If you are self-employed and pay a tax preparer to complete your Form 1040 income tax return, make sure that you get an itemized bill showing the portion of the tax preparation fee allocated to preparing your Schedule C (and any other business tax forms you have to file).

K.   Taxes and Licenses

Most taxes that you pay in the course of your business are deductible.

1.   Income Taxes

Federal income taxes that you pay on your business income are not deductible. However, a corporation or partnership can deduct state or local income taxes it pays. Individuals may deduct state and local income taxes only as an itemized deduction on Schedule A, Form 1040. This is a personal, not a business deduction.

However, you can deduct state tax you pay on gross business income as a business expense. For example, Michigan has a Single Business Tax of 2% on business gross receipts over $250,000. This tax is a federally deductible business operating expense. Of course, you can't deduct state taxes from your income for state income tax purposes.

2.   Self-Employment Taxes

If you are a sole proprietor, partner in a partnership, or an LLC member, you may deduct one-half of your self-employment taxes from your total net business income. This deduction reduces the amount of income on which you must pay personal income tax. It's an adjustment to gross income, not a business deduction. You don't list it on your Schedule C; instead, you take it on page one of your Form 1040.

The self-employment tax is a 15.3% tax, so your deduction is equal to 7.65% of your income. To figure out your income after taking this deduction, multiply your net business income by 92.35% or .9235.

> **EXAMPLE:** Billie, a self-employed consultant, earned $70,000 from her business and had $20,000 in business expenses. Her net business income was $50,000. She multiplies this amount by .9235 to determine her net self-employment income, which is $46,175. This is the amount on which Billie must pay federal income tax.

This deduction is intended to help ease the tax burden on the self-employed.

3. Employment Taxes

If you have employees, you must pay half of their Social Security and Medicare taxes from your own funds and withhold the other half from their pay. These taxes consist of a 12.4% Social Security tax, up to an annual salary cap ($87,900 in 2004); and a 2.9% Medicare tax on all employees' pay. You may deduct half of this amount as a business expense. You should treat the taxes you withhold from your employees' pay as wages paid to your employees on your tax return.

> **EXAMPLE:** You pay your employee $18,000 a year. However, after you withhold employment taxes, your employee receives $14,500. You also pay an additional $1,500 in employment taxes from your own funds. You should deduct the full $18,000 salary as employee wages and deduct the $1,500 as employment taxes paid.

4. Sales Taxes

You may not deduct state and local sales taxes that you are required to collect from the buyer and turn over to your state or local government. Do not include these taxes in your gross receipts or sales.

However, you may deduct sales taxes that you pay when you purchase goods or services for your business. The amount of the tax is added to the cost of the goods or services for purposes of your deduction for the item.

> **EXAMPLE:** Jean, a self-employed carpenter, buys $100 worth of nails from the local hardware store. She had to pay $7.50 in state and local sales taxes on the purchase. She may take a $107.50 deduction for the nails. She claims the deduction on her Schedule C as a purchase of supplies.

If you buy a long-term business asset, the sales taxes must be added to its basis (cost) for purposes of depreciation or expensing under IRC Section 179.

EXAMPLE: Jean buys a $2,000 power saw for her carpentry business. She pays $150 in state and local sales tax. The saw has a useful life of more than one year and is therefore a long-term business asset for tax purposes. She can't currently deduct the cost as a business operating expense. Instead, Jean must depreciate the cost over several years or expense the cost (deduct the full cost in one year) under Section 179. The total cost to be depreciated or expensed is $2,150.

5.   Real Property Taxes

You can deduct your current year's state and local property taxes on business real property as business expenses. However, if you prepay the next year's property taxes, you may not deduct the prepaid amount until the following year.

a.   Home Offices

The only real property most home businesspeople own is their home. If you are a homeowner and take the home office deduction, you may deduct the home office percentage of your property taxes. However, as a homeowner, you are entitled to deduct all of your mortgage interest and property taxes, regardless of whether you have a home office. Taking the home office deduction won't increase your income tax deductions for your property taxes, but it will allow you to deduct them from your income for the purpose of calculating your self-employment taxes. You'll save $153 in self-employment taxes for every $1,000 in property taxes you deduct (15.3% self-employment tax x $1,000 = $153).

b.   Charges for Services

Water bills, sewer charges, and other service charges assessed against your business property are not real estate taxes, but they are deductible as business expenses. If you have a home office, you can deduct your home office percentage of these items.

However, real estate taxes imposed to fund specific local benefits such as streets, sewer lines, and water mains, are not deductible as business expenses. Because these benefits increase the value of your property, you should add what you pay for them to the tax basis (cost for tax purposes) of your property.

c. Buying and Selling Real Estate

When real estate is sold, the real estate taxes must be divided between the buyer and seller according to how many days of the tax year each held ownership of the property. You'll usually find information on this in the settlement statement you receive at the property closing.

6. Other Taxes

Other deductible taxes include:

- excise taxes—for example, Hawaii imposes a general excise tax on businesses ranging from 5% to 4% of gross receipts
- state unemployment compensation taxes or state disability contributions
- corporate franchise taxes
- occupational taxes charged at a flat rate by your city or county for the privilege of doing business, and
- state and local taxes on personal property—for example, equipment or machinery that you use in your business.

You can deduct taxes on gasoline, diesel fuel, and other motor fuels that you use in your business. However, these taxes are usually included as part of the cost of the fuel. For this reason, you usually do not deduct these taxes separately on your return. However, you may be entitled to a tax credit for federal excise tax that you pay on fuels used for certain purposes—for example, farming or off-highway business use. See IRS Publication 378, *Fuel Tax Credits and Refunds* (available from the IRS website, www.irs.gov).

7. License Fees

License fees imposed on your business by your local or state government are deductible business expenses. For example, some cities and counties require home business owners to obtain business licenses; the fees for such licenses are deductible. ∎

Chapter 15

Record Keeping and Accounting

When you incur business expenses, you can take tax deductions and save money on your taxes. But those deductions are only as good as the records you keep to back them up.

This is what Alton Williams, a schoolteacher with a sideline business selling new and used books, found out when he was audited by the IRS. Over a four-year period, he claimed over $70,000 in business deductions and inventory costs from his business. Unfortunately, he had no records or receipts tracking these expenses. His excuse: "A receipt is something I never thought I would actually need." The auditor reduced his deductions for each year by 50% to 70%, and Williams ended up owing the IRS almost $10,000 (*Williams v. Commr.*, 67 T.C.M. 2185 (1994)).

Any expense you forget to deduct, or lose after an IRS audit because you can't back it up, costs you dearly. Every $100 in unclaimed deductions costs the average midlevel income person (in a 25% tax bracket) $43 in additional federal and state income and self-employment taxes.

Luckily, it's not difficult to keep records of your business expenses. This chapter shows you how to document your expenditures so you won't end up losing your hard-earned deductions.

A.   Basic Record Keeping for Tax Deductions

This section explains how to set up a basic system for keeping track of your deductible expenses. All you need is:

- a business checking account
- an appointment book
- an expense journal, and
- supporting documents, such as receipts.

This system will get you started, but it is by no means everything you'll need for your business record keeping. For example, every business must keep track of its income. If you make or sell merchandise, you will have to also keep inventory records. And if you have employees, you must create and keep a number of records, including payroll tax records, withholding records, and employment tax returns.

Need help with bookkeeping? For an excellent overall guide to small business bookkeeping, see *Small Time Operator*, by Bernard B. Kamoroff (Bell Springs Press).

1. Business Checkbook and Credit Cards

One of the first things you should do (if you haven't done it already) is set up a separate checking account for your business. Your business checkbook will serve as your basic source of information for recording your business expenses and income. Deposit all of your business receipts (checks you receive from clients, for example) into the account and make all business-related payments by check from the account. Don't use your business account to pay for personal expenses or your personal account to pay for business items.

You are legally required to have a separate business checkbook if you've formed a corporation, partnership, or an LLC. Keeping a separate business account is not legally required if you're a sole proprietor, but it will provide these important benefits:

- It will be much easier for you to keep track of your business income and expenses if you pay them from a separate account.
- Your business account will clearly separate your personal and business finances; this will prove very helpful if you're audited by the IRS.
- Your business account will help convince the IRS that you are running a business and not engaged in a hobby. Hobbyists don't generally have separate bank accounts to fund their pursuits. This is a huge benefit if your business incurs losses because losses from hobbies are not fully deductible. (See Chapter 2 for more on the hobby loss rule.)

a. Setting Up Your Bank Account

Your business checking account should be in your business name. If you're a sole proprietor (like the vast majority of home business owners), you can use your own name. If you've formed a corporation, partnership, or limited liability company, the account should be in your corporate, partnership, or company name. If you're a sole proprietor doing business under an assumed name, you'll probably have to give your bank a copy of your fictitious business name statement.

You don't have to open your business checking account at the same bank where you have your personal checking account. Shop around and open your account with the bank that offers you the best services at the lowest price. If you're doing business under your own name, consider opening up a second personal account in that name and using it solely for your business instead of creating a separate business account. You'll usually pay lower fees for a personal account than for a business account.

If you've incorporated your business, call your bank and ask what documentation you'll have to present to open the account. You will probably need to show the bank a corporate resolution authorizing the opening of a bank account and showing the names of the people authorized to sign checks. Typically, you will also have to fill out, and impress your corporate seal on, a separate bank account authorization form provided by your bank. You will also need to have a federal employer identification number. If you've established a partnership or limited liability company, you'll likely have to show the bank a resolution authorizing the account.

You may also want to establish interest-bearing accounts for your business, in which you can place cash you don't immediately need. For example, you may decide to set up a business savings account or a money market mutual fund in your business name.

b.   When You Write Checks

If you already keep an accurate, updated personal checkbook, do the same for your business checkbook. If, however, you tend to be lax in keeping up your checkbook (as many of us are), you're going to have to change your habits. Now that you're in business, you can't afford this kind of carelessness. Unless you write large numbers of business checks, maintaining your checkbook won't take much time.

When you write business checks, you may have to make some extra notations besides the date, number, amount of the check, and the name of the person or company to which the check is written. If the purpose of the payment is not clear from the name of the payee, describe the business reason for the check—for example, the equipment or service you purchased.

You can use the register that comes with your checkbook and write in all this information manually, or you can use a computerized register. Either way works fine as long as the information is complete and up to date. (See Section B, below, to find out what information you need to record for various types of expenses.)

Don't Write Checks for Cash

Avoid writing checks payable to cash, because this makes it hard to tell whether you spent the money for a business purpose. Writing cash checks might lead to questions from the IRS if you're audited. If you must write a check for cash to pay a business expense, be sure to include the receipt for the cash payment in your records.

c. Use a Separate Credit Card for Business

Use a separate credit card for business expenses instead of putting both personal and business items on one card. Credit card interest for business purchases is 100% deductible, while interest for personal purchases is not deductible at all (see Chapter 14). Using a separate card for business purchases will make it much easier for you to keep track of how much interest you've paid for business purchases. The card doesn't have to be in your business name; you can just use one of your personal credit cards.

2. Appointment Book

The next item you need is an appointment book, day planner, tax diary, or calendar. You can find inexpensive ones in any stationery store. Many computerized calendars are available as well. However, a calendar completed by hand in ink will always be more convincing to the IRS than one you create on a computer, because it is very easy to forge or alter a computerized calendar.

Properly used, this humble item will:

- provide solid evidence that you are serious about making a profit from your business, and thereby avoid an IRS claim that your activity is a hobby (see Chapter 2)
- help show that the expenses you incur are for business, not personal purposes
- help verify entertainment, meal, and travel expenses
- enable you to use a sampling method to keep track of business mileage, instead of keeping track of every mile you drive all year (see Section B, below), and
- if you claim a home office deduction, help show that you use your office for business.

EXAMPLE: Tom, a self-employed advertising copywriter who worked out of his Florida home, kept a detailed appointment book. He devoted a page to each day, listing all of his business activities. He also kept a mileage log to record his business mileage. When he was audited by the IRS, the auditor picked out a trip from his mileage log at random and asked him the purpose of the trip. Tom looked at his appointment book entry for that day, and was able to truthfully and credibly tell the auditor that the trip was to visit a client. The auditor accepted his explanation and the rest of his business mileage deductions.

Every day you work, you should write down in your appointment book (in ink):

- the name of every person you talk to for business
- the date, time, and place of every business meeting,
- every place you go for business
- the amount of all travel, meal, and entertainment expenses that are less than $75, and
- if you claim the home office deduction, the time you spend working in your office.

Here's a sample page from an appointment book for a self-employed real estate salesperson (you'll find information in Section B, below, on what information you need to list for different types of expenses):

Sunday	Monday	Tuesday	Wednesday	Thursday	Friday	Saturday
	1 Meeting with Earl Crowler	*2*	*3* Show 111 Green St.	*4* Answer phones	*5* Sales Meeting	*6* Prepare for open house— Green St.
7 Open House 111 Green St.	*8*	*9* Sales Meeting	*10* Lunch Gibbons	*11*	*12* Meeting Kim Mann	*13*
14 Open House 222 Blue St.	*15*	*16* Show Gibbon 222 Blue St.	*17*	*18* Lunch Mortgage Broker	*19* Sales Meeting	*20*
21 Open House 456 Main St.	*22*	*23* Sales Meeting	*24* Lunch Mortgage Broker	*25* Breakfast Kiwanis Club	*26* Sales Meeting	*27*
28 Open House 826 3rd St.	*29* Continuing education seminar	*30*	*31*			

3. Expense Journal

You can track your expenses by creating what accountants call a chart of accounts—a listing of all your expenses by category. This will show what you buy for your business and how much you spent. It's very easy to do this. You can write your chart out on paper or you can set up a computer spreadsheet program, such as *Excel* or *Lotus*, to do it. Or, if you already have or would prefer to use a financial computer program such as *Quicken*, you can do that instead.

a. Creating a Paper Expense Journal

You can easily create an expense journal by using paper divided into columns or a professional multicolumn book you can get from any stationery or office supply store. These multicolumn pages are also called "ledger sheets." Get ledger sheets with at least 12 or 14 columns. Devote a separate column to each major category of expense you have. Alternatively, you can purchase accounting record books with the expense categories already printed on them. These cost more, however, and may not offer categories that meet your needs.

To decide what your expense categories should be, sit down with your bills and receipts and sort them into categorized piles. IRS Schedule C, *Profit or Loss from Business,* the tax form sole proprietors must use to claim their deductions, lists common categories of business expenses. These categories are a good place to start when you devise your own list, because you'll have to use them when you complete your Schedule C for your taxes. The Schedule C categories include:

- advertising
- bad debts
- car and truck expenses
- commissions and fees
- depletion (rarely used by most small business)
- depreciation and Section 179 expense deductions
- employee benefit programs
- insurance (other than health)
- interest
- legal and professional services
- meals and entertainment
- office expenses
- pension and profit-sharing plans
- rent or lease—vehicles, machinery, and equipment
- rent or lease—other business property
- repairs and maintenance
- supplies
- taxes and licenses
- travel
- utilities, and
- wages.

The Schedule C list of business categories is by no means exclusive. (In fact, it used to contain more categories.) It just gives you an idea of how to break down your expenses. Depending on the nature of your business, you may not need all these categories or you might have others. For example, a graphic designer might have categories for printing and typesetting expenses, or a writer might have a category for agent fees. Be sure not to use multiple categories for the same expenses—for example, you don't need both an "office supplies" and "office expenses" category; one will do.

You should always include a final category called Miscellaneous for various and sundry expenses that are not easily pigeonholed. However, you should use this category sparingly, to account for less than 10% of your total expenses. Unlike "travel" or "advertising," "miscellaneous" is not a type of business expense. It's just a heading under which you can lump together different types of expenses that don't fit into another category.

You can add or delete expense categories as you go along—for example, if you find that your miscellaneous category contains many items for a particular type of expense, add it as an expense category. You don't need a category for automobile expenses, because these expenses require a different kind of documentation for tax purposes.

In separate columns, list the check number, date, and name of the person or company paid for each payment. If you pay by credit card or check, indicate it in the check number column.

Once a month, go through your check register, credit card slips, receipts, and other expense records and record the required information for each transaction. Also, total the amounts for each category when you come to the end of the page and keep a running total of what you've spent for each category for the year to date.

The following example shows a portion of an expense journal.

Expense Journal

Date	Check No.	Transaction	Amount	Advertising	Outside Contractors	Utilities	Supplies	Rent	Travel	Equipment	Meals & Entertainment	Misc.
5/1	123	ABC Properties	500					500				
5/1	124	Office Warehouse	150				150					
5/10	VISA	Computer World	1,000							1,000		
5/15	VISA	Cafe Ole'	50								50	
5/16	Cash	Sam's Stationery	50				50					
5/18	125	Electric Co.	50			50						
5/30	126	Bill Carter	500		500							
Total This Page			2,300		500	50	200	500		1,000	50	
Total Year to Date			7,900	200	2,000	250	400	2,500	300	1,500	250	500

b.   Using Computer Financial Programs

There are many computer programs designed to help people and businesses keep track of their finances. These range from relatively simple checkbook programs like *Quicken*, to complex and sophisticated accounting programs like *QuickBooks Pro* and *MYOB*. You can use these in place of the handwritten ledger sheets or simple spreadsheets described above. However, you'll be better off using handwritten ledger sheets, which are easy to create and simple to keep up to date, instead of a complicated computer program that you can't understand or use properly. So, if you're not prepared to invest the time to use a computer program correctly, don't do it!

This book doesn't explain how to use these programs in detail. You'll need to read the manual and/or tutorial that comes with the program you choose. There are also books that explain how to use them—for example, *Using Quicken In a Business*, by Stephen Nelson, C.P.A. (Redmond Technology Press).

Before You Purchase a Program

You don't want to spend your hard-earned money on a financial program only to discover that you don't like it. Before you purchase a program:

- Talk to others in similar businesses to find out what they use (if they don't like a program, ask them why).
- Think carefully about how many features you need—the more complex the program, the harder it will be to learn and use it.
- Obtain a free demo version to see if you like it—you can usually download one from the software company's website.

The simplest financial programs are those that work off of a computerized checkbook, like *Quicken* and *MS Money*. When you buy something for your business, you write a check using the program. It automatically inputs the data into a computerized check register, and you print out the check using your computer (payments can also be made online). You'll have to input credit card and cash payments separately.

You create a list of expense categories just like you do when you create a ledger sheet or spreadsheet. Programs like *Quicken* come with preselected categories, but these are not adequate for many businesses, so you'll probably have to create your own. The expense category is automatically noted in your register when you write a check.

The program can then take this information and automatically create income and expense reports—that is, it will show you how much you've spent or earned for each category. This serves the same function as the expense journal. It can also create profit and loss statements. You can even import these amounts into tax preparation software, such as *TurboTax*, when it's time to do your income taxes.

Quicken or *MS Money* provides all the tools many small service businesses need. However, if your business involves selling goods or maintaining an inventory, or if you have employees, you'll need a more sophisticated program. Other programs (such as *MYOB Account Edge* and *Plus* by MYOB, *Peachtree Accounting* by Peachtree Software, and *QuickBooks* by Intuit) can accomplish more complex bookkeeping tasks, such as double-entry bookkeeping, tracking inventory, payroll, invoicing, handling accounts receivable, and maintaining fixed asset records.

4.   Supporting Documents

The IRS lives by the maxim that "figures lie and liars figure." It knows very well that you can claim anything in your books and on your tax returns, because you create or complete them yourself. For this reason, the IRS requires that you have documents to support the deductions you claim on your tax return. In the absence of a supporting document, an IRS auditor may conclude that an item you claim as a business expense is really a personal expense, or that you never bought the item at all. Either way, your deduction will be disallowed.

The supporting documents you need depend on the type of deduction. However, at a minimum, every deduction should be supported by documentation showing:

- what you purchased for your business
- how much you paid for it, and
- who (or what company) you bought it from.

You must meet additional record-keeping requirements for local transportation, travel, entertainment, meal, and gift deductions, as well as for certain long-term assets that you buy for your business (Section B, below, covers these rules).

You can meet the basic requirements by keeping the following types of documentation:

- canceled checks
- sales receipts
- account statements
- credit card sales slips
- invoices, or
- petty cash slips for small cash payments.

Keep your supporting documents in a safe place. If you don't have a lot of receipts and other documents to save, you can simply keep them all in a single folder. If you have a lot of supporting documents to save or are the type of person who likes to be extremely well organized, separate your documents by category—for example, income, travel expenses, or equipment purchases. You can use a separate file folder for each category or get an accordion file with multiple pockets.

a.   Canceled Check + Receipt = Proof of Deduction

Manny, a self-employed photographer, buys a $500 digital camera for his business from the local electronics store. He writes a check for the amount and is given a receipt. How does he prove to the IRS that he has a $500 business expense?

Could Manny simply save his canceled check when it's returned from his bank? Many people carefully save all their canceled checks (some keep them for decades), apparently believing that a canceled check is all the proof they need to show that a purchase was a legitimate business expense. This is not the case. All a canceled check proves is that you spent money for something. It doesn't show what you bought. Of course, you can write a note on your check stating what you purchased, but why should the IRS believe what you write on your checks yourself?

MANNY FARBER   **2345**
123 SHADY LANE
ANYTOWN, IL 12345   Date Feb. 1, 2005   12-34/5780

Pay to the
order of   Acme Camera Store $ 500.00

Five hundred and 100/100 ⸺⸺⸺⸺⸺⸺⸺⸺ Dollars

Piggy Bank
100 Main Street
Anytown, IL 12345

Memo   Digital Camera   Manny Farber

⑆ 5780003581: 5355 ⑈ 05556 ⑈ 05555 ⑈

Does Manny's sales receipt prove that he bought his camera for his business? Again, no. A sales receipt only proves that somebody purchased the item listed in the receipt. It does not show who purchased it. You could write a note on the receipt stating that you bought the item, but you could easily lie. Indeed, for all the IRS knows, you could hang around stores and pick up receipts people throw away to give yourself tax deductions.

509257

CUSTOMER'S ORDER NO. 14601		DATE February 1, 2005				
NAME						
ADDRESS						
CITY, STATE, ZIP						

SOLD BY SF	CASH	C.O.D.	CHARGE	ON ACCT.	MDSE. RETD.	PAID OUT

QUAN.		DESCRIPTION		PRICE	AMOUNT
1	1	Minolta Digital Camera		500	500
2					
3					
4					
5					
6					
7					
8					
9					
10					
11				Total	500
12					
RECEIVED BY					

KEEP THIS SLIP FOR REFERENCE

However, when you put a canceled check together with a sales receipt (or an invoice, a cash register tape, or a similar document), you have concrete proof that you purchased the item listed in the receipt. The check proves that you bought something, and the receipt proves what that something is.

This doesn't necessarily prove that you bought the item for your business, but it's a good start. Often, the face of a receipt, sales slip, or the payee's name on your canceled check will strongly indicate that the item you purchased was for your business. But if it's not clear, note the purpose of the purchase on the document. Such a note is not proof of how you used the item, but it will be helpful. For some types of items that you use for both business and personal purposes—cameras are one example—you might be required to keep careful records of your use. (See Section B, below, for the stricter rules that apply to these types of expenses.)

b.   Credit Cards

Using a credit card is a great way to pay business expenses. The credit card slip will prove that you bought the item listed on the slip. You'll also have a monthly statement to back up your credit card slips. You should use a separate credit card for your business.

c.   Account Statements

Sometimes, you'll need to use an account statement to prove an expense. Some banks no longer return canceled checks, or you may pay for something with an ATM card or another electronic funds transfer method. Moreover, you may not always have a credit card slip when you pay by credit card—for example, when you buy an item over the Internet. In these situations, the IRS will accept an account statement as proof that you purchased the item. The chart below shows what type of information you need on an account statement.

Proving Payments With Bank Statements	
If payment is by:	**The statement must show:**
Check	Check number Amount Payee's name Date the check amount was posted to the account by the bank
Electronic funds transfer	Amount transferred Payee's name Date the amount transferred was posted to the account by the bank
Credit card	Amount charged Payee's name Transaction date

B. Records Required for Specific Expenses

The IRS is particularly suspicious of business deductions people take for local transportation, travel, meals, gift, and entertainment expenses. It knows that many people wildly inflate these deductions—either because they're dishonest or because they haven't kept good records and instead estimate how much they think they must have spent. For this reason, special record-keeping requirements apply to these deductions. Likewise, there are special requirements for long-term assets that can be used for both personal and business purposes. If you fail to comply with the requirements discussed below, the IRS may disallow the deduction, even if it was legitimate.

1. Automobile Mileage and Expense Records

If you use a car or other vehicle for business purposes, you're entitled to take a deduction for gas and other auto expenses. You can either deduct the actual cost of your gas and other expenses or take the standard rate deduction based on the number of business miles you drive. In 2004, the standard rate was 37.5 cents per mile. (See Chapter 8 for more on car expenses.)

Either way, you must keep a record of:

- your mileage
- the dates of your business trips
- the places you drove for business, and
- the business purpose for your trips.

The last three items are relatively easy to keep track of. You can record the information in your appointment book, calendar, or day planner. Or, you can record it in a mileage logbook—you can get one for a few dollars from any stationery store and stash it in your car glove compartment.

No Documentation Needed for Utilitarian Vehicles

All this documentation is not required for vehicles that ordinarily are not driven for personal use—for example, ambulances, hearses, trucks weighing more than 14,000 pounds, cement mixers, cranes, tractors, garbage trucks, dump trucks, forklifts, moving vans, and delivery trucks with seating only for the driver (with or without a folding jump seat). But you still need to keep track of your gas, repair, and other expenses.

Calculating your mileage takes more work. The IRS wants to know the total number of miles you drove during the year for business, commuting, and personal driving other than commuting. Commuting is travel between home and your office or other principal place of business. If you work from a home office, you'll have no commuting mileage. Personal miles include, for example, trips to the grocery store, personal vacations, or visits to friends or relatives.

Claiming a Car Is Used Solely for Business

If you use a car 100% for business, you don't need to keep track of your personal or commuting miles. However, you can successfully claim to use a car 100% for business only if you:

- work out of a tax deductible home office
- have at least two cars, and
- use one car just for business trips.

There are several ways to keep track of your mileage; some are easy and some are a bit more complicated.

a.   52-Week Mileage Book

The hardest way to track your mileage—and the way the IRS would like you to do it—is to keep track of every mile you drive every day, 52 weeks a year, using a mileage logbook or business diary. This means you'll list every trip you take, whether for business, or personal reasons. If you enjoy record keeping, go ahead and use this method. But there are easier ways.

b.   Tracking Business Mileage

An easier way to keep track of your mileage is to record your mileage only when you use your car for business. Here's what to do:

- obtain a mileage log book and keep it in your car with a pen attached
- note your odometer reading in the logbook at the beginning and end of every year that you use the car for business (if you don't know your Jan. 1 odometer reading for this year, you might be able to estimate it by looking at auto repair receipts that note your mileage)
- record your mileage and note the business purpose for the trip every time you use your car for business, and

- add up your business mileage when you get to the end of each page in the logbook (this way, you'll only have to add the page totals at the end of the year instead of all the individual entries).

Here's an example of a portion of a page from a mileage logbook.

Mileage Log

Date	Business Purpose	Odometer Reading Begin	End	Business Miles
5/1	Visit Art Andrews—potential client	10,111	10,196	85
5/4	Delivered documents to Bill James in Stockton	10,422	10,476	54
5/5	Picked up office supplies	10,479	10,489	10
5/8	Meeting—Acme Corp.—Sacramento	10,617	10,734	117
5/10	Lunch with Stu Smith—client	10,804	10,841	37
5/13	Meeting—Acme Corp.—Sacramento	10,987	11,004	117
5/15	Breakfast—Mary Moss—client	11,201	11,222	21
5/15	Lunch—Sam Simpson—potential client	11,222	11,247	25
5/15	Attend sales seminar—Hilton Hotel	11,247	11,301	54
5/17	Bank	11,399	11,408	9
5/18	Meeting—ABC Company	11,408	11,436	28
5/20	Sales presentation—Smith Bros. & Co.	11,544	11,599	55
Total				604

At the end of the year, your logbook will show the total business miles you drove during the year. You calculate the total miles you drove during the year by subtracting your January 1 odometer reading from your December 31 reading.

If you use the actual expense method, you must also calculate your percentage of business use of the car. You do this by dividing your business miles by your total miles.

EXAMPLE: Yolanda uses her car extensively for her home business. At the beginning of the year her odometer reading was 34,201 miles. On December 31, it was 58,907 miles. Her total mileage for the year was therefore 24,706. She recorded 62 business trips in her mileage logbook for a total of 9,280 miles. Her business use percentage of her car is 37% (9,280 ÷ 24,706 = .366).

Record Your Mileage Electronically

If writing your mileage down in a paper mileage logbook seems too primitive, you can keep your records in electronic form with a Palm Pilot or computer. There is special software available for recording business mileage. However, be warned: Although the IRS's official policy is that electronic records are acceptable, many IRS auditors are old-fashioned. They like to see paper and ink mileage records because they are much harder to alter, forge, or create in a hurry than electronic records.

c.   Sampling Method

There is an even easier way to track your mileage: use a sampling method. Under this method, you keep track of your business mileage for a sample portion of the year and use your figures for that period to extrapolate your business mileage for the whole year.

This method assumes that you drive about the same amount for business throughout the year. To back up this assumption, you must scrupulously keep an appointment book showing your business appointments all year long. If you don't want to keep an appointment book, don't use the sampling method.

Your sample period must be at least 90 days—for example, the first three months of the year. Alternatively, you may sample one week each month—for example, the first week of every month. You don't have to use the first three months of the year or the first week of every month; you could use any other three-month period or the second, third, or fourth week of every month. Use whatever works best for you—you want your sample period to be as representative as possible of the business travel you do throughout the year.

You must keep track of the total miles you drove during the year by taking odometer readings on January 1 and December 31 and deduct any atypical mileage before applying your sample results.

EXAMPLE: Tom, a traveling salesman, uses the sample method to compute his mileage, keeping track of his business miles for the first three months of the year. He drove 6,000 miles during that time, and had 4,000 business miles. His business use percentage of his car was 67%. From his January 1 and December 31 odometer readings, Tom knows he drove a total of 27,000 miles during the year. However, Tom drove to the Grand Canyon for vacation, so he deducts this 1,000 mile trip from his total. This leaves him with 26,000 total miles for the year. To calculate his total business miles, he multiplies the yearlong total by the business use percentage of his car: 67% x 26,000 = 17,420. Tom claims 17,420 business miles on his tax return.

d.   Keeping Track of Actual Expenses

If you take the deduction for your actual auto expenses instead of using the standard rate (or if you are thinking about switching to this method), keep receipts for all of your auto-related expenses, including gasoline, oil, tires, repairs, and insurance. You don't need to include these expenses in your ledger sheets; just keep them in a folder or envelope. At tax time, add them up to determine how large your deduction will be if you use the actual expense method. Also add in the amount you're entitled to deduct for depreciation of your auto. (See Chapter 8 for more on using the actual expense method, including vehicle depreciation.)

Use a Credit Card for Gas

If you use the actual expense method for car expenses, you should use a credit card when you buy gas. It's best to designate a separate card for this purpose. The monthly statements you receive will serve as your gas receipts. If you pay cash for gas, you must either get a receipt or make a note of the amount in your mileage logbook.

Costs for business-related parking (other than at your office) and for tolls are separately deductible whether you use the standard rate or the actual expense method. Get and keep receipts for these expenses.

2. Entertainment, Meal, Travel, and Gift Expenses

Deductions for business-related entertainment, meals, and travel are hot-button items for the IRS because they have been greatly abused by many taxpayers. You need to have more records for these expenses than for almost any others, and they will be closely scrutinized if you're audited.

Whenever you incur an expense for business-related entertainment, meals, gifts, or travel, you must document the following five facts:

- The date: The date you incurred the expense will usually be listed on a receipt or credit card slip; appointment books, day planners, and similar documents have the dates preprinted on each page, so entries on the appropriate page automatically date the expense.
- The amount: How much you spent, including tax and tip for meals.
- The place: The nature and place of the entertainment or meal will usually be shown on a receipt, or you can record it in an appointment book.
- The business purpose: Show that the expense was incurred for your business—for example, to obtain future business, encourage existing business relationships, and so on. It is not sufficient merely to write "lunch with client" on a receipt. What you need to show depends on whether the business conversation occurred before, during, or after entertainment or a meal. (See Chapter 7 for more information about these rules.)
- The business relationship: If entertainment or meals are involved, you should record the business relationship among the people at the event—for example, list their names and occupations and any other information needed to establish their business relation to you.

Proof Required for Travel, Entertainment, and Gift Deductions

Records must show:	Amount	Time	Place or Description	Business Purpose and Relationship
Travel	Cost of each separate expense for travel, lodging, and meals. Incidental expenses may be totaled in categories such as taxis, daily meals, and so on.	Dates you left and returned for each trip, and the number of days spent on business.	Name of city, town, or other destination.	Business purpose for the expense, or the benefit gained or expected to be gained.
Entertainment (including meals)	Cost of each separate expense. Incidental expenses such as taxis, telephones, etc. may be totaled on a daily basis.	Date of entertainment.	Name and address or location of place of entertainment. Type of entertainment, if not otherwise apparent. For entertainment directly before or after business discussion: date, place, nature, and duration.	Nature of business discussion or activity. Identities of people who took part in discussion and entertainment. Occupations or other information (such as names or titles) about the participants that shows their business relationship to you. Proof you or your employee was present at business meal.
Gifts	Cost of gift.	Date of gift.	Description of gift.	Same as for Entertainment.

The IRS does not require you to keep receipts, canceled checks, credit card slips, or any other supporting documents for entertainment, meal, gift, or travel expenses that cost less than $75. However, *you must still document the five facts listed above.* This exception does not apply to lodging—that is, hotel or similar costs—when you travel for business. You do need receipts for these expenses, even if they cost less than $75.

⚠️ **The $75 rule applies only to travel, meals, gifts, and entertainment.** The rule that you don't need receipts for expenses of less than $75 applies *only* to travel, gift, meal, and entertainment expenses. It does not apply to other types of business expenses. For example, if you go to the office supply store and buy $50 worth of supplies for your business and then spend $70 for lunch with a client, you need a receipt for the office supplies, but not the business lunch. If you find this rule hard to remember, simply keep all of your receipts.

All this record keeping is not as hard as it sounds. You can record the five facts you have to document in a variety of ways, and the information doesn't have to be all in one place. Information that is shown on a receipt, canceled check, or other item need not be duplicated in a log, appointment book, calendar, or account book. Thus, for example, you can record the five facts with:
- a receipt, credit card slip, or similar document alone
- a receipt combined with an appointment book entry, or
- an appointment book entry alone (for expenses less than $75).

However you document your expense, you are supposed to do it in a timely manner. You don't need to record the details of every expense on the day you incur it. It is sufficient to record them on a weekly basis. However, if you're prone to forget details, it's best to get everything you need in writing within a day or two.

Using Electronic Records to Document Travel Deductions

These days, many of us fly without an actual airline ticket, using "paperless travel." When you book a flight this way, you will receive a receipt and itinerary (via download from a Website, email, or fax), but no actual ticket. The IRS says it's perfectly fine to use copies of these types of electronic records to document a travel deduction, as long as they show the amount spent, date, location, and business purpose of the expenditure. Make sure you save these records, in either digital or hard copy format. (Ltr. Ruling 98050007.)

a.   Receipt or Credit Card Slip Alone

An easy way to document an entertainment, gift, travel, or meal expense is to use your receipt, credit card slip, invoice, or bill. A receipt or credit card slip will ordinarily contain the name and location of the place where the expense was incurred, the date, and the amount charged. Thus, three of the five facts you must document are already covered. You just need to describe the business purpose and business relationship (if entertainment or meals are involved). You can write this directly on your receipt or credit card slip.

> **EXAMPLE:** Mary, a freelance computer programmer, has lunch with Harold, president of Acme Technologies, Inc., to discuss doing some programming work for Acme. Her restaurant bill shows the date, the name and location of the restaurant, the number of people served, and the amount of the expense. Mary just has to document the business purpose for the lunch and identify her dining companion. She writes on the receipt: "Lunch with Harold Lipshitz, President Acme Technologies, Inc. Discussed signing contract for programming services." All five facts Mary must prove are on the receipt. This is all Mary needs. She need not duplicate the information elsewhere—for example, in an appointment book or dayplanner.

CESAR Lunch

Check No Tab Cov Server Time Date
262603 7 2   83 12:38:29 PM 1/28/0
4

                                    8.75
1   PETRALE   5.25
1   FRIED POTATOES   7.75
1   JAMON PLATE

                                   21.75
     Food Sub-Total
                                    2.75
1   ROOT BEER   3.00
1   ICED TEA

                                    5.75
     Beverage Sub-Total
                                   27.50
     SUB TOTAL
                                    2.27
     Sales Tax
                                  29.77
     TOTAL
           THANK YOU
           DYLAN

Lunch with Harold Lipshitz, President,
Acme Technologies, Inc. Discussed signing
contract for programming services.

b.   Receipt Plus Appointment Book

You can also document the five facts you need to record for an expense by combining the information on a receipt with entries in an appointment book, day planner, calendar, diary, or similar record.

> **EXAMPLE:** Assume that Mary from the above example saves her receipt from the restaurant where she had her business lunch. She writes nothing on the receipt. She still needs to document the five facts. Her receipt contains the date, the name and location of the restaurant, and the cost of the lunch. She records who she ate with and the business purpose of the lunch by writing a note in her appointment book: "Lunch—Harold Lipshitz, President Acme Technologies, Inc. Discussed signing contract for programming services."

```
                        Appointment Book

 19   Thursday         232/134

   7
   8
   9
  10
  11
  12   Lunch—Harold Lipshitz, President, Acme Technologies. Cesar Restaurant.
   1   Discussed signing contract for programming service.
   2
   3
   4
   5
   6

 20   Friday           233/133

   7
   8
```

c.   Appointment Book Alone

If your expense is for less than $75, you don't need to keep a receipt (unless the expense is for lodging). You may record the five facts in your appointment book, dayplanner, daily diary, calendar, or on any other sheet of paper.

> **EXAMPLE:** Assume that Mary from the above examples doesn't keep her receipt from her lunch. Because lunch cost less than $75, she does not need it. Instead, she documents the five facts she needs to record in her appointment book. She writes: "Lunch — Cesar Restaurant, with Harold Lipshitz, President Acme Technologies, Inc. Discussed signing contract for programming services. $29.77." This short entry records the place of the lunch, who she ate with, the business purpose, and the amount. She doesn't need to add the date because this is already shown by her appointment book.

Receipts to Keep	
Type of Expense	**Receipts to Save**
Travel	Airplane, train, or bus ticket stubs, travel agency receipts, rental car, and so on.
Meals	Meal check, credit card slip.
Lodging	Statement or bill from hotel or other lodging provider. Your own written records for cleaning, laundry, telephone charges, tips, and other charges not shown separately on hotel statement.
Entertainment	Bill from entertainment provider; ticket stubs for sporting event, theatre, or other event; credit card slips.

3. Listed Property

Listed property refers to certain types of long-term business assets that can easily be used for personal as well as business purposes. Listed property includes:

- cars, boats, airplanes, motorcycles, and other vehicles
- computers
- cellular phones, and
- any other property generally used for entertainment, recreation, or amusement—for example, VCRs, cameras, and camcorders.

Because all listed property is long-term business property, you cannot deduct it like a business expense. Instead, you must depreciate it over several years or deduct it in one year under Section 179. (See Chapter 5 for detailed information on deducting listed property.)

a. Special Record-Keeping Requirements

The IRS fears that taxpayers might claim business deductions for listed property, but use it for personal reasons. That's why you're required to document how you use listed property. Keep an appointment book, log book, business diary, or calendar showing the dates, times, and reasons for which the property is used—both business and personal. You also can purchase log books for this purpose at stationery or office supply stores.

EXAMPLE: Bill, an accountant, purchases a computer he uses 50% for business and 50% to play games. He must keep a log showing his business use of the computer. Following is a sample from one week in his log.

Usage Log for Personal Computer			
Date	Time of Business Use	Reason for Business Use	Time of Personal Use
5/1	4.5 hours	Prepared client tax returns	1.5 hours
5/2			3 hours
5/3	2 hours	Prepared client tax returns	
5/4			2 hours

b.   Exception to Record-Keeping Rule for Computers

You usually have to document your use of listed property even if you use it only for business. However, there is an exception to this rule for computers: If you use a computer or computer peripheral (such as a printer) only for business and keep it at your business location, you need not comply with the record-keeping requirement. This includes computers that you keep at your home office if the office qualifies for the home office deduction. (The home office deduction is covered in Chapter 6.)

EXAMPLE: John, a freelance writer, works full time in his home office, which he uses exclusively for writing. The office is clearly his principal place of business and qualifies for the home office deduction. He buys a $4,000 computer for his office and uses it exclusively for his writing business. He does not have to keep records showing how he uses the computer.

This exception applies only to computers and computer peripheral equipment. It doesn't apply to other items such as calculators, copiers, fax machines, or typewriters.

C. How Long to Keep Records

You need to have copies of your tax returns and supporting documents available in case you are audited by the IRS or another taxing agency. You might also need them for other purposes—for example, to get a loan, mortgage, or insurance.

You should keep your records for as long as the IRS has to audit you after you file your returns for the year. These statutes of limitation range from three years to forever—they are listed in the table below.

To be on the safe side, you should keep your tax returns indefinitely. They usually don't take up much space, so this shouldn't be a big hardship. Your supporting documents probably take up more space. You should keep these for at least six years after you file your return. If you file a fraudulent return, keep your supporting documents indefinitely (if you have any). If you're audited, they will show that at least some of your deductions were legitimate.

Keep your long-term asset records for three years after the depreciable life of the asset ends. For example, keep records for five-year property (such as computers) for eight years. You should keep your ledger sheets for as long as you're in business, because a potential buyer of your business might want to see them.

Scanning Your Records

If you don't want to keep paper copies of your tax records, you can make digital copies by scanning them and storing them on a computer hard disk or CD-ROM. The IRS has approved the use of electronic storage systems for this purpose. (Rev Proc 97-22, 1997-1 CB 652 .)

IRS Statute of Limitations	
If:	**The limitations period is:**
You failed to pay all the tax due	3 years
You underreported your gross income for the year by more than 25%	6 years
You filed a fraudulent return	No limit
You did not file a return	No limit

D. What If You Don't Have Proper Tax Records?

Because you're human, you may not have kept all the records required to back up your tax deductions. Don't despair, all is not lost—you may be able to fall back on the Cohan rule. This rule (named after the Broadway entertainer George M. Cohan, who was involved in a tax case in the 1930s) is the taxpayer's best friend. The Cohan rule recognizes that all business people must spend at least some money to stay in business, and so must have at least some deductible expenses, even if they don't have adequate records to back them up.

If you're audited and lack adequate records for a claimed deduction, the IRS can use the Cohan rule to make an estimate of how much you must have spent, and allow you to deduct that amount. However, you must provide at least some credible evidence on which to base this estimate, such as receipts, canceled checks, notes in your appointment book, or other records. Moreover, the IRS will allow you to deduct only the smallest amount you must have spent, based on the records you provide. In addition, the Cohan rule cannot be used for travel, meal, entertainment, or gift expenses, or for listed property.

If an auditor claims you lack sufficient records to back up a deduction, you should always bring up the Cohan rule and argue that you should still get the deduction based on the records you do have. At best, you'll probably get only part of your claimed deductions. If the IRS auditor disallows your deductions entirely or doesn't give you as much as you think you deserve, you can appeal in court and bring up the Cohan rule again there. You might have more success with a judge. However, you can't compel an IRS auditor or a court to apply the Cohan rule in your favor. They have discretion to decide whether to apply the rule and how large a deduction to give you.

> **EXAMPLE:** Ajuba Gaylord had a part-time business as a home-based salesperson. One year, she took a $474 deduction for postage and over $1,100 for meals and entertainment. The IRS disallowed both deductions because she had no documentary evidence showing that the expenses were for her business. However, the tax court applied the Cohan Rule and allowed her a $75 deduction for postage. It reasoned that this was the least that she must have spent, given the nature of her business. However, the court would not use the Cohan Rule to grant her a deduction for meal and entertainment expenses. (*Gaylord v. Comm'r.*, T.C. Memo 2003-273.)

Reconstructing Tax Records

If you can show that you possessed adequate records at one time, but now lack them due to circumstances beyond your control, you may reconstruct your records for an IRS audit. Circumstances beyond your control include acts of nature such as floods, fires, earthquakes, or theft. (Treas. Reg. 1.275.5(c)(5).) If you lose your tax records while moving, that doesn't constitute circumstances beyond your control. Reconstructing records means you either create brand new records just for your audit or obtain other evidence to corroborate your deductions—for example, statements from people or companies from whom you purchased items for your business.

E.   Accounting Methods

An accounting method is a set of rules used to determine when and how your income and expenses are reported. Accounting methods might sound like a rather dry subject, but your choice about how to account for your business expenses and income will have a huge impact on your tax deductions. You don't have to become as expert as a C.P.A. on this topic, but you should understand the basics.

You must choose an accounting method when you file your first tax return. If you later want to change your accounting method, you must get IRS approval. The IRS requires some types of businesses to use the accrual method. If your business doesn't fall into this group, you are free to choose the method you want, as long as it clearly shows your income and expenses. If you operate two or more separate businesses, you can use a different accounting method for each. (A business is separate for tax purposes only if you keep a separate set of books and records for it.)

There are two basic methods of accounting: cash basis and accrual basis. Most home businesses can use either method.

Personal and Business Accounting Methods May Differ

You can account for business and personal items using different accounting methods. For example, you can figure your business income under an accrual method, even if you use the cash method to figure personal items. Almost everyone uses the cash basis method of accounting for personal finances, so it might be convenient to continue to use it for personal items even if you want or are required to use the accrual method for your business.

---

1.   Cash Method

The cash method is by far the simplest method. It is used by individuals who are not in business and by most small businesses that provide services and do not maintain inventory or offer credit. The cash method is based on this common sense idea: You haven't earned income for tax purposes until you actually receive the money, and you haven't incurred an expense until you actually pay the money. Using the cash basis method, then, is like maintaining a checkbook. You record income only when the money is received and expenses only when they are actually paid. Although it's called the "cash" method, payments by check, credit card, or electronic funds transfer also count as cash payments

> **EXAMPLE 1:** Helen, a home-based marketing consultant, completes a market research report on September 1, 2004, but isn't paid by the client until February 1, 2005. Using the cash method, Helen records the payment as income in February 2005—when she receives it.

> **EXAMPLE 2:** On December 1, Helen goes to the Acme electronics store and buys a laser printer for her consulting business. She buys the item on credit from Acme—she's not required to make any payments until March 1, 2005. Helen does not record the expense until 2005 when she actually pays for the printer.

a.   Constructive Receipt

Under the cash method, payments are "constructively received" when an amount is credited to your account or otherwise made available to you without restrictions. Constructive receipt is as good as actual receipt. If you authorize someone to be your agent and receive income for you, you are considered to have received it when your agent receives it.

> **EXAMPLE:** Interest is credited to your business bank account in December 2005, but you do not withdraw it or enter it into your passbook until 2006. You must include the amount in gross business income for 2005, not 2006.

b.   No Postponing Income

You cannot hold checks or other payments from one tax year to another to avoid paying tax on the income. You must report the income in the year the payment is received or made available to you without restriction.

> **EXAMPLE:** On December 1, 2005, Helen receives a $5,000 check from a client. She holds the check and doesn't cash it until January 10, 2006. She still has to report the $5,000 as income for 2005 because she constructively received it that year.

c.   No Prepayment of Expenses

Just as you can't delay receipt of income using the cash method, you can't hurry up the payment of expenses by paying them in advance. An expense you pay in advance can be deducted only in the year to which it applies.

> **EXAMPLE:** Helen pays $1,000 in 2005 for a business insurance policy that is effective for one year, beginning July 1st. She can deduct $500 in 2005 and $500 in 2006.

2.   Accrual Method

In accrual basis accounting, you report income or expenses as they are earned or incurred, rather than when they are actually collected or paid. With the accrual method, you count income when a sale occurs and expenses when you receive the goods or services. You don't have to wait until you see the money or actually pay money out of your checking account. The accrual method can be difficult to use because complex rules determine when income or expenses accrue.

a.   When Expenses Are Incurred

Under the accrual method, you generally deduct a business expense when:

- you are legally obligated to pay the expense
- the amount you owe can be determined with reasonable accuracy, and
- you have received or used the property or services involved.

> **EXAMPLE:** Bill, the owner of a home-based furniture refinishing business, borrows $10,000 from his bank to help pay his business

operating expenses. He signs a promissory note on December 15, 2005 and receives the money the same day, but doesn't start making payments to the bank until the following January. Bill can deduct the expense in 2005 because he became legally obligated to pay the expense upon signing the note, the amount of the expense can be determined from the note, and he received the money that day.

Thus, when you use the accrual method, you can take a deduction for an expense you incur even if you don't actually pay for it until the following year. You can't do this under the cash basis method. There are obvious advantages to getting a tax deduction this year without actually having to shell out any money until a future year.

b.   When Income Is Received

While the accrual method lets you deduct expenses that you haven't paid for yet, it also requires you to report payments you haven't yet received as income. Transactions are counted as income when an order is made, an item is delivered, or services are provided, regardless of when the money for them (receivables) is actually received or paid.

> **EXAMPLE:** Andrea repairs watches in her home workshop as a part-time business. She is hired to repair an antique watch and finishes the job on December 15, 2005. She bills the customer for $250, which she receives on January 20, 2005. Because she uses the accrual method of accounting, Andrea must count the $250 as income in December 2004, because that's when she earned the money by finishing the job. She must report this income in her 2004 tax return, even though she did not receive the money that year.

c.   Businesses That Must Use the Accrual Method

Any business, however small, may use the accrual method. Some types of businesses are required to use it, including C corporations with average annual gross receipts exceeding $5 million. As a general rule, you are required to use the accrual method if you produce, purchase, or sell merchandise and are required to maintain an inventory (see Chapter 10). However, there are two big exceptions that relieve most home businesses from having to use the accrual method.

Exception #1—Businesses That Earn Less Than $1 Million: Even if you deal in merchandise, you may use the cash basis method if your average annual gross receipts were $1 million or less for the three tax years ending with the prior tax year. This includes the vast majority of home businesses that have inventories.

Exception #2—Some Businesses That Earn Less Than $10 Million: Even if your home business earns more than $1 million per year, you may use the cash basis method if your average annual gross receipts were $10 million or less for the three tax years ending with the prior tax year, *and*:

- your principal business is providing services
- your principal business is making or modifying personal property according to customers' specifications, or
- your business does not involve mining, manufacturing, wholesale or retail trade, or certain information services (see IRS Publication 538, *Accounting Periods and Methods,* for more details).

3. Which Is Better—Accrual or Cash Method Accounting?

There is no single best accounting method. Each method has its advantages and disadvantages. The cash basis method is much simpler to use and easier to understand. Because you don't report income until it's actually received, it's more advantageous than the accrual method if you're in a business in which you are paid slowly.

EXAMPLE: Tom is a freelance writer who usually must wait months until he is paid for his articles by magazines and newspapers. He contracts with the *Podunk Review* to write an article about inventions created by people in jail. He is to be paid $1,000 within 60 days after the article is accepted. The article is accepted by the *Podunk Review* on September 1, 2004, but Tom doesn't receive his check until March 2005. If he used the accrual method, he would have to recognize the $1,000 as income for 2004, even though he didn't receive it that year. If he used the cash basis method, he wouldn't recognize the income until 2005, when he gets the check.

The accrual method is more complicated than the cash basis method and harder to use, but it shows the ebb and flow of business income and debts more accurately than the cash basis method. Moreover, the accrual method is more advantageous than the cash basis method if you are paid promptly by your clients or customers, because you are allowed to deduct expenses when you incur them, not when you actually pay for them.

EXAMPLE: Dick is a home-based sex therapist who requires all of his patients to pay him by cash or check after each appointment. In 2004, he received $100,000 from his patients. To help offset this income, he buys a $50,000 SUV in December 2004, which he drives solely for his business. He signs a three-year car loan in 2004, and puts $5,000 down. Under the accrual method, he may deduct the entire $50,000 car expense from his 2004 income, even though he didn't actually pay it all that year. If Dick used the cash method, he could only deduct his car expenses in the year they were actually paid. (Note: Dick may deduct the SUV, a long-term business asset, in one year by using IRC Section 179; see Chapter 5 for more information.)

It's Not Easy to Change Your Mind

You choose your accounting method by checking a box on your tax form when you file your tax return. Once you choose a method, you can't change it without getting permission from the IRS. You must file IRS Form 3115, *Application for Change in Accounting Method*, 180 days before the end of the year in which you want to make the change. Changing your accounting method can have serious consequences, so consult a tax professional before filing this form.

F.   Tax Years

You are required to pay taxes for a 12-month period, also known as the tax year. Sole proprietors, partnerships, limited liability companies, S corporations, and personal service corporations (see Chapter 1) are required to use the calendar year as their tax year—that is, January 1 through December 31.

However, there are exceptions that permit some small businesses to use a tax year that does not end in December (also known as a fiscal year). You need to get the IRS's permission to use a fiscal year. The IRS doesn't want businesses to use a fiscal year, but it might grant you permission if you can show a good business reason for it.

One good reason to use a fiscal year is that your business is seasonal. For example, if you earn most of your income in the spring and incur most of your expenses in the fall, a tax year ending in July or August might be better than a calendar tax year ending in December because the income and expenses on each tax return will be more closely related. To get permission to use a fiscal year, you must file IRS Form 8716, *Election to Have a Tax Year Other Than a Required Tax Year.* ■

Chapter 16

Claiming Tax Deductions for Prior Years

S am, a self-employed genealogy researcher, has worked out of his home office for the last four years. However, he has never taken the home office deduction because he was afraid it would increase his chances of being audited. After reading this book, he realizes that he should have claimed the deduction on his last three tax returns. Had he done so, he would have saved thousands on his taxes. But what can he do now?

Fortunately, tax returns are not engraved in stone. If, like Sam, you realize that you failed to claim tax deductions to which you were entitled, you may be able to amend your tax returns for those years and get the IRS to send you a refund check.

A. Reasons for Amending Your Tax Return

It's very common for taxpayers to file amended tax returns. Here are some reasons why you might want to amend a tax return:

- You forgot to take a deduction.
- You have a net operating loss for the year and want to apply it to prior years.
- You claimed a deduction to which you were not entitled.
- You entered incorrect information on your return.
- A retroactive change in the tax laws makes you eligible for an additional deduction.

You need not amend your return if you discover that you made a simple math error. These will be corrected by the IRS computers, and you'll be notified of the change by mail.

However, if you made a mistake in your favor, failed to report income, or took deductions to which you were not entitled, amending your return may avoid all or some fines, interest, and penalties if you're later audited by the IRS.

⚠ **Filing an amended return makes an audit more likely.** You don't have to file an amended return if you don't want to. Filing an amended tax return increases the chances that your tax return for the year involved will be audited by the IRS. Thus, it may not be worth doing unless you are entitled to a substantial refund. If you're not sure whether to amend, consult a tax professional for advice.

1.   Net Operating Losses

Some home business owners pay out more for expenses than they take in as income. When a business's expenses for a tax year exceed its income, it has a "net operating loss" (NOL for short). Although it may not be pleasant to lose money over an entire year, an NOL has some important tax benefits: You can apply the NOL to reduce your taxable income from other sources for the same tax year—for example, income from a job, your spouse's income, or investment income. If you still have all or part of your NOL left over, you have the option of applying it to future tax years. This is called carrying a loss forward. You can carry the NOL forward for up to 20 years and use it to reduce your taxable income in the future.

Alternatively, you may apply the loss to past tax years by filing an amended return for those years. Ordinarily, you may elect to carry back the loss for the two years before the year you incurred the loss. However, if you had an NOL for 2001 or 2002, you may carry back the loss five years before the NOL year. The loss is used to offset the taxable income for the earliest year first, and then applied to the next year(s). This will reduce the tax you had to pay for those years and result in a tax refund. This is called carrying a loss back.

As a general rule, it's advisable to carry a loss back, so you can get a quick refund from the IRS on your prior years' taxes. However, you may elect not to carry an NOL back if you paid no income tax in prior years, or if you expect your income to rise substantially in future years and you want to use your NOL in the future, when you'll be subject to a higher tax rate.

Need to know more about NOLs? Refer to IRS Publication 536, *Net Operating Losses*, for more information. You can download it from the IRS website at www.irs.gov, or obtain a paper copy by calling the IRS at 800-TAX-FORM.

2.   Retroactive Tax Laws

Sometimes, Congress or the IRS changes the tax laws or regulations and makes the change retroactive—that is, the change applies to returns filed some time before the change was made. If a retroactive change is more favorable to you than the laws that were in effect when you filed your return, you might be entitled to a refund for prior years.

a.   House Sales After May 6, 1997

By far the most important retroactive tax change affecting home businesses in recent years involves the home office deduction. Under the tax law in effect before 2003, home business owners who took the home office deduction often had to pay extra tax when they sold their homes. If they took a home office deduction for more than three of the five years before they sold their house, they had to pay capital gains tax on the profit from the home office portion of their home.

Fortunately, effective December 24, 2002, the IRS changed its regulations to eliminate this requirement. As long as you live in your home for at least two of the five years before you sell it, the profit you make on the sale—up to $250,000 for single taxpayers and $500,000 for married taxpayers filing jointly—is not taxable. (See Chapter 6 for more information on this change.) Moreover, the change was made retroactive to May 6, 1997. If you sold your house after this date and paid capital gains tax on the home office portion, and you meet the two-out-of-five-year requirement, you are entitled to a refund of the tax. You obtain your refund by filing an amended tax return for the year.

> **EXAMPLE:** Greta, the owner of a home-based crafts business, sold her house in 2001 for a $50,000 profit. She used 20% of the space in her house as a home workshop, and took a home office deduction every year. Thus, she had to pay a $2,000 capital gains tax on her profit from the house sale (20% x $50,000 = $10,000 x 20% = $2,000). In 2005, she amends her 2002 tax return to eliminate the capital gains tax, and receives a refund from the IRS of the $2,000.

However, it may be too late for you to claim this refund, because there are limits on how far back you can go to amend your returns. See Section B, below, for information on these time limits.

b.   Bonus Depreciation

Another instance of a retroactive change in the tax laws involves bonus depreciation. In March 2002, Congress enacted a law allowing business owners to take an additional 30% (later increased to 50%) first-year depreciation deduction for business assets purchased after 9/11/01, the date of the attack on the World Trade Center. If you filed your 2001 income taxes before March 2002, you would not have been able to take this deduction because the law had not yet been enacted. You may amend your 2001 tax return to take the deduction; but you must act by April 15, 2005. (For more on this time limit, see Section B, below; see Chapter 5 for a detailed discussion of bonus depreciation.)

Not every taxpayer wants to take bonus depreciation. However, it applies automatically for tax years 2002 through 2004 unless you file a statement with your tax return that you wish to opt out of the deduction (it is scheduled to end on 12/31/04). (See Chapter 5, Section I1.) If you failed to do so, you should file an amended tax return including such a statement. If you don't file the statement, the IRS will act as if you took a bonus depreciation deduction, even though you really didn't. This could result in your having to pay extra taxes if you sell long-term assets you purchased during 2002-2004. You must file your amendment within the six month period described above. (Write "Filed pursuant to Section 301.9100-2" on the amended return.)

3.   Casualty Losses

There is a special rule for certain types of casualty losses—losses to business property caused by things like fire, floods, or earthquakes. If you suffer a loss to your business property or home office due to a disaster that occurs in an area the President declares to be a disaster area, you have the option of deducting the loss from your previous year's taxes. You do this by filing an amended tax return for the year and deducting the amount of the loss from your taxable income for that year. This will reduce the taxes you had to pay for the year, and the IRS will send you a refund check for the difference. Alternatively, you can wait and deduct your loss from the current year's taxes. But if you want to get some money from the IRS quickly, you should file an amended return (unless you paid no tax the prior year). (See Chapter 14 for a detailed discussion of casualty losses.)

John Kerry Amends His Tax Return

In the midst of the 2004 presidential campaign, Senator John Kerry released his 2003 tax return to the public. A Texas CPA who analyzed the return discovered an error. Kerry and his wife had sold a rare Dutch painting they co-owned for $1,350,000. Kerry's share of the profit on the sale was $175,000. For some reason, his accountant thought this gain should be taxed at the 20% capital gains rate then in effect. However, this was clearly wrong. Kerry's profit should have been taxed at his 28% income tax rate, because the painting was not a capital asset. Soon after this was brought to his attention, Kerry filed an amended tax return for 2003 and paid an extra $11, 577 in income tax for the year.

B. Time Limits for Filing Amended Returns

Unfortunately, you can't wait forever to amend a tax return for a prior year. If you wait too long, you'll forever lose your right to file an amended return for the year, even if it means you'll be forced to give up a deduction for that year to which you were legally entitled.

1. Three-Year Amendment Period

The general rule is that you must file an amended return within three years after the date you filed the original return, or two years after the date you paid the tax, whichever is later. The three-year period applies in most cases. Even if you filed your return for the year before April 15, it is deemed to be filed on that date for amendment purposes. For example, you have until April 15, 2005 to file an amended return for your 2001 taxes, which are deemed to have been filed on April 15, 2002 (even if you filed them earlier).

EXAMPLE: Recall Greta from the example above. She sold her house in 2001, and paid capital gains tax on her profit that a subsequent retroactive law change made refundable. She filed her original 2001 tax return on April 1, 2002. How long does Greta have to amend her 2001 tax return to claim her refund? Until April 15, 2005, three years after she is deemed to have filed her original tax return for 2001 (April 15, 2002). If she fails to meet the deadline, she loses her right to a refund.

However, if you obtained an extension of time to file your original return for the year involved, you may add that time to the three-year period. You can get an automatic extension of time to file your return until August 15, and you can get a further extension until October 15 if the IRS agrees, which it usually does.

EXAMPLE: Assume that Greta from the above example obtained an extension of time to file her 2001 tax return to August 15, 2002. That would give her until August 15, 2005 to amend her tax return for 2001.

2.   Section 179 Deductions

You have much less time to amend your return to claim a Section 179 deduction, which is an extremely valuable deduction for many home business owners. (See Chapter 5 for more information on Section 179.) You must file your amended return within six months after the due date for the return for the tax year involved, including any extensions of time you received. Because tax returns are ordinarily due on April 15, you must file your amended return by October 15 to claim a Section 179 deduction for the prior year, unless you received an extension of time to file your return.

EXAMPLE: Jill bought a $3,000 computer for her home medical record transcription business during 2004. When she did her taxes for the year in early 2005, she thought she had to depreciate the computer's cost over five years. She took a depreciation deduction for the computer on her 2004 tax return. However, she learns later that she could have deducted the entire cost in one year using Section 179. She has until October 15, 2005 to file an amended 2004 return to claim the deduction. If she fails to do so, she loses the right to claim a Section 179 deduction for the property and must use depreciation instead.

3. Net Operating Losses

There are two ways to claim a refund of a prior year's taxes due to a later net operating loss: you can file IRS Form 1040X, *Amended U.S. Individual Income Tax Return* (see Section C, below) within the usual three-year limitation period, or you can seek a quick refund by filing IRS Form 1045, *Application for Tentative Refund*. If you file Form 1045, the IRS is required to send your refund within 90 days. However, you must file Form 1045 within one year after the end of the year in which the NOL arose.

4. Bad Debts

In some instances, you may be able to deduct a business bad debt as a business operating expense. A debt doesn't become "bad" until it is clearly worthless. This may occur years after the loan was originally made. (See Chapter 14 for more on the requirements for deducting bad debts.) If you failed to claim a bad debt deduction on your original tax return for the year the debt became totally worthless, you have up to seven years to file an amended return listing the bad debt. However, the seven-year term applies only to debts that are completely worthless. If a debt is only partially worthless, you must amend your return within the usual three-year period.

5. Business Start-Up Expenses

If you want to deduct your business start-up expenses, you must file an election with the IRS on or before the due date of your first tax return after you start your business. For example, if your business begins in

2005, you must file the election with your 2005 tax return, due April 15, 2006 (or later if you receive an extension). If you miss this deadline, you have one last chance to make your election: You may file an amended return making the election within six months after the date your original return was due (April 15, or later if you got an extension). If you fail to do this, you will lose your right to deduct your start-up expenses and you'll have to treat them as capital expenses. (See Chapter 3 for a detailed discussion of deducting business start-up expenses.)

Should You File Your Amendment As Late As Possible?

The IRS ordinarily has only three years after a return is filed to audit the return. Filing a Form 1040X does not extend this period. Thus, if you file your Form 1040X near the end of the three-year period, the IRS will have very little time to audit your return for the year involved. As a result, it might accept your claim without auditing your return. However, it might also refuse to accept your 1040X unless you agree to extend the time it has to audit your return for the year.

C. How to Amend Your Return

If you, like the vast majority of home business owners, are a sole proprietor, you amend your income tax return by filing IRS Form 1040X, *Amended U.S. Individual Income Tax Return*. When you file Form 1040X to obtain a refund of taxes you've already paid, it is called a "claim for refund."

Filing an amended tax return is not terribly difficult. You can usually do it yourself, with or without the aid of a computer tax-preparation program. The heart of the form consists of three columns: A, B, and C. You record the relevant figures from your original tax return in Column A; the corrected information is listed in Column C; and the difference between the two is listed in Column B. You must also provide a brief explanation for the changes. For example, Senator Kerry included the following explanation when he filed a Form 1040X to amend his 2003 taxes: "The tax on the one-half interest in the Adam Willerts painting was inadvertently calculated at the 20% rather than the 28% rate."

If you're amending your previous year's tax return and are entitled to an additional refund for that year, tax experts suggest that you wait until you receive your original refund check for that year. You can go ahead and cash the first refund check as soon as you receive it. Of course, you can file your amended return immediately if you were not entitled to a refund on your original return.

You must mail or hand deliver Form 1040X to the IRS. You can't file it electronically. If you mail it, send it by certified mail, with postal return receipt requested. This will let you know when the IRS received it. If you amend your returns for more than one year, mail each 1040X in a separate envelope. The 1040X instructions show where to mail the form.

You may also hand deliver the form to the IRS service center where you file your tax returns. If you do this, be sure to get a stamped copy as your filing receipt.

To obtain a refund due to an NOL, you may file either IRS Form 1045 alone, or along with Form 1040X. You can often get your refund faster by using Form 1045 alone. The calculations required to figure out how much you can deduct from your income in prior years can be complicated. Tax preparation programs like *TurboTax* aren't designed to handle net operating losses, so it's a good idea to get some help from a tax professional. Refer to IRS Publication 536, *Net Operating Losses*, for more information.

⚠️ **Don't forget your state tax returns.** The IRS routinely shares information with states that impose income taxes (every state except Alaska, Florida, Nevada, South Dakota, Texas, Washington, and Wyoming). Thus, your state tax department will probably learn that you amended your federal tax return. For this reason, tax experts advise that you also amend your state tax returns for the years affected.

D. How the IRS Processes Refund Claims

The IRS doesn't like paying back money to taxpayers. When you file a Form 1040X, your tax return for that year will receive extra special attention. An IRS employee will pull your return and examine it and your 1040X to decide whether you're really entitled to a refund; and if so, how much. Your claim may be denied or accepted as filed, or the amended items may be audited. If a claim is audited, the procedures are almost the same as in the audit of a regular tax return. Moreover, the IRS has the option of extending the audit to your entire tax return, not just the amended items. Thus, *filing an amended tax return increases your chances of an audit.*

You should receive your refund, if you're entitled to one, in about 12 weeks. However, your refund may be reduced by amounts you owe for past-due child support, debts you owe to another federal agency, or past-due state income tax obligations. You will be notified if this happens.

If the IRS denies your claim, it must explain why—for example, because you filed it late. You have the right to appeal such a denial. For a detailed discussion of IRS appeals, refer to *Stand Up to the IRS*, by Frederick W. Daily (Nolo). ■

Chapter 17

Staying Out of Trouble With the IRS

M ost taxpayers have at least some concern about the possibility of facing an IRS audit. You may be wondering how the IRS decides to audit, how likely it is that you'll be audited, and what you can do to avoid being one of the unlucky ones. This chapter explains IRS audits and provides tips and strategies that will help you avoid attracting the attention of the IRS—or come out of an audit unscathed, if you find yourself in the government's crosshairs.

Need more information on dealing with the IRS? For a detailed discussion of audits and other IRS procedures, see *Stand Up to the IRS*, by Frederick Daily (Nolo).

A. What Every Home Business Owner Needs to Know About the IRS

Just as you should never go into battle without knowing your enemy, you should never file a tax return without understanding what the IRS plans to do with it.

1. Anatomy of an Audit

You can claim any deductions you want to take on your tax return—after all, you (or your tax preparer) fill it out, not the government. However, all the deductions you claim are subject to review by the IRS. This review is called a tax audit. There are three types of audits: correspondence audits, office audits, and field audits.

- **Correspondence audits.** As the name indicates, correspondence audits are handled entirely by mail. These are the simplest and shortest type of IRS audit, usually involving a single issue. The IRS sends you written questions about a perceived problem, and may request additional information and/or documentation. If you don't provide satisfactory answers or information, you'll be assessed additional taxes. Correspondence audits are often used to question a home business about unreported income—income the IRS knows the taxpayer received because an IRS Form 1099 listing the payment has been filed by a client or customer.

- **Office audits.** Office audits take place face-to-face with an IRS auditor at one of the 33 IRS district offices. These are more complex than correspondence audits, often involving more than one issue or more than one tax year. If you make less than $100,000 per year, this is the type of in-person audit you're likely to face.

- **Field audits.** The field audit is the most comprehensive IRS audit, conducted by an experienced revenue officer. In a field audit, the officer examines your finances, your business, your tax returns, and the records you used to create the returns. As the name implies, a field audit is normally conducted at the taxpayer's place of business; this allows the auditor to learn as much about your business as possible. Field audits are ordinarily reserved for taxpayers who earn a lot of money. You probably won't be subjected to one unless your home business earns more than $100,000 per year.

a.   How Home Business Owners Get in Trouble With the IRS

When auditing self-employed home business owners, the IRS is most concerned about whether you have:

- **Underreported your income.** Unlike employees who have their taxes withheld, sole proprietor business owners have no with-holding—and many opportunities to underreport how much they earn, particularly if they run a cash business.

- **Claimed tax deductions to which you were not entitled.** For example, you claimed that nondeductible personal expenses, such as a personal vacation, were deductible business expenses.

- **Properly documented the amount of your deductions.** If you don't have paperwork to back up the amount of a deduction, the IRS may reduce it, either entirely or in part. Lack of documentation is the main reason small business owners lose deductions when they get audited.

- **Taken business deductions for a hobby.** If you continually lose money, or you are involved in a fun activity such as art, photography, crafts, or writing and don't earn profits every year, the auditor may also question whether you are really in business. If the IRS claims you are engaged in a hobby, you could lose every single deduction for the activity. (See Chapter 2 for more on the hobby loss rule.)

b.   Records Available to Auditors

An IRS auditor is entitled to examine the business records you used to prepare your tax returns, including your books, check registers, canceled checks, and receipts. The auditor can also ask to see records supporting your business tax deductions, such as a mileage record if you took a deduction for business use of your car. The auditor can also get copies of your bank records, either from you or your bank, and check them to see whether your deposits match the income you reported on your tax return. If you deposited a lot more money than you reported earning, the auditor will assume that you didn't report all of your income, unless you can show that the deposits you didn't include in your tax return weren't income. For example, you might be able to show that they were loans, inheritances, or transfers from other accounts. This is why you need to keep good financial records.

2.   The IRS: Clear and Present Danger or Phantom Menace?

A generation ago, the three letters Americans feared most were I-R-S. There was a simple reason for this: the IRS, the nation's tax police, enforced the tax laws like crazy. In 1963, an incredible 5.6% of all Americans had their tax returns audited. Everybody knew someone who had been audited. Jokes about IRS audits were a staple topic of night-club comedians and cartoonists.

In 2002, only .65% of all Americans were audited, and an IRS audit was a relatively rare event. There are several reasons for the change:

- A decline in the IRS workforce: Between 1992 and 2001, the IRS workforce declined by 16%; the number of revenue agents dropped by 21%.

- An increase in workload: At the same time the IRS workforce was declining, its workload was increasing; it grew 16% between 1992 and 2001.
- A new emphasis on taxpayer service, rather than enforcement: Starting in the mid-1990s, the IRS began to emphasize taxpayer service rather than enforcement. Staff was shifted from doing audits to performing service functions like answering taxpayer questions.
- Legal changes: Congress enacted new laws in 1998 that were intended to prevent perceived abuses by IRS agents and auditors. These new protections also made it more difficult for the IRS to go after tax cheats.

According to the IRS Oversight Board, the IRS does not have the resources to pursue at least $30 billion worth of known taxes that are incorrectly reported or not paid. In 2001, the nation's "tax gap"—the total inventory of taxes that are known and not paid—was estimated at $311 billion. Pulitzer Prize-winning *New York Times* reporter David Cay Johnston, in his book *Perfectly Legal*, a detailed analysis of the IRS's woes, commented: "The IRS budget has been restrained so severely that only one in five of the tax cheats it identifies is pursued to make him pay. The other four pay nothing. Tax law enforcement became so weak that businessmen were quoted on the front page of *The New York Times* in the year 2000 boasting about how they neither paid taxes nor withheld them from their employees' paychecks. More than two years later, not one of them had been indicted or even forced through civil court action to pay up."

Both the IRS and the Congress are aware of the IRS's enforcement problems and have taken some steps to ameliorate them. The IRS has received moderate budget increases in the past few years and has placed a renewed emphasis on enforcement. The precipitous decline in audit rates that began in the mid-1990s has been stopped, but audit rates remain at very low levels. With budget deficits yawning as far as the eye can see, Congress could still decide to fund substantial increases in IRS enforcement efforts. But it hasn't happened yet.

Aggressive or Dishonest?

Given the relatively low audit rates in recent years, many tax experts say that this is a good time to be aggressive about taking tax deductions. In this context, "aggressive" means taking every deduction to which you might arguably be entitled. If a deduction falls into a gray area of law, you would decide the question in your favor. This is *tax avoidance*, which is perfectly legal.

However, being aggressive does not mean being dishonest—that is, taking phony deductions that you are clearly not entitled to take or falsely increasing the amount of the deductions to which you are entitled. This is *tax evasion*, which is a crime.

3.   You Are the IRS's Number One Target

Although the IRS is a troubled agency and audit rates are at or near all-time lows, tens of thousands of people still get audited every year. In 2003, the IRS audited 928,725 tax returns for tax year 2002. Moreover, the sad fact is that self-employed people, including home business owners, are the IRS's number one target. This is shown by audit rate statistics: 162,206 of the 928,725 tax returns audited in 2003 belonged to sole proprietors, a category that includes 90% of all home business owners.

Every year, the IRS releases statistics about who got audited the previous year. Here are the most recently available audit statistics.

IRS Audit Rates		
	2001 Audit Rate	**2002 Audit Rate**
Sole Proprietors		
Income under $25,000	2.67%	3.00%
$25,000 to $100,000	1.18%	1.33%
$100,000 and over	1.45%	1.47%
Partnerships	0.26%	0.35%
S Corporations	0.39%	0.30%
C Corporations		
Assets under $250,000	0.24%	0.24%
$250,000 to $1 million	0.76%	0.64%
$1 million to $5 million	2.08%	1.55%
$5 million to $10 million	4.63%	3.40%
Individuals (not in business)		
Income under $25,000	0.64%	1.09%
$25,000 to $50,000	0.23%	0.30%
$50,000 to $100,000	0.28%	0.41%
$100,000 and over	0.75%	0.98%

This chart shows that in 2002, 3% of sole proprietors earning less than $25,000 from their businesses were audited. This category includes substantial numbers of home businesses. Only corporations with assets worth more than $5 million were audited more often. Only corporations with assets over $1 million were audited more often than sole proprietors earning $25,000 to $100,000. In 2002, sole proprietors earning less than $25,000 were three times more likely to face an audit than individuals not in business who earned $100,000 or more.

These statistics undoubtedly reflect the IRS's belief that sole proprietors habitually underreport their income, take deductions to which they are not entitled, or otherwise cheat on their taxes. The lesson these numbers teach is that you need to take the IRS seriously. This doesn't mean that you shouldn't take all the deductions you're legally entitled to take, but you should understand the rules and be able to back up the deductions you do take with proper records.

4.   How Tax Returns Are Selected for Audits

It's useful to understand how tax returns are selected for audit by the IRS. (By the way, if you are audited, you are entitled to know why you were selected. You ordinarily have to ask to find out.)

a.   DIF Scores

One way the IRS decides who to audit is by plugging the information from your tax return into a complex formula to calculate a "discriminate function" score (DIF). Returns with high DIFs have a far higher chance of being flagged for an audit, regardless of whether or not you have done anything obviously wrong. Anywhere from 25% to 60% of audited returns are selected this way. The exact percentage is not entirely clear, but it appears to be declining, partly because the current DIF formula, which was created in the 1980s, is badly out of date. As a result, fully one-third of audits conducted in recent years through the DIF formula resulted either in no change or a tax refund!

Exactly how the DIF is calculated is a closely guarded secret. Some of the known factors the formula takes into account are:

- **The nature of your business.** Businesses that deal with large amounts of cash are scrutinized more closely than those that don't.
- **Where you live.** Audit rates differ widely according to where you live. In 2000, for example, taxpayers in Southern California were almost five times more likely to be audited than taxpayers in Georgia. The IRS no longer releases information on audit rates by region, but according to the latest available data, the state with the highest audit rate is Nevada; other high-audit states include Alaska, California, and Colorado. Low-audit states include Illinois, Indiana, Iowa, Maryland, Massachusetts, Michigan, New York (not including Manhattan), Ohio, Pennsylvania, and West Virginia.
- **The amount of your deductions.** Returns with extremely large deductions in relation to income are more likely to be audited.

For example, if your tax return shows that your business is earning $25,000, you are more likely to be audited if you claim $20,000 in deductions than if you claim $2,000.

- **Hot-button deductions.** Certain types of deductions have long been thought to be hot buttons for the IRS, especially auto, travel, and entertainment expenses. Casualty losses and bad debt deductions may also increase your DIF score. Some people believe that claiming the home office deduction makes an audit more likely, but the IRS denies this.

- **Businesses that lose money.** Businesses that show losses are more likely to be audited, especially if the losses are recurring. The IRS may suspect that you must be making more money than you are reporting—otherwise, why would you stay in business?

- **Peculiar deductions.** Deductions that seem odd or out of character for your business could increase your DIF score—for example, a plumber who deducts the cost of foreign travel might raise a few eyebrows at the IRS.

- **How you organize your business.** Sole proprietors get higher DIF scores than businesses that are incorporated or owned by partnerships or limited liability companies. As a result, sole proprietors generally are most likely to be audited by the IRS. Partnerships and small C corporations are 10 times less likely to be audited than sole proprietors.

b.   IRS Matching Program

Whenever a client pays you $600 or more for your services during the year, it must report the payments to the IRS on IRS Form 1099. IRS computers match the information on 1099s with the amount of income reported on tax returns, using Social Security and other identifying numbers. Discrepancies usually generate correspondence audits.

c.   Groups Targeted for Audit

Every year, the IRS gives special attention to specific industries or groups of taxpayers that it believes to be tax cheats. Businesses that receive a lot of cash are a perennial audit favorite. Other IRS favorites include doctors, dentists, lawyers, CPAs, and salespeople.

The IRS also targets taxpayers who use certain tax shelters or have offshore bank accounts or trusts. But you don't have to be rich to be an audit target. The IRS also heavily audits low-income taxpayers who claim the earned income tax credit.

d.   Tips and Referrals

You could also get audited as a result of a referral from another government agency, such as your state tax department. The IRS also receives tips from private citizens—for example, a former business partner or ex-spouse.

e.   Bad Luck

A certain number of tax returns are randomly selected for audit every year. If you find yourself in this category, there's not much you can do about it. As long as you have adequate documentation to support your deductions, you should do just fine.

State Tax Audits Grow Increasingly Common

Although most people (and books) focus on IRS audits, audits by state income tax agencies are becoming increasingly common. Many states are facing deficits, and are therefore desperate to collect more taxes. For example, Idaho increased income tax audits by 25% in 2003, while Kansas upped them by 30%. Many states have increased fines and late-payment penalties. Others have adopted severe—and highly effective—punishments against delinquent taxpayers. For example, some states refuse to issue drivers' licenses to people who owe back taxes. Others are hiring private tax collectors and publishing names of tax evaders online.

B.   Ten Tips for Avoiding an Audit

Here are ten things you can do to minimize your chances of getting audited.

1.   Tip #1: Be Neat, Thorough, and Exact

If you file by mail (as you should), submit a tax return that looks professional; this will help you avoid unwanted attention from the IRS. Your return shouldn't contain erasures or be difficult to read. Your math should be correct. Avoid round numbers on your return (like $100 or $5,000). This looks like you're making up the numbers instead of taking them from accurate records. You should include, and completely fill out, all necessary forms and schedules. Moreover, your state tax return should be consistent with your federal return. If you do your own taxes, using a tax-preparation computer program will help you produce an accurate return that looks professional.

2.   Tip #2: Mail Your Return by Registered Mail

Mail your tax return by certified mail, return receipt requested. In case the IRS loses or misplaces your return, your receipt will prove that you submitted it. The IRS also accepts returns from four private delivery services: Airborne Express, DHL Worldwide Express, Federal Express, and United Parcel Service. Contact these companies for details on which of their service options qualify and how to get proof of timely filing.

3.   Tip #3: Don't File Early

Unless you're owed a substantial refund, you shouldn't file your taxes early. The IRS generally has three years after April 15 to decide whether to audit your return. Filing early just gives the IRS more time to think about whether you should be audited. You can reduce your audit chances even more by getting an extension to file until August 15 or October 15 (the latest extension you can obtain). Note, however, that filing an extension does not extend the date by which you have to pay any taxes due for the prior year—these must be paid by April 15.

4.   Tip #4: Don't File Electronically

The IRS would like all taxpayers to file their returns electronically—that is, by email. There is a good reason for this: It saves the agency substantial time and money. Every year, the IRS must hire thousands of temp workers to enter the numbers from millions of paper returns into its computer system. This is expensive, so the IRS only has about 40% of the data on paper returns transcribed. The paper returns are then sent to a warehouse where they are kept for six years and then destroyed. The IRS makes its audit decisions based on this transcribed data. By filing electronically, you give the IRS easy access to 100% of the data on your return instead of just 40%.

5.   Tip #5: Form a Business Entity

The audit rate statistics in Section A3, above, show that partnerships and small corporations are audited far less often than sole proprietors. In 2002, for example, the IRS audited 0.35% of partnerships, 0.30% of S corporations, and only 0.24% of regular C corporations with assets worth less than $250,000. In contrast, 3% of sole proprietors earning less than $25,000 were audited. 90% of home business owners are sole proprietors, but no law says they have to be. Incorporating your business or forming a limited liability company will greatly reduce your audit risk. However, you must balance this against the time and expense involved in forming a corporation or an LLC. Moreover, in some states—most notably California—corporations and LLCs have to pay additional state taxes.

6.   Tip #6: Explain Items the IRS Will Question

If your return contains an item that the IRS may question or that could increase the likelihood of an audit, include an explanation and documentation to prove everything is on the up and up. For example, if your return contains a substantial bad debt deduction, explain the circumstances and attach copies of loan documents or other paperwork showing that the debt is a legitimate business expense. This won't necessarily avoid an audit, but it may reduce your chances. Here's why:

If the IRS computer gives your return a high DIF score, an IRS classifier screens it to see whether it warrants an audit. If your explanations and documentation look reasonable, the screener may decide you shouldn't be audited after all.

7.   Tip #7: Avoid Ambiguous or General Expenses

Don't list expenses under vague categories such as "miscellaneous" or "general expense." Be specific. IRS Schedule C lists specific categories for the most common small business expenses. If an expense doesn't fall within one of these classifications, create a specific name for it.

8.   Tip #8: Report All of Your Income

The IRS is convinced that self-employed people, including many home business owners, don't report all of their income. Finding such hidden income is a high priority. As mentioned above, IRS computers compare 1099 forms with tax returns to determine whether there are any discrepancies. Not all income home business owners receive is reported to the IRS on Form 1099—for example, if you sell a product to customers rather than providing a service, your receipts will not be reported on Form 1099. However, if you are audited, the auditor may examine your bank records to see whether you received any unreported income.

9.   Tip #9: Watch Your Income-to-Deduction Ratio

Back in the 1990s, a statistics professor named Amir D. Aczel got audited by the IRS. The experience proved so unpleasant that he decided to conduct a statistical study of how and why people get selected for IRS audits. He carefully examined more than 1,200 returns that were audited and reported his findings in a book (now out of print) called *How to Beat the IRS At Its Own Game* (Four Walls Eight Windows, 1995). He concluded that the key factor leading to an audit was the ratio of a taxpayer's expenses to his or her income.

According to Aczel, if your total business expenses amount to less than 52% of your gross business income, you are "not very likely" to be audited. If your business expenses are 52% to 63% of your business income, there is a "relatively high probability" that the IRS computer will tag you for an audit. Finally, if your expenses are more than 63% of your income, Aczel claims you are "certain to be computer tagged for audit." Of course, this doesn't necessarily mean that you *will* be audited. Less than ten percent of returns that are computer tagged for audit are actually audited. But being tagged considerably increases the odds that you'll be audited.

Whether Aczel's precise numbers are correct or not is anyone's guess. However, his basic conclusion—that your income-to-deduction ratio is an important factor in determining whether you'll be audited—is undoubtedly true. (A former IRS commissioner admitted as much in a CNN interview in 1995.)

10. Tip #10: Beware of Abnormally Large Deductions

It is not just the total amount of your deductions that is important. Very large individual deductions can also increase your audit chances. How much is too much? It depends in part on the nature of your business. A $2,000 foreign travel deduction might look abnormal for a plumber, but not for a person in the import-export business.

The Government Accounting Office released a report in 2004 that shows the dollar range for common deductions claimed by sole proprietors in 2001 who earned less than $25,000 from their businesses.

Looking at this chart, you can see that in 2001, the home office deduction ranged from a low of $40 (the amount claimed by taxpayers in the 1st percentile) to a high of $10,130 (the amount claimed by taxpayers in the 99th percentile). The average deduction (mean) was $1,800. The median deduction (half of the sample size claimed more than this number, while the other half claimed less) was $1,120. This tells you that if you claim a $15,000 home office deduction, the IRS will think something is wrong. This does not necessarily mean you will get audited, but it increases your chances. Of course, if you're entitled to a $15,000 home office deduction, you should claim it. But be prepared to back it up with good documentation.

Range of Expenses for Sole Proprietorships With Gross Income Less Than $25,000 (Tax Year 2001)						
Expense category	Mean	1st	10th	Median	90th	99th
Advertising	$ 600	$ 10	$ 40	$ 220	$1,200	$5,290
Bad debts	1,700	10	50	300	2,020	18,480
Car/truck	2,300	30	190	1,420	5,480	12,530
Commissions	1,600	10	60	440	3,480	14,060
Depletion	1,400	0	70	770	2,850	6,060
Depreciation	2,000	20	130	950	4,560	17,150
Employee benefit programs	2,300	180	310	1,540	4,460	7,300
Insurance	800	20	100	460	1,780	4,830
Interest on mortage	3,400	10	320	1,840	7,210	25,960
Interest on other business debt	1,800	10	70	480	2,830	11,770
Legal/professional services	400	20	50	160	680	3,790
Office	600	10	40	250	1,360	4,510
Pension/profit sharing plans	1,500	0	10	800	3,480	6,950
Rent on machinery/ equipment	1,800	10	100	750	4,810	9,120
Rent on other business property	2,800	30	200	1,990	6,170	13,970
Repairs	900	10	60	370	2,330	7,110
Supplies	1,100	10	70	500	2,710	8,410
Taxes	400	10	30	140	860	2,960
Travel	1,200	20	80	560	2,800	8,520
Meals/ entertainment	500	10	30	200	1,140	3,560
Utilities	900	10	110	580	2,030	5,370
Wages	4,500	30	190	1,190	8,000	29,940
Other	2,200	10	110	860	4,480	16,320
Home office	1,800	40	280	1,120	3,900	10,130
All categories	$7,000	$ 60	$ 590	$4,400	$14,970	$36,260

Source: GAO analysis of IRS data

Range of Expenses for Sole Proprietorships With Gross Income From $25,000 to $100,000 (Tax Year 2001)						
Expense category	Mean	1st	10th	Median	90th	99th
Advertising	$1,600	$ 20	$ 80	$ 680	$4,290	$10,920
Bad debts	1,500	20	70	580	2,680	15,530
Car/truck	6,100	100	880	4,200	12,990	30,910
Commissions	5,200	20	140	1,670	13,910	51,330
Depletion	6,000	40	280	4,960	13,780	24,490
Depreciation	4,300	50	330	2,400	9,900	27,870
Employee benefit programs	2,700	90	160	1,830	6,890	10,500
Insurance	1,600	60	250	990	3,610	8,060
Interest on mortage	4,100	30	410	2,190	9,020	32,400
Interest on other business debt	1,900	10	140	970	4,750	11,910
Legal/professional services	700	40	90	250	1,290	7,820
Office	1,300	20	100	580	3,020	10,150
Pension/profit sharing plans	3,100	0	100	1,170	9,020	10,440
Rent on machinery/ equipment	3,100	20	130	1,260	7,600	21,950
Rent on other business property	6,400	40	600	4,790	14,400	26,610
Repairs	2,200	30	110	900	5,700	18,250
Supplies	3,000	30	180	1,250	7,110	26,840
Taxes	1,000	10	50	400	2,540	7,520
Travel	2,300	30	140	1,070	5,490	17,930
Meals/ entertainment	1,000	20	70	500	2,440	6,070
Utilities	2,100	60	370	1,500	4,400	11,690
Wages	10,500	100	750	6,640	26,160	48,090
Other	6,200	40	410	2,880	15,110	45,530
Home office	3,000	110	550	2,060	6,910	12,960
All categories	$26,200	$1,560	$ 7,240	$21,420	$51,140	$90,100

Source: GAO analysis of IRS data

The chart above shows the amounts for the same deductions claimed in 2001 by sole proprietors who earned $25,000 to $100,000. As you'd expect, these amounts are somewhat higher than the deductions claimed by proprietors who earned less than $25,000. For example, the average home office deduction claimed by these taxpayers was $3,000.

These deductions were claimed back in 2001, so you must correct for inflation when using the charts today. In recent years, inflation has averaged between 2% and 3% per year. Therefore, you'd expect these deductions to be about 10% higher for sole proprietors in 2005. ■

Chapter 18

Help Beyond This Book

There are many resources available to supplement and explain more fully the tax information covered in this book. Many of these resources are free; others are reasonably priced. The more expensive tax publications for professionals are often available at public libraries or law libraries—and a lot of tax information is available free on the Internet.

If you have a question about a specific tax deduction or any other tax-related matter, you can:

- consult a secondary tax source (see Section A)
- review the tax law (see Section B), or
- see a tax professional (see Section C).

You can do these suggested steps in any order you wish, depending on how much time and money you want to spend. For example, you can see a tax professional right away instead of doing any research yourself. Although this will save you time, it will cost you money.

Need more information on legal research? Before you try to research tax law on your own, it's a good idea to learn how to do legal research first. An excellent resource is *Legal Research: How to Find and Understand the Law*, by Stephen Elias and Susan Levinkind (Nolo). You can also find information at Nolo's Legal Research Center at www.nolo.com.

A.   Secondary Sources of Tax Information

You might think that the easiest place to find answers to your tax questions is in the tax code—after all, that's where the actual laws are collected. However, the tax code can be dry and difficult to decipher—particularly if you're trying to figure out how a particular law or rule applies to your situation. Instead of diving right into the code books, your best bet is usually to start with one of the many secondary sources that try to make the tax law more understandable.

Unlike the primary sources listed in Section B, below, these sources are not the law itself or the IRS's official pronouncements on the law. Instead, they are interpretations and explanations of the law, which are intended to make it more understandable to those who aren't tax experts. Often, you'll be able to find the answer to your question in one or more of these sources. You can also learn about topics not covered in this book—for example, what constitutes income for tax purposes, how to complete your tax returns, or how to deal with an IRS audit.

1. Information From the IRS

The IRS has made a huge effort to inform the public about the tax law, creating hundreds of informative publications, an excellent website, and a telephone answering service. However, unlike the regulations and rulings issued by the IRS, these secondary publications and assistance are for informational purposes only. They are not official IRS pronouncements, and the IRS is not legally bound by them.

Reading IRS publications is a useful way to get information on IRS procedures and learn how the agency views the tax law. But keep in mind that these publications only present the IRS's interpretation of the law, which may be different from how a court might rule on the same issue. That's why you shouldn't rely exclusively on IRS publications for information.

a. IRS Website

The IRS has one of the most useful Internet websites of any federal government agency. Among other things, almost every IRS form and informational publication can be downloaded from the site. The Internet address is www.irs.gov.

The IRS website has a special section for small businesses and the self-employed, categories that include virtually all home businesses (www.irs.gov/businesses/small/index.html). It includes:

- answers to basic tax questions and a calendar of tax deadlines
- online access to most IRS forms and information booklets
- industry-specific tax information for certain industries like construction and child care
- tips on how to avoid common tax problems
- announcements of new IRS policies and procedures of particular interest to small businesses
- links to court opinions and to rulings and regulations on specific industries
- links to non-IRS sites for general tax information, and
- links to helpful small business resources.

b.   IRS Booklets

The IRS publishes over 350 free booklets explaining the tax code, called IRS Publications ("Pubs," for short). Many of these publications are referenced in this book. Some are relatively easy to understand, others are incomprehensible or misleading. As with all IRS publications, they only present the IRS's interpretation of the tax laws—which may or may not be upheld by the federal courts.

You can download all of the booklets from the IRS website at www.irs.gov. You can also obtain free copies by calling 800-TAX-FORM (800-829-3676), or by contacting your local IRS office or sending an order form to the IRS.

c.   IRS Telephone Information

The IRS offers a series of prerecorded tapes of information on various tax topics on a toll-free telephone service called TELETAX (800-829-4477). See IRS Publication 910, *Guide to Free Tax Services,* for a list of topics.

You can talk to an IRS representative on the telephone by calling 800-829-1040. (It is difficult to get though to someone from January through May.) Be sure to double check anything an IRS representative tells you over the phone—the IRS is notorious for giving misleading or outright wrong answers to taxpayers' questions, and the agency will not stand behind oral advice that turns out to be incorrect.

d.   Free IRS Programs

In larger metropolitan areas, the IRS offers small business seminars on various topics, such as payroll tax reporting. You can ask questions at these half-day meetings, which are often held at schools or federal buildings. Call the IRS at 800-829-1040 to find out whether programs are offered near you and to get on the IRS small business mailing list. The IRS also has an online tax workshop for small businesses; you can find it at the online classroom on the IRS website. You can also order a free CD-ROM with a video presentation of the workshop through the IRS website.

2.   Other Online Tax Resources

In addition to the IRS website, there are hundreds of privately created websites on the Internet that provide tax information and advice. Some of this information is good; some is execrable. A comprehensive collection of web links about all aspects of taxation can be found at: www.taxsites.com. Here are some other pages listing links to sites that offer tax information:

- www.willyancey.com/tax_internet.htm
- www.abanet.org/taxes
- www.natptax.com/tax_links.html
- www.el.com/elinks/taxes

Some useful tax related websites include:

- www.accountantsworld.com
- www.unclefed.com
- www.smbiz.com/obwduy.html
- http://aol.smartmoney.com/tax/filing
- www.taxguru.net

Nolo's Website

Nolo maintains a website that is useful for small businesses and the self-employed. The site contains helpful articles, information about new legislation, book excerpts, and the Nolo catalog. The site also includes a legal encyclopedia with specific information for businesspeople, as well as a legal research center you can use to find state and federal statutes, including the Internal Revenue Code. The Internet address is www.nolo.com.

3.   Tax Publications

If you like to read books, you'll be happy to know that there are enough books about tax law to fill a library. Tax publications vary from the broadly focused to the highly detailed. You can find answers to most tax questions in one or more of these resources.

a.   Publications for the Nonexpert

There are many books (like this one) that attempt to make the tax law comprehensible to the average person. The best known are the paperback tax preparation books published every year. These books emphasize individual taxes, but also have useful information for small businesses. Two of the best are:

- *The Ernst and Young Tax Guide* (John Wiley & Sons), and
- *J.K. Lasser's Your Income Tax* (John Wiley & Sons).

J.K. Lasser publishes other useful tax guides, many of which are targeted at small businesses. You can find a list of these publications at: www.wiley.com/WileyCDA/Section/id-103210.html.

Tax guides designed for college courses can also be extremely helpful. Two good guides to all aspects of income taxes that are updated each year are:

- *Prentice Hall's Federal Taxation Comprehensive* (Prentice Hall), and
- *CCH Federal Taxation Comprehensive Topics* (Commerce Clearing House).

Nolo also publishes several books that deal with tax issues:

- *Stand Up to the IRS*, by Frederick W. Daily (Nolo), explains how to handle an IRS audit.
- *Tax Savvy for Small Business*, by Frederick W. Daily (Nolo), provides an overview of the entire subject of taxation, geared to the small businessowner.
- *Hiring Independent Contractors*, by Stephen Fishman (Nolo), shows small businesses how to hire independent contractors without running afoul of the IRS or other government agencies.
- *Working for Yourself,* by Stephen Fishman (Nolo), covers the whole gamut of legal issues facing the one-person business.
- *Creating Your Own Retirement Plan*, by Twila Slesnick and John C. Suttle (Nolo), covers retirement planning for the self-employed.
- *IRAs, 401(k)s & Other Retirement Plans: Taking Your Money Out*, by Twila Slesnick and John C. Suttle (Nolo), covers the tax implications of withdrawing funds from retirement accounts.
- *Inventor's Guide to Law, Business, and Taxes*, by Stephen Fishman (Nolo), covers tax aspects of inventing.

b. Publications for Tax Professionals

You may have a question that you can't answer by looking at websites or tax publications for the layperson. In this event, you can consult one or more publications for tax professionals—accountants, CPAs, and attorneys. These are the most detailed and comprehensive secondary sources available.

There are six main publishing companies that publish reference materials for tax professionals:

- Business News Association (BNA); www.bna.com
- Commerce Clearing House (CCH); www.cch.com
- Klienrock Publishing; www.kleinrock.com
- Research Institute of America (RIA); www.riahome.com
- Tax Analysts; www.taxanalysts.com, and
- West Group; http://west.thomson.com

These publishers produce an incredible volume of tax information, ranging from detailed analyses of the most arcane tax questions to brief, one-volume guides to the entire federal tax law. Among their publications are:

Tax Services: These are highly detailed discussions of the tax law, organized by IRC section or topic and updated frequently—every week, or at least every month. The most authoritative is *The Law of Federal Income Taxation*, published by West Group (it's also called "Mertens" by tax professionals because it was originally edited by Jacob Mertens). Other tax services include the *United States Tax Reporter* (published by RIA) and *Standard Federal Tax Reporter* (published by CCH).

Tax Treatises: Tax treatises provide in-depth, book-length treatment of a particular tax topic. Among the most useful are the *Tax Management Portfolios*, a series of paperback booklets published by BNA. If you're looking for information on a very precise tax issue, you might find what you need in a portfolio.

Tax Citators: Tax citators summarize tax cases and compile and organize them by subject matter and IRC section. By using a citator, you can find all the tax cases that have addressed a specific tax topic. Both CCH and RIA publish citators.

Tax Deskbooks: CCH publishes a well-known one-volume tax "deskbook" called the *Master Tax Guide* that provides an overview of the tax law. It's updated each year.

You can find a good discussion on how to use these tax materials in *West's Federal Tax Research* (South-Western College Publishing).

All of these publications are available in print form, on CD-ROMs, and on subscriber websites (notably, Westlaw and Lexis, subscriber databases containing legal information). As you might expect, they are generally very expensive. You can also find them in a law library, some large public libraries, or a tax professional's office.

c.   Trade Association Publications

There are hundreds of trade associations and organizations representing every conceivable occupation—for example, the American Society of Home Inspectors, the Association of Independent Video and Filmmakers, and the Graphic Artists Guild. Most of these have specialized publications and newsletters that track tax issues of common interest. You can learn about specific tax issues in your industry that even your tax professional might not know about—perhaps a new case or IRS ruling. Also, you can often find speakers on tax topics at programs offered to members at conventions and trade shows.

If you don't know the name and address of an association relevant to your business, ask other businesspeople in your field. Or check out the *Encyclopedia of Associations* (Gale Research); it should be available at your public library. Also, many of these associations have websites on the Internet, so you may be able to find the one you want by doing an Internet search.

4.   Tax Software

Today, millions of taxpayers use tax preparation software to complete their own income tax returns. The best-known programs are *Turbotax* and *TaxCut*. These programs contain most IRS tax forms, publications, and other tax guidance. Both have helpful websites—www.turbotax.com and www.taxcut.com.

B. The Tax Law

If you can't find an answer to your question in a secondary source, you might be able to find help in the tax law itself. Or, you may want to consult the tax law to verify (or clarify) what you've learned from secondary sources.

The "tax law" of the United States comes from several sources:

- the Internal Revenue Code
- IRS regulations
- court cases, and
- IRS rulings, interpretations, and tax advice.

Every branch of the federal government is involved in creating the tax law. The Internal Revenue Code is enacted by Congress (the legislative branch), IRS regulations and rulings are issued by the IRS (a department of the executive branch), and taxpayers may appeal the IRS's actions to the federal courts (the judicial branch).

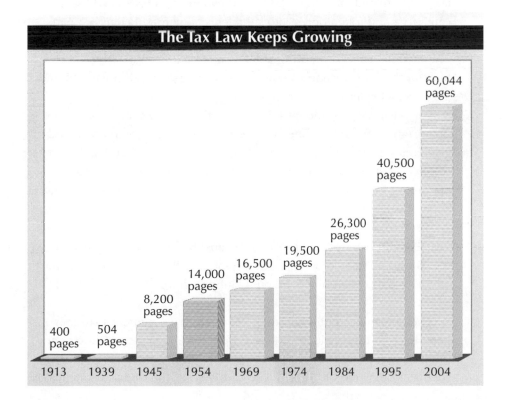

The Tax Law Keeps Growing

1913	400 pages
1939	504 pages
1945	8,200 pages
1954	14,000 pages
1969	16,500 pages
1974	19,500 pages
1984	26,300 pages
1995	40,500 pages
2004	60,044 pages

The Tax Law Versus *War and Peace*

	Number of pages
Internal Revenue Code	3,653
IRS Regulations	13,079
War and Peace, by Leo Tolstoy	1,444

1.   Internal Revenue Code

The Internal Revenue Code (IRC) is the supreme tax law of the land. The IRC (also called "the code" or "the tax code") is written, and frequently rewritten, by Congress. The first tax code, adopted in 1913, contained 14 pages. Today, the tax code is more than 3,500 pages long.

The IRC is found in Title 26 of the United States Code (USC, for short). The USC encompasses all of our federal laws. "Title" simply refers to the place within the massive USC where the IRC is found.

The entire tax code covers income taxes, Social Security taxes, excise taxes, estate and gift taxes, and tax procedure. It is organized by category and broken down into subtitles, chapters, subchapters, parts, subparts, sections, subsections, paragraphs, subparagraphs, and clauses. The income tax laws are in Chapter 1 of Subtitle A of the Tax Code. Most of the laws dealing with tax deductions are found in Parts VI and VII of Subchapter B of Chapter 1.

For our purposes, the most important thing to remember about the organization of the tax code is that each specific tax law is contained in a separate numbered section. For example, Section 179 covers first-year expensing of long-term business assets. For the sake of convenience, tax professionals will often refer to these numbered sections of the tax code.

> **EXAMPLE:** "IRC § 179(b)(4)(A)" means that this particular tax law is found in Title 26 of the USC (the Internal Revenue Code), Section 179, Subsection b, Paragraph 4, Subparagraph A.

The tax code is published each year in a two-volume set (usually in paperback). You should be able to find it in the reference section of any public library. You can also purchase a set from various tax publishers, such as Commerce Clearing House and Research Institute of America. A complete set of the tax code costs more than $80. You can also purchase a one-volume abridged version for much less. This will likely contain all the tax code provisions you'll want to read. The entire United State Code (including the IRC) is also available on CD-ROM from the Government Printing Office for less than $40.

Fortunately, the IRC is available free on the Internet. You can get to the entire IRC from Nolo's Legal Research Center—go to www.nolo.com2. Portions are also available on the IRS website (www.irs.gov) and several other websites.

Make sure your tax code is current. The IRC is amended every year; in recent years, these amendments have made major changes to the law. Make sure that any copy of the IRC you use in your research is current.

2. IRS Regulations

Even though the Internal Revenue Code contains over 3,600 pages, it does not provide adequate guidance for every situation that arises in real life. To supplement the IRC, the IRS issues regulations, called "Treasury Regulations," "Regulations," or "Regs." Although written by the IRS, not Congress, these regulations have almost the same authoritative weight as the tax code itself.

While the tax code is usually written in broad and general terms, the regulations get down and dirty, providing details about how tax code provisions are intended to operate in the real world. Regulations are slightly easier to read than the tax code on which they are based and often include examples that can be helpful. The regulations cover many (but not all) of the tax code provisions.

To see if a particular IRC section is supplemented by a regulation, start with the number of the IRC section. If there is a corresponding regulation, it will bear the same number, usually preceded by the number "1."

EXAMPLE: "Reg. 1.179" refers to a Treasury regulation interpreting IRC Section 179.

The regulations are published in a multivolume set by the Government Printing Office and tax publishers such as CCH and RIA. These are available in law libraries and in some large public libraries. You can download many (though not all) regulations from the IRS website.

3.   Court Cases

When a dispute arises between a taxpayer and the IRS, the taxpayer may take the matter to federal court. The courts are the final arbiters of tax disputes. A court may overrule the IRS if the court concludes that the IRS applied the tax code in a manner contrary to the United States Constitution or different from what Congress intended.

Tax disputes are tried in three different courts: a special tax court that handles only tax disputes; the regular federal trial courts (called U.S. District Courts); and the Court of Federal Claims. If either the taxpayer or the IRS doesn't like the outcome of the trial, it may appeal to the federal appellate courts (called the U.S. Court of Appeals), and even to the United States Supreme Court.

Decisions of these courts are published, along with explanations and discussions of the tax law. These court decisions provide valuable interpretations of the tax laws. Many, but not all, of these court interpretations are binding on the IRS. Thousands of court decisions dealing with tax law have been published, so chances are good that there is at least one decision on the issue that interests you.

To locate a published court decision, you must understand how to read a case citation. A citation provides the names of the people or companies involved on each side of the case, the volume of the legal publication (called a reporter) in which the case can be found, the page number on which it begins, and the year in which the case was decided. Here is an example of what a legal citation looks like: *Smith v. Jones*, 123 F.3d 456 (1995). Smith and Jones are the names of the people in the legal dispute. The case is reported in volume 123 of the Federal Reporter, Third Series, beginning on page 456; the court issued the decision in 1995.

Opinions by the federal district courts are in a series of reporters called the Federal Supplement, abbreviated as F.Supp. Any case decided by a federal court of appeals is found in a series of books called the

Federal Reporter. Older cases are contained in the first series of the Federal Reporter, or F. More recent cases are contained in the second or third series of the Federal Reporter, F.2d or F.3d. Cases decided by the U.S. Supreme Court are found in three publications: United States Reports (identified as U.S.), the Supreme Court Reporter (identified as S.Ct.), and the Supreme Court Reports, Lawyer's Edition (identified as L.Ed.). Supreme Court case citations often refer to all three publications.

Many, but not all, of these legal decisions are available free on the Internet. Tax court decisions from 1999 on can also be accessed at www.ustaxcourt.gov. Generally, only decisions issued after the mid-1990s are available free. The website www.findlaw.com is a good place to start a search for a free copy of any court decision. Virtually all legal decisions are available on the subscriber websites Lexis.com and Westlaw.com. You may be able to access these websites through a library or tax professional's office.

Hard copies of published decisions by the United States Tax Court can be found in the Tax Court Reports, or TC, published by the U.S. Government Printing Office. You can also find tax court decisions in a reporter called Tax Court Memorandum Decisions, or TCM, published by Commerce Clearing House, Inc. You can find tax decisions from all federal courts in a reporter called U.S. Tax Cases, or USTC, published by Commerce Clearing House, Inc. These are available in law libraries.

For a detailed discussion of how to research court cases, see *Legal Research: How to Find and Understand the Law*, by Stephen Elias and Susan Levinkind (Nolo), or go to Nolo's Legal Research Center at www.nolo.com.

4.   IRS Rulings, Interpretations, and Tax Advice

It might seem like the tax code, regulations, and court decisions would provide everything anyone ever wanted to know about tax law. But even more IRS guidance is available. The IRS publishes several types of statements (besides Regs) of its position on various tax matters. These pronouncements guide IRS personnel and taxpayers as to how the IRS will apply specific tax laws.

Unlike the tax code and regulations, these statements do not have the force of law. Rather, they are the IRS's own interpretation of the tax law, which is not necessarily binding on the courts (or on you, should you choose to challenge the IRS's interpretation in court). However, they give you a good idea of how the IRS would handle the situation involved.

a. Revenue Rulings

IRS Revenue Rulings (Rev. Rul.) are IRS announcements of how the tax law applies to a hypothetical set of facts. The IRS publishes over 100 of these rulings every year. These rulings represent the IRS's view of the tax law, and the IRS presumes that they are correct. If an auditor discovers that you have violated a revenue ruling, you will probably have to pay additional tax. On the other hand, if you can show an auditor that a revenue ruling supports your position, you probably won't have to pay more tax. Even if you have violated a revenue ruling, all is not necessarily lost. Revenue rulings are not binding on the courts, which can (and do) disregard them from time to time. Thus, it's possible you could win your case on appeal even if a revenue ruling goes against you.

You can download free copies of all IRS Revenue Rulings from 1954 to date from: www.taxlinks.com. Revenue rulings also appear in the weekly Internal Revenue Cumulative Bulletin, which is published by the U.S. Government Printing Office. Tax book publishers Prentice-Hall, Commerce Clearing House, and Research Institute of America also reprint IRS Revenue Rulings. They are indexed by IRC section and subject matter.

> **EXAMPLE:** "Rev. Rul. 03-41" refers to IRS Revenue Ruling number 41, issued in 2003.

b. Revenue Procedures

Revenue procedures ("Rev. Procs.") are IRS announcements dealing with procedural aspects of tax practice. Rev. Procs. are used primarily by tax return preparers. They often explain when and how to report tax items, such as how to claim a net operating loss on a tax form or return. Revenue procedures are contained in the weekly Internal Revenue Cumulative Bulletin, which you can find in larger public and law libraries, and also are reprinted by tax book publishers and on the IRS website.

> **EXAMPLE:** "Rev. Proc. 99-15" refers to a published Revenue Procedure number 15, issued in 1999.

c.   Letter Rulings

IRS letter rulings are IRS answers to specific written questions from taxpayers about complex tax situations. The only person who is entitled to rely on the ruling as legal authority is the taxpayer to whom the ruling is addressed; even if you find yourself in a similar position, the IRS is not legally required to follow the guidance it gave in the letter. However, letter rulings offer valuable insight into the IRS's position on tax treatment of complex transactions. Since 1976, letter rulings have been made available to the general public. They are published by tax publishers.

> **EXAMPLE:** "Ltr. Ruling 9913043 (April 3, 1999)" refers to a letter ruling issued on April 3, 1999. The first two numbers of the seven-digit identifier show the year it was issued, the next two indicate the week of the year, and the last three show the ruling for that week. Thus, this letter ruling was the 43rd issued during the 13th week of 1999.

d.   IRS General Guidance

From time to time, the IRS gives general guidance and statements of policy in official "announcements" and "notices" similar to press releases. They appear in the weekly Internal Revenue Cumulative Bulletin. It usually doesn't pay to search IRS announcements or notices because they are too broad to answer specific questions.

e.   Internal Revenue Manual

The Internal Revenue Manual (IRM) is a series of handbooks that serve as guides to IRS employees on tax law and procedure. The IRM tells IRS employees (usually auditors or collectors) how specific tax code provisions should be enforced. The manual is for IRS internal use, but most of it is public and reprinted by private tax book publishers. It is available to the public in the Freedom of Information Act reading rooms of larger IRS offices, and in law libraries and some tax professionals' offices. Portions of the IRM are also available on the IRS website.

The IRM is revealing of IRS attitudes in certain areas—for example, Section 4.10.3 of the Manual describes the techniques IRS auditors are supposed to use when they examine the depreciation deductions claimed by a business.

f.   IRS Forms and Instructions

IRS forms are well known to us all, especially Form 1040, the annual personal income tax return. There are more than 650 other IRS forms, listed in Publication 676, *Catalog of Federal Tax Forms*. You can get them free at IRS offices or by calling 800-829-FORM or 800-829-1040. You can also download them from the IRS website, www.irs.gov. Many IRS forms come with instructions and explanations of the tax law.

C.   Consulting a Tax Professional

You don't have to do your own tax research. There are hundreds of thousands of tax professionals (tax pros) in the United States ready and eager to help you—for a price. A tax pro can answer your questions, provide guidance to help you make key tax decisions, prepare your tax returns, and help you deal with the IRS if you get into tax trouble.

1.   Types of Tax Pros

There are several different types of tax pros. They differ widely in training, experience, and cost.

- **Tax preparers.** As the name implies, tax preparers prepare tax returns. The largest tax preparation firm is H & R Block, but many mom-and-pop operations open for business in storefront offices during tax time. In most states, anybody can be a tax preparer; no licensing is required. Most tax preparers don't have the training or experience to handle taxes for businesses and, therefore, are probably not a wise choice for tax preparation services or advice.

- **Enrolled agents.** Enrolled agents (EAs) are tax advisors and preparers who are licensed by the IRS. They must have at least five years of experience or pass a difficult IRS test. They can represent taxpayers before the IRS, and in administrative proceedings, circuit court, and, possibly, tax court, if they pass the appropriate tests. Enrolled agents are the least expensive of the true tax pros but are reliable for tax return preparation and more routine tax matters. They can be quite adequate for many home businesses.

- **Certified public accountants.** Certified public accountants (CPAs) are licensed and regulated by each state. They undergo lengthy training and must pass a comprehensive exam. CPAs represent the high end of the tax pro spectrum. In addition to preparing tax returns, they perform sophisticated accounting and tax work. CPAs are found in large national firms or in small local outfits. The large national firms are used primarily by large businesses. Some states also license public accountants. These are competent, but are not as highly regarded as CPAs.

- **Tax attorneys.** Tax attorneys are lawyers who specialize in tax matters. The only time you'll ever need a tax attorney is if you get into serious trouble with the IRS or another tax agency and need legal representation before the IRS or in court. Some tax attorneys also give tax advice, but they are usually too expensive for home businesses. You're probably better off hiring a CPA if you need specialized tax help.

2. Finding a Tax Pro

The best way to find a tax pro is to obtain referrals from business associates, friends, or professional associations. If none of these sources can give you a suitable lead, try contacting the National Association of Enrolled Agents or one of its state affiliates. You can find a listing of affiliates at the NAEA website at www.naea.org. Local CPA societies can give you referrals to local CPAs. You can also find tax pros in the telephone book under "Accountants, Tax Return." Local bar associations can refer you to a tax attorney. Be aware that CPA societies and local bar associations refer from a list on a rotating basis, so you shouldn't construe a referral as a recommendation or certification of competence.

Your relationship with your tax pro will be one of your most important business relationships, so be picky about the person you choose. Talk with at least three tax pros before hiring one. You want a tax pro who takes the time to listen to you, answers your questions fully and in plain English, seems knowledgeable, and makes you feel comfortable. Make sure the tax pro works frequently with small businesses. It can also be helpful if the tax pro already has clients in businesses similar to yours. A tax pro already familiar with the tax problems posed by your type of business can often give you the best advice for the least money. ■

Index

Phone line for the business, for IRS
behavior test, 2/11
Photographer's deductible day
example, operating expenses, 4/10
Physical inventory, 10/9–10
Principal place of business, home as,
6/9–12
Professional organizations, IRS
behavior test and, 2/11–12
Profit limitation
home office deduction, 6/26–28
Section 179 deductions, 5/15–16
Profit test, for determining business
activity, 2/5–7
Property taxes
deductions for, 14/30
home office deduction and,
6/21–22

R

Real estate activities, 2/25–26
Real property
depreciation, 5/43–44
taxes and deductions, 14/30–31
Reasonable in amount requirement,
4/9
Recapture
depreciation, 5/45–46
Section 179, 5/19–20
Receipts
$75 rule for receipts, 15/23
as supporting documentation,
15/12–14
See also Record keeping
Reconstructing tax records, 15/31

Record keeping
appointment book, 15/5–7
business checkbook and credit
cards, 15/3–5
car expenses and actual expenses,
8/11
car expenses and mileage records,
8/7
depreciation, 5/51–52
expense journal, 15/7–11
failure to retain records, 15/30–31
gifts, 15/21–27
home office deduction expense
records, 6/32–33
and IRS behavior test, 2/10
listed property rules, 15/27–29
meals and entertainment expenses,
15/21–27
reconstructing, 15/31
scanning of records, 15/29
Section 179 deductions, 5/51–52
$75 rule for receipts, 15/23
supporting documents, 15/11–15
time for retaining records, 15/29–30
travel expenses, 15/21–27
Recovery periods, 5/31–33
Reimbursed expenses
of employees, 11/14–20
entertainment deduction and,
7/14–15
excess payment to employee,
return of, 11/18
of independent contractors,
11/32–34
travel expense deduction and, 9/11
See also Medical reimbursement
plans

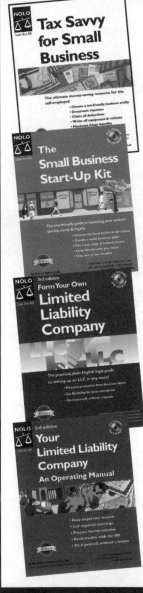

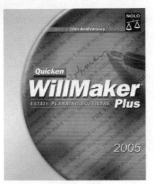

Remember:

Little publishers have big ears.
We really listen to you.

Take 2 Minutes & Give Us Your 2 cents

Your comments make a big difference in the development and revision of Nolo books and software. Please take a few minutes and register your Nolo product—and your comments—with us. Not only will your input make a difference, you'll receive special offers available only to registered owners of Nolo products on our newest books and software. Register now by:

PHONE	**FAX**	**EMAIL**	or **MAIL** us
1-800-728-3555	1-800-645-0895	cs@nolo.com	this registration card

fold here

Registration Card

NAME _____ DATE _____

ADDRESS _____

_____

CITY _____ STATE _____ ZIP _____

PHONE _____ EMAIL _____

WHERE DID YOU HEAR ABOUT THIS PRODUCT? _____

WHERE DID YOU PURCHASE THIS PRODUCT? _____

DID YOU CONSULT A LAWYER? (PLEASE CIRCLE ONE)   YES   NO   NOT APPLICABLE

DID YOU FIND THIS BOOK HELPFUL?   (VERY)   5   4   3   2   1   (NOT AT ALL)

COMMENTS _____

_____

_____

WAS IT EASY TO USE?   (VERY EASY)   5   4   3   2   1   (VERY DIFFICULT)

We occasionally make our mailing list available to carefully selected companies whose products may be of interest to you.
❑ If you do not wish to receive mailings from these companies, please check this box.
❑ You can quote me in future Nolo promotional materials.
   Daytime phone number _____.

DEHB 1.0

Nolo *in the* NEWS

"Nolo helps lay people perform legal tasks without the aid—or fees—of lawyers."
—USA TODAY

Nolo books are ..."written in plain language, free of legal mumbo jumbo, and spiced with witty personal observations."
—ASSOCIATED PRESS

"...Nolo publications...guide people simply through the how, when, where and why of law."
—WASHINGTON POST

"Increasingly, people who are not lawyers are performing tasks usually regarded as legal work... And consumers, using books like Nolo's, do routine legal work themselves."
—NEW YORK TIMES

"...All of [Nolo's] books are easy-to-understand, are updated regularly, provide pull-out forms...and are often quite moving in their sense of compassion for the struggles of the lay reader."
—SAN FRANCISCO CHRONICLE

fold here

- -

**Place
stamp here**

Nolo
950 Parker Street
Berkeley, CA 94710-9867

Attn: DEHB 1.0